PRACTICAL VISUAL TECHNIQUES IN SYSTEM DESIGN

With Applications to Ada

R.J.A. Buhr

Department of Systems and Computer Engineering
Carleton University
Ottawa, Canada

Prentice Hall
Englewood Cliffs, New Jersey 07632

AAW 7990

Library of Congress Cataloging-in-Publication Data

Buhr, R. J. A.
    Practical visual techniques in system design : with applications
to Ada / by R.J.A. Buhr.
        p.   cm. -- (Prentice-Hall software series)
    Includes bibliographical references (p.
    ISBN 0-13-880808-2
    1. System design. 2. Ada (Computer program language)   I. Title.
II. Series.
QA76.9.S88B84 1990
005.13'3--dc20   90-6913
                                                        CIP

Editorial/production supervision
  and interior design: Harriet Tellem
Cover design: Wanda Lubelska
Manufacturing buyer: Kelly Behr

Prentice Hall Software Series
Brian Kernighan, Advisor

© 1990 by Prentice-Hall, Inc.
A division of Simon & Schuster
Englewood Cliffs, New Jersey 07632

The publisher offers discounts on this book when ordered
in bulk quantities. For more information, write:

> Special Sales/College Marketing
> College Technical and Reference Division
> Prentice Hall
> Englewood Cliffs, New Jersey 07632

Printed in the United States of America
10 9 8 7 6 5 4 3 2 1

ISBN 0-13-880808-2

Prentice-Hall International (UK) Limited, *London*
Prentice-Hall of Australia Pty. Limited, *Sydney*
Prentice-Hall Canada Inc., *Toronto*
Prentice-Hall Hispanoamericana, S.A., *Mexico*
Prentice-Hall of India Private Limited, *New Delhi*
Prentice-Hall of Japan, Inc., *Tokyo*
Simon & Schuster Asia Pte. Ltd., *Singapore*
Editora Prentice-Hall do Brasil, Ltda., *Rio de Janeiro*

DEDICATION

To Sheila, my wife and best friend,
for her love, laughter, and support over the years.

Contents

PREFACE

GENESIS OF THE BOOK

This book is an evolutionary development of material in an earlier book of mine — *System Design With Ada*, Prentice Hall, 1984 — that introduced a visual notation for Ada design that has subsequently been widely accepted in the Ada community under the name "Buhr Diagrams", and is now supported by several CASE tools.

Practical Visual Techniques in System Design addresses three areas that were undeveloped in the earlier book:

- It shows that the notation is not Ada-bound, but can be effectively used both to design for different target implementation technologies, and to learn about design in an Ada-independent way.

- It provides more expressiveness relative to some features of practical implementation technologies, including Ada, but not restricted to Ada.

- It places considerable emphasis on viewing diagrams as "visual prototypes" of the system under design that capture not only structure but also temporal behaviour (as opposed to viewing them as just visual shorthand for code).

It addresses these points through a new notation called MachineCharts that is an evolution of Buhr Diagrams.

The material in this new book is based on 6 years of personal experience, since *System Design With Ada* was written, using, stretching, and extending "Buhr Diagrams" in the classroom, the research laboratory, and the workplace. This experience included considerable interaction with users of the notation among students, former students now in industry, colleagues, and members of the Ada community; it also included frequent consultations with tool developers. At Carleton University, my colleagues and I developed a designer's workbench call CAEDE (CArleton Embedded system Design Environment) that supported the techniques of *System Design With Ada*, as well as including prototype temporal behaviour analysis and performance analysis capabilities of a kind that have still not made their way into commercial tools; extensions of this work continue as this is being written, in a project called TimeBench, which is based on the material in this new book.

GENERAL NATURE OF THE MATERIAL

This book is a personal statement on how to use visual techniques to organize one's thinking during the design process, based on the above experience, interpreted in light of many years of practical involvement with real time systems, multiprocessor systems, and computer communication systems. It is not an academic dissertation on visual techniques in general, and it therefore provides no survey of the literature. In a way, it is a requirements definition for a designer's workbench that does not exist yet that would treat visual representations of systems under design as prototypes that can be directly "executed" (or analyzed) to investigate temporal behaviour.

The MachineCharts notation presented in this book provides a framework for conceptualizing software design in common sense, physical terms that owes much to the way communication engineers and hardware engineers conceptualize the operation and interaction of the physical black boxes of their domains (e.g., network nodes, front ends, devices, boards, chips). A contribution of this book is that it extends this way of conceptualizing systems into the domain of software design in a manner that is independent of any specific software implementation technology.

I believe that workbenches should provide such common sense representations as "windows" through which practical engineers may view formal methods for specifying temporal behaviour; in other words, formal methods should be supported by a designer's workbench in a manner that is relatively transparent to its users. Therefore I have taken pains not only to give the design abstractions in this book a common sense character, but also to make them precise, so that formalism can be added. However, formal methods are outside the scope of this book.

This material has evolved independently of developments in the "object-oriented" community. Nevertheless, some readers of prepublication drafts have pointed out that the book may be viewed as being about "object-oriented system design". In spite of this view, I have made an effort to avoid object-oriented terminology, because I do not treat the subject of inheritance, which the object-oriented community thinks of as a cornerstone of object-oriented methods, but which I regard as a side-issue for the kinds of problems I am trying to address with this book. Where object-oriented terms are used, they are mostly used with their everyday English meaning; for example, the term "object" itself may be used in the sense of "thing"; and the term "actor" is used to identify a particular kind of concurrent component that is defined in terms particular to the material in the book, but that has no particular relationship to actor models in the object oriented world.

BACKGROUND NEEDED TO READ THE BOOK

This book uses a visual notation to explore some deep issues in concurrent systems. It assumes that readers can start from the premise that such systems are composed of interacting, concurrent black boxes. To cope with this starting point, the reader needs to have encountered black boxes and concurrency before, and dealt with them in enough depth to be ready to grapple with the design-level issues they raise. A sufficient appreciation of black box ideas can come either from familiarity with programming constructs and abstractions like units, modules, packages, objects, and abstract data types, or from familiarity with hardware black boxes, such as chips, boards, and so forth. A sufficient appreciation of concurrency ideas can come either from programming in a high level concurrent programming language like Ada, or in a lower level programming language used with a real time executive. In either case, experience with interrupt level programming is advantageous because it imparts a "gut feel" for how computer systems really work that is hard to get in any other way.

This minimal background may be found in a wide variety of people: university undergraduates in computer science, in computer system engineering and in electrical engineering, usually past the second year level; professional programmers in many different environments; hardware engineers with some software knowledge (deep knowledge of hardware replaces much of the need for concurrent software concepts, because hardware is inherently concurrent); consultants; project managers; educators.

Ada is not a prerequisite (or even a corequisite). The Ada program examples may be skipped by the non-Ada reader without loss of continuity, so there is no need to rush out and learn Ada to profit from this book; the Ada examples are there mainly to show that the ideas are concrete by relating them to one practical implementation technology (for this purpose, many of the Ada examples are easy to understand, even without any detailed knowledge of Ada, given the notational preliminaries). However, no tutorial material on Ada is given in the book and the coverage of Ada is selective, so Ada knowledge is required to place this Ada material in a larger Ada context and to use it effectively in that context.

DIFFERENCES BETWEEN MACHINE CHARTS AND BUHR DIAGRAMS

Ada readers who are familiar with the older Buhr Diagrams will notice the following cosmetic changes to the old notation, expressed here in Ada terms (otherwise, the features of the new notation that look the same as the old one may be interpreted for Ada design as having the same meaning):

- Arrowheads on connections corresponding to the old call-path arrows are missing; this is because the arrowheads were redundant in the first place — call direction is always implied by context — and leaving them out has the twin advantages of making diagrams less cluttered, and eliminating possible confusion with arrows used for data flows in requirements analysis. Arrow connections shaped like the old Buhr Diagram connections never appear for any reason between components in structure charts in the new notation, so users of the old notation who want to keep their arrowheads can do so without danger of causing confusion between the two notations.

- There is a simpler representation for selective accepts: a line drawn across entry icons, instead of a parallelogram enclosing them.

- Timeouts on calls and accepts are now indicated by clock icons.

Otherwise, Ada readers who are familiar with Buhr Diagrams should note the following new features:

- Terminology is entirely new, and Ada-independent. However, for Ada readers, Ada words are used below to explain the other new features.

- The interpretation of filled-in circles marking waiting places on interfaces has been generalized to mean any designer-designated waiting place, not just a guarded select alternative.

- A new notation is provided for exceptions.

- There is a new icon called an "engine" that represents the mainline program of any component (procedure, entry, task, or package).

- Entries appear procedure-like, in the sense that they appear in diagrams as if they had a separate existence from task "engines". Connections to entries exist not only to show call-paths from callers, but also accept-paths from accepting engines. In general, entries may be detached from tasks, like procedures, and may have multiple acceptors. The result is a more general interaction model than Ada's that can be constrained to Ada by requiring that entries be attached to task interfaces, or mapped to Ada using transformations given in the book.

- Asynchronous interactions are included.

- A visual distinction is made between "actors" that always map for implementation to active tasks in Ada, and "reactors" that may map either to passive multitasking objects like semaphores, mailboxes, and monitors, or to tasks programmed to behave passively, of a kind that a smart Ada compiler might be able to optimize away.

- Notations for templates and instances have been added that treat all program components (including packages) in a uniform way as first class objects that may be dynamically installed, passed around, and removed. The notation can be constrained to Ada by not using the features that do not represent Ada directly, or mapped to Ada using transformations given in the book. A relationship is drawn between dynamically installable packages (possibly containing tasks) that cannot be programmed as such in Ada, but that are useful design-level abstractions, and abstract data types that can be programmed directly in Ada.

- A notation is provided for nested rendezvous, and a relationship is drawn between this notation and a more general representation for multi-party "meetings" that is not directly supported by Ada.

- A number of new annotation icons are provided that enrich the notation both structurally and temporally.

- Events, timing diagrams, timing threads, and channels have been added to the notation.

- A process framework for using the notation is described in some detail.

SOFTWARE USED TO PREPARE THE BOOK

I used Latex for formatting the text, Autosketch for drawing the diagrams, and Postscript for printing the combined results. The combination, although not without its disadvantages, was very flexible to work with, enabling me to work easily on different machines and different parts of the book in different places, and to combine the results easily. Although Autosketch diagrams may not appear as stylish as those produced by some integrated desktop publishing systems, the relative ease of producing and modifying complicated, engineering-drawing-style diagrams with Autosketch was more important for my purposes.

PRESENTATION CONVENTIONS

All readers should note the following conventions relating to the way some material is presented:

- Although the book has been run through a spelling checker, there are some Canadian spellings that may look wrong to American eyes (e.g., "neighbour"). Otherwise, the only possibly controversial spelling that I am aware of is "reuseable", instead of "reusable", which I have chosen to spell with the extra "e" — in the good old Canadian tradition of having too many vowels in some words — because my dictionary gives both "useable" and "usable" as correct.

- Although an effort has been made to keep the forms of names in figures, text and code in correspondence, there are occasional lapses, such as upper case being used in one place but not another, or a dash being used in text as a separator instead of the underscore that appears in a program. Differences like these are not significant; e.g., decodeEVENT, DecodeEvent, DECODE_EVENT, and DECODE-EVENT are all equivalent.

- Dotted, dashed, or otherwise broken lines are not part of the structural notation, except for customizable parts of templates; therefore, when they are used in non-template structure charts (which is to say in most of the structure charts in the book), they are used only for emphasis or contrast. The notation tries to do all its work through shape alone.

- Diagrams are not always complete. Sometimes they show only just enough to illustrate a particular point, but no more; components or parameters required for a fully formed design may be missing.

- Ada program fragments used for illustration are not necessarily complete; details may be missing that would be needed for compilation.

VIDEOTAPES

Professionally-made videotapes are available of courses I have given to industry on this material (see card inserted at the back of the book).

ACKNOWLEDGEMENTS

Many individuals helped in various ways at different stages of this project by using the ideas, providing opportunities to try out the material, offering suggestions or criticisms, or giving encouragement; I would particularly like to thank Angel Alvarez, Gerry Cohen, Moshe Cohen, Herm Fischer, Mark Gerhardt, Gerald Karam, Dennis Mackinnon, Bob Satnik, Salim Ramji, and Murray Woodside.

Thanks are due to several readers of the first drafts who offered many suggestions for improvements. I would particularly like to thank Don Bailey, whose penetrating comments caused me much rewriting pain. Other individuals who made helpful comments on the drafts are Ron Casselman, Nick Dawes, Herm Fischer, Gerald Karam, Avi Lior, Mark Vigder, and Murray Woodside. Thanks are also due to the many students who had to cope with incomplete, error-riddled drafts as textbooks while the material was being refined.

Industrial tool makers and users provided encouragement and in some cases more substantial support: I would particularly like to thank Boeing Advanced Systems Division, Cadre, GE Research Laboratories, I-Logix, and MarkV Systems. Industrial users of Buhr Diagrams and MachineCharts provided enthusiasm, criticism and that invaluable commodity, practical use; I would particularly like to thank Boeing Advanced Systems Division, TRW/ESL, Computing Devices of Canada, and Canadian Marconi.

My colleagues in the Department of Systems and Computer Engineering at Carleton University provided support, encouragement, criticism, and stimulation. I would like to thank them for making the department such a supportive and interesting place to be.

Research funding that contributed to the development of the material was provided by the National Research Council of Canada (NSERC), the Telecommunications Research Institute of Ontario (TRIO), and Boeing Advanced Systems Division.

My son, Michael, helped with diagram drawing, program example writing and early production aspects. My wife, Sheila, kept me going during the much too long period in which the book was finally put together.

Elena Keen assisted with final editing and prepared the index, coping cheerfully and efficiently with an author who kept making revisions while the indexing was in progress.

Part I

NATURE OF THE BOOK

Chapter 1

INTRODUCTION

1.1 INTRODUCTION

It has been said that inside every large problem is a small problem struggling to get out. This books aims to help with the struggle, in the domain of system design, by providing visual techniques for conceptualizing the essence of system organization and operation (the small problems struggling to get out), while providing a precise framework to serve as the starting point for detailed design and implementation of whole systems (the large problem).

1.1.1 WHAT IS "SYSTEM DESIGN"?

Here is what the key words "system" and "design" mean in this book:

- The word *system* identifies a philosophical viewpoint: that the techniques of the book are at a level of abstraction above implementation technology, whether software or hardware. The book describes how to design systems in terms of interacting *black boxes* that may, in general, have interfaces, internal state, and internal passive or active machinery, and that may be expressed in reuseable form. Much of the design thinking that has to go on at this level of abstraction is independent of whether black boxes are to be implemented in software or hardware.

- A second connotation of the word *system* is an orientation of the material of the book towards a problem domain characterized by terms like *reactive system*, *real time system*, *embedded system*, and *distributed system*. Important characteristics of this domain are the unavoidable presence of *autonomous components* that may generate events at unpredictable times that require attention by other components, and the importance of *time* as a requirements factor.

- The word *design*, as engineers well know, implies a process of *synthesis*, not just analysis (in engineering design, analysis using principles of science and mathematics can only occur after synthesis has been performed). Synthesis is concerned with determining the particular *form* of a system from among a possibly bewildering variety of very different forms. Engineers use pictures to express the form of physical systems, and would find it hard to imagine how to perform synthesis of form without

1

pictures. One of the problems in system design is the non-physical nature of one of the most important parts of a system, its software. This book takes the view that, for design purposes, all the parts of a system should be treated as if they were physical objects to which standard engineering techniques apply, including the use of pictures to synthesize form.

Remaining above the level of abstraction of particular implementation technologies during the design process is particularly appropriate today in the system domain for several reasons:

- Problems are getting larger (it is no longer unusual to hear talk of millions of lines of code in high level languages like Ada), but ways of conceptualizing them to expose their essence are not keeping pace. Powerful means of conceptualization are needed to build confidence in the correctness of designs and implementations as early in the process as possible.

- As problems get larger, it becomes increasingly important to improve the productivity of software implementors by reusing, not just pieces of code, but also the design ideas underlying the code.

- Object oriented thinking is becoming increasingly recognized as important, but often becomes mired in the tar pit of implementation technology, making it easy to lose sight of the essence of the problem. (Although the term "object" rarely appears in this book, the book may be viewed as being about "object oriented system design".)

- The distinction between software design and hardware design is becoming less sharp-edged; software engineers may draw wiring-diagram-like pictures to represent program structures, hardware engineers may write programs to specify hardware, and both may sit at identical workstations to do the work. Means of design capture that span both worlds are highly desirable.

This philosophical viewpoint means that, in this book, programming languages, like Ada, combinations of programming languages and real time executives, like C and Harmony, object oriented software systems and languages, like Smalltalk, Objective-C, and C++, and hardware description languages, like VHDL, are all viewed as "implementation technologies" to which, in principle, "system"-level designs may be mapped. This philosophical viewpoint is implicit in the material of the book, which, however, stops short of actually treating all of these implementation technologies explicitly; as the title indicates, implementation examples are restricted to Ada.

This philosophical viewpoint, it must be emphasized, is not the only possible one in general. For example, Ada itself might be viewed as above the level of implementation technology if it were used, say, as a specification language for hardware, rather than an implementation language for software; or full Ada might be viewed as above the level of implementation technology if it were used, say, as a specification language for a program to be implemented in taskless Ada with a separate real time executive; or the visual techniques of this book might be viewed in a limited way simply as providing means of documenting the organization of programs, rather than as the primary means of deriving them. These are not the viewpoints of this book, however.

1.1.2 VISUAL TECHNIQUES

This book is about practical visual techniques for system design that aim to range in usefulness from sketching ideas quickly and economically "on the back of an envelope", through capturing and testing designs in a workbench, to serving as a basis for automatically generating prototype implementations.

A strong motivation for the use of visual techniques is the improved conceptualization they provide for many people, relative to programming or specification languages.

The visual notation of this book is called "MachineCharts". The term "machine" is deliberately used to suggest that components and systems represented by the notation have the property of physical machines of being describable in a common sense fashion from the *outside*. Physical machines have parts that are visibly connected together, that visibly do work, and that visibly move through externally observable sequences of events and states. These aspects of physical machines can be described, in a common sense fashion, to people who are not experts in the implementation technology of the machines, simply by pointing to the parts of the machine, tracing structural relationships among parts, and indicating operating sequences in relation to parts. Furthermore, the same common sense descriptions serve as the starting point for the work of technical specialists who must design, analyze, implement, test, and maintain the machines; all that is required for the specialists to be able to do their work is the fleshing out of details. The black-box model of MachineCharts provides a pseudo-physical representation of systems that is intended to serve much the same purposes.

Note that saying that MachineCharts provide a common sense description capability is not the same as saying that creating designs using MachineCharts is easy. Not only is the full notation quite rich, requiring a while to learn to use correctly, sensibly and effectively, but also the synthesis aspect of engineering design (of which designing with MachineCharts is a special case) always requires experience and expertise. Untrained persons may easily produce nonsense or fantasy MachineChart designs, just as you or I might produce fantasy designs for bridges that, to us, would look perfectly sensible.

The approach draws its inspiration from traditional engineering, where design conceptualization is aided by the existence of visual notations that serve not only to capture the essence of a design, but also to provide a framework for detailed design refinement, rigourous analysis in terms of underlying scientific principles, and implementation in terms of standard or custom components. For example, drawings of a bridge can be used as basis for exploring the essence of different alternatives during early design synthesis, for explaining to others how the bridge is intended to respond to static and dynamic loads, for analyzing its strength in response to such loads, and for showing how it is to be built in terms of standard and custom girders, beams, plates and so forth. It would be hard for a design engineer in a traditional engineering discipline to imagine dealing with a typically complex engineering system without such visual aids to conceptualization.

There are some differences between traditional engineering and system design (as defined by this book) that may make visual techniques even more desirable for system design:

- In system design, the artifacts being described are often logical rather than physical (e.g., software), so that diagrams may not represent anything that can be touched or held. Having no physical form, software can easily take on an amorphous, jelly-like

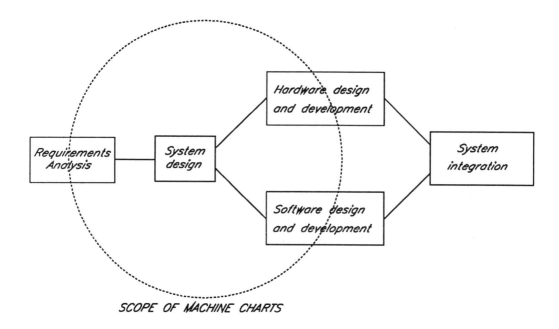

Figure 1.1: THE PLACE OF THE VISUAL TECHNIQUES OF THIS BOOK IN THE BIG PICTURE

character. Perhaps this character is not inevitable, but is a product of the way we conceptualize software while we are building it. Visual techniques, like the ones of this book, that conceptualize software as if it were composed of physical components, may help in producing software that is less amorphous and jelly-like than has been the case in the past, and therefore subject to fewer problems.

- Underlying analysis methods for system "strength" (correctness, response time, speed, reliability, safety,...) are not as well developed yet in the computer field as they are in traditional engineering. This suggests that visual aids to conceptualization may be even more important in the systems field than in traditional engineering, not less important, as they are in typical industrial practice now, because of the need to rely more on the human designer to get things right.

Although the visual techniques of this book are for system design, they may also, as suggested by Figure 1.1, extend part way up into requirements analysis (as an alternative to, or in alignment with, widely used requirements analysis techniques), and part way down into implementation (by providing a starting point for automatic generation of, for example, code skeletons, and by providing test sequences for implementations).

1.1.3   CAD-ORIENTATION

The ultimate objective is to have the visual techniques serve as the framework for design capture and evaluation in a *designer's workbench* like the CAD workstations currently used for engineering design in a variety of fields. Then one can combine the advantages of understandable sketches in "back of the envelope" style with automated support for using them for designing large systems. In the software domain, the acronym CASE (Computer Aided Software Engineering) tends to be preferred to CAD (Computer Aided Design). However, CASE applies to programming tools as well as software design tools, whereas CAD has a strong connotation of visual design capture that seems more appropriate for the techniques of this book.

CAD of software and systems is an idea whose time has come. Its timeliness arises in part because of the relatively recent insertion of abstractions which used to be viewed as being at the design level into programming languages (Ada, Modula-2, Turbo Pascal, BNR-Pascal, Mesa, Concurrent Euclid, Occam, Smalltalk, Objective-C, C++, Eiffel, ...) and hardware specification languages (VHDL, ...). This frees the designer to concentrate on conveying the intended nature of a system under design in a way that focuses more on the relationships among abstractions than on detailed descriptions of the nature of the abstractions themselves, or the detailed algorithms required to make them work. Graphical representations in a CAD system are natural ones for this purpose. Graphics technology is making it practical.

A CAD workbench may translate a complete design into a prototype implementation that can be completed by adding details in a manner constrained by the design detail already held in the workbench. The implementation may then be retested with the same test sequences that were used to test the design. In this way, confidence can be built that behaviour already tested at the design level has not been changed by the implementation process.

1.1.4   TIME-INTENSIVE SYSTEMS

INTRODUCTION

The term *TIME*-intensive is used in this book to identify systems for which concerns about time dominate the requirements, such as timely response to real time events, ability to deal with bursts of events, execution of important items of work at prescribed times (e.g., periodically), ability to take appropriate action when expected events fail to occur within expected times, correct sequencing of events and responses when many parallel components are interacting at unpredicatable times, and ability to handle unexpected events at any time. In this book, "*TIME*" refers to the domain of design concerns of this nature, and "time" to a quantity that is measured in terms of hours, minutes and seconds.

Two other domains of concern to the designer besides the *TIME*-domain are identified in this book, namely the *WORK*-domain and the *PLACE*-domain. Briefly, the *TIME*-domain is concerned with *when* things happen, the *WORK* domain with *what* gets done (e.g., computation and data processing), and the *PLACE domain* with *where* all of this occurs relative to the black boxes of the system. Chapter 2 describes a design process in terms of these domains.

The visual techniques of this book are particularly oriented towards *TIME*-intensive systems, because they explicitly separate *TIME*-domain concerns from other concerns at the design level. This separation facilitates conceptualization of temporal behaviour, enabling designers (and others) to gain confidence early in the process, before implementation, that design errors have not been made that will produce incorrect *TIME*-domain behaviour; and it enables testing of *TIME*-domain aspects of a system under design during the design stage, where errors can be found more quickly and corrected less expensively than after implementation has been completed.

CONCURRENCY AND INDETERMINISM

Autonomous components that operate concurrently are a central feature of reactive systems and of this book. So it may be helpful at this stage to recall why concurrency is important:

- Concurrency is inherent in hardware.

- Concurrency is useful in software if the hardware on which it runs is multiprocessing. Building explicit concurrent components (tasks) into the software makes it possible to allocate these components to different processors. This provides modularity by separating what the software does from *where* it runs, enabling the latter decision to be postponed until system configuration time, and possibly until run time, if dynamic allocation is supported.

- Concurrency is useful in the software of reactive systems. Unpredictable event arrival rates in such systems may sometimes cause overload. Using concurrent components (tasks) provides modularity by separating what the software does from *when* it runs in an overload situation, enabling the latter decision to be postponed until run time, and decided then based on priority.

- Concurrency is inherent in the system level view of reactive systems. Even without tasks, such systems have other concurrent components: in particular, concurrent hardware devices may interact with software by means of interrupts.

- Concurrency provides a better conceptualization of some problems (for example, telephone call processing, "fly-by-wire" control of aircraft, computer communications).

The twin of concurrency is indeterminism. Indeterminism comes from the following sources:

- Rates of event arrival and work completion at and in particular components are inherently unpredictable (e.g., messages sent from one task to another, interrupts sent from hardware devices to tasks, computations of unknown duration performed by a particular task that make it impossible to interact with other tasks until they are finished).

- Implementation technologies (e.g., multitasking executives) rely on priority schedulers to sort out urgent from less urgent work during periods when the system is temporarily overloaded, making it impossible to know *when* a particular component will run.

Indeterminism makes exhaustive testing even more impossible than it normally is without it.

A way of dealing with indeterminism is to eliminate it entirely by scheduling everything in advance, taking into account the maximum time required for work to be performed, thus eliminating the need for priority schedulers. This is done in some practical systems, but the results are not modular (small changes may easily require the entire schedule to be changed). Furthermore, the approach presents technical problems in distributed systems.

The perspective of this book is that concurrency and indeterminism are unavoidable features of *TIME*-intensive systems that have to be dealt with up front, at the design level.

SYNTHESIS OF TIME-INTENSIVE SYSTEMS

This book is concerned with techniques that enable human designers to synthesize the *form* of *TIME*-intensive systems using representations that capture this form not only in the *PLACE* domain, but also in the *TIME* domain, so that they help in thinking about concurrency and indeterminism. The techniques are visual because *form* is often best expressed visually, and because visual forms provide a solid basis for humans to gain confidence in the correctness of a design. With proper annotation, they can also provide the basis for computers to analyze a design, execute it at the design level, and compile it to a prototype implementation. The idea is to use formal specifications where they can be used effectively in design, for parts of systems, rather than whole systems.

Synthesizing the form of a *TIME*-intensive system is a particularly difficult problem because it involves not only the *PLACE* domain, but also the *TIME* domain. Concern with form in the *PLACE* domain involves issues like application domain abstraction, and information hiding. These aspects are given visual form by drawing diagrams that show structure. Concern with form in the *TIME* domain involves issues like the amount of concurrency required, the protocols required for communicating among concurrent components, and the patterns of correct and incorrect processing of transactions that may be threaded through many concurrent components. These aspects are given visual form in the *PLACE*-domain by annotating structure diagrams to indicate patterns of waiting, timeout, and periodicity, and in the *TIME*-domain by threading temporal paths through structures, and by drawing diagrams like timing diagrams and state transition diagrams that show intended temporal behaviour.

The assumption in much of this book is that details in the *WORK* domain can be deferred while synthesizing form in the *PLACE* and *TIME* domains. As much of the bulk of the code in multitasking software implementations of *TIME*-intensive systems is often in the *WORK* domain, this may have the desirable effect of reducing the size of the problem (thereby helping to expose the "small problem struggling to get out").

The holy grail in the domain of *TIME*-intensive systems is the automatic production from formal specifications of practical implementations with guaranteed-correct *TIME*-domain behaviour. This would completely sidestep the problem of testing. However, there are no methods yet available to do this on a large scale.

1.1.5 IMPLEMENTATION-TECHNOLOGY-INDEPENDENCE OF THE DESIGN MODEL

The MachineCharts model is deliberately independent of implementation technology. Its *PLACE*-domain, or structural, aspect provides an intuitively appealing *black-box-with-buttons* model. The notion of a black box is a familiar one in engineering and computer science. It is an easy step to imagine that black boxes have buttons on their interfaces (like the buttons that are pushed to summon an elevator in a building). Now visualize black boxes as having projecting fingers that may connect to buttons on other black boxes, to provide paths for interaction, imagine connecting the fingers and buttons together in a static structure, and you have the essence of the MachineCharts model. The model is recursive, because the insides of black boxes may be decomposed into further black boxes. The model requires thinking in terms of interactions among black boxes, not use of shared memory, as the the means of communicating information. Some of the constraints of this model may be relaxed, for generality, but much can be done with this constrained model. Here are some examples of features of the model:

- Black boxes used simply as enclosures, for information hiding purposes, are called, simply, *boxes*; they may be interpreted in terms of packages in Ada, modules in Modula-2, units in Turbo Pascal, objects in object oriented programming, and so forth.

- Black boxes that are autonomous, self-directing machines are called *robots*. Robots are of two kinds: *actors* model concurrent objects like tasks in Ada, and as supported by real time executives; *reactors* model objects that provide services to robots in a mutually exclusive fashion, like semaphores, mailboxes, and monitors supported by real time executives (and sometimes by programming languages). Reactors are classified as robots, because the may be modelled as actors that are constrained to behave passively, just as semaphores, for example, may be modelled by Ada tasks that are programmed to behave passively.

- Buttons are of two kinds: *work buttons*, and *gate buttons*. Work buttons do work immediately upon being pushed by a visitor; they correspond to procedures and functions in any programming language. Gate buttons require two visitors, one to *push* the button, and the other to *pull* it, before anything happens; then a *meeting* occurs, during which work may be done; they correspond to task entries in Ada, and to other mechanisms in other implementation technologies, like message services offered by some programming languages and real time executives.

- The basic interaction concept is the *visit*, which nicely models a variety of software mechanisms built around *calls*. The visit model requires thinking in terms of an active component inside a black box interacting with another black box by visiting a button on its interface. A variation of the notation provides latching buttons that allow a visitor to leave information there for someone else to pick up; this nicely models asynchronous communication mechanisms in software, and latching outputs in hardware.

- Common forms of synchronous and asynchronous communication found in implementation technologies are easily modelled by combining these components in standard ways.

As can be seen, the terminology is not overwhelming, and is explainable in intuitive and common sense terms. For readers bound to a particular implementation technology, such as Ada, this new terminology will be a small hurdle to overcome. However, it should prove worth it, because even Ada is not a monolithic implementation technology, as is discussed further in the following section.

1.1.6 ADA AS THE REFERENCE IMPLEMENTATION TECHNOLOGY OF THIS BOOK

INTRODUCTION

As indicated by the title, and as mentioned above, the specific implementation examples in this book are all in Ada. [1] Ada occupies such an important place in this book for several reasons: it is an important implementation technology in its own right; it is a widely known, well understood language containing good system-level abstractions; and earlier versions of the visual techniques of this book, known as *Buhr Diagrams*, are already widely used in the Ada community for design, so an audience exists for this new material in that community. However, Ada is used in this book only as an example implementation technology, not as the foundation of the visual techniques.

The visual techniques may be used to design for Ada or for other implementation technologies, including ones that may have mechanisms that are very different from Ada (for example, asynchronous message sends instead of synchronous rendezvous for task interactions).

HOW AN ADA READER SHOULD VIEW THE BOOK

An Ada reader may view the book as having three foundations, illustrated by the solid outlines in Figure 1.2: annotated structure, temporal behaviour, and Ada. The structural and behavioural abstractions are joined by a design process called *Architectural Design*. These abstractions may be mapped to Ada, but are not dependent on it. The Ada language is seen by the Ada reader as one of the foundations of the book because of the presence in the book of examples of such mappings.

Figure 1.3 emphasizes the point that MachineCharts design abstractions cover Ada design abstractions, but also go beyond them. This has some desirable consequences for the Ada community. One desirable consequence springs from the fact that even Ada is not a monolithic implementation technology. For example, for multitasking implementations, one may use full Ada, with tasks, or taskless Ada with a separate real time executive; or one may obtain packages to support real time extensions to the language. Freeing the notation from

---

[1]Wherever Ada is referred to in this book, the version implied is that of the 1983 Ada Reference Manual. As this is being written, at the end of Ada's first five years, a review process called ADA-9X is underway that will result in some detailed changes to the language; however, they are unlikely to be major and are, in any case, likely to be in directions that will make the interpretation of MachineCharts in Ada terms easier and more natural, rather than the reverse.

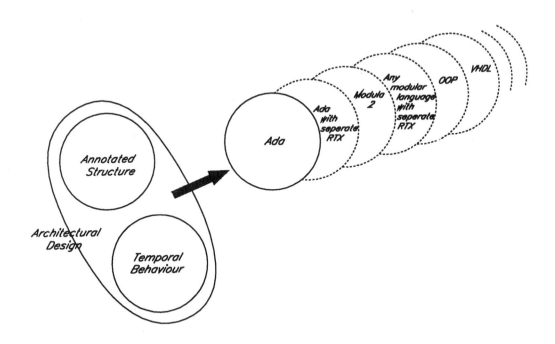

Figure 1.2: RELATIONSHIP OF THE MATERIAL OF THIS BOOK TO IMPLEMEN-
TATION TECHNOLOGY

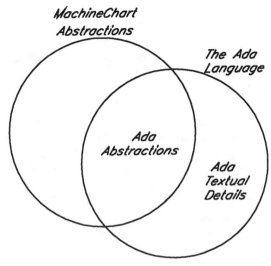

Figure 1.3: MACHINE CHART ABSTRACTIONS AND ADA

the constraints of the language allows such extensions to be expressed in a compact and direct fashion. Another desirable consequence arises from the fact that Ada expresses some useful behavioural idioms in a clumsy and complex fashion; the notation allows them to be expressed elegantly and simply, and later expanded into the more complex form required by Ada (two examples are *out-of-order* termination of rendezvous, and *anonymous-host* task interactions).

HOW A NON-ADA READER SHOULD VIEW THE BOOK

For non-Ada readers, Figure 1.2 indicates that the methods and abstractions of this book are expressed in a manner that is independent of Ada, and that provides them with the capability to be mapped to other implementation technologies, although, as suggested by the dotted outlines of the parts of this figure that represent different possible implementation technologies, these mappings are not explicitly illustrated by examples in this book.

Non-Ada readers should particularly note that features of Ada that may be regarded from outside the Ada community as constraining, such as rendezvous being the only method of intertask communication, are not properties of the notation at the design level, but only of the interpretation of the notation in terms of Ada.

Non-Ada readers may skip the Ada examples without loss of continuity. But even without any particular interest in Ada, these readers should find the Ada examples helpful in providing guidance for mapping to their own implementation technologies, because Ada is standardized, widely disseminated and by now well understood.

1.2   APPROACH OF THE BOOK

System design is a very large subject. Constraining the subject matter to visual techniques actually increases its size, by combining two subject areas: how to design; and how to represent what is being designed visually.

This book is as much about how to represent what is being designed, as it is about how to design. The author's experience has been that a big part of the problem people have with design is the lack of good representation techniques by means of which alternative forms of the system under design may be expressed, and that once good people learn a good representation technique, they become quite effective at discovering alternate forms in requirements, and analyzing them in a systematic way. How can one represent the *form* of a system under design visually? What do the components of the visual representation mean? How can one avoid creating nonsense or fantasy forms that do not mean anything? Considerable attention has to be paid to questions like these for the particular visual notation of this book, because of the extent to which it includes *TIME*-domain semantics. Without a solid grounding in the principles of the notation, one cannot proceed to use it effectively for design. This aspect of the book requires many detailed examples, rather than large case studies. Some of the detailed examples are a source of standard components that may be used in a bottom-up fashion in larger problems.

Form is expressed in terms of *peer machines*, *interfaces*, and *glue structures*, and many reuseable ideas for each are provided. The only unfamiliar term here is *glue structure*; in this book, it indicates the structure that binds peer concurrent machines together, and supports the protocols by means of which they may interact. Glue structures are a distinguishing feature of concurrent systems.

The book treats representation issues in the context of a design process that has identifiable steps, requiring particular kinds of diagrams at each step; there are several examples of this process applied to small problems.

The larger issue of how to map a possibly vague set of requirements for a practical system into a set of candidate alternative forms for the system under design is treated by giving examples of how to do it, drawing lessons and guidelines from the examples, and offering a paradigm of design experimentation using the notation.

In a sense, the content of this book is in its diagrams, and there are many of them. Certainly, the subject matter requires diagrams, but even making allowance for this, the number is large. There are so many because of the book's focus on *TIME*-intensive systems. The book aims to help the reader to develop an eye for seeing temporal behaviour while drawing or observing structure, and for spotting temporal behavioural problems that may be implicit in bad structures. Many of the diagrams aim to show the unfolding of temporal behaviour in the way an expert would visualize it while mentally walking through a design, or explaining it to others, as an aid to helping the reader to develop the same expertise.

1.3   ORGANIZATION OF THE BOOK

Part I, titled NATURE OF THE BOOK contains only the chapter you are now reading.

Part II, titled PRINCIPLES OF METHOD AND NOTATION contains Chapters 2, 3, 4, and 5. All of these contain basic material for all readers.

- Chapter 2 sets the stage by discussing issues in design, and outlining the general nature of the *Architectural Design* method of the book.

- Chapter 3 is a fundamental chapter that paves the way for everything that follows, by giving an overview of the highlights of a subset of the *MachineCharts* notation in relation to the *Architectural Design* method, illustrated by simple examples. It devotes a lot of space to showing how to use diagrams as a basis for thinking about and exploring temporal behaviour of systems.

- Chapter 4 fleshes out the basic black-box-with-buttons subset of MachineCharts that was introduced in Chapter 3, and illustrates the fleshed-out notation with deeper examples that continue the visual approach to temporal behaviour.

- Chapter 5 gives the notation greater expressiveness for both Ada and non-Ada technologies. It stretches the notation, without introducing any new icons, to show how it provides a general conceptual framework for very different implementation technologies. It also extends the notation with new icons for handling unusual events outside of normal operating structures (e.g., exceptions), and specifying reuseable components and dynamic structures.

Part III, titled CASE STUDIES IN SYSTEM DESIGN, contains Chapters 6 and 7. These two chapters are important for understanding how to synthesize the form of a system. They are dependent on all of the chapters of Part II except Chapter 5 (there are only a few, non-critical backward references to this chapter).

- Chapter 6 consolidates the method and notation by providing a case study that demonstrates the design of sequential and concurrent versions of a system to play the game of LIFE, in the process raising many design issues associated with interfaces and glue structures.

- Chapter 7 shows how to explore alternative forms for a system under design by visually examining the behaviour and performance of compositions of subsystems and components in terms of their interfaces and glue structures. It contains a substantial case study of a communications example that illustrates design transformation to improve performance.

Part IV, titled EXERCISING THE NOTATION ON TIME-INTENSIVE PROBLEMS, contains Chapters 8 and 9.

- Chapter 8 explores a number of issues in *TIME*-intensive systems, using a series of small case studies; the issues include busy-waiting, non-busy-waiting, deadlocks, flow control, critical races, timeouts, and real time. Some of these have been treated before, but here they are treated either in greater depth, or from a different perspective.

- Chapter 9 is a case study of a particular, *TIME*-intensive problem, that of concurrent readers and writers accessing a shared resource. The problem is simple, but worth studying in detail because it contains ample scope for demonstrating ways in which inappropriate behaviour may be inadvertently designed-in, and because it provides a vehicle for a thorough treatment of the relationships between timing diagrams, state machines, component interfaces, and component internal details. A particular feature of this chapter is its presentation of several examples of plug-in state machines, using an Abstract Controller Machine (ACM) abstraction.

Part V, titled COMPONENTRY, contains only Chapter 10.

- Chapter 10 is on principles of designing for reuseability, centering around a common concept of a template for both passive and active components. There are many Ada examples, involving task typing and generics, both of which are special cases of the template concept. Static and dynamic instance structures are covered.

Part VI, titled CONCLUSIONS, contains only Chapter 11.

- Chapter 11 makes concluding remarks and suggests vectors for the future.

The book closes with several appendices:

- Appendix A gives an overview of an annotation approach for MachineCharts being developed for the TimeBench project at Carleton University, to give an idea of how the visual approach presented here is seen as fitting into a designer's workbench.

- Appendix B provides supplementary problems to give the reader something on which to practice.

- Appendix C identifies supplementary reading associated directly with the material of the book.

- Appendix D provides a glossary of key terms relating to MachineCharts and Architectural Design.

For readers who want a quick overview of how much visual notation there is to learn, the pivotal method figures are 2.2, 2.3, 3.1, and 3.43, and the pivotal notation figures are 3.2, 4.1, 4.5, 4.7, 5.1, 5.2, 5.5, 5.8, 5.16, 5.25, and 5.36. Tables 4.1 and 4.2 give some basic mappings to Ada. The rest is mostly explanation, application, and illustration.

The only important topic in the book that is not consolidated in one place is that of Abstract Controller Machines (ACMs). ACMs provide a standard way of "plugging in temporal behaviour". They are introduced in Chapter 3, and illustrated in Chapters 6 and 9. The pivotal figures are 3.37, 3.38, 3.39, 3.40, 6.10, 9.12, 9.35, and 9.46.

Throughout the book, design material is explicitly distinguished from implementation examples or comments by putting the latter in insets headed IMPLEMENTATION IMPLICATIONS; these insets are scattered throughout every chapter, and contain specifically Ada-related examples or comments, often supplemented by informal remarks on relationships to other implementation technologies.

Part II

PRINCIPLES OF METHOD AND NOTATION

Chapter 2

THE ARCHITECTURAL DESIGN PROCESS

2.1 SEPARATION OF CONCERNS

To enable humans to cope with practically complex problems, separation of concerns is essential. For example, the computer industry depends on separating concerns into software and hardware domains; software concerns are often separated into operating system and application program domains; individual programs are often separated into files that may be worked on by different persons independently; projects are often separated into teams that work on different aspects of a problem; and so forth. The point is that without separation of concerns, complex problems cannot be managed, either intellectually or operationally.

This chapter is about separation of design concerns, and about a design process called *Architectural Design* that results from a particular separation. The rest of the book is about this Architectural Design process.

The Architectural Design process is based on separating concerns associated with the following three domains of design:

- The *WORK* domain is concerned with *what* the system must do to satisfy application requirements (e.g., numeric computation, or data processing); in other words, with *functional behaviour*.

- The *TIME* domain is concerned with *when* interactions occur between the system and its environment, and between the parts of the system itself, to accomplish the work; in other words, with *temporal behaviour*.

   (Throughout this book, "*TIME*" refers to this domain of design, which may require drawing diagrams of various kinds to express temporal relationships, in contrast to "time", which has its ordinary meaning in terms of seconds, minutes, hours, etc.).

- The *PLACE* domain is concerned with *where* work is to be performed, and *where* interaction paths exist, in relation to the parts of the system; in other words, with system *structure*.

17

This separation of concerns is a common sense one inspired by how we view machines in the physical world. Physical machines have parts that are visibly connected together (the *PLACE* domain), that visibly do work (the *WORK* domain), and that visibly move through externally observable sequences of events and states (the *TIME* domain). It seems desirable to separate design concerns for the systems of this book into the same domains, provided this is practical.

Figure 2.1 represents the three domains by orthogonal axes, suggesting that design refinement can proceed independently along each axis. In fact the concerns are not orthogonal in a global sense, because decisions in the different domains cannot be made completely independently of each other. However, a stepwise design process that proceeds for a while with design refinement in one domain, while fixing concerns in the other two, is eminently practical. Any such process of stepwise refinement may be viewed as tracing a zig-zag path in the 3-dimensional space defined by the three axes. At any point in the process, the path establishes a vector from the origin to a point in this space. The length of the vector is proportional to the amount of information that has been placed in the design data base up to that point. Projections of the vector along the axes have lengths proportional to the amount of information accumulated relative to that axis.

From a behavioural perspective, we may view total system behaviour as having a *WORK* component and a *TIME* component. Design of these components can initially be separated, but eventually must be merged. A designer may appropriately work on the *TIME*-domain aspects of behaviour first for *TIME*-intensive systems, deferring details in the *WORK* domain. For as long as *WORK*-domain concerns can be deferred, we are left with a joint stepwise refinement process between the *TIME* and *PLACE* domains called *Architectural Design* in this book.

A further separation of concerns is once again inspired by how we view machines in the physical world. Physical machines have *outside* and *inside* aspects in all three domains. We can describe how they are constructed and operate from the *outside* in terms of these aspects, without being specialists in the technology of the machines; designers and specialists are concerned with how machinery *inside* a machine causes its *outside* aspects.

The notion that there are *outside* and *inside* concerns along each of the dimensions of Figure 2.1 that may be treated separately is illustrated by Figure 2.2:

- *OUTSIDE* refers to the *what* of each domain. As suggested by Figure 2.2, *outside* aspects of a design are developed first, before *inside* ones. Relative to each of the axes, outside aspects are as follows:

    - *WORK*: *What* work is to be done?
    - *PLACE*: *What* system parts are required to perform the work and *what* are the interaction pathways among them?
    - *TIME*: *What* interactions occur at *what* times and in *what* sequences?

- *INSIDE* refers to the *how* of each domain. As suggested by Figure 2.2, *inside* aspects are developed after *outside* ones. Relative to each of the axes, inside aspects are as follows:

    - *WORK*: *How* is work to be done inside parts?

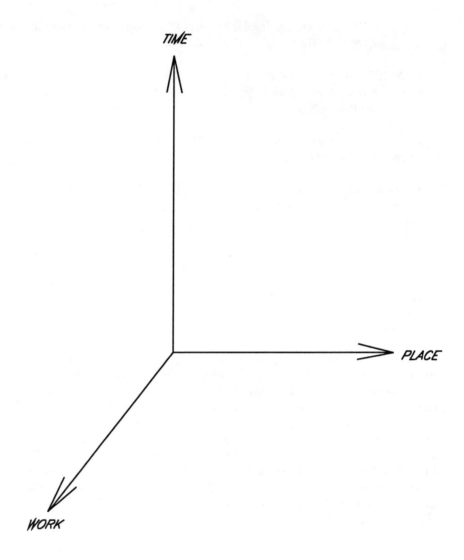

Figure 2.1: SEPARATION OF CONCERNS INTO WORK, TIME AND PLACE

> – *PLACE*: *How* are the insides of parts to be organized to perform work?
>
> – *TIME*: *How* are the insides of parts to be organized to make interactions occur at the right times and in the right sequences?

- *INSIDE* a subsystem may be a set of *OUTSIDES* for subsubsystems; thus subsystems, subsubsystems, etc., may themselves be treated as systems, in a process of recursive decomposition.

Notice the absence of both *data* and *control* from these definitions. This is because, in the approach of this book, both are regarded as aspects of *TIME* and *PLACE*:

- The *flow* of control and data are *outside* aspects of *TIME* and *PLACE*. In other words, they are aspects of interactions.

- *Exercising* control is an *inside* aspect of both *TIME* and *PLACE*.

- The *storage* of data is an *inside* aspect of *PLACE*.

An important feature of the approach presented in this book is its insistence on both *outside* and *inside* aspects for the *TIME* domain. This enables common sense descriptions of *behaviour* to be provided in terms of *outside* aspects of system parts, without reference to their internal details.

Programming languages provide well established means for separating *WORK* and *PLACE* concerns, and for separating each into *outside* and *inside* aspects. For example, the name of a procedure, together with its arguments, may identify the *outside* aspect a unit of work, with the body giving the details of how the work is to be done (the *inside* aspect). The specification of an Ada package gives *outside* aspects of *PLACE* and *WORK*, and its body gives corresponding *inside* aspects. Object oriented programming systems like Smalltalk additionally provide means of reusing *inside* aspects of *WORK* in different *PLACES*, through inheritance expressed in terms of *outside* aspects of classes.

Programming languages provide very limited means of separating *TIME* concerns. Multitasking languages like Ada enable *TIME*-domain to be partitioned into concurrent timelines, using tasks, but do not provide means of specifying behaviour of tasks from the *outside*. In programming, *inside* aspects of *WORK* and *TIME* are typically intertwined in algorithms *inside* a *PLACE*. This makes reasoning about *outside* patterns in *TIME*, while writing or reading the text of a program, conspicuously difficult, particularly for multitasking software, in which interaction patterns between concurrent *TIME* threads may be buried in the bodies of tasks spread over many pages of program text.

Hardware engineers recognize the value of having separate *outside* descriptions relating to the *TIME* domain and have put the facilities for doing so into the hardware specification language, VHDL. This language provides for separate descriptions of a part in terms of its *inside* "structure" and its *outside* "behaviour". The latter is a just a joint description of *WORK* and *TIME*, seen from the *outside* of a part, which is exactly the kind of *TIME*-domain *outside* description missing from programming languages, but desirable for design.

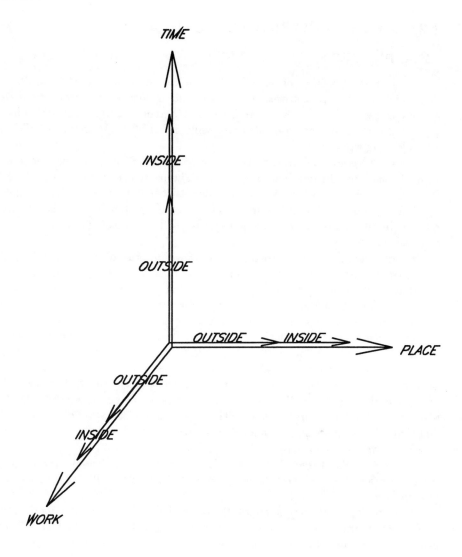

Figure 2.2: FURTHER SEPARATION OF CONCERNS INTO INSIDE
AND OUTSIDE ASPECTS

2.2 ARCHITECTURAL DESIGN

2.2.1 PROCESS

The separation of *TIME* concerns from *WORK* ones enables *TIME* and *PLACE* aspects to be jointly refined in a process which is called, in this book, *Architectural Design*. This process proceeds jointly in the *PLACE* and *TIME* domains, paying attention first to *outside* aspects of each, and then to *inside* ones, while deferring *inside* details of *WORK* (in other words leaving work in *stub* form).

The *Architectural Design* process may be visualized as tracing a path in *WORK-TIME-PLACE* space, as illustrated by Figure 2.3. The particular path shown in the figure fixes *WORK* in *outside* stub form and then proceeds to refine details of *TIME* and *PLACE* in a zig-zag fashion, first refining details in one of these dimensions, then fixing them and refining details in the other dimension relative to them, dealing with *outside* aspects first, and then *inside* ones.

Designs produced by this process are expressed in terms of communicating "black boxes" that may, in general, have interfaces, internal state, and internal passive or active machinery, and that may be expressed in reuseable form. Such black boxes may also be called "objects", so Architectural Design may be viewed as a form of process that has come to be known as "Object Oriented Design" in the software community.

At some point on this path short of implementation, enough information will be available about *WORK* (in stub form), *TIME* and *PLACE* to make the design complete enough to evaluate its behaviour in skeletal form, either by analysis, or execution. The behaviour will be incomplete, because details of *WORK* have been deferred, but it will be capable of demonstrating work item sequencing and timing. Execution may be by manual walk-through or by visual animation in a workbench. In either case, the visual nature of the execution and the fact that what is executing is, in a sense, a prototype of the system under design, suggests that the term *Visual Prototyping* be applied to the process.

In other words, *Visual Prototyping* is the animation (manually, or automatically) of design diagrams that are mostly concerned with *PLACE* and *TIME*, and that leave *WORK* in stub form.

The Architectural Design approach forms the backbone of the method part of this book. The separation of concerns that it provides into *WORK*, *TIME* and *PLACE* aspects gives a desirable modularity to the processes of design capture, design experimentation and mapping to implementation technology.

Figure 2.4 gives a perspective on transforming requirements into implementations that shows the place of the techniques of this book as being squarely in the middle, in the area of capturing design ideas in human-comprehensible form. From this point, compiling human-created designs into partial implementations is currently technically feasible. The holy grail is to completely bypass the design step by compiling formal requirements directly into implementations, as shown by the dotted arrows in the figure. Research has shown that it is technically feasible to generate small fragments of code in this way. However, it seems likely that human designers will need to provide a design framework for such automatically generated fragments for the forseeable future, because of the difficulty of taking into account constraints and experience in the compilation process. The implementation phase may be separated into partial implementation and complete implementation steps, with the former

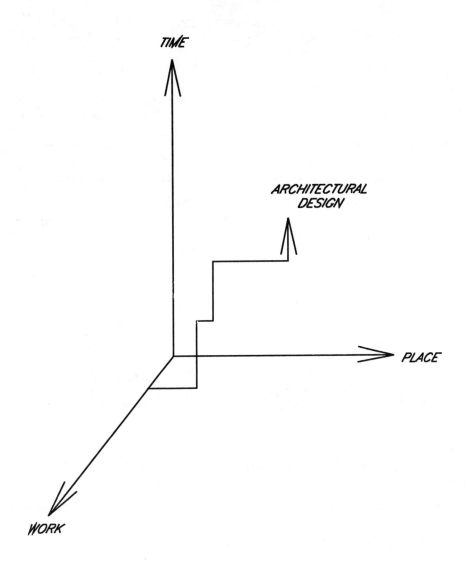

Figure 2.3: THE ARCHITECTURAL DESIGN PATH

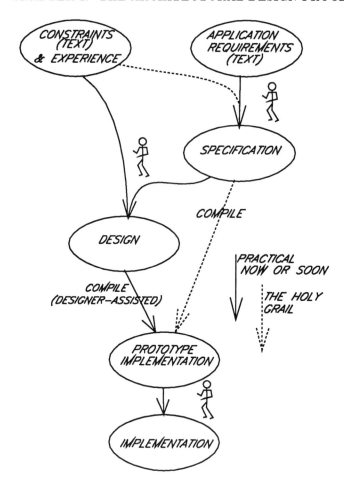

Figure 2.4: TRANSFORMING SPECIFICATIONS INTO IMPLEMENTATIONS

being compilable from design input, and the latter requiring human intervention.

2.2.2   PRELIMINARY DESIGN

Preliminary design is concerned with partitioning the system under design into subsystems (possibly recursively), informally allocating work items to each, and exploring the nature of the interactions that need to take place among the subsystems to do the work, while deferring details of both work and interfaces. Deferring interface details is particularly important for *TIME*-intensive systems, because the underlying nature of interactions needs to be explored first, to ensure that inappropriate overheads are not built in at the interface level. At this stage, work aspects appear explicitly as textual comments in *PLACE* diagrams, and implicitly as time fillers in *TIME* patterns.

Recursive decomposition of subsystems may be carried out in many ways. One may proceed in a preliminary way through all levels of decomposition, and then make a second pass for detailed design. One may begin with detailed design at some deeply nested level, because design parts are available at that level, and move up to preliminary design at higher levels, and then back downwards for detailed design. The reader may imagine other possibilities.

> IMPLEMENTATION IMPLICATIONS: The approach of exploring interactions before committing to interfaces is at odds with the approach one often hears advocated for Ada of writing package specifications as a first step in "design".

The reader may ask how preliminary design differs from requirements analysis. The answer is that it is a form of requirements analysis that expresses the requirements for detailed design. Whether or not one thinks of this forming a continuum with higher level requirements analysis depends on whether or not one thinks that higher level requirements analysis must be free of *PLACE*-domain commitments. If not, then an object-oriented perspective is in place, and a continuum between requirements analysis and preliminary design is possible.

2.2.3   DETAILED DESIGN

Detailed design is concerned with defining interfaces of black boxes, and internal details. It has two major phases, as follows:

- DETAILED OUTSIDE DESIGN: Interfaces are configured to provide the means for achieving the intent of preliminary design. Behaviour patterns are checked in concrete interface terms.

- DETAILED INSIDE DESIGN: Inside details of components are designed with the intent of achieving the desired *TIME* and *WORK* patterns; that they actually do so is verified by testing the detailed design, at the design level.

2.2.4   DESIGN PATHS IN WORK-TIME-PLACE SPACE

The general nature of design paths in *WORK-TIME-PLACE* space is indicated by Figure 2.3, but different paths may be followed in different parts of the same project, or by different designers in different projects. For example, the figure suggests a *PLACE*-first path, in which one decides on subsystems before deciding on their *TIME*-domain nature, but a *TIME*-first path is also possible, in which one decides on concurrency and on event patterns among concurrent components, deferring grouping of them into subsystems until a later *PLACE*-domain step.

2.2.5   TIME GRANULARITY IN ARCHITECTURAL DESIGN

To wrap up this chapter, it may be helpful to point out that the separation of *TIME*-domain concerns from *WORK*-domain ones that is central to the Architectural Design approach amounts to viewing the *TIME* domain at different levels of granularity. Sequencing and timing of interactions among *PLACE*-domain parts are *TIME*-domain concerns at a coarse level of granularity. Sequencing of statements in sequential algorithms to do work inside parts, which is actually a *TIME*-domain concern at a fine level of granularity, is treated as a *WORK*-domain concern instead.

Chapter 3

AN INTRODUCTION TO MACHINECHARTS FOR ARCHITECTURAL DESIGN

3.1 INTRODUCTION

This chapter gives the essence of the *Architectural Design* method and the *MachineCharts* notation, in one place. The notation is fleshed out in Chapters 4 and extended in Chapter 5 but, with only the material of this chapter in mind, the essential nature of the design process, and of most diagrams, can be understood, and basic designs can be drawn.

This chapter follows the steps of a particular Architectural Design path, introducing MachineChart notations and concepts as they are required, and illustrating them by examples, where appropriate. Recall from Chapter 2 that in the Architectural Design process, design concerns are separated into *WORK*, *TIME*, and *PLACE* domains, and that the focus is on joint refinement of the *TIME* and *PLACE* domains, proceeding with *outside* aspects first. A further separation of concerns is achieved by separating preliminary design from detailed design.

The *PLACE*-domain diagrams introduced in this chapter are *operational*, in the sense that they show the parts of the system that run, and the relationships among the parts that enable them to interact while they are running. The *TIME*-domain diagrams introduced in this chapter continue this operational theme by showing (or specifying) the temporal patterns that may occur in relation to the parts of the system, while the system is running.

This operational theme continues throughout the book. Even when templates are introduced, in Chapters 5 and 10, the diagrams show only how operational parts are derived from templates, not how templates may be derived from each other by, say, inheritance (the latter subject is outside the scope of this book).

3.2   VISUAL MILESTONES ALONG A DESIGN PATH

3.2.1   A REFERENCE ARCHITECTURAL DESIGN PATH

For reference purposes, the kind of diagrams drawn for each step of a reference Architectural Design path that zig-zags between the *PLACE* and *TIME* domains are illustrated in Figure 3.1; this is a *PLACE-FIRST* path that will be discussed in the following sections. The reader should not conclude that this is the best, or only, path just because it is illustrated first.

A point to be kept in mind while following the steps of this path in this chapter, is that the path applies equally well to sequential or concurrent systems. In fact, after the reader has understood the notation, close examination of the diagrams in the steps of Figure 3.1 will reveal that it depicts the design of a sequential system. On the other hand, the example used to illustrate it in this chapter is a simple concurrent system. To bring the point home even more strongly, Chapter 6 provides a case study that follows exactly these steps to develop designs for sequential and concurrent versions of the same system.

The steps of this path, or something like them, are essential parts of the thinking patterns that lead to capturing design details in implementable form. However, the formal drawing of all the diagrams associated with all of the design steps may not always be necessary, although it may often be desirable. Only concrete structure charts and associated details are really necessary to capture implementation intent. However, the information in other diagrams is useful to provide redundant information against which details can be checked.

A subsystem may itself be viewed as a system, with the consequence that the design steps may apply recursively to it. This may be carried out for as many levels of recursive decomposition as may be deemed appropriate for the problem at hand.

3.2.2   GENERAL OVERVIEW OF THE VISUAL NOTATION OF THE REFERENCE DESIGN PATH

The icons in the diagrams of the reference design path of Figure 3.1 are as follows, introduced in the order in which they appear in the numbered steps of the path:

- **(Steps 1,5,6,7)** Rectangles are *boxes*, representing *PLACE*-domain partitioning into subsystems.

- **(Steps 1,2,5)** Double headed arrows are *events*, having both *PLACE*-domain and *TIME*- domain presence (the former indicating possible paths and the latter indicating occurrence).

- **(Steps 1,5)** *PLACE*-domain diagrams containing faceless boxes and events are *abstract structure charts*, useful in preliminary design.

- **(Step 2)** Sets of parallel lines are *timelines*, representing *TIME*-domain partitioning into potentially concurrent activity threads. With events added, they are *event scenarios*, useful in preliminary design. A good starting point is to draw one timeline per peer component in a diagram (in the end there may be fewer or more timelines than this, depending on concurrency decisions, and the judgement of the designer about how to best represent temporal behaviour for the particular system under design).

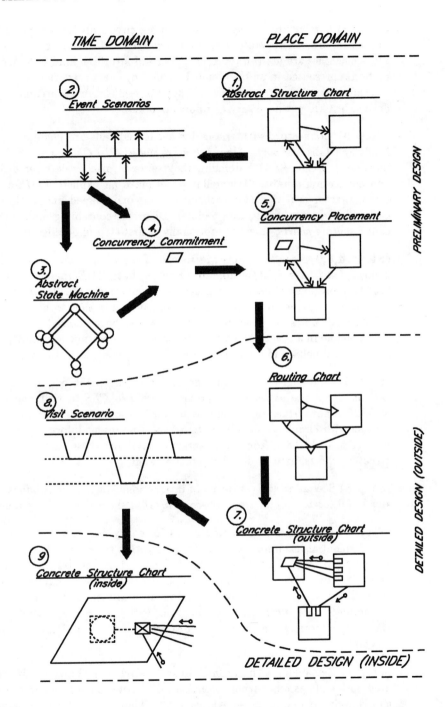

Figure 3.1: HIGHLIGHTS OF A PLACE-FIRST APPROACH TO ARCHITECTURAL DESIGN

- **(Step 3)** Circles are *states*. Arrows joining circles are *transitions*. Diagrams containing these icons are *state transition diagrams* used to show state machines visually. State machines are used to represent, in closed form, the kind of *TIME*-domain information represented in an open-ended fashion by event scenarios; such state machines are called *abstract state machines*. They are useful in both preliminary and detailed design, but are not necessary components of either.

- **(Step 6)** Connectors with triangular heads and tails are *channels*. The triangular heads and tails are *ports*. Channels have mixed *PLACE*-domain and *TIME*-domain purposes. In the *PLACE*-domain, they serve as placeholders for deferred interface and connection details. Triangular ports make an explicit *TIME*-domain commitment, that of *visit direction* (otherwise, diamond shaped endpoints are used, indicating bidirectional visits are possible). Diagrams containing boxes and channels are called *routing charts*; they are, optionally, a first step of detailed outside design.

- **(Steps 4,5,9)** Parallelograms are *robots*. They are autonomous, self-directing machines. They have *PLACE*-domain presence, but *TIME*-domain purpose, indicating that temporal behaviour is partitioned into concurrent threads, one thread per robot. If there is only one robot in a system, the system is said to be sequential; multiple robots make a system concurrent. A robot may be visualized as a machine with its own timeline in a scenario, which it controls (this does not necessarily imply that the number of timelines in scenarios is restricted to be equal to the number of robots).

- **(Step 7)** Rectangles or parallelograms attached to the edges of similarly shaped machine icons are *buttons* that provide both *PLACES* to visit and means of doing *WORK*. Lines connecting machines to buttons are *fingers* that provide visit paths. Arrows with circular tails adjacent to fingers represent information carried with the visit or brought back from it. Diagrams containing these icons are *concrete outside structure charts*, used in detailed outside design.

- **(Step 8)** Scenarios with patterns of interaction shown as continuous waveforms, instead of discrete events, are *visit scenarios* that show visit threads among machines.

- **(Step 9)** Rectangles with their corners joined by diagonal lines are *engines*: primitive sequential machines, without inside *PLACE* structure, that drive, via *agendas*, the visit patterns of machines. The "X" formed by the diagonals may be regarded as symbolizing their lack of internal *PLACE* structure. Engines, like robots, have *PLACE*-domain presence, but *TIME*-domain purpose; unlike robots, they cannot be further decomposed structurally. Diagrams with engines are *concrete inside structure charts*; they normally make their appearance only during detailed inside design of a machine.

- **(Step 9)** Rectangles with internal circles are *Abstract Controller Machines (ACMs)*, used optionally as sequencers by engines. The notation symbolizes a box (the rectangle) containing a state machine (the circle). They may be used to "plug in" abstract state machines developed during preliminary design into a concrete context during detailed inside design. Like robots and engines, they have *PLACE*-domain presence, but *TIME*-domain purpose; they have implicit internal *PLACE*-domain structure, but this structure is normally a standard one, used as a framework for "plugging-in" an abstract state machine.

Abstract structure charts and event scenarios are optional in general, but useful for exploring temporal behaviour patterns in *TIME*- intensive systems, before committing to concrete interface details. Abstract state machines and ACMs are optional in general, but useful for separating interaction control from sequencing and timing logic, when there are intricate temporal behaviour patterns. Routing charts are optional in general, but useful for indicating the general nature of a system's structure, with partial commitment to interfaces and connections. Visit scenarios are optional in general, but useful for confirming intended temporal behaviour at the interface level, and as later test cases.

3.3   SOME KEY CONCEPTS

3.3.1   INTRODUCTION

This section explains the visit and event models of interactions. The concepts underlying these models are needed before delving deeper into the notation and method.

3.3.2   THE CONCRETE INTERACTION MODEL: VISITS

Concrete interactions among black boxes are conceptualized in the *TIME* domain as *visits*. For example, one may visualize a robot visiting a box to obtain service, or visiting another robot to announce, or wait for, some event. A box normally does not initiate visits on its own, but may do so if it has internal robots to do the visiting. The concept of a visit is essentially one-to-one (i.e., when a machine visits somewhere, it cannot be visiting elsewhere at the same time); to have multiple visits going on simultaneously, a machine needs multiple internal robots.

Visits trigger *WORK* at some other place. The work may take a short time, in which case it may be completed entirely during the visit; or it may take a long time, in which case it may be broken up into a request part, a work part, and a result part, with one visit required to pass the request, and another to get the result, in between which the work is done. Visits always take the visitor away from its home place for some length of time.

Later, we shall see explicit notations for representing different visiting mechanisms, but for the time being, the concept of a visit is sufficient to keep us going.

IMPLEMENTATION IMPLICATIONS:

The visit concept covers a wide range of practical software interaction mechanisms:

- The simplest visit is a procedure call, in which case the work is done immediately and the visitor leaves when it is done.

- An Ada entry call is a procedure-like visit, except that it requires the active cooperation of an acceptor to complete. A 2-way meeting, called a rendezvous, occurs.

- Message sends and receives directly between tasks have different visit models, depending on whether they are asynchronous or synchronous.

  - Asynchronous message sends require implicit intermediate places to visit to deposit messages. Visits to these places by the sender and receiver do not result in meetings between them. The intermediate places may be hidden in real time executives, or may be designed as explicit components, but in either case they may be conceptualized at the design level as explicit black boxes.

  - Synchronous message sends to tasks may be conceptualized as direct visits to a robot representing the receiving task. In this case, the message is transferred during a meeting between the sender and receiver

- Semaphores and mailboxes are intermediate places to visit that are typically hidden in a real time executive, but that may be conceptualized at the design level as black boxes in their own right.

- Message sending between objects in object oriented programming is procedure-call-like, and may be conceptualized as direct visiting.

- Monitor calls are visits to monitor black boxes.

The visit concept works well for any system composed of cooperating sequential machines, whether implemented in software or hardware. It is important to note that, in multitasking implementations, visits between robots *do not* necessarily imply task context switching (a context switch is when one running task is replaced by another on the same processor); whether they do, or not, depends on the implementation technology.

In a concurrent system, visit direction becomes an important interface issue that is better left until detailed design, because it may have a profound effect on waiting and response patterns. For example, to pass a request and get a result, the following visit patterns are possible:

- The requestor visits the worker with the request, and visits again to get (and possibly wait for) the result.

- The requestor visits the worker with the request, and the worker makes a return visit to deliver the result.

- The worker visits the requestor to get (and possibly wait for) the request, and visits again to deliver the result.

- The worker visits the requestor to get (and possibly wait for) the request, and the requestor visits the worker to get (and possibly wait for) the result.

- All visit some intermediate place (or places) to deposit requests and results, and to get (and possibly wait for) them.

- Messengers move requests and results from place to place.

During preliminary design, it is better to think of the request and the result as abstract *events*, and to defer until later the issue of which of these concrete mechanisms for getting them from place to place is appropriate for the problem at hand.

3.3.3 THE ABSTRACT INTERACTION MODEL: EVENTS

Events are used during preliminary design to indicate *what* interactions take place, without commitment to *how* they take place by means of visits.

The term *event* is widely understood to imply a quantity that occurs instantaneously, and indivisibly, at some time. However, in addition to this *TIME*-domain aspect, events also have *PLACE*-domain aspects; they must originate at some place (the source) and be absorbed at some other place (the sink). There are many interpretations in common use of the relationship between the *TIME* and *PLACE* aspects of events. An event may be constrained to occur at the same time in the source and sink places, in which case it is either a *transient* event, that disappears if the sink place is not ready for it, or a *rendezvous* event, that cannot occur until both the source and sink places agree that it should occur. Alternatively, an event may be, in effect, stretched out in time, by allowing it to be *queued* after leaving the source, until it can be absorbed by the sink, in the meantime allowing other activity to go on at the source, and other events to occur.

Different communities may tend to think of one or the other of these event models as fundamental. Computer communications practitioners tend to think in terms of a *queued* event model, in which events are messages that may be queued at a receiver while the sender continues with other activities. Concurrent system theorists tend to think in terms of a *rendezvous* event model, in which rendezvous interactions are instantaneous in time, because it is easier to make formal statements and draw formal conclusions from such a model. Ada is based on an *extended rendezvous* model, in which the start of the rendezvous and the end of the rendezvous are distinct events. Hardware engineers may think in terms of a *transient* event model, in which events may be lost if there is no receiver ready for them.

Many methods and tools for specifying temporal behaviour are constrained to a particular event model, to make execution and/or analysis of specifications easier. Unfortunately, sticking to one particular event model for preliminary design may make conceptualization of temporal behaviour harder, if the model does not match the way the designer thinks of the system as "really" behaving. This is because the constraints of a particular model may force the addition of machinery to capture what is "really" meant. For example, if events are "really" queued, then a transient event model requires adding queuing mechanisms explicitly, in terms of transient events; if they are "really" rendezvous, then a queued event model requires adding rendezvous mechanisms explicitly, in terms of queued events; and so forth. Such added machinery makes conceptualizing what is "really" meant more difficult than is desirable.

Accordingly, the MachineCharts event model is not constrained *a priori*. It is up to the designer to indicate which interpretation is intended for particular events, and it allows different interpretations for different events. The notation of this book does not provide distinct event icons for different event models, so this indication must be conveyed by comments and by the way event scenarios are drawn (examples throughout the book illustrate how to do this). Using specific event models during preliminary design to gain the advantage of executability and/or analysis is not precluded. However, the issue of aligning such models with concrete event transfer machinery developed by the Architectural Design process during detailed design is outside the scope of this book. Therefore, events are treated only as a means of organizing thinking during the preliminary design stage.

The MachineCharts event model is as follows:

- An event is a named, abstract unit of communication between components that is independent of the concrete interface details of the components.

- An event may have data associated with it (thus an event may be, in effect, a message).

- The *PLACE* aspect of an event defines an interaction path, with *source* and *sink* ends.

- The *TIME* aspect of an event defines points on timelines when the event is *sourced* and *sunk*.

- Event sourcing and sinking are viewed as occurring instantaneously at timelines, but as, *possibly* taking some time to transfer between timelines, so that the sourcing and sinking times for the same event are not necessarily identical; during the transfer time, activity may or may not continue at the source. Thus transient, rendezvous, or queued interpretations are allowed, depending on the patterns shown in scenarios.

A distinctive arrow notation for events is deliberately used to distinguish abstract structure charts from the ubiquitous data flow diagrams used in industry for requirements analysis. The difference from data flow diagrams is that events represent only *outside* manifestations of control and data; all control is assumed to be exerted from the *inside* of black boxes, and all data is assumed to be stored *inside* them.

3.4   THE BLACK-BOX-WITH-BUTTONS MODEL OF COMPONENTS

3.4.1   INTRODUCTION

The abstraction of a "black box" is an enduring one in electrical engineering and computing. The MachineCharts model has two basic kinds of black boxes appropriate for system level partitioning, one without any *TIME*-domain semantics, called simply a *box*, and one with *TIME*-domain semantics, called a *robot*. Boxes are for *PLACE*-domain partitioning, and robots for *TIME*-domain partitioning (in the sense that they partition temporal behaviour into concurrent time threads). Buttons and fingers are attached to black boxes to provide visit paths.

3.4.2   BOXES: "BLACK-BOXES" THAT PROVIDE ONLY PARTITIONING AND CONTAINMENT

Boxes are shown in Steps 1, 5, 6, and 7 of Figure 3.1. They model packaging and information-hiding structures in software and hardware that provide only partitioning and containment, without having any implicit temporal behaviour of their own. During design, they may be used as passive enclosures, providing either data abstraction or passive machinery (e.g., the right-hand or bottom boxes of Step 7); or they may be made into active machines that may have any kind of external temporal behaviour, by placing appropriate machinery inside them (e.g., the top, left-hand box of Steps 5 and 7).

The visual representation of a box is a rectangle, the empty inside of which is a place where internal machinery may be hidden, and the periphery of which is a place to which to attach interface components. A faceless box (in other words, one without interface components, as in Steps 1 and 5) is an incomplete machine, that can exist in this form only during preliminary design. Interfaces like those in Step 7 are created during detailed design by adding buttons (as places to visit) and fingers (as paths for outgoing visits), along with appropriate parameters

> IMPLEMENTATION IMPLICATIONS: In programming terms, boxes map to the likes of Ada packages, Modula-2 modules, Turbo Pascal units, and objects in object oriented programming languages like Smalltalk, or Objective-C. There are no explicit equivalents in earlier programming languages like C, Fortran or Pascal, but experienced programmers often create implicit equivalents by grouping related program components in separate files. For hardware design using VHDL, boxes are entities. For hardware-software codesign, one might also interpret boxes as devices, boards, chips, or cells. Depending on interfaces and internal details, boxes may degenerate to other constructs such as variables, procedures or tasks. The interface of a box does not necessarily correspond to a specification in a programming language, like Ada's package specifications, because it contains more information.

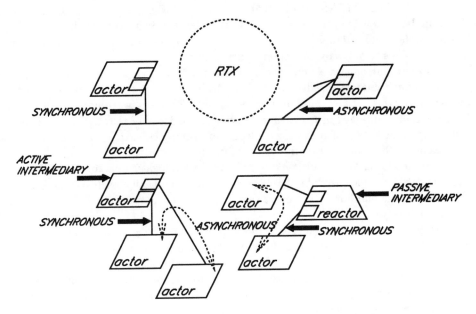

Figure 3.2: HOW TO THINK ABOUT ROBOTS

3.4.3 ROBOTS: AUTONOMOUS "BLACK-BOXES"

Robots are shown in Steps 5, 7, and 9 of Figure 3.1. They model active tasks and passive multitasking objects in software; they also model autonomous, sequential machines and shared devices in hardware.

The general property of robots that distinguishes them from boxes is their autonomy, making it possible for them to operate concurrently relative to each other, and to have control over when they interact with each other; otherwise, they have identical properties to boxes of enclosure and information hiding. The name "robot" follows naturally from the fact that robots in the automated factories of the present, and in science fiction stories of the future, are *autonomous, self-directed machines* that may operate concurrently with each other.

The default visual representation for a robot is a parallelogram, which may be viewed as symbolizing parallelism (in other words concurrency), hinted at by the word "parallelo-gram". Alternatively, the shape itself, like a box leaning over as if in motion, may be taken to symbolize activity.

Faceless robots (Step 5), like faceless boxes, are incomplete machines that can appear in this form only during preliminary design. Interfaces are created during detailed design by adding buttons (as places to visit) and fingers (as paths for outgoing visits), along with appropriate parameters (Steps 7 and 9 show only fingers on the interface, but in general there may also be buttons).

Figure 3.2 shows how to think about relationships among robots. The implicit relationship to a real time executive *RTX* hinted at in this figure is discussed under "IMPLEMENTATION IMPLICATIONS". Note that the circle representing the real time executive is shown in dashed outline, to emphasize that it is never drawn explicitly in design diagrams; it is drawn here only to indicate that a real time executive implicitly underlies the mapping of robot designs to software implementation technologies.

This figure introduces a new icon — a trapezoid — for a new kind of robot, a passive one, henceforth characterized as a *reactor*. Robots that are not reactors — represented by parallelograms — are characterized as *actors*. Reactors were not shown explicitly in Figure 3.1, or mentioned in the earlier overview of the icons of that figure, because they are just a specialized form of robot that introduces nothing essentially new; an actor may act as a reactor. The visual distinction is nice but not necessary.

Actors model tasks in multitasking software technologies. Reactors model passive multitasking objects that provide shared services in a mutually exclusive fashion, such as semaphores and mailboxes; however, they may also be mapped to tasks programmed to behave passively.

Just as a parallelogram suggests the nature of an actor, so a trapezoid suggests the nature of a reactor. The trapezoid looks like the icon for an actor with an elongated base, suggesting that it is solidly in place instead of on the move (a visual synonym for the trapezoid will be introduced later that is useful for conceptualizing reactors in relation to Ada, or for indicating that a component that was originally characterized as an actor is more appropriately a reactor).

The salient points in Figure 3.2 are as follows:

- Actor robots are represented by parallelograms, reactor ones by trapezoids.

- Actor robots may have both buttons and fingers on their interfaces. Reactors often only have buttons, but may also have fingers (although the latter possibility is not shown in the figure).

- Direct connections between robots normally indicate synchronous interactions, whether the robots are actors or reactors. "Synchronous" means interlocked.

- Asynchronous interactions between peers are normally shown as indirect, via intermediary actors or reactors that act as the "glue" between them.

- Direct connections between actors and reactors are not different in kind from those between actors — both imply meetings between the directly-connected robots during which mutual exclusion is enforced — but because the internal machinery of a reactor is highly constrained, they may have quite different mappings to implementation technology.

- An extension to the notation described in Chapter 5 enables asynchronous interactions between peers to be shown as direct, using a "jab" icon (however, a reactor intermediary conveys the same intent in a more general fashion).

IMPLEMENTATION IMPLICATIONS:

Robots model *multitasking objects* supported by multitasking programming languages or real time executives, like tasks, semaphores, mailboxes, monitors, and so forth. Figure 3.2 hints that all of these objects, and the relationships among them, are supported by an underlying real time executive. Actors map to tasks. Reactors may map either to non-task objects, or to tasks programmed to behave passively. The underlying real time executive that supports such multitasking objects is not shown in design diagrams.

The notation does not constrain design thinking to synchronous task interactions that always require task context switching, like the Ada rendezvous, in spite of the fact that the subset notation of this chapter and Chapter 4 constrains direct robot interactions to be synchronous. This is so because synchronous interactions between actor and reactor robots may be mapped to non-context-switching interactions at the implementation level, given an appropriate implementation technology. For example, if an actor is mapped to a task and a reactor to a semaphore supported by a real time executive, then the task-semaphore interaction required to signal the semaphore does not necessarily imply a task context switch (sometimes it implies one if tasks are of different priorities and a higher priority task is signalled). Furthermore, asynchronous peer interactions are easily expressed at the design level by introducing explicit reactors as intermediaries between actors.

For Ada, visualizing the executive as implicit is natural, because the underlying real time executive is hidden from the programmer in the run time system for the language, and all multitasking objects are explicit at the language level (they are all programmed as tasks).

However, for languages that do not support multitasking objects, the real time executive is not hidden from the programmer, and visualizing it as hidden, and the objects it supports as explicit components, takes a deliberate mental effort.

Passive multitasking objects (e.g., semaphores and mailboxes) may often be provided as standard components by real time executives. Such standard components would be shown in design diagrams as reactors alongside custom actors and reactors that have been specially designed for the problem at hand. The notation of this chapter does not distinguish visually between standard and custom components, and there is no need to do so when only temporal behaviour is the issue. However, Chapter 4 has a marking for "foreign" components in structure charts that does the job.

3.4.4 BUTTONS AND FINGERS

INTRODUCTION

Buttons and fingers are shown as interface components in Steps 7 and 9 of Figure 3.1. Buttons and fingers are objects in the physical world with simple, common sense temporal behaviour patterns. They have essentially the same common sense nature in the MachineCharts world.

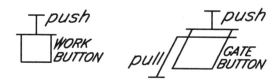

Figure 3.3: THE SHAPES OF BUTTONS AND FINGERS

GENERAL PROPERTIES OF BUTTONS AND FINGERS

Buttons are machines that do work when *visited* by other machines. *Fingers* indicate the paths over which visits may take place. A machine does not necessarily have to visit a button to get work done; it may do work itself. But such self-done work becomes part of the agenda of the engine of a machine, and is not shown in structure charts. Thus, buttons provide the means of explicitly identifying important work items in structure charts. Work is a very general term here, including such matters as incrementing counters, interpreting parameters, preparing results, and doing lengthy computations.

Buttons may stand alone as machines to do work in their own right (not shown in Figure 3.1), or be attached to boxes or robots (but not other buttons) as interface components.

Figure 3.3 shows how buttons and fingers are drawn, in isolation from other machines.

The salient points illustrated by Figure 3.3 are as follows:

- A button is represented visually from the *outside* by an icon that is intended to look like a side view of a physical button such as one might find on a television receiver, or in an elevator: namely a body, with an extended edge representing an edge-on view of a face that can be pushed. There are two kinds of buttons, visually distinguished by body shape; these are *work* buttons and *gate* buttons. They will now be described.

- Fingers identify visit paths from machines to buttons. With fingers, you see is what you get; they have no internal structure. Fingers may project from any machine (including a button) to connect to buttons. A finger is represented visually by a line drawn from a potential visitor machine to a button. When viewed in isolation, the tail of the finger is "T"-shaped, representing an attachment point to the edge of a machine. Directional arrows are not needed on fingers, because a finger-button path is directional, by inspection. There are two kinds of fingers, distinguished visually by the way their heads are shown in relationship to buttons; these are *push* fingers and *pull* fingers. They will now be described.

WORK BUTTONS AND PUSH FINGERS

A *work button* is one that does work immediately upon being pushed (it may also be called a *push button*, or an *immediate button*). The visual shape of its body conforms to that of a box, symbolizing that it may be only attached to a box.

Push fingers indicate paths for performing push visits to any kind of button. Visually, the head of the finger touches the face of the visited button.

Ways of visualizing interactions at work buttons are given later, in Section 3.5.

> IMPLEMENTATION IMPLICATIONS: Work buttons correspond to procedures or functions in any programming language. A push finger represents a call path in any programming language. Whether a button is implemented as a procedure or a function is purely an implementation decision.

GATE BUTTONS AND PULL FINGERS

A *gate button* is one that requires two visitors before work will be done by the button. One visitor must *push* the button, and the other *pull* it (therefore, gate buttons may also be called *push-pull* buttons). When a push and a pull both occur, a 2-way meeting between the visitors at the button occurs, during which the button does all the work and the visitors wait; when the button has finished its work, the visit is over and the visitors leave.

The visual shape of the body of a gate button conforms to that of a robot, symbolizing that it it may only be attached to a robot.

Pull fingers indicate paths for performing pull visits to gate buttons. In the notational subset of this chapter, they indicate a pull path between a robot's internal engine and one or more of its gate buttons, by means of which the engine controls meetings with external visitors to the robot. Visually, the head of a pull finger crosses the body of a gate button in a way that symbolizes pulling.

Ways of visualizing interactions at gate buttons are given later, in Section 3.12.

> IMPLEMENTATION IMPLICATIONS:
>
> For Ada, gate buttons attached to robots correspond to entries of Ada tasks. Visiting a gate button to push it corresponds to an entry call. Visiting a gate button to pull it corresponds to an entry accept. However, the concept this gives of a gate button being procedure-like does not quite correspond to Ada, although it is a good design abstraction. In Ada, entry bodies are coded in-line in accept statements in the executable part of a task body, and not defined as separate entities like procedures, as the button model seems to suggest. A consequence is that the same entry may have different bodies for it scattered throughout the program text. The MachineChart model of separately defined gate buttons is more structured than Ada (and leads naturally to more regular Ada program structures than inventive programmers might create by exploiting the full freedom of Ada).
>
> Outside Ada, gate buttons may be used as a abstractions of places where messages and answers may be exchanged in messaging systems, or where interactions may take place with non-task objects supported by real time executives,

like semaphores and mailboxes. Note that with these interpretations, a meeting at a gate button does not always imply a task context switch at the implementation level. There are various possible ways of representing such structures, and various possible mappings of them to implementations, that will be discussed in later chapters. For example, a single button might represent a message send-receive place, with push fingers representing message sending paths and pull fingers representing message receiving ones. Or different buttons might be used to represent send and receive places, with push fingers representing the paths for these operations, and a pull finger representing the visit path from an implicit controller that makes them mutually exclusive (the latter approach may also be interpreted in Ada terms).

PARAMETERS ASSOCIATED WITH BUTTONS AND FINGERS

Parameters are visually associated with fingers and buttons as arrows with circular tails visually close to and parallel with fingers. Parameters pointing towards the button are transferred at the beginning of the visit, and ones pointing away at the end; if the parameter points both ways, then a value goes in at the beginning and out at the end of the visit.

> IMPLEMENTATION IMPLICATIONS: Parameters associated with push fingers have the same meaning as call parameters in programming languages. Parameters associated with pull fingers may also have distinct meaning in some implementation technologies (e.g., a selector for the kind of message to be received). However, in Ada there is no concept of parameters associated with an accept being distinct from those associated with a call.

3.4.5   ENGINES

THE NATURE OF ENGINES

Engines are the driving force inside robots and buttons, and optionally inside boxes, as shown by Figure 3.4. Engines do work and make visits in much the same way for every kind of machine (although the engines in the figure have no projecting fingers, one may imagine that they will have such fingers in general, by means of which they may make visits). Each machine has at most one engine (a box may have none). If a machine has no other internal structure than its engine, then the engine may be assumed to exist, but need not be drawn, because only its agenda is of interest (agendas specify when the work is to be done and the visits to be made).

Because engines are the internal source of all visits by machines, diagrams to explain temporal behaviour will often be drawn showing only engines as visitors, omitting enclosing machines, thus leaving the reader to imagine appropriate ones.

As indicated by the annotations in the Figure 3.4, the nature of the enclosing machine affects only whether the operation of the engine is transient (non-cyclic), or persistent (cylic):

- Engines of boxes are transient, used only as initializors. It is a design mistake to provide a persistent agenda for a box, or to arrange visits to a box before initialization

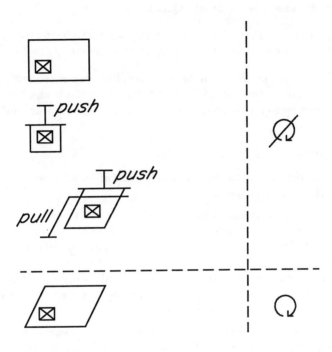

Figure 3.4: THE RELATIONSHIP OF ENGINES TO MACHINES

is completed. In concurrent systems, it is better to perform initialization via buttons on the box's interface, so that the sequencing of initialization and use can be controlled; in this case, boxes are left without engines.

- Engines of buttons are transient, starting only when the button is pushed, or pushed and pulled. It is a design mistake to provide a persistent engine for a button.

- Engines of robots are persistent by default, providing their autonomy and self-direction. However, it is not a design mistake to overide this default and to make the engine of a robot transient (this is done in dynamic systems, which are not covered in this chapter).

IMPLEMENTATION IMPLICATIONS:

A box engine corresponds to the executable body of an Ada package (or similar constructs in other languages).

A button engine corresponds to the executable part of a procedure or the critical section of an entry accept statement in Ada. Note that Ada, because entry bodies are not defined separately from the task mainline, allows the existence of different critical sections for the same entry. The visual notation makes it unnatural to exploit this feature of Ada to the full, which is an advantage of the notation, not a disadvantage, because pushing this feature to the limit can result in code that is very hard to understand.

In implementation technologies using an explicit real time executive, the engines of buttons representing services (like waits and signals) provided by objects supported by the executive (like semaphores) are actually coded in the body of the executive, and so outside the control of the designer. However, the model of a button with an engine provides a useful way of conceptualizing them in a manner consistent with the parts of the system over which the designer has control.

A robot engine corresponds to the executable part of a task body, unless the robot is a reactor that is mapped to an object supported by a real time executive (e.g., a semaphore). The engine in the latter case is coded in the body of the executive, and the engine model provides only a consistent way of conceptualizing operation.

AGENDAS OF ENGINES

Agendas are not shown in Figure 3.1 because there are no diagrams for them; however, their preparation is part of Step 9.

An agenda specifies the sequence in which engines do work and make visits; thus it is just a sequential program of particularly simple kind. Sometimes an engine may passively wait for an event (say the arrival of a data item, or the occurrence of a timeout), but such waiting is always accomplished through a visit to a waiting place, so waiting is bundled in with visiting. There is little more to be said about agendas. They are shown in this book either as pseudo-code fragments in Ada syntax, or as actual Ada code fragments.

For agendas with simple logic, a visual notation is hardly necessary. Because agendas are always simple in this book, no visual notation is presented for them. The reason agendas are always simple in this book is that complicated scheduling logic is placed in separate Abstract Controller Machines (ACMs). A visual notation (state machines) is provided for describing this separate scheduling logic. ACMs are described later, in Section 3.14.

3.4.6 STORES

Stores are not shown in Figure 3.1 because they only appear at the stage of preparing agendas. The intent is that boxes will be used for data abstraction during the steps of the process up to Step 9. Thus the designer is encouraged to think of data as residing in machines with interfaces, and not to think of communicating data among machines by means of shared memory.

A *store* is primarily a place for keeping data. The concept is that data flows at the beginning and/or end of visits between places, and is kept in stores in those places. A store is not a good system level design abstraction, because it fails to include permitted operations on the store; for system design, a box with interface buttons and an internal store should be used (thus the designer specifies a complete data abstraction, including operations). Because of this, the icon for a faceless box may sometimes be used to indicate a store in this book, the implication being that the store will eventually be fleshed out with an interface indicating an appropriate data abstraction; otherwise an ellipse represents a store.

IMPLEMENTATION IMPLICATIONS: Stores correspond to variables in any programming language.

3.5   VISUALIZING TEMPORAL BEHAVIOUR: WORK BUTTONS

3.5.1   INTRODUCTION

This section introduces a way of visualizing temporal behaviour while looking at structure that will be useful later for thinking about interactions among concurrent components. It uses visits to a single work button as the example. The point is not to give an elaborate description of procedure calling and parameter passing mechanisms in pictures, but to pave the way for visualizing deeper temporal behaviour later. We defer discussion of the deeper behaviour until after the need for it has been motivated by a design example (see particularly Section 3.12).

3.5.2   VISITS TO WORK BUTTONS

In Figure 3.5, assume that the engine on the left is inside the visiting machine; the button on the right may or may not be on the interface of some other machine. The engine of the button on the right does the work of the button. The salient points of the figure are as follows:

- Engines are shown as "vibrating" when working, and not otherwise.

- The moving hand with the pointing finger shows visiting and leaving.

- The visit model is slightly different from what one might assume by thinking of a person using a finger to push a button, because in that relationship the connection is established, and the visit made, in one motion. In MachineCharts, there must be a connection in place (represented by a finger in a structure chart) for a visit to be possible. Furthermore, a MachineChart visit, once started, must continue until the button has finished its work; in other words, there is an interlock. It is as if a person's finger became temporarily locked to the buttons it visits, until the button chooses to release it.

- The waveform at the bottom is a visit scenario with numbered segments indicating which parts of the waveform correspond to the visit steps shown above it.

Figure 3.6 conveys the same information as Figure 3.5 in two different forms. The form on the left is useful for visualizing the earlier figure in simpler terms:

- Active engines are shown filled in.

- Visits not yet at the interlock stage, are shown with a heavy line drawn part way along the finger's length, starting from an active engine (this is equivalent in meaning to, but visually simpler than the moving finger in Figure 3.5).

- An interlock is shown by drawing a heavy line for the entire finger, and showing the engine at its tail as inactive (no longer filled in). At this stage, for a work button, the button engine becomes active (filled in).

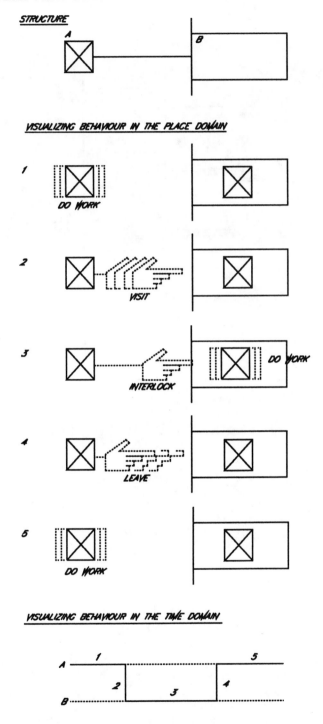

Figure 3.5: VISUALIZING VISITS TO BUTTONS

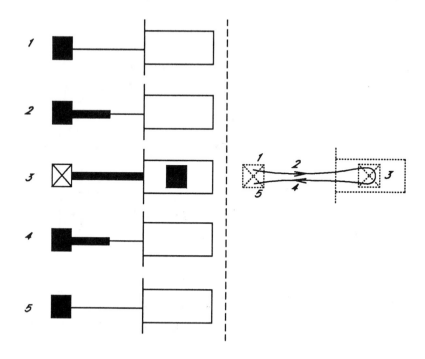

Figure 3.6: A STYLIZED WAY OF SHOWING VISIT PATTERNS

The form on the right in Figure 3.6 shows how to think about these patterns in terms of a visit thread. Visit threads are particularly useful for visualizing the temporal behaviour of concurrent systems while looking at structure charts; in such systems, there may be many independent threads that come together from time to time. This figure only introduces the concept.

Figure 3.7 shows, in the stylized form of the left hand side of Figure 3.6, how to visualize the case when visits include parameters. The significant points are that data is transferred **in** just as the internal engine starts to run and **out** just as it stops.

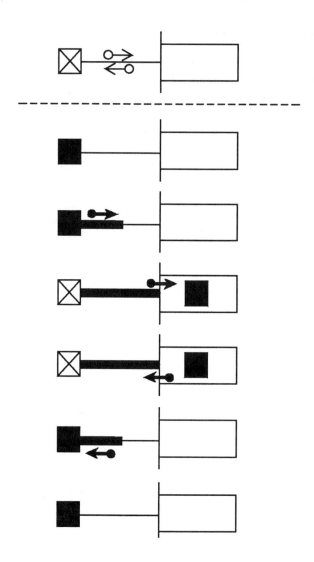

Figure 3.7: VISUALIZING VISITS WITH PARAMETERS

3.6 PRELIMINARY DESIGN

3.6.1 THE PRELIMINARY DESIGN PROCESS

The preliminary design process is concerned with *finding* both system parts, and appropriate patterns of interaction among the parts, while deliberately deferring interface commitments.

3.6.2 PRELIMINARY PLACE PARTITIONING INTO SUBSYSTEMS

Step 1 of Figure 3.1 first draws faceless boxes, representing peer subsystems, in an *abstract structure chart* (faceless means with empty interfaces). The character of a faceless box is indicated by its icon, its name, and an informal, textual description, which includes a list of the allocated work items.

> IMPLEMENTATION IMPLICATIONS: A faceless box in an abstract structure chart does not directly correspond to any implementation technology construct; in particular, it does not indicate an Ada package with an empty specification.

Drawing a set of faceless boxes does not seem, at first glance, to convey much information. However, this is actually a profound and far-reaching step, because it has defined the existence and general nature of the major components of the system. Doing it right the first time requires a deep understanding of the requirements, and considerable insight into how particular partitionings may best satisfy them. In other words, the designer must have an overall design concept in mind, including *WORK* and *TIME* aspects, to get the *PLACE* partitioning right the first time. The ability to do this only comes with experience of similar problems, and even experienced designers may not always manage it.

The designer must follow principles of application domain abstraction and information hiding that are well documented in any textbook on software engineering. However, principles are not algorithms; creativity and insight are required in applying them.

Our present state of knowledge about the creative aspects of the design process for *TIME*-intensive systems is inadequate to allow us to be confident about prescribing rules or algorithms for *discovering*, in the requirements definition, appropriate partitionings into subsystems. It is only easy when subsystems are already identified in the requirements, either explicitly or implicitly, as they may sometimes be in the *TIME*-intensive domain.

So what is the novice designer to do? Even a novice can make a first pass at a particular partitioning in terms of faceless boxes. This is the suggested approach here. Make a first pass; then explore the consequences visually in the *TIME*-domain, using the techniques to follow; then revise the partitioning, based on the knowledge gained from this exploration.

3.6.3 EVENTS AND EVENT PATHS IN PRELIMINARY PLACE PARTITIONING

Step 1 of Figure 3.1 also finds events. Events do not appear explicitly in later concrete structure charts (e.g., Step 7); they are simply a means of exploring interaction patterns in a manner that is free of commitment to interface details. In particular, events do not commit to visit directions. One is free to choose them to represent *what* should occur rather than *how* it should occur.

Judgment is required in the early stages of design to *discover* appropriate events. The choice is important because it will, like the initial choice of subsystems, influence the rest of the design process. However, discovering events for a set of machines of known character is easier than discovering the machines in the first place, either because the nature of the machines will suggest their own events, or because the designer had certain events in mind when finding the machines in the first place.

3.6.4   EVENT METHODS VS. DATA FLOW METHODS

Anyone familiar with data flow diagrams (*DFDs*) will recognize that changing the rectangular nodes into circular ones and the event arrows into data flow arrows in an abstract structure chart like Figure 3.8 gives a diagram that looks like a traditional data flow diagram. However, the intent of abstract structure charts is different, as described below. (The difference does not necessarily mean that *DFD*-based requirement analysis methods are inappropriate as a prelude to Architectural Design).

The important distinction is that the peer nodes of an abstract structure chart are assumed to be capable of controlling themselves, by means of event protocols that include both control and data, whereas the peer nodes in a DFD are usually assumed to require external control (sometimes indicated explicitly by adding control arcs, controlled by a state machine common to a set of peer nodes). To appreciate the importance of this distinction, imagine how a DFD would be used to describe interactions between communicating computers in a computer network, in which the nodes of the DFD represent the nodes of the network. Instead of a communications protocol between autonomous machines which combines data and control events, data would be described as flowing between machines under control of a central state machine. One could certainly specify temporal behavioural requirements for such a system in this way, but the specification would be troublesome as a starting point for design, because the state machine would have to be pulled apart to achieve distributed control via a communication protocol.

It seems better to start with requirements specification as one intends to continue for design; this is the intent of abstract structure charts. Note that some users of *DFD*-based requirements analysis methods may interpret *DFDs* in the manner of abstract structure charts, and this is a perfectly viable approach.

3.6.5   EXPLORING INTERACTION PATTERNS

As suggested by Step 2 of Figure 3.1, the next step is exploring interaction patterns in the *TIME* domain from the *outside*, using events in a form of timing diagram called an *event scenario*.

At the stage of *PLACE* refinement reached in Step 1, there would be a timeline for each subsystem. Even without knowing about robots, one may imagine that, in general, machinery within subsystems might operate concurrently, and might even spontaneously generate events going in opposite directions between subsystems at the same time. The scenarios can show whether such concurrency is intended, or not.

A constraint for non-concurrency is that active segments of timelines must not be overlapped in time. Then the system is a sequential one of a kind familiar to any programmer, with the subsystems simply providing *PLACE* modularity, rather than concurrent activity.

In a sequential system, one of the subsystems will act as a master (and must contain a robot).

The nature of events may be indicated in scenarios as follows:

- Transient events are indicated by showing them as lost if they are not sunk immediately.

- Queued events are shown as taking some time to transfer between timelines; in the meantime, activity may continue at the source timeline, and other events may occur.

- Rendezvous events are like transient events, except that activity cannot continue at the source timeline until the event is sunk.

There are two different types of event scenarios possible: *complete* and *mixed*. A complete event scenario has explicit start and stop events for all work activities. A mixed scenario (illustrated in Chapter 9), has the start and stop events of work activities implicit, and the activities themselves explicit. This reduces scenario clutter (by getting rid of some event arrows) and also allows deferring commitment to the *PLACE* where the work activity occurs (because, without explicit start and stop events, no sources and sinks for them have to be explicitly identified).

In general, event scenarios are useful for capturing inter-machine communication protocols, such as the following:

- An *interface scenario* for an isolated machine shows time sequences of events that may be sourced and sunk at that machine, as seen from *outside* it. They form a kind of *TIME*-domain interface specification for the machine.

- An *interaction scenario* for a set of machines shows time sequences of events between them, as seen from *outside* them.

- A *transaction scenario* for a set of machines traces the progress of a transaction through the machines.

As we shall see later, a different kind of scenario may be drawn during detailed design to show visiting patterns among machines via their interfaces; these are called visit scenarios and have the shape of a continuous waveform.

3.6.6 REMARKS ON SCENARIOS

REASONS FOR DRAWING SCENARIOS

Drawing scenarios is a labour-intensive activity (more because of the thinking required than the actual drawing, but the drawing too takes time and effort, although here a workbench can help). As one develops expertise in system thinking, constructing scenarios by mentally walking through design diagrams becomes second nature. For this reason, expositions of earlier versions of this notation did not include explicit scenarios as a central feature; instead, structure charts were presented as a framework for constructing mental scenarios (or verbal or textual descriptions of them). However, subsequent experience has shown explicit scenarios to be very useful.

Here are some good reasons why the labour is worthwhile:

- Scenarios encourage thinking in a common sense way about temporal behaviour patterns in the *TIME* domain. Such thinking is always necessary, and often occurs in design walk-throughs, but its results are not always recorded.

- Scenarios provide an *easy-to-understand record of the results* of such thinking that serve as reminders of *why*, from a *TIME* perspective, certain design decisions were taken. Failing to record such results may have possibly serious consequences later in a project, when the early *whys* have been forgotten, and details are inadvertently changed in ways that violate them.

- Scenarios are useful as test sequences for later *inside* details of designs, and for implementations. Such test sequences must be developed at some point in any project, so why not do it early?

GUIDELINES FOR DEVISING SCENARIOS

Devising scenarios that will capture the essence of the *outside* aspect of the *TIME* domain for a machine is essentially the same problem as devising black box test cases for a software package. Devising good black box tests cases is known to be a difficult art, so the reader should not expect any magic here that would make devising scenarios easy.

The problem of devising scenarios is eased by good partitioning that keeps the coupling between subsystems weak, so that interface and interaction scenarios may be kept simple. This might be stated the other way round: a criterion of good partitioning is that it produces simple interface and interaction scenarios.

The basic guideline for devising scenarios is to ask pointed, *what-if* questions about temporal event patterns, and then to draw scenarios to answer them; one stops when one can no longer think of questions. Exposing scenarios to a peer review group may result in further questions. Eventually, a team of knowledgeable people can be satisfied that they have covered the essentially different temporal behaviour patterns.

SCENARIOS AND RECURSIVE DECOMPOSITION

A consequence of recursive decomposition is that one can use scenarios for describing *outside* aspects of both subsystems and subsubsystems. But *outside* aspects of subsubsystems are *inside* aspects of subsystems. Then the designer must ensure that the following conditions are satisfied:

- The various levels of scenarios must be consistent with each other.

- The subsubsystems must be designed internally to satisfy their own scenarios.

- The combination of subsubsystems must be designed to satisfy the subsystem scenarios.

Such conditions are deep, requiring nothing less than ensuring that redundant specifications of temporal behaviour at the different levels are consistent. Automatic tests for these conditions would be desirable, but in the present state of knowledge are not available. Therefore, for the time being, the designer must laboriously verify that these conditions are satisfied. However, this verification must be performed anyway during unit and integration testing of implementations, so there is nothing here that is more complicated than what already has to happen in implementation projects. There is only the suggestion that the thinking that goes into devising black box unit and integration tests be moved earlier in the process, to help with design.

3.6.7 CAPTURING EVENT PATTERNS IN CLOSED FORM

INTRODUCTION

Step 3 of Figure 3.1, which captures *abstract state machines*, is optional in general. If it is skipped, then the event scenarios are treated simply as information to guide detailed design, or as test sequences for a completed design.

STATE MACHINES

State machines are particularly attractive in the context of visual techniques for *TIME*-intensive systems, because they have simple, widely-understood visual representations, and because they describe *TIME* aspects in a manner that may be cleanly separated from the details of *WORK*.

The essence of the state machine model used in this book is as follows: there are a number of possible states, only one of which can be the current state; transitions between states are triggered by events; only one event occurs at a time; when an event occurs, only one transition is possible, and the next state is a function only of the current state and the event. Thus, the current state represents the cumulative effect of the history of past events. Actions can be associated with transitions. What happens to events if the state machine is not ready to receive them is outside the scope of the state machine model; the state machine only deals with events that it is given; the assumption is that events will be delivered to it by concrete machinery designed during the detailed inside design phase.

The visual state machine notation used for illustrative purposes in this book is the simplest one possible. Circles represent states, arrows represent transitions, and textual labels on arrows represent events and actions (in the form event/action). Auxiliary variables are allowed that affect choices between transitions for the same event (only one transition is allowed, so if more than one has the same triggering event, then an auxiliary variable must be used to determine which one will be selected). Changing the value of an auxiliary variable is done in the action part of the transition label; the effect of a value on a transition is expressed by including it in a boolean condition in the event part (e.g., in the form "event=x AND value=y"). Transitions resulting solely from auxiliary variable changes are not included in this model, because we want the state machines to be purely passive, always requiring an external event before a transition will occur. Mealy machine semantics are assumed; i.e., actions are always performed during transitions, not while in states.

For complex state machines that may cause this simple visual state machine notation to break down, because of too many states and transitions, there are more sophisticated state machine notations available (e.g., Harel's StateCharts). The methods of this book are not bound to any particular state machine notation.

ABSTRACT STATE MACHINES (ASM)

Abstract state machines (ASMs) may be used to express the kind of temporal behaviour shown in one or more event scenarios. ASMs are called "abstract" because their events and actions are expressed in the abstract terms of preliminary design, not in the concrete terms of detailed design. They may be of two kinds:

- Test-sequence ASMs: These capture a single event scenario in state machine form, instead of timing diagram form. They may be useful as test sequence generators when using a state machine tool to investigate temporal behaviour. They are identified here only as a possibility that will not be explored further in this book.

- Composite ASMs: These aim to capture the complete temporal behaviour implied by a number of event scenarios (although perhaps incompletely expressed by them). All the ASMs drawn in this book are composite ones.

Composite ASMs derived from complete event scenarios (as opposed to mixed ones) adopt the perspective of one of the components in an abstract structure chart, or, equivalently, the corresponding timelines in a set of event scenarios. From this perspective, the events of an ASM are the events sunk at the timelines, and the actions are the triggers of events sourced at the timelines. Being abstract, the actions are not expressed in terms of button operations.

Abstract state machines may be *discovered* in event scenarios by analyzing them to find states in the inter-event gaps and transitions in the event sequences. An experienced person may be able to develop them from scratch, by inspiration, without first drawing scenarios explicitly; however, there are implicit scenarios in such a person's mind during such a process.

In spite of the fact that, once an ASM is drawn, the scenarios from which it was derived become formally redundant, and in spite of the attractive, closed form nature of state machines, care should be taken not to be too quick to start developing ASMs too early, because of the danger of becoming preoccupied with fine details at the expense of larger issues. Devising good state machines requires some creativity, making it easy to become preoccupied with exploring the fine details of different possibilities. Scenarios have the advantage of being incomplete, thereby allowing fine details to be deferred.

The term "Abstract State Machine" (ASM) should not be confused with the term "Abstract Controller Machine" (ACM). An ASM is a state machine that is abstract in the sense of not being explicitly coupled into a concrete design context. An ACM is (in this book) a box that puts a standard interface around an ASM, so that an engine may use it to get scheduling information. ACMs are described later, in Section 3.14.

Once one starts using state machines to express the temporal behaviour of some parts of a system under design, the question naturally arises: Why not use them everywhere, and investigate temporal behaviour with a state machine tool that executes coupled state machines? This is indeed possible, and is appropriate for requirements analysis. However, experience has shown that forcing everything into a state machine mold is not the best approach for design. So this book takes the stance that state machines are useful, but optional, components in the designer's parts kit. Where used, they are expressed initially as ASMs that may later be "plugged-in" to a detailed design via ACMs.

3.6.8 CONCURRENCY COMMITMENT

Step 4 of Figure 3.1 is a *TIME*-domain step that decides whether the system is concurrent or sequential, by deciding how many robots there are. This decision might be implied by earlier scenarios, or implicit judgments made by the designer, but this step makes it explicit. The robots are placed in the system in Step 5, but the decision about how many is a *TIME*-domain one. This particular figure illustrates a decision for a sequential system, because only one robot is shown; however, the thinking is the same whether the decision is for a sequential or concurrent system.

Remember that although robots are shown in *PLACE* diagrams as structural parts, and although they have structural aspects (namely interface and enclosure), their *purpose* is *TIME*-domain partitioning of temporal behaviour, to achieve *TIME*-modularity through concurrency. In *TIME*-intensive systems, this kind of modularity is as important as *PLACE*-modularity achieved by structural partitioning with boxes; it provides for the possibility of multiprocessing or distributed implementations, and localizes the effects of timing changes, such as speeding up or slowing down execution rates, adding new events and/or functionality, changing event rates, and so forth.

3.6.9 CONCURRENCY PLACEMENT

Step 5 of Figure 3.1 places robots in the system. In this particular figure, a decision has been made that the top, left-hand box is the driver of the system.

3.6.10 RECURSIVE DECOMPOSITION

Remember that preliminary design proceeds recursively through all levels of decomposition of the system under design, until one arrives at a point where primitive internal machinery (engines and stores) is required. It is not only performed at the system level.

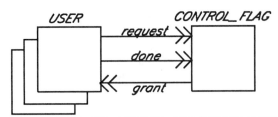

Figure 3.8: ABSTRACT STRUCTURE CHART FOR GRANTING PERMISSION

3.7   EXAMPLE: PRELIMINARY DESIGN OF A CONTROL FLAG

3.7.1   INTRODUCTION

A running example throughout this chapter is a control flag abstraction used for permission-granting purposes. The notion of a flag is a well known concept in either software or hardware; it is an indicator of some changing condition that needs to be tested from time to time (for example, "output done", or "permission granted"). In some ways, this is a bad example to lead off with, because it uses a paradigm that is generally rejected by the book for reactive systems, namely busy waiting (also known as polling). Therefore, a cautionary word is in order here. View the example as a vehicle for understanding the steps of the method, and the expressivity of the notation. The example is a good one for this purpose for several reasons: its simplicity prevents the details of the problem from getting in the way; it is sufficiently *TIME*-intensive to provide a good springboard for dealing with more complex *TIME*-intensive problems later; and exploring alternative solutions enables us to cover the basics of the black-box-with-buttons model provided by the notation. Wait until Chapter 4 to see how to do it right, without polling. Remember also that this is a pedagogical example that deliberately brings to bear the full weight of the stepwise process of Figure 3.1 on a problem that is really too simple for such a heavy approach.

3.7.2   ABSTRACT STRUCTURE CHARTS

Step 1 of the design process of Figure 3.1 has already been done for this problem simply by stating the problem. Figure 3.8 captures the problem statement in an abstract structure chart. The multiple "shadows" of the **USER** box indicate that there may be many users that are all identical from the point of view of their interaction with the **CONTROL_FLAG** box (a more general meaning for "shadow" components is introduced in Chapter 5, in conjunction with templates, but here the more general meaning is not intended, because there is no template icon in evidence).

The problem that remains is to design the **CONTROL_FLAG** box so to take input events **request** and **done** and deliver output **grant** events at the appropriate times. What the permission is for is not shown in the diagram and is not of concern to our purpose here; it might be to access a shared resource, like a data base. The subsystems from which the requests come may have internal concurrency.

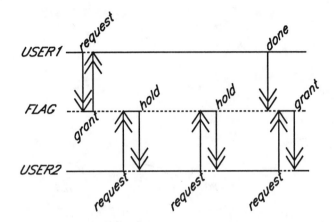

Figure 3.9: EVENT SCENARIOS FOR GRANTING PERMISSION

3.7.3   PERMISSION-GRANTING SCENARIOS

Proceeding with Step 2 of the design process of Figure 3.1, an example of a possible temporal pattern of events is given by the scenario of Figure 3.9 (this is a complete event scenario, rather than a mixed one). The general protocol expressed by this scenario is that the first **request** event produces an immediate **grant**, but that subsequent **request** events are denied **grants** until a **done** occurs. In the meantime the flag delivers a **hold** event to users, telling them to hold off doing anything, and to retry later (this is a new output event, not contemplated in Figure 3.8, illustrating that new events may sometimes be introduced in thinking about scenarios); the temporal behaviour demonstrated by this scenario is sometimes called "spin locking".

3.7.4   ASM FOR THE PERMISSION-GRANTING PROBLEM

Step 3 of the design process of Figure 3.1 is illustrated by the abstract state machine of Figure 3.10. The **YES** and **NO** states correspond to the sections of the flag timeline after a **done** event, and after a **grant** event, respectively. The state machine is obvious, except for the implications of the **hold** action. It would need to be transformed into an output event of the flag box, because the state machine obviously does not keep track of **holds** (it always goes directly from **NO** to **YES** when a **done** occurs, implying that it does not know whether or not there were previous **requests** while in the **NO** state).

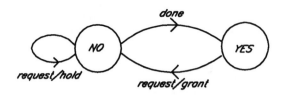

Figure 3.10: AN ABSTRACT STATE MACHINE FOR GRANTING PERMISSION

3.8 DETAILED OUTSIDE DESIGN

3.8.1 THE DETAILED OUTSIDE DESIGN PROCESS

Detailed outside design is concerned with devising concrete *outside* representations of machines to enable the abstract interaction patterns of preliminary design to be realized by visits.

3.8.2 ROUTING CHARTS

Step 6 of Figure 3.1 shows a useful first step in detailed design, drawing a *routing chart*, employing *channel* icons to indicate visit directions. Visit direction is an important starting point for detailed design, because it establishes client-server relationships (by definition, a client visits a server to obtain service).

Structurally, a channel is a placeholder for interface details that will enable visiting to take place; in other words it presents an *outside* view of the interaction structure between a pair of machines.

> IMPLEMENTATION IMPLICATIONS: Channels rarely map to programming constructs directly (for reasons having to do with implementation modularity, programming languages rarely require complete definition of client-server relationships at the specification, as opposed to the body, level); but they have obvious correspondence to wiring harnesses and buses in hardware.

3.8.3 CONCRETE STRUCTURE CHARTS

Step 7 of Figure 3.1 finally resolves concrete interface mechanisms. This may be done on a channel-by-channel basis, showing details of each port, or on a system basis, as shown in the figure.

3.8.4 VISIT SCENARIOS

Step 8 of Figure 3.1, draws *visit scenarios* to confirm that expected temporal behaviour will occur for the newly designed interfaces and connections, and to provide test cases for use later.

Visit patterns may be conceptualized as drawing temporal threads through structure charts. One often indicates *threaded visit scenarios* during presentations, discussions, walk-throughs, etc., by pointing and tracing on a structure chart. One might even draw them for the record, although this would not be satisfactory for extended patterns, particularly cyclic ones, because threads would cross and overlay each other. For recording purposes, visit scenarios are more appropriately drawn in *linearized* form, showing waveform shapes that trace visit patterns from timeline to timeline. A waveform that leaves its timeline indicates an attempted visit. If it joins another timeline, it indicates a successful visit. If the visit requires cooperation of the visitee, then there may be a delay before an attempted visit is successful, represented by the waveform going into limbo between timelines, during which its shape conveys no semantics other than delay.

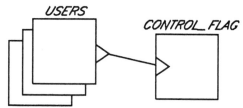

Figure 3.11: A ROUTING CHART FOR THE CONTROL FLAG PROBLEM

3.9   EXAMPLE: DETAILED OUTSIDE DESIGN OF A CONTROL FLAG

Step 6 of the design process of Figure 3.1 requires no new thinking for this problem. Figure 3.11 simply records the final result, that robots in the **USER** boxes always visit the **CONTROL_FLAG** box.

A possible result of Step 7 of the design process of Figure 3.1 is shown in Figure 3.12. This interface represents a simple abstraction of a flag that does not explicitly represent the permission-granting event model of our example design problem. This is not perverse, but normal; interfaces may be specified with an eye to providing general purpose components, useable in as wide variety of applications as possible.

The **CONTROL_FLAG** box of Figure 3.12 provides two buttons that "toggle" a "flag" between two positions, identified by **0** and **1**, starting from an initial position of **0**, the idea being that visitors finding the flag set at **0** have permission, but visitors finding it set at **1** do not.

- **TEST_AND_SET** returns the current value of the flag, so that the visitor can see whether it is **0** or **1**, and sets the flag to **1**. If the flag is already **1**, it has no effect other than to return the current value.

- **CLEAR** sets the flag to **0**.

The events of Figure 3.9 are mapped to visits to this black box as follows:

- **request** is mapped to at least one, and possibly many, visits to **TEST_AND_SET** (in other words, a not-granted **request**, indicated by the return of a **1**, forces busy-waiting, also known as polling, which is *not* a recommended approach).

- **grant** and **hold** are mapped to returns from visits to **TEST_AND_SET** with values of **0**, or **1**, respectively, for the tested value of the flag).

- **done** is mapped to a visit to **CLEAR**.

Step 8 of the design process of Figure 3.1 is illustrated by Figure 3.13, which is a visit scenario showing the expected temporal behaviour pattern for the control flag, specifically showing polling. Note how this scenario could be used as an external specification that might be put in a requirements document, or a components manual, of how the black box is supposed to behave, replacing the textual description above.

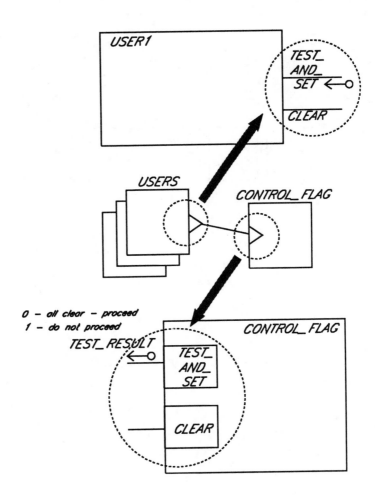

Figure 3.12: DETAILING CHANNEL PORTS GIVES INTERFACES

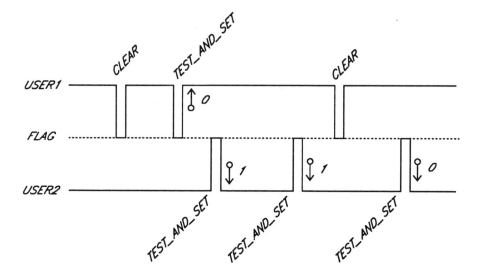

Figure 3.13: EXPECTED VISIT SCENARIO FOR A CONTROL FLAG

3.10 DETAILED INSIDE DESIGN

3.10.1 THE DETAILED INSIDE DESIGN PROCESS

Step 9 of Figure 3.1 illustrates the nature of this process at the point where recursive decomposition stops and we must finally get down to saying *how* all of the machinery prepared so far will be made to work. Engines are the ultimate source of the *how*, optionally in combination with Abstract Controller Machines (ACMs).

Either an engine (or an engine-ACM combination) stands alone as the only non-interface component of a machine, as shown in Step 9, in which case, detailed inside design is only concerned with specifying agendas, or there is other internal machinery as well. By virtue of the recursive nature of the design process, there is nothing new in designing internal machinery relative to designing external machinery, so we are left with engine agendas and ACMs as the only new concerns of detailed inside design. ACMs are deferred until Section 3.14, so we are left with agendas. Agendas are simple sequential programs, as will now be explained for the **CONTROL_FLAG** example.

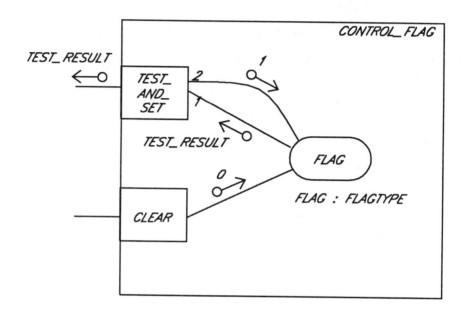

$0 - all\ clear - proceed$

$1 - do\ not\ proceed$

Figure 3.14: A PLAUSIBLE, BUT UNSAFE, INTERNAL STRUCTURE FOR THE CONTROL FLAG

3.11 EXAMPLE: DETAILED INSIDE DESIGN OF A CONTROL FLAG

3.11.1 AN UNSAFE FIRST PASS

Suppose we start Step 9 of the design process of Figure 3.1 by elaborating the internal structure of the **CONTROL_FLAG** of Figure 3.12 in the plausible manner shown in Figure 3.14. This design puts all the logic directly in the agendas of engines, without making use of either the abstract state machines developed during preliminary design, or the ACM concept. However, the logic is equivalent to the state machine of Figure 3.10.

Figure 3.15 continues with Step 9 by elaborating the internal structure of the user robots in the user subsystems. Their only internal components are engines that make visits from time to time to the flag's buttons. The point here is that they do so autonomously, so there is no way of predicting when they will arrive at the flag, and it would therefore be quite possible for several of them to arrive at the same time, causing the kind of trouble illustrated by Figure 3.16. Note that we have not evolved a description of what users do, other than interact with the flag, so we cannot do anything more with them.

Looking at Figure 3.14 and Figure 3.15 together, we can see that overlapping visitors

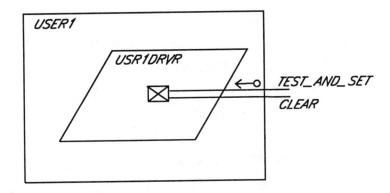

Figure 3.15: INTERNAL STRUCTURE OF THE USER ROBOTS

to the flag box might be able to interfere with each other at the point of accessing the flag store that is in the box, but outside the buttons.

Figure 3.16 shows, using the stylized representation of Figure 3.6, how to visualize the resulting temporal behaviour in the structure chart. When a second visitor arrives at an active work button, the agenda starts for the new visitor from the beginning (symbolized in the figure by showing a second, overlapped, active engine), without disturbing the progress of the already-active agenda. The different activations may start at different times, and interleave agenda items in unpredictable ways. Because the store exists as a component in its own right, outside the button, the different activations may operate on it in inconsistent ways.

Figure 3.17 shows how to represent the same temporal behaviour in the time domain by a visit scenario. This scenario shows explicitly that more than one visitor may inspect the flag before any of them have a chance to change it. Particularly unpleasant is the fact that this kind of erroneous temporal behaviour will only occur sometimes, particularly under heavy load conditions, so it might be missed by testing.

The problem may be seen from a another perspective by examining the engine agendas given (in Ada syntax) in Figure 3.18 and Figure 3.19. Note that agendas are purely operational components, so declarations for the flag store are not included in them (a workbench would generate these declarations automatically for an implementation from the graphics). Incorrect temporal behaviour is possible because the agenda of **TEST_AND_SET** in Figure 3.18 has two sequential parts, one to test the flag and the other to set it; in particular, more than one user may execute the testing part of the agenda at the same time, enabling more than one to see a value of **0**.

IMPLEMENTATION IMPLICATIONS: Although the solution it provides to the permission-granting problem is unsafe, the **CONTROL_FLAG** box still provides a perfectly good example of the nature of a box-with-buttons representation of a data abstraction that can be mapped to an Ada package, so it is worth completing the mapping, just to see how it is done. Putting all the pieces of the

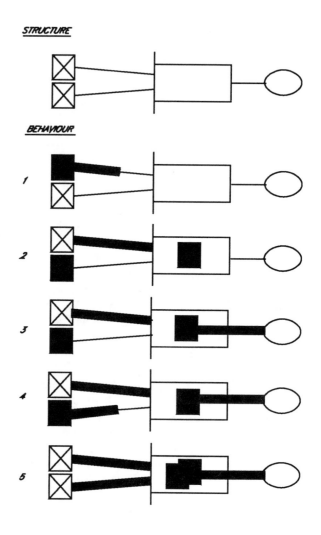

Figure 3.16: INTERFERENCE AT SHARED COMPONENTS

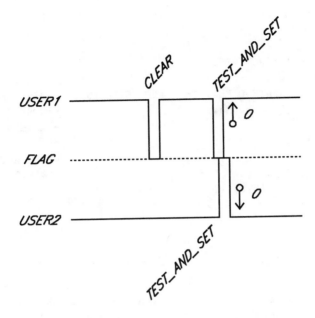

Figure 3.17: ERRONEOUS TEMPORAL BEHAVIOUR OF AN UNSAFE CONTROL FLAG ABSTRACTION

```
--TEST_AND_SET agenda
    begin
        TEST_RESULT := FLAG;  --WORK
        FLAG:= 1;             --WORK
    end;
--CLEAR agenda
    begin
        FLAG:= 0;             --WORK
    end;
```

Figure 3.18: AGENDAS FOR THE BUTTONS OF AN UNSAFE CONTROL FLAG AB-STRACTION

```
--TYPICAL USER agenda
    begin
      loop;
        ...   --ANY ACTIVITY
        loop
          push  CONTROL_FLAG.TEST_AND_SET(FLAG);   --VISIT FLAG
          if FLAG=0 then exit;                      --WORK
          ...                                       --ALTERNATE ACTIVITY
        end loop;
        ...                                         --PROTECTED ACTIVITY
        push CONTROL_FLAG.CLEAR;                     --VISIT FLAG
        ...   --ANY ACTIVITY
      end loop;
    end;
```

Figure 3.19: TYPICAL AGENDA FOR A USER OF THE CONTROL FLAG

CONTROL_FLAG together (the structure of Figure 3.14 and the agendas of Figure 3.18) gives the Ada program of Figure 3.20. The structural components of the chart map to declarations in the code: the box to a package; the buttons to procedures. The agendas map to **begin ... end** parts in places in the program bodies corresponding to the places where the engines are shown in the charts. The charts say nothing about where the package specification should go in relation to the body. Here the specification and body are next to each other in the same place in the text, whereas the charts do not show interfaces and internal structures next to each other in the same diagram. This indicates that the concept of an interface in MachineCharts is not the same as the concept of an Ada specification. To complete the picture, an actor robot like a typical user robot in this problem (in other words, one with only projecting fingers on its interface, but no buttons) maps to a task with an empty specification and an infinitely looping body, like the one shown in Figure 3.21.

```
package CONTROL_FLAG is
  type FLAGTYPE is range 0..1;
  procedure TEST_AND_SET (TEST_RESULT: out FLAGTYPE);
  procedure CLEAR;
end CONTROL_FLAG;

package body CONTROL_FLAG is
    FLAG: FLAGTYPE := 0;
    procedure TEST_AND_SET(TEST_RESULT: out FLAGTYPE) is
      begin
        TEST_RESULT := FLAG;
        FLAG:= 1;
      end TEST_AND_SET;
    procedure CLEAR is
      begin
        FLAG:= 0;
      end CLEAR;
end CONTROL_FLAG;
```

Figure 3.20: ADA CODE FOR AN UNSAFE CONTROL FLAG ABSTRACTION

```
task User1 is --NO ENTRIES, SO AN EMPTY SPECIFICATION
end User1;
task body User1 is
  FLAG: CONTROL_FLAG.FLAGTYPE;
  begin
    loop
      ...    --ANY ACTIVITY
      loop
        CONTROL_FLAG.TEST_AND_SET(FLAG);
        exit when  FLAG = 0;
        ...
      end loop;
      ...
      CONTROL_FLAG.CLEAR;
      ...
    end loop;
end User1;
```

Figure 3.21: ADA USER TASK

3.12   MORE ON VISUALIZING TEMPORAL BEHAVIOUR: GATE BUTTONS AND ROBOTS

3.12.1   INTRODUCTION

Before trying to fix the control flag design, we need to understand more about gate buttons and robots.

3.12.2   VISUALIZING MEETINGS AT GATE BUTTONS

Figure 3.22 indicates how to visualize interactions with gate buttons in the manner of Figure 3.6, to which it should be compared.

Assume that the engine on the left of the button is inside a robot that is visiting the button to push it, and that the gate button is attached to the interface of a robot containing the engine on its right. In general, both robot engines may be assumed to operate concurrently some of the time, and to visit the button from time to time. Showing the underlying machinery separate from the enclosing robots like this lays bare the nature of gate buttons as meeting places.

As shown by the left hand side of the figure, a visit to a gate button from the push side looks a lot like a visit to a work button, except that the interlock implies a possible delay until there is also a visitor from the pull side. Not shown, but similar in pattern, is the case where the pull visitor arrives first and must wait for a meeting with a push visitor. The arrival of both a push visitor and a pull one, whether at the same or different times, triggers a *meeting* between them, during which both are interlocked while the button engine does its work.

Considering that the pull visitor is assumed to be the engine of the robot to which the gate button is attached, it is clear from the figure that this engine will allow only one meeting at a time, thereby providing mutual exclusion, and consequential protection against interference of the kind illustrated in Figure 3.16.

Because only one meeting at a time is allowed, there has to be an implicit queuing mechanism associated with a gate button to hold visitors that cannot be serviced immediately. Time in this queue is part of the interlock time.

The right hand side of this Figure 3.22 illustrate how to think about meetings in terms of visit threads. Here there are two independent visit threads, each originating in the engine of a robot, that meet at the gate button. The numbers on the thread segments correspond to the numbers on the interaction phases in the left hand side of the figure. In general, such independent threads may trace paths all over the system, meeting each other from time to time at gate buttons.

Figure 3.23 maps the visiting patterns shown in relation to structure in Figure 3.22 into an equivalent visit scenario. A pairwise meeting like this between two threads is called a rendezvous; in this book, the term rendezvous is used only when it is clear that the meeting robots are both actors.

Because of the temporal behaviour patterns illustrated by these figures, button-pushing visitors will sometimes be referred to just as visitors, and button-pulling visitors as hosts.

IMPLEMENTATION IMPLICATIONS: This is a good model of Ada opera-

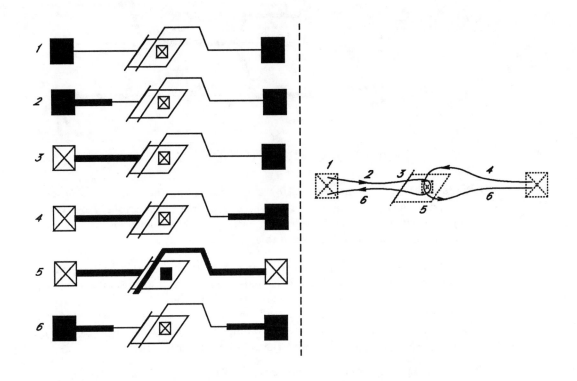

Figure 3.22: VISUALIZING VISITS TO AND MEETINGS AT GATE BUTTONS

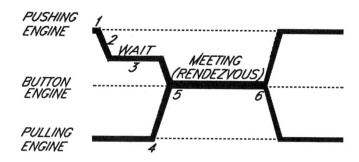

Figure 3.23: A GATE BUTTON VISIT SCENARIO

tional semantics, with the gate button engine modelling the critical section of an entry and the meeting between two robots modelling a rendezvous. However, in Ada the structure is slightly different, because the critical sections of entries are programmed in line in the executable body of a task.

Figure 3.24 shows how to visualize the same gate button operations with parameters. There is a significant point in this figure. A parameter going into the button via a push does not get to the button engine until it starts to run, which will not happen until a pull has also occurred. A parameter going out of the button to a push visitor will go out at the end of the engine's operation as before. Parameters may also be associated with pull fingers, although care must be taken with the Ada interpretation of this.

> IMPLEMENTATION IMPLICATIONS: The Ada interpretation of parameters associated with pull fingers is that there is an internal store of the robot from which the button may get values or to which it may put values, as illustrated by Figure 3.25, which shows two sensible MachineChart structures, only the second of which directly represents what can be done in Ada.

What if a robot has many gate buttons? Then the simple push/pull model of Figure 3.22 requires that, at any particular time, a particular button must be selected on the push side, and also on the pull side. This may result in the situation shown by the highlighted push and pull fingers in Figure 3.26, in which a pushing engine might be waiting for a pull at one gate button while the pulling engine is waiting for a push at the other. This may or may not be desirable; if it is desirable, then the notation is fine as it stands. However, if it is not desirable, then a means is needed for the designer to indicate something different.

3.12.3   CHOICE FRAMES

Figure 3.27 shows how to indicate that the situation of Figure 3.26, in which buttons are implicit waiting places relative to each other, is not desired. The choice frame in this figure is an example of an annotation on a structure chart that allows the designer to indicate temporal behavioural intent (more such annotations will be introduced in Chapter 4). This particular annotation indicates a *pull-first-push* protocol that is illustrated in the figure.

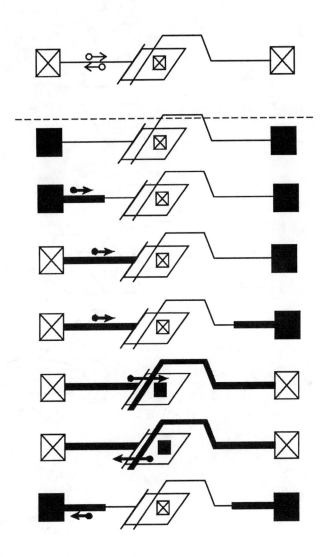

Figure 3.24: VISUALIZING VISITS WITH PARAMETERS TO GATE BUTTONS

THIS:

MAY IMPLY THIS:

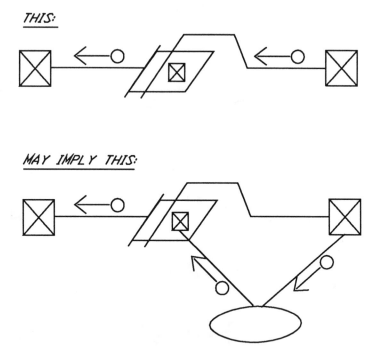

Figure 3.25: PARAMETERS OF GATE BUTTONS

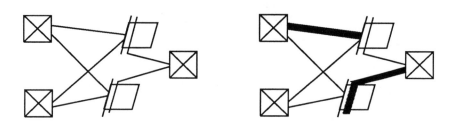

Figure 3.26: THE PROBLEM OF PICKING WHAT TO PUSH AND PULL

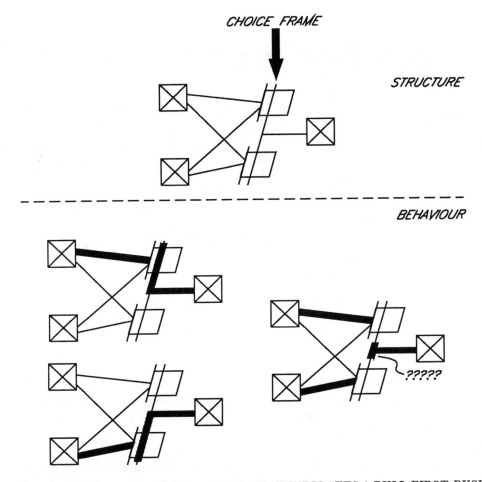

Figure 3.27: AN INTERFACE ANNOTATION THAT INDICATES A PULL-FIRST-PUSH PROTOCOL

As shown, indeterminism may arise if visitors happen to be waiting on the push side of more than one button when a pull occurs. Such indeterminism may be resolved in several ways: by random choice; by choosing among waiting visitors on the basis of time of arrival (implying a single FIFO queue for all the buttons of the choice frame); or by prioritizing buttons.

IMPLEMENTATION IMPLICATIONS: A choice frame maps to a selective accept in Ada. Ada's rule for resolving indeterminism may be assumed to be random choice. Ada only chooses visitors on a time-of-arrival basis in individual entry queues, not between entries in the same selective accept. Entries cannot be prioritized by declaration in Ada.

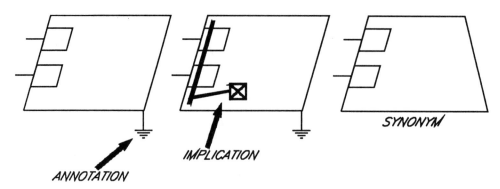

Figure 3.28: NOTATIONS FOR REACTORS

3.12.4   REACTOR ROBOTS

A reactor is a robot that has all of its activity in its button engines, so that it is active only during meetings. Its engine does nothing except serialize meetings, thereby providing mutual exclusion. The concept of the engine doing this provides a model for thinking, not necessarily a mechanism for implementation.

> IMPLEMENTATION IMPLICATIONS: The mutual exclusion effect of reactor robots may be achieved by mapping them to tasks programmed to behave passively, or by mapping them to non-task objects for which mutual exclusion is achieved in other ways.

As shown by Figure 3.28, there are two alternative forms of visual representation that will be used in an interchangeable fashion in this book. One is the trapezoid of Figure 3.2. The other is a parallelogram with an attached ground symbol (borrowed from electrical engineering), directly symbolizing a "grounded" actor (i.e., one that is constrained to act passively). These two different visual forms are offered because one or the other may be more natural when designing with a particular implementation technology in mind. When designing for Ada, which requires that reactors be programmed as tasks, a ground symbol attached to a parallelogram may be most natural. When designing for a technology based in an explicit real time executive that offers standard reactors directly, the trapezoid symbol may be most natural.

In either case, all of the buttons of the reactor are implicitly grouped in a choice frame drawn around the entire periphery of the reactor icon and there is an implication that the reactor behaves externally *as if* it were an actor the engine of which did nothing else but pull the choice frame after every meeting, to start, or wait for, the next meeting. The existence of an explicit engine to provide this external temporal behaviour does not necessarily have to be taken literally, unless the reactor is to be implemented as a task. Nor does the implicit choice frame have to be drawn.

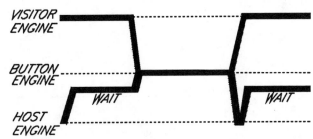

Figure 3.29: CONCEPTUAL SCENARIO OF A REACTOR MODELLED BY A CON-
STRAINED ACTOR

A way to conceptualize the temporal behaviour of a reactor as that of an actor with an
implicit main engine of this kind is given by Figure 3.29. Observe that the only sustained
activity of the robot is in its buttons, unlike the more general case shown in Figure 3.23.
The activity of the engine is momentary, and is concerned only with triggering the next
meeting.

There is a strong similarity and one significant difference between a box with work
buttons and a reactor with gate buttons. Both may offer identical services from a work
perspective. With both, the engines of the buttons do all the work. Both may have internal
stores that are shared among the buttons. The significant difference is that with boxes we
have only *visits* that may overlap, not meetings (because there is nothing to control visitors),
whereas with reactors we have sequential *meetings* that may not overlap, because their
sequencing is controlled by the internal machinery of the reactor. The internal machinery
arranges that the reactor is always ready for a meeting, unless another meeting is already
in progress.

Figure 3.30 illustrates the difference between the internal machinery of an actor and
a reactor, when both are viewed as robots with internal engines. Note that, because the
buttons of a reactor can visit other machines, there is no reason why reactors cannot visit
each other.

IMPLEMENTATION IMPLICATIONS:

Reactor robots are useful models of protected, non-task objects supported by
real time executives, like semaphores, mailboxes, and monitors. They may also
be mapped to tasks that are programmed to behave passively, although this is
likely to be an inefficient way of doing the job, because it forces a task context
switch for every visit and every return.

Note particularly that the concept of a meeting with a reactor implies only mutual exclusion, and not necessarily a task context switch. Unless implementation
is by means of a task programmed to behave passively, task context switching
would occur in an implementation only in cases where waiting is explicitly required, such as waiting for a signal at a semaphore, or a message at a mailbox.

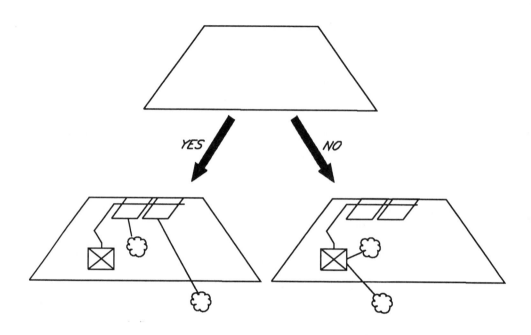

Figure 3.30: REACTOR ROBOTS PROVIDE MUTUAL EXCLUSION, NOT AUTONOMY

3.13 EXAMPLE: A SAFE VERSION OF THE CONTROL FLAG

3.13.1 INTRODUCTION

One way of getting the control flag right is to redo its detailed outside design, as described here (another way is to change the internal machinery).

3.13.2 REVISITING DETAILED OUTSIDE DESIGN

Figure 3.31 represents the control flag as a reactor with gate buttons **TAS** and **CLR** implicitly grouped in a choice frame (the names of the buttons have been changed to emphasize that they have different effects from before).

The visit scenario of Figure 3.32 shows how the underlying semantics of gate buttons ensure that interactions on TAS are serialized even when clients try to visit it simultaneously.

3.13.3 RETURNING TO DETAILED INSIDE DESIGN

Now we may return to detailed inside design. An appropriate internal structure for this black box is shown in Figure 3.33.

Figure 3.34 shows the implied agendas of the engines in Figure 3.33.

> IMPLEMENTATION IMPLICATIONS:
>
> A reactor like **CONTROL_FLAG** would not necessarily map to a task in some other implementation technology than Ada, and might even be provided as a standard service by software or hardware. However, for Ada, it must be mapped to a task, programmed to behave passively (instead of actively, like the user task of Figure 3.21). Note that Ada tasks with entries are not constrained to be passive, in general.
>
> Figure 3.35 puts the pieces together in a plausible-looking program for a task that mirrors the structure chart of Figure 3.33, but is not actually a legal Ada program because of the separately defined entries. The choice construct of MachineCharts maps to a selective accept statement that says, in effect, **select** the first call on either one entry **or** the other. In spite of the illegality of this program, it expresses the intent better than the corresponding real Ada program that follows. Note how the passivity of the task is obvious. All the mainline does is loop around, accepting entry calls one after the other, but leaving all the work to the entries. Thus, all it accomplishes is mutual exclusion of callers; in some other implementation technology, this mutual exclusion would be accomplished in some other way.
>
> To make a legal Ada program, the separate entry definitions have to be eliminated and their executable parts placed in the mainline of the task, as shown in Figure 3.36. Thus, mapping structure charts to Ada leads naturally to Ada programs in which there is only one **do..end** body for each entry.

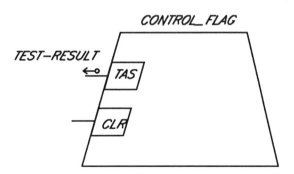

Figure 3.31: INTERFACE OF A SAFE CONTROL FLAG ABSTRACTION

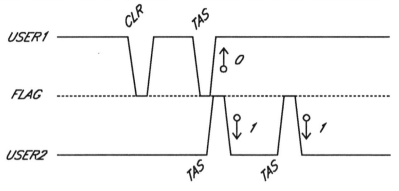

Figure 3.32: SCENARIO FOR A SAFE CONTROL FLAG ABSTRACTION

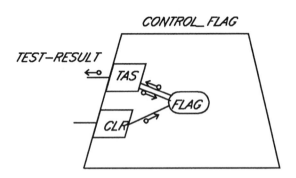

Figure 3.33: INTERNAL STRUCTURE OF A SAFE CONTROL FLAG ABSTRACTION

```
--TAS agenda
   begin
     TEST_RESULT := FLAG;        --WORK
     FLAG:= 1;                   --WORK
   end;
--CLR agenda
   begin
     FLAG:= 0;                   --WORK
   end;
--MAIN ENGINE agenda
   begin
     loop
       pull choice(TAS,CLR);     --VISIT
     end loop;
   end;
```

Figure 3.34: AGENDAS FOR A SAFE CONTROL FLAG ABSTRACTION

```
type FLAGTYPE is range 0..1;
task CONTROL_FLAG is
  entry TAS (TEST_RESULT: out FLAGTYPE);
  entry CLR;
end CONTROL_FLAG;

task body CONTROL_FLAG is
  FLAG: FLAGTYPE;
  entry TAS (TEST_RESULT: out FLAGTYPE) is
    begin
      TEST_RESULT:= FLAG;
      FLAG:= 1;
    end TAS;
  entry CLR is
    begin
      FLAG:=0;
    end CLR;
  begin
    loop
      select
        accept TAS
      or
        accept CLR
      end select;
    end loop;
end CONTROL_FLAG;
```

Figure 3.35: PSEUDO ADA CODE FOR A SAFE CONTROL FLAG ABSTRACTION

```
type FLAGTYPE is range 0..1;
task CONTROL_FLAG is
  entry TAS (TEST_RESULT: out FLAGTYPE);
  entry CLR;
end CONTROL_FLAG;

task body CONTROL_FLAG is
  FLAG: FLAGTYPE;
  begin
    loop
      select
        accept TAS(TEST_RESULT: out FLAGTYPE)
          do TEST_RESULT:= FLAG;
            FLAG:= 1; end;
      or
        accept CLR
          do FLAG:= 0; end;
      end select;
    end loop;
  end CONTROL_FLAG;
```

Figure 3.36: ADA CODE FOR A SAFE CONTROL FLAG ABSTRACTION

3.14   ABSTRACT CONTROLLER MACHINES (ACM)

3.14.1   INTRODUCTION

ACMs separate the scheduling from the doing by putting the scheduling in a separate machine and the doing in an engine that uses the machine to determine what to do next. Reasons for performing this separation are as follows:

- Reuse of abstract state machines developed during preliminary design is enabled.

- Reuse of the same scheduling logic in different concrete contexts is enabled.

- Mapping from designs to implementations is facilitated by the regularity of structure of both the ACMs and the associated agendas.

- The visual approach can be carried right down to the agenda level, by using visual representations for the scheduling logic (e.g., state transition diagrams).

- The emphasis is shifted in creating agendas from ad hoc programming to plugging in abstractions developed during design in an organized manner.

The ability to use ACMs is quite independent of whether the system under design is sequential or concurrent. In either case they may be used by main engines, as suggested by Step 9 of Figure 3.1, and as exemplified by the user robots in the **CONTROL_FLAG** problem, or they may be used by the engines of buttons on the interface of machines like the **CONTROL_FLAG** box or robot. The concept is that there are one or more master engines that interface with an ACM to determine what to do next.

3.14.2   NATURE OF ACMS

Figure 3.37 illustrates the nature of ACMs. Internal details of the ACM may be assumed to be automatically generated from a state transition diagram. The passive nature of ACMs means that they are visited by their master engines, but do not themselves do any visiting; this is left up to the agendas of the master engines. They are passive because this leaves it up to the designer to use ACMs, or not, for particular components. The only internal actions ACMs perform, apart from identifying output events, are related to maintaining their own internal state (for example, to update counters or change enabling predicates on transitions, neither of which is illustrated here). Thus concrete visit control is kept separate from timing logic.

As shown by Figure 3.38, ACMs are, implicitly, boxes with standard interfaces to which master engines pass abstract events (input events of the enclosing machine), and from which master engines receive abstract actions (identifying output events of the enclosing machine). The internal engine of the box is an initializor for the state and state table. The internal engine of the button does the decoding.

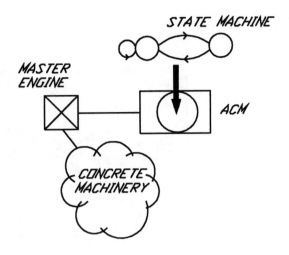

Figure 3.37: THE NATURE OF ABSTRACT CONTROLLER MACHINES (ACMS)

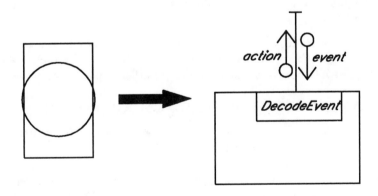

Figure 3.38: IMPLIED STANDARD INTERFACE FOR ABSTRACT CONTROLLER MACHINES (ACMs)

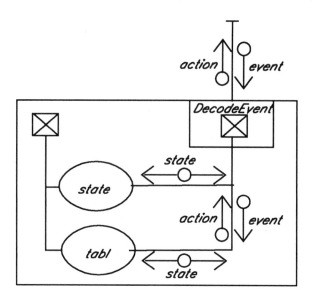

Figure 3.39: INTERPRETING AN ACM AS A BOX

3.14.3   INTERNAL STRUCTURE OF ACMS

Figure 3.39 illustrates one possible form for the internal structure of an ACM box. The idea is that ACMs are not represented in this way directly by the designer, unless the conversion of design diagrams to code is to be performed manually, in which case this form might be drawn by the designer as an intermediate step.

> IMPLEMENTATION IMPLICATIONS: Such ACM boxes may be mapped to Ada packages, following the pattern illustrated earlier for the unsafe **CON-TROL_FLAG** box, or to the equivalent in other implementation technologies.

3.14.4   ALTERNATIVES TO THE ACM APPROACH

If the scheduling logic is kept in the agendas, instead of placed in ACMs, then well known means for visually specifying sequential program logic are available. Even flow charts, which have major disadvantages for describing program organization in a larger sense, might be suitable for this purpose, because they express only what is needed here, namely sequential logic (for this purpose, structured versions of such charts are best — GOTOs are still to be avoided). However, this approach does not have the attributes of regularity and modularity of the ACM approach.

Instead of giving state machines a passive role, as in the ACM approach, they might be given an active role, by using them to specify agendas directly. This approach has not been incorporated in this notation, for the following reasons:

- It does not separate concrete interface control from timing logic; both would be contained in the same state machine.

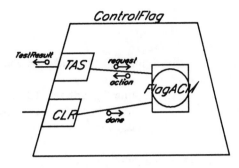

Figure 3.40: AN ACM-BASED VERSION OF THE CONTROL FLAG

- It does not provide a natural way of describing simple, sequential agendas, because every line in the agenda becomes a state, making it annoying rather than helpful to use state machine conventions.

- It does not provide a means of allowing different temporal behaviour specification techniques to be used in such a way that the technique being used is hidden.

- It provides a less uniform conceptual model.

3.15 EXAMPLE: AN ACM VERSION OF THE SAFE CONTROL FLAG

3.15.1 INTRODUCTION

Let us put an ACM in the **CONTROL_FLAG** box of Figure 3.14 simply as an example of how to do it, recognizing from the start that the internal machinery is so simple to begin with that we can do nothing but complicate it with this approach. The point is not to demonstrate that ACMs are good for control flag problems, but to illustrate the nature of ACMs with a very simple example.

3.15.2 REVISED CONTROL FLAG STRUCTURE

Figure 3.40 shows the revised internal structure of the **CONTROL_FLAG** robot. The engines of TAS and CLR are the master engines of the ACM and the events and actions of the ACM are those of the state machine of Figure 3.10. Notice that there is no longer storage for a value of a flag (the state of the ACM replaces it).

3.15.3 AGENDAS AND CODE

Because ACMs have a standard interface, this is all we need to write the agendas of the master engines. The resulting agendas are given, in Ada syntax, in Figure 3.41 (compare with Figure 3.34). The concrete/abstract mappings must be hand-crafted by examining the

```
--TAS agenda
  begin
    push FlagACM.DecodeEvent(request,action);
    case action is
      when grant => TEST_RESULT:= 0;
      when hold  => TEST_RESULT:= 1;
    end case;
  end;
--CLR agenda
  begin
    push FlagACM.DecodeEvent(done,action)
  end;
```

Figure 3.41: NEW, ACM-BASED AGENDAS FOR THE BUTTONS OF THE CONTROL FLAG

state machine in relation to the concrete interface of the **CONTROL_FLAG**; they are as follows:

- A push of **TAS** is mapped to a **request** passed to **FlagACM**.

- A **grant** returned by **FlagACM** is mapped to a **0** returned by **TAS**.

- A **hold** returned by **FlagACM** is mapped to a **1** returned by **TAS**.

- A push of **CLR** is mapped to a **done** passed to **FlagACM**.

IMPLEMENTATION IMPLICATIONS: For implementation, **FlagACM** is mapped to an Ada package, the assumption being that this could be done automatically, given a fully specified state machine. Figure 3.42 gives an Ada package for the ACM that fills in the details, following the general structure of Figure 3.39, and incorporating the state machine of Figure 3.10. Note the introduction of two new actions: one is an error identifying an event/state combination that will never occur (the previous agendas ignore it); the other is a **nop** action indicating "no operation", allowing the ACM to return a value for **action** in cases where no value is needed, as with the **done** event. Note that the initialization mechanism for the state machine table is handled by a procedure called from the package mainline, instead of by an Ada aggregate, following the structure of Figure 3.39; this is not a programming book, so we are not attempting to show how to program elegantly in Ada; certainly, an Ada aggregrate would be more elegant.

```
package FlagACM is
  type  EventType is (request,done);
  type  ActionType  is (grant,hold,nop,error);
  procedure DecodeEvent(event:in EventType,action:out ActionType);
end FlagACM;

package body FlagACM is
  type
    StateType is (YES,NO);
  type EntryType is
    record
      sta : StateType ;
      act : ActionType ;
    end record;
  tabl   : array  (EventType, StateType) of EntryType ;
  state  : StateType ;
  procedure InitTabl is
   begin
   tabl(request, YES).sta:= NO ; tabl (request,YES).act:= grant;
   tabl(request, NO ).sta:= NO ; tabl (request,NO ).act:= hold;
   tabl(done,    YES).sta:= YES; tabl (done,   YES).act:= error;
   tabl(done,    NO ).sta:= YES; tabl (done,   NO ).act:= nop;
   end InitTabl ;
  procedure DecodeEvent(event:in EventType,action:out:ActionType) is
    begin
      action := tabl( event,state ).act ;
      state  := tabl( event,state ).sta ;
    end DecodeEvent ;
  begin
    InitTabl;
    state  := YES;
 end FlagACM;
```

Figure 3.42: AN ADA PACKAGE FOR FlagACM

3.16   REFLECTIONS ON METHOD AND NOTATION

3.16.1   OTHER DESIGN PATHS

Figure 3.1 is not the only possible design path. Figure 3.43 illustrates a different one that follows a *TIME*-first, instead of a *PLACE*-first pattern. This pattern could have been followed in developing the control flag example, and is followed in the case study of Chapter 9. Note that many of the steps are conceptually the same, but numbered differently from Figure 3.1. This is why step numbers were not elevated to the level of section headings in earlier discussions.

A brief explanation of each step follows:

- Step 1 decides on the basic level of concurrency, by identifying peer actor robots. It draws an abstract structure chart, associating a minimal set of events with its components, but not showing event connections (this step is in the *TIME* domain because its primary decision content is a concurrency commitment, in contrast to Step 5, which is also an abstract structure chart, which is in the *PLACE* domain because it commits to event connections).

- Step 2 explores event patterns, using event scenarios.

- Step 3 extracts abstract state machines from the scenarios, if the event patterns are complicated enough to warrant it.

- Step 4 is particular to concurrent systems: it commits to whether the *glue* that binds peer actor robots together is formed only of connections, or includes machinery. We may speak of *glue structures* as ones that provide connections among peer robots.

- Step 5 commits fully to structural event patterns among peer robots and glue robots, including identifying sources and sinks for all events.

- Step 6 confirms with elaborated event scenarios that the new event patterns will work.

- Step 7 commits to the nature of channels among the components of the peer and glue machinery.

- Step 8 decides on interfaces and connections.

- Step 9 explores visiting behaviour in terms of the interface details, using visit scenarios.

- Step 10 specifies agendas, including plugging in abstract state machines as ACMs, where appropriate.

- Step 11 verifies temporal behaviour against Step 9.

- Step 12 gathers robots into boxes, to form subsystems.

There is nothing about this pattern or the earlier one that is cast in concrete. Variations are possible, and steps may be shuffled, left out, or added, depending on the requirements

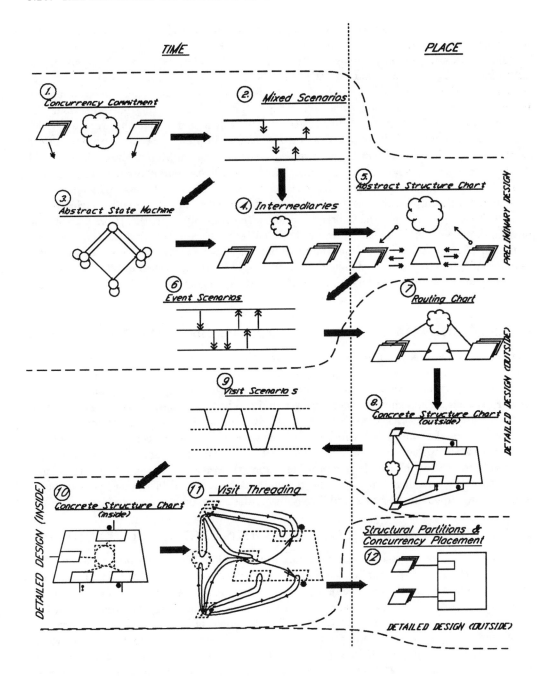

Figure 3.43: HIGHLIGHTS OF A TIME-FIRST DESIGN PATH

of the problem at hand. However, these particular patterns provide a conceptual framework for proceeding with the rest of the material in this book.

The relationship of these steps to the control flag problem is as follows (steps in the *PLACE*-first approach of Figure 3.1 are identified as PF1, PF2, ...): In Step 1, the user robots would be drawn and the **request** events indicated, but no commitment would be made yet to **grant** and **done** events. In Step 2, permission granting patterns would be explored (as in PF2), but with mixed scenarios, in which there would be work activities shown on timelines, in place of **grant** and **done** events. In Step 3, the same state machines would be constructed (as in PF3), with some details missing. In Step 4, the decision would be made to use a control flag, or some other mechanism, like a semaphore (this exposes this more appropriately as a glue structure decision, unlike PF1, where the flag was shown as a peer structural component). In Step 5, the events omitted from the mixed scenarios would be added and given structural sources and sinks (corresponding to PF1). In Step 6, the missing details of mixed scenarios would be filled in, producing the kind of scenarios seen earlier (PF2). Steps 7-10 would be similar to before (PF6-PF9). Step 11 was not explicitly performed before, but would be done by walk throughs of a fully-fleshed out design. Step 12 was done at the faceless box level of commitment at the beginning (PF1), and the interface added later (PF7); here it is left to the end.

3.16.2   REDUNDANCY OF TIME DOMAIN INFORMATION

Figure 3.44 identifies, in an impressionistic way, three aspects of design captured by MachineCharts diagrams, which may be viewed as particular projections of a more complete, underlying representation of a system under design, details of which are either suppressed in the projections, or not shown because they remain to be determined. There is redundancy in these three aspects. All three contain *TIME*-domain information; even structure charts do, because of the underlying semantics of components, and also because of annotations that make declarations about intended temporal behaviour. Once detailed internal design is completed, the structure chart annotations and the scenarios become formally redundant. However, this does not mean they should not be recorded in the design data base. Redundancy provides a means of validating inside decisions against outside intent.

3.16.3   PRACTICAL USE OF SCENARIOS AND STATE MACHINES

A number of visual ways of specifying temporal behaviour have been introduced in this chapter: event scenarios, visit scenarios, and abstract state machines (ASMs). The intent has not been to suggest that people should draw independent diagrams in all of these ways to describe the same temporal behaviour, as has been done in this book; this would be far too labour-intensive (as the author can testify). People should only have to draw the meaning once, using whatever form is appropriate, and have a tool draw other compatible forms when desired, for explanation, presentation, documentation, design execution, or implementation purposes. Furthermore, a tool should be able to integrate the temporal behaviour forms with structural forms stored in a design data base, and provide visual projections of the information from different perspectives to help the designer see relationships. This kind of workbench assistance involves only information retrieval, static analysis and drawing, not actual design execution; therefore, it can be performed on incomplete designs.

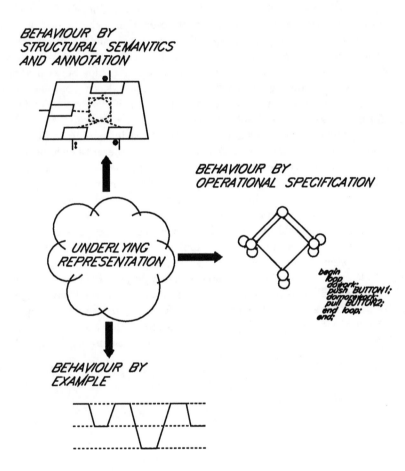

Figure 3.44: MACHINE CHARTS AS PROJECTIONS

For example, given an event scenario, and a cross reference listing of events corresponding to visits or returns from visits, a tool should be able to draw a visit scenario, or its equivalent threaded form on a structure chart. A person should be able to "draw" visit scenarios in linearized form by tracing patterns on a structure chart with a mouse, or follow patterns on a structure chart in threaded form by moving a cursor along the time axis of a linearized scenario. A tool should provide assistance in creating ASMs from scenarios by enabling a person to move a cursor along the time axis of a linearized scenario, identifying segments of the scenario with states; the tool could then draw a preliminary transition diagram itself. Or a tool could show visit threads on a structure chart corresponding to state transitions in a requirements ASM, by making use of the event-visit cross reference list and other information in the design data base. Relationships between structure charts, scenarios and state machines could be shown in the context of a complete set of structure charts representing all levels of recursive decomposition of the system under design, or in projected form, perhaps showing only robots at all levels of decomposition, leaving out all boxes and work buttons. Assistance could be provided in helping the designer to ensure that interface, interaction and transaction scenarios at different levels of recursive decomposition are compatible with each other, by displaying them in relation to each other in revealing ways. Assistance could be provided to the designer in composing ACMs from sets of test-sequence ASMs that describe different examples of required external behaviour. The reader may imagine other possibilities.

Still more assistance could be provided by a workbench that can execute or analyze fully annotated designs. For example, the temporal behaviour of the detailed design could be checked for consistency with requirements scenarios (expressed either in scenario or test-sequence ASM form), and additional nuances of temporal behaviour could be explored by generating new scenarios to answer *what-if* questions. MachineCharts components have temporal semantics that makes them executable for this purpose when properly annotated, although the mechanism of execution is not discussed in this book. However, observe that executability is only part of the picture; a workbench also needs to provide the kind of pre-execution support indicated above.

Chapter 4

MORE ON THE SUBSET BLACK-BOX-WITH-BUTTONS NOTATION

4.1 INTRODUCTION

4.1.1 OBJECTIVES

The purpose of this chapter is to add flesh to the bones of the subset structure chart notation introduced in Chapter 3 by giving

- more explanation of the fine points of the notation,

- more examples of visual thinking that aim to strengthen the reader's ability to *think temporal behaviour*, while drawing or observing structure, and to *assume temporal behaviour*, while devising agendas, and

- more examples of mapping to Ada that aim to strengthen the reader's ability to *think Ada* while drawing or observing pictures, and to indicate how a workbench might help with the process of mapping designs to code.

Extensions that lift some of the restrictions of the subset notation, and that generalize it in both the *TIME* and *PLACE* domains, are provided in Chapter 5. However, the subset notation can go a long way towards helping the designer to gain confidence in the correctness of the structure and temporal behaviour of a system under design.

4.2 RECAP OF THE SUBSET NOTATION

Recall that subset notation (summarized in Figure 4.1) captures designs as static structures with all components custom-designed, and all interactions between black boxes taking place by means of synchronous visits to buttons on their interfaces.

The correspondence between the icons in this figure and our reference implementation technology, Ada, is summarized in Table 4.1.

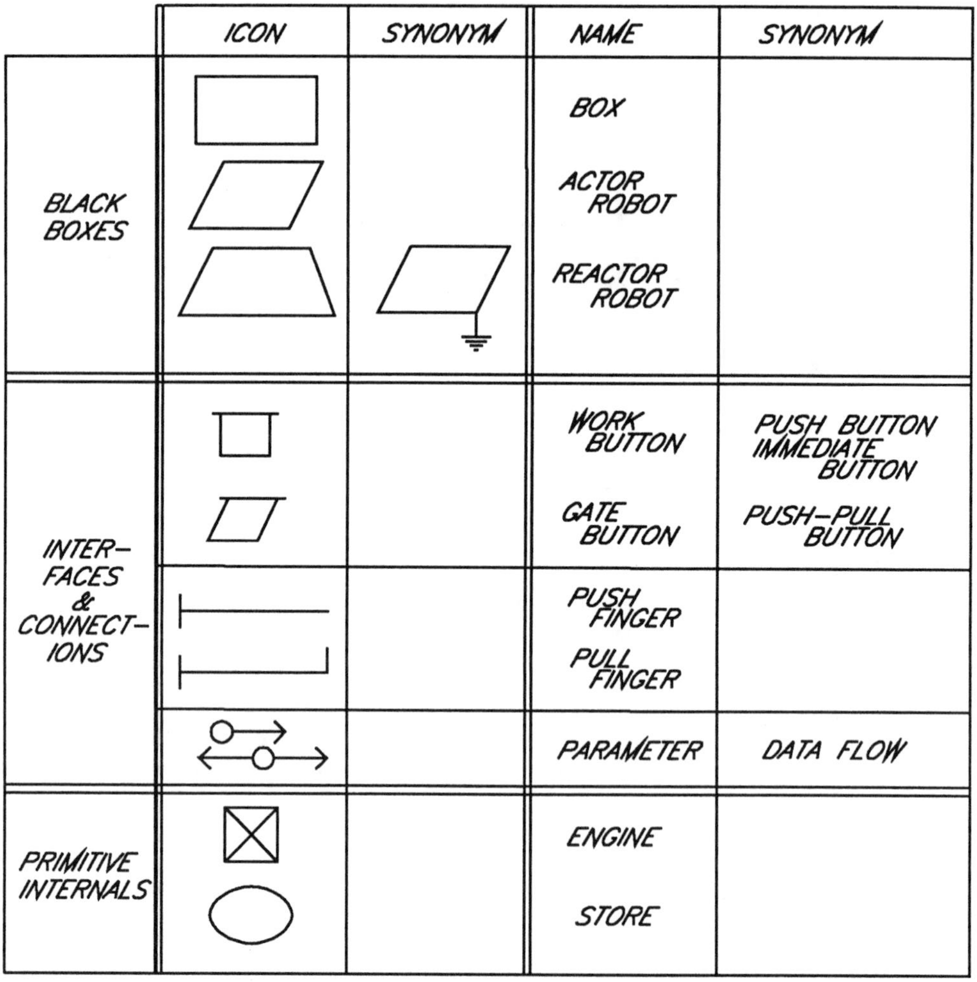

	ICON	SYNONYM	NAME	SYNONYM
BLACK BOXES			BOX	
			ACTOR ROBOT	
			REACTOR ROBOT	
INTERFACES & CONNECTIONS			WORK BUTTON	PUSH BUTTON IMMEDIATE BUTTON
			GATE BUTTON	PUSH–PULL BUTTON
			PUSH FINGER	
			PULL FINGER	
			PARAMETER	DATA FLOW
PRIMITIVE INTERNALS			ENGINE	
			STORE	

Figure 4.1: A BASIC SUBSET OF STRUCTURE CHART ICONS

ICON	ADA MEANING	COMMENTS
box	package,subsystem	an Ada environment may provide subsystems
robot-actor	task	
robot-reactor	task, acts passively	or passive RTX object called from Ada
work button	procedure, function	
gate button	entry	visualized as having procedure-like form
push finger	call path	
pull finger	accept path	no literal accept path in Ada
parameter	parameter	
engine	executable mainline of a body	includes do..end in accept
store	variable	

Table 4.1: CORRESPONDENCE BETWEEN THE SUBSET ICONS AND ADA

Although the subset notation maps nicely to Ada, it is not restricted to Ada. In particular, the restriction to synchronous visits does not force the interpretation to be in terms of Ada tasking and rendezvous, although that is the correct interpretation for Ada, because the notation provides reactors that can represent non-task objects supported by real time executives.

Recall from the control flag example of Chapter 3 that this notation visually indicates the different properties of different machines with respect to *concurrency*, *protection* (i.e., mutual exclusion), and *hiding*. Hiding implies containment of internal machinery that is not visible on the interface, but that may possibly be accessible indirectly through it. Protection implies prevention of concurrent access to a hidden internal machinery. Figure 4.2 shows how to see these properties in pictures, as follows:

- Boxes provide only hiding as an inherent property. Their lack of *TIME*-domain semantics means that they provide neither protection nor concurrency as inherent properties (although the designer may explicitly add such properties by appropriate design of the inside of the box).

- Buttons inherently provide both hiding and protection of what is inside their bodies (as opposed to inside the bodies of machines to which they may be attached).

- Reactor robots inherently provide both hiding and protection of all internal components accessed by all interface buttons. They are concurrent only in the limited sense that the button engines of different reactors may run concurrently during disjoint meetings.

- Actor robots inherently provide all the hiding and protection properties of reactors, plus active concurrency.

Figure 4.3 enlarges our view of the difference between hiding and protection, by showing explicitly where interference, due to lack of protection, may or may not occur in different structures. Failure to choose the right structure among these was the reason for failure of the first control flag attempt in Chapter 3.

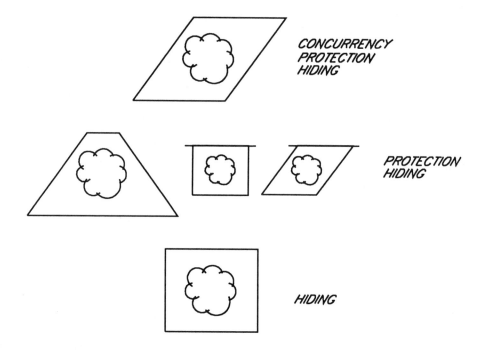

Figure 4.2: MACHINES PROVIDE CONCURRENCY, PROTECTION AND HIDING

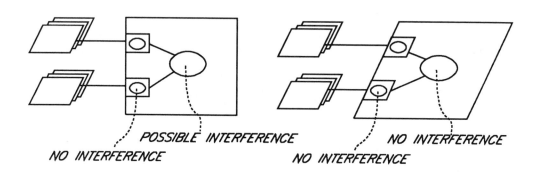

Figure   4.3:   STRUCTURES   DISPLAYING   INTERFERENCE   AND
NON-INTERFERENCE

4.3 REPRESENTING SYSTEM STRUCTURE

4.3.1 INTRODUCTION

Figure 4.4 illustrates some structural features of charts. Descriptions of these features follow.

4.3.2 HIERARCHIES OF CHARTS

System structure is described by a downward-branching tree of structure charts, tied together by interfaces. Peer machines in the same chart are connected via their interfaces. Internal machinery is hidden underneath interfaces in separate charts. The tree may be created from the top down by a process of recursive decomposition, or from the bottom up by a process of composition from parts. A chart at one level of the tree (e.g., MC1) has possibly many charts at the next lower level (e.g., MC2, MC3, and MC4), showing the internal machinery hidden underneath each interface. Showing details of more than one level of the tree in one diagram is called "flattening", and would be an information retrieval function in a workbench, not a design capture one.

This figure illustrates that a machine's *interface* shows everything that is required to connect peer machines together. This enables us to conceptualize structure charts as like "wiring diagrams": machines are constructed by "wiring" internal components to their interfaces; systems are constructed by "wiring" peer interfaces together; temporal behaviour is described in terms of visits via the "wires" joining interfaces. One never needs to see internal details to know how a machine may be "wired" to its peers.

Note how components of any kind at any level may have similar, rich internal structure.

IMPLEMENTATION IMPLICATIONS:

An interface is different in concept from, for example, an Ada specification, and contains more information. In MachineChart terms an Ada specification only shows the buttons, not the fingers.

The main engine in the top level chart of Figure 4.4 may be interpreted for Ada purposes as the mainline program of a main procedure that is never called that implicitly defines a master task for the system. Calls from its mainline program to other tasks anywhere in the program are inter task calls just like those between explicitly defined tasks. Because the master task is not drawn as a task, it is often convenient to leave out the main engine of a design for a multitasking program, in order to make all tasks explicit in the charts.

Gate buttons are not shown in Figure 4.4 as examples of components that can have internal *PLACE*-domain structure. This mirrors Ada, but is not a constraint of MachineCharts.

4.3.3 STRUCTURAL ANNOTATIONS

Figure 4.5 shows some annotations relating to structure that may be added to structure charts; examples of their use are contained in the earlier Figure 4.4.

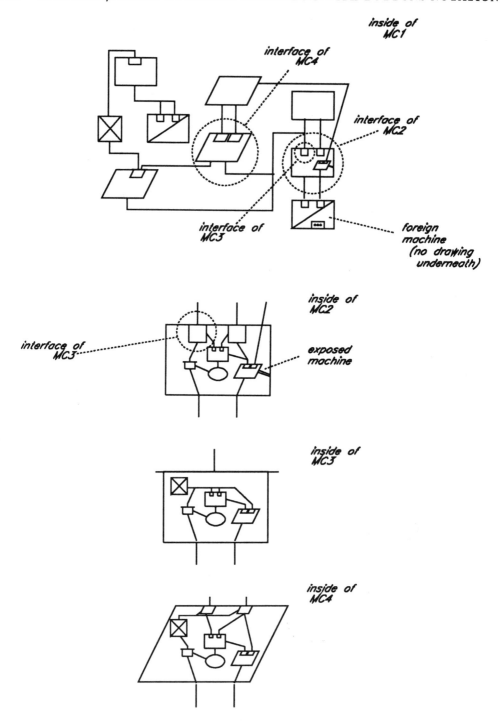

Figure 4.4: EXAMPLES OF STRUCTURE

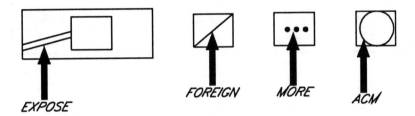

Figure 4.5: STRUCTURAL ANNOTATIONS FOR STRUCTURE CHARTS

- Expose: This connector enables one to promote an internal component to the interface level; in other words, it makes the interface of the exposed machine part of the interface of the enclosing machine. Buttons attached to interfaces are implicitly so exposed (in fact an alternative notation is to draw them inside the visual frame of a machine and then connect them to the frame using the expose icon). This icon enables a more complicated object than a button to be made part of the interface in a visually natural manner. The expose icon enables one to distinguish charts in which internal components are promoted to the interface level from flattened charts in which internal machinery is merely shown, for explanatory or thinking purposes.

- Foreign: A single diagonal line across a component indicates that it is foreign, in other words, not designed here, but only used here. It mimics the international road sign convention in which a diagonal line indicates prohibition of some kind; what is prohibited here is changing the inside of the component.

- More: This symbol indicates that something is left out of a chart; in other words, that there is more here than meets the eye in this particular chart. It is particularly useful when only part of the interface of a foreign component is used.

- ACM: The circle in this symbol annotates a box to indicate that it is of a special, constrained kind that implements an Abstract Controller Machine (ACM). Like a foreign box, the internal machinery of an ACM box is not accessible for design, but, unlike a foreign box, the wherewithall to generate the internal machinery is provided by the designer, in the form of an annotated state transition diagram.

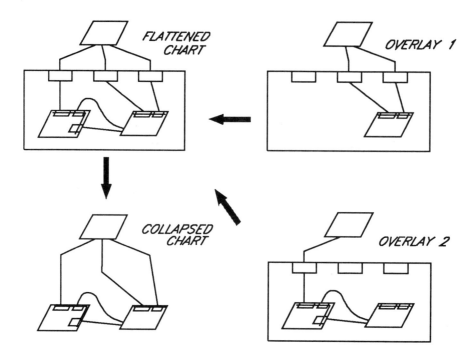

Figure 4.6: OVERLAID, FLATTENED, AND COLLAPSED CHARTS

4.3.4   VIEWS OF CHARTS

As illustrated by Figure 4.6, charts may be split into *overlays* to provide less cluttered presentations of particular aspects, *flattened* to show two or more levels of the hierarchy on the same diagram, or *collapsed* to show only robot interactions. A collapsed chart is missing some detail, but retains the essence of the robot interactions, and so is useful for reasoning about temporal behaviour.

Overlays show different aspects of the same chart on different diagrams that may be superimposed to form a complete diagram, as one would superimpose transparencies on an overhead projector.

One may approach flattening and collapsing the other way round from that shown in the diagram: one may start, in a bottom up fashion, with a robot structure like that in the collapsed chart, and then partition it to give the structure shown in the flattened chart.

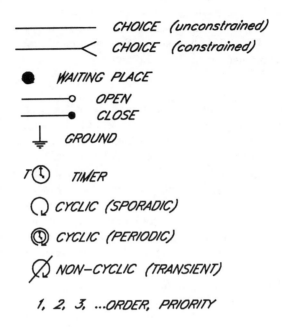

Figure 4.7: TIME DOMAIN ANNOTATIONS FOR STRUCTURE CHARTS

4.4 TEMPORAL ANNOTATIONS ON STRUCTURE

4.4.1 TIME-DOMAIN ANNOTATION ICONS

The *TIME*-domain annotations for structure charts shown in Figure 4.7 provide a means for the designer to indicate intent regarding some key aspects of temporal behaviour. Their use is declarative in nature, and provides a similar kind of redundancy to that provided by type declarations in programming languages; i.e., a means of checking that later agenda detail does not violate the declaration. Some of them have already been seen in Chapter 3 (specifically choice frames, ground icons, and cycle icons).

Unconstrained choice implies a first-come-first-served selection criteria among a set of alternatives (e.g., an unconstrained choice frame drawn across a set of gate buttons, or across a set of fingers connected to a set of gate buttons, indicates that the first possible meeting is desired). Choice frames indicating unconstrained choice may be given names, to identify them as destinations for visits. Their use in conjunction with waiting places will be explored in Section 4.5. *Constrained choice* implies picking a specific alternative based on some condition (e.g., drawing a constrained choice frame across a set of fingers indicates that one finger will be picked for a visit based on some condition in effect prior to the visit).

Waiting places are gate buttons (or choice frames) where non-busy waiting occurs *by design*, rather than by accident. They are visually marked as such by placing filled-in circles near them on the side where a visitor may wait. Waiting place markers may be given names to identify waiting conditions. Not all gate buttons are waiting places in the sense defined above; accidental waiting may also occur at any gate button, due to congestion (many other visitors on the same side of the button) or latency (a sluggish visitor on the other side of the button), but these possibilities do not qualify a gate button as a waiting place. A central problem in the design of event driven systems is using waiting places effectively; therefore considerable space is given in this book to the issues surrounding them, starting in Section 4.5.

Open and *close* directed arcs indicate patterns of opening and closing waiting places. These are not fingers indicating visiting paths, but annotations indicating where the opening or closing action is performed (at the tail of the arc) and what it affects (the waiting place at the head of the arc). The head of the arc has an empty circle at the end touching the affected waiting place if the action is opening, and a filled circle if it is closing.

Ground icons are attached to actors to symbolize that they are "grounded" from a temporal behaviour viewpoint, making them into reactors. This way of showing reactors may be preferred to the visually cleaner trapezoid notation because the identification can be performed as an afterthought, after a structure chart has already been drawn, without having to change any existing details of the chart. It also indicates the state of affairs in Ada more directly, when designing for Ada (recall that reactors map to Ada tasks that must be constrained by programming to behave passively).

A *timer* is a clock icon that may be attached to fingers or choice frames, where a timeout condition may be required. The timeout action is indicated by a finger with its tail offset from the timer icon (or from the finger or choice frame to which the timeout icon is attached).

A *cycle* is a circular arrow that may be attached to any place where cyclic behaviour is intended. A diagonal line drawn across the circular arrow indicates the opposite, that transient behaviour is intended. Cyclic engines have infinitely looping agendas; in other words, they are persistent. Non-cyclic engines have agendas that eventually terminate; in other words, they are transient. A combination of a *cycle* and a *timer* indicates periodicity.

An *integer* associated with a finger, or a gate button not in a choice group, indicates temporal order of visiting, relative to other fingers. An *integer* associated with a robot, or with a gate button in a choice group, indicates priority (smaller integers indicate higher priorities).

4.4.2   USING THE TIME-DOMAIN ANNOTATIONS

Figure 4.8 illustrates some ways of combining these annotations with the basic icons of Figure 4.1. The meaning of these will be described in detail later in this chapter and the book, both visually, and with Ada examples. For the moment, there is enough information in this figure to suggest meaning. Choice frames may be drawn across components or fingers. Gate buttons may be marked as waiting places. Opening or closing patterns may be indicated. (Although not used in the rest of this book, the convention of indicating an opening action with an open circle and a closing action with a closed, or filled, circle, may be extended to the marking of the waiting place itself, by showing an initially-open place with an open circle, and an initially-closed place with a closed circle.) Timers may be used to indicate timeout on a choice, timeout on a push or pull visit, periodicity, or

ICON	ADA MEANING	COMMENTS
choice frame	selective call or accept	unconstrained
	if-then-else or case	constrained
waiting place	guarded or avoided entry	declared or programmed
open, close	not Ada operations	side effects on guard variables
ground	passive task	usually remains a task
timer	timeout on selective call or accept	
	self-delay	
balk	else on selective call or accept	
cyclic	loop	
periodic	not declarable	achieve approx. effect only
non-cyclic(transient)	a task that terminates	
order	accomplished by programming	
priority - robot	static declaration for tasks	
priority - button	not declarable for entries	

Table 4.2: CORRESPONDENCE BETWEEN THE TIME-DOMAIN ANNOTATIONS AND ADA

self-delay for a period. Alternate actions on timeout or balking are indicated by offset fingers. A special symbol is used for a balking visit that gives up if no meeting can take place immediately; it is a synonym for timeout with zero time. Order and priority may be indicated by numbering (numbering choice alternatives indicates priority, not order). Cyclic behaviour may be associated with various components.

To give a glimpse of possible uses of the *TIME*-domain annotations to indicate temporal properties at interfaces and in internal structures, Figure 4.9 crowds most of them into one overloaded robot that is *not* intended to exemplify recommended design style. The particular usages demonstrated by this figure will not be explained further here, but will be illustrated by examples in the remainder of the book.

Note that all of the ways of using these annotations involve robots, gate buttons and associated fingers. They do *not* apply to boxes and work buttons. Why not, considering that these may sometimes contain active internal machinery (i.e., including robots), making them, in effect, robots themselves, or "super-robots", composed of teams of cooperating robots? The answer is that the *TIME*-domain behaviour implied by internal active machinery can be very complex, and impossible to indicate in a meaningful way at the interface level by simple markings on an interface; one must look at outside scenarios, or internal organization, or both, to understand it. The most that the notation can meaningfully do is mark a box or work button that has internal active machinery in a special way, indicating that this component is not as simple as it looks from the outside. Although it will not be used further in this book, Figure 4.10 illustrates a way of marking a box that will identify it in this way.

Table 4.2 cross references these annotations to Ada.

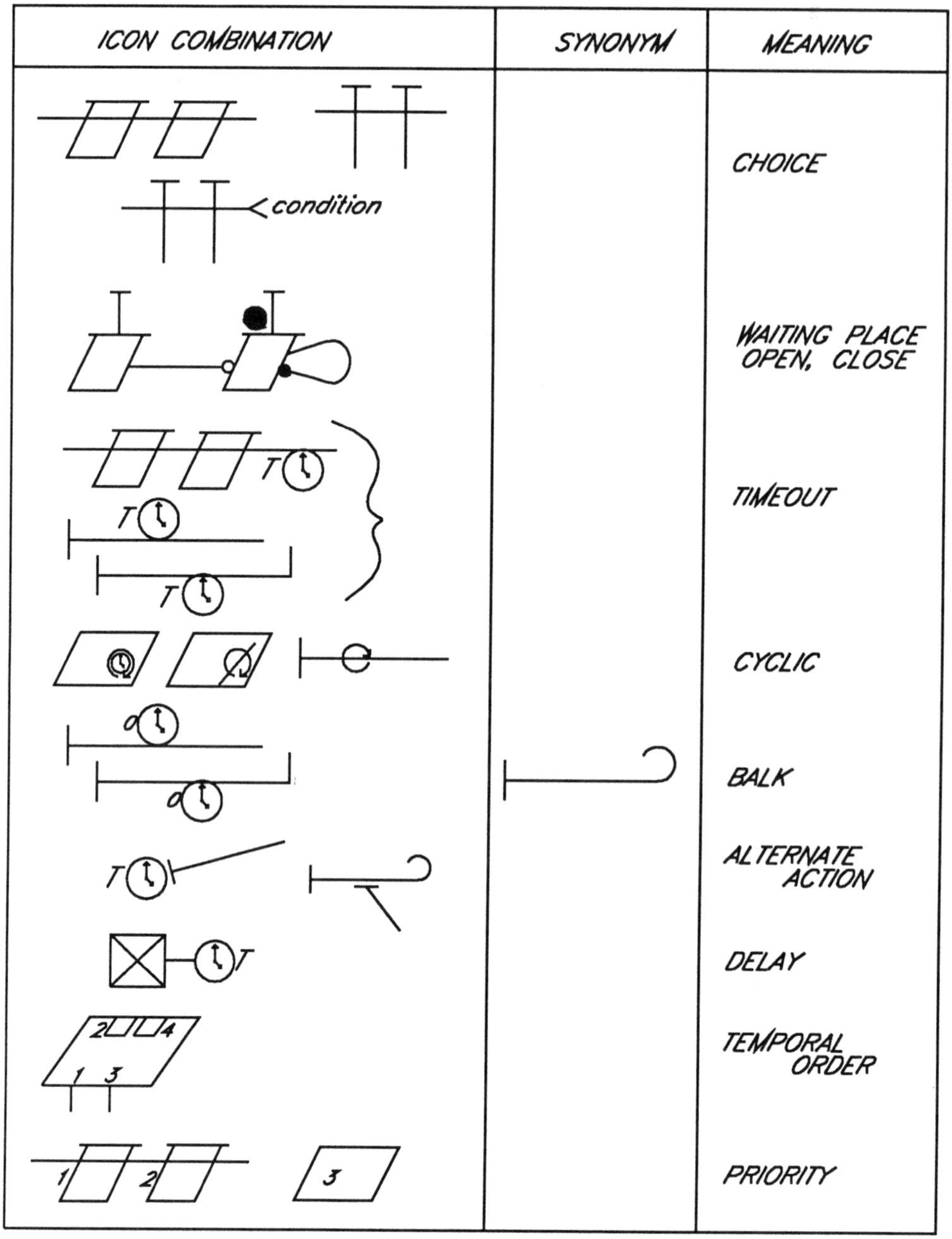

Figure 4.8: COMBINING TIME-DOMAIN ANNOTATIONS WITH BASIC ICONS

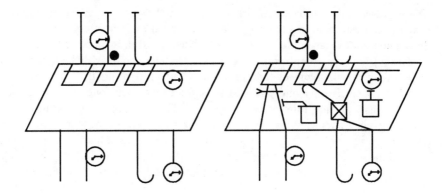

Figure 4.9: SOME USES OF TIME-DOMAIN ANNOTATIONS TO INDICATE INTENDED TEMPORAL BEHAVIOUR AT INTERFACES

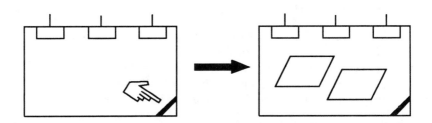

Figure 4.10: A BOX WITH INTERNAL ROBOTS

4.5   WAITING PLACES AND WAITING PARADIGMS

4.5.1   INTRODUCTION

Non-busy waiting is the central organizing rule of event-driven systems. Non-busy waiting is at the opposite end of the design spectrum from busy-waiting, or polling, as exemplified by the control flag example of Chapter 3. Busy-waiting is undesirable because it generates overhead that may compromise performance, and introduces behavioural complexity that may make achieving correct temporal behaviour more difficult.

When there is only one place to wait for events, and one responder for these events, the non-busy waiting rule is easy to follow. However, in typical practical systems, there are many places to wait for events, both at the edges of systems, and internal to them, and many responders. It becomes a challenge to organize patterns of waiting places and responders so that non-busy waiting is used throughout, while avoiding such problems as waiting somewhere where nothing is happening while things are happening elsewhere, and mutual waiting leading to deadlock. This section begins an in-depth treatment of waiting places that will continue throughout the book.

4.5.2   THE WAITING PLACE NOTATION

Figure 4.11 illustrates the use of waiting places in the subset notation of this chapter, in which all interaction between robots is by means of gate buttons on their interfaces. The figure shows the meaning of waiting places, without necessarily indicating how the waiting conditions are imposed and lifted, as follows:

- Parts I and IV show how gate buttons on interfaces may be marked as such on the push side, either by themselves, or in association with choice frames. The meaning to a push-side visitor to a waiting place is that a pull may not occur for an unpredictable length of time, while the host waits for other events that will enable it to perform the pull. A typical use of a push-side waiting place is to **receive** some item that must arrive from somewhere else first; such a button would not be pulled by the host until it had an item for a **receiver**. The difference between Parts I and IV is that in the former, the waiting is enforced by avoidance, and in the latter by screening, as explained below.

- Parts II and V show that the corresponding pull-side structure is drawn in the usual way with an engine pulling the individual buttons, or pulling a choice frame joining the buttons. The convention for the subset notation is that buttons are not normally marked on their pull sides as waiting places, because the pull-side waiting place pattern may normally be assumed by default to be the inverse of the push side one.

- Parts III and VI show the default waiting place patterns on the pull side. For example, in Part III, **a** and **b** are push-side waiting places, so they are not pull-side ones; whereas **c** is not a push-side waiting place, so it is a pull-side one. The implication is that the host engine may have to wait for an unpredictable length of time for a visitor at **c**, but can expect visitors to be waiting at **a** and **b** when it pulls them. In Part VI, the host engine waits for any visitor at the choice frame, so the choice frame itself is the default pull-side waiting place. A fundamental difference between the situations with and without the choice frame is indicated by Part VII.

- Part VII shows a special case that overides the default of Part III to change fundamentally the designer's intent expressed by the push-side waiting place markers. Suppose a gate button is a waiting place on both its push and pull sides (button **a** here). The difference from the default case is that the host engine cannot assume that there will be a visitor at **a** when it pulls it. But if there is not, then the host engine may be waiting at **a** while a visitor pushes **c**, implicitly making **c** into a push-side waiting place, in violation of the original intent; this means that **c** should now be marked as a push-side waiting place. The whole issue can be avoided by using choice frames, because the late arrival of a visitor to push **a** will not affect visitors at **c**.

4.5.3   IMPOSING A WAITING CONDITION BY AVOIDANCE OR SCREENING

Imposing a waiting condition at a waiting place is called *closing* it; releasing the waiting condition is called *opening* it. While a button is closed, a visitor must join the button queue until the button is opened again (unless it chooses to balk or time out). Note that closing is done "blind" on one side of a button, without reference to visitors on the other side. There must be queues on both sides of gate buttons. However, when the buttons are on robot interfaces, there may be many visitors on the push side, but only one on the pull side, namely the main engine of the host robot.

Closing may be accomplished by avoidance or screening:

- Avoidance: Closing may be accomplished by avoiding a button, and opening by visiting it; avoidance strategies must be programmed into the agendas of engines.

- Screening: Closing may be accomplished by screening out certain buttons before visiting a choice frame, and opening by removing the screening conditions before some later visit. The notation provides icons identifying the opening and closing patterns associated with the screening.

IMPLEMENTATION IMPLICATIONS: There are no explicit *open* and *close* operations in Ada; everything is done by side effects of variable changes on guard expressions. Although this may be fine for programming, it does not separate *TIME*-domain behaviour from *WORK*-domain behaviour for design purposes, whereas the Architectural Design process requires this separation. The open and close operations provide a convenient fiction for doing this for Ada design. Later it will be shown how their assumed existence may be helpful in mapping designs into programs.

If the clutter of open and close icons makes design pictures too complex, the same information may be entered via a dialogue with a designer's workbench to establish which engines are responsible for opening or closing which waiting places. In either case, the workbench can use this information to insert

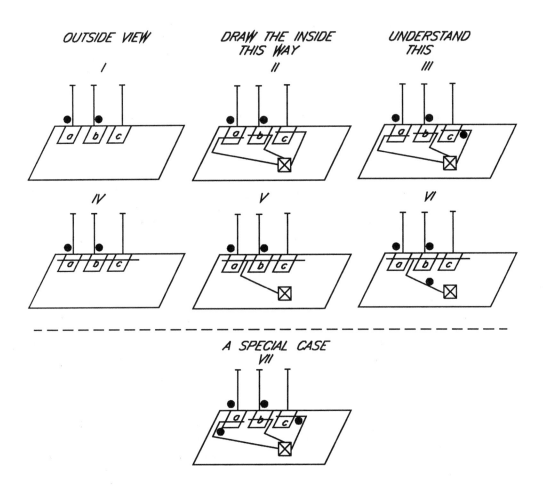

Figure 4.11: WAITING PLACES IN THE SUBSET NOTATION

functions in appropriate places to perform the opening and closing, and by inserting textual comments in the bodies of these functions to guide later detailed programming. Examples are given in Section 4.6.

Accidental waiting differs from place waiting, as follows:

- *Congestion*: Waiting may occur at places not designated as waiting places, due to congestion. Many visitors may happen to arrive simultaneously at a single place. Then waiting occurs simply because the interactions must be serialized. The possibility of congestion is visible in structure charts because of the presence of many fingers pointing from many different potential visitors to the same place. Congestion waiting occurs at times when the system is very active; it is strongly affected by implementation technology (e.g., multitasking on a uniprocessor). It is aggravated by synchronous modes of interaction, requiring visitors always to wait for meetings.

- *Latency*: Latency occurs when a visitor on one side of a button is waiting for a sluggish visitor on the other side who should be ready for a meeting. The possibility of latency is not directly visible in structure charts, so the designer must try to make latency small, in order that it can be assumed negligible. A large latency delay associated with a nominally non-waiting place should be a hint to change the design (perhaps by splitting visits to the place into two parts, to form a request-wait pair).

Figure 3.24 in Chapter 3 showed how to visualize temporal behaviour associated with gate buttons. Now reexamine this figure from the perspective that the gate button is a waiting place. Note particularly that parameters carried by the visitor *to* a gate button are not seen until a meeting occurs there, which may be delayed for some time when the button is a waiting place, even though the host is not busy at the time of the visit. Consequences are as follows:

- The host sees neither visitors nor parameters while the waiting place is closed, so a visitor cannot use a parameter to carry a request to a closed waiting place, expecting that the answer will be delivered at the end of the wait; nor can the visitor know in advance when the waiting place is closed, to avoid visiting it at that time.

- If, on the other hand, the waiting place is open when the visitor arrives, then the request will be seen immediately and the answer returned, if it is available. But what if the answer is not available at that time? Then the visitor must leave empty handed and visit again to wait for the answer. We are back to where we started.

Generalized waiting places that lift this restriction are discussed in Chapter 5.

IMPLEMENTATION IMPLICATIONS: The restricted waiting places of this chapter accurately mirror how Ada entries may be used as waiting places. In particular, the use of **in** parameters to pass a request to an entry and **out** parameters to get an answer does not mean that one can use the entry to both place the request and wait for the answer in one call, if producing the answer requires rendezvousing with other callers, as it often may. In general, one rendezvous is required for the request and one for the answer, with other rendezvous allowed in between.

4.5.4   AN EXAMPLE: A LINE-TO-CHARACTER CONVERTER

Figure 4.12 illustrates some of these waiting issues with a simple example of a **LINE2CHAR** robot that receives lines from a line source and delivers characters to a character sink. Both buttons of **LINE2CHAR** are marked as push-side waiting places, because they may be pushed at any time, but not serviced at any time. The two cases in the figure illustrate the avoidance and screening approaches to enforcing waiting place conditions. The former requires the main engine to have an agenda that imposes the desired waiting pattern (forcing **LINE2CHAR** to be an actor), while the latter requires of the main engine only that it pull the choice to cause the next meeting, leaving it up to buttons to change the opening and closing conditions that will enforce waiting (enabling **LINE2CHAR** to be a reactor). Opening is done by one button on the other (shown in the figure); closing is done by each button on itself (not shown in the figure, because self-closing may be assumed, unless otherwise specified).

The visual representations follow the conventions of Chapter 3 that a reactor implicitly has a choice frame that includes all its buttons, so the frame does not need to be shown as part of the interface.

Figure 4.13 gives the agendas for the engines in Figure 4.12 in pseudo-Ada style. Note that **open** and **close** are agenda operations applied to gate buttons that are marked as waiting places.

IMPLEMENTATION IMPLICATIONS:

The structure charts and agendas may be mapped into Ada in the manner illustrated in Chapter 2 for the Control Flag example. Only the screening approach offers anything new, so a skeleton form of it is given in Figure 4.14, omitting variable declarations and initializations, which the reader should have no trouble filling in based on earlier figures and discussions. Observe that, although there is a lot of code in the mainline of the task, it is all in critical sections, so it is all executed during rendezvous; therefore, the task is passive; in other words it does nothing outside of its rendezvous with callers. The **openPUT** and **openGET** boolean variables may be replaced by expressions involving buffer variables, but the program as shown has a more obvious mapping from the structure chart.

A notational issue arises here. Ada users of the notation may wish to reserve the waiting place marker for guarded selective accept alternatives, as exemplified by this program. With this convention, the avoidance approach would have no waiting place markers. A problem with this convention, which is not used in this book, is that it results in inconsistent behavioural cues at interfaces.

AVOIDANCE

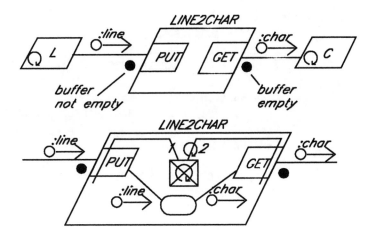

SCREENING

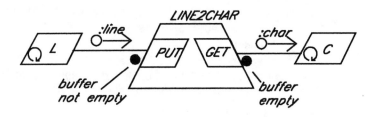

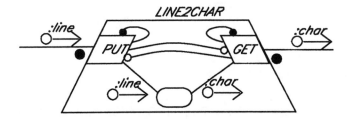

Figure 4.12: A LINE-TO-CHARACTER EXAMPLE

```
--AVOIDANCE
    --BUTTON AGENDAS
      gatebutton PUT(...) is
      ... -- PUT LINE IN INTERNAL LINE STORE
      end PUT;
      gatebutton GET(...) is
        ...-- GET NEXT CHARACTER FROM INTERNAL LINE STORE
      end GET:
    --MAINLINE
    --loop
        pull PUT; --CLOSES GET
        while MORE_CHARACTERS loop
          pull GET --CLOSES PUT
        end loop;
    --end loop;


--SCREENING
    --BUTTON AGENDAS
      gatebutton PUT(...) is
      ... -- PUT LINE IN INTERNAL LINE STORE
      close PUT; open GET;
      end PUT;
      gatebutton GET(...) is
        ...-- GET NEXT CHARACTER FROM INTERNAL LINE STORE
        if not MORE_CHARACTERS then
          close GET; open PUT;
        end if;
      end GET:
    --MAINLINE
    --loop
        pull choice (PUT,GET);
    --end loop;
```

Figure 4.13: AGENDAS FOR THE LINE TO CHARACTER EXAMPLE

```
loop
  select
    when openPUT =>
      accept PUT(...) do
      ... -- PUT LINE IN INTERNAL LINE STORE
      openPUT:=FALSE; openGET:=TRUE; end;
  or
    when openGET =>
      accept GET(...) do
      ...-- GET NEXT CHARACTER FROM INTERNAL LINE STORE
      if not MORE_CHARACTERS then
      openPUT:=TRUE; openGET:=FALSE; end if; end;
  end select;
end loop;
```

Figure 4.14: ADA MAINLINE FOR A PASSIVE LINE-TO-CHARACTER TASK

4.6   SEMAPHORES AND WAITING PLACES

4.6.1   INTRODUCTION

Semaphores are generalizations of control flags that provide waiting places, instead of requiring busy waiting. The world of semaphores is a microcosm of the world of concurrent systems that displays many general behavioural properties of the larger world. Therefore, it is well worth studying in detail, as a vehicle for gaining deeper understanding of both the MachineCharts way of thinking about such properties, and the relationship of the visual approach to implementation. Semaphores are useful components to have in a designer's parts kit, but not so useful that they deserve the level of detailed inspection given them here for that reason alone. However, the style of representation and thinking developed here will be found to scale up to more powerful components.

In general, semaphores are used either to enforce mutually exclusive access to some shared object that cannot enforce mutual exclusion itself (this was the function of the control flag in Chapter 3), or to pass events in an asynchronous manner between peer robots. In the bigger world of concurrent system design, these objectives can often be achieved without semaphores; for example, mutual exclusion may be achieved by enclosing the shared object in a reactor with buttons that provide operations on it, and event signalling by providing buttons for events on a robot that has a larger purpose in the system under design than just transfer of a single event. However, the semaphore function is still there in the larger component, only mixed in with other functions. Here we study it in its pure state.

4.6.2   A GENERAL NOTATIONAL SHORTHAND FOR VISIT SCENARIOS

Visit scenarios will be used extensively in this section and throughout the rest of the book. Although the general representation for visit scenarios has a timeline for each push-side visitor, a timeline for each button, and a timeline for each pull-side visitor, the shorthand representation of Figure 4.15 may be used when buttons are attached to robots, as they are in this chapter and also in many examples in later chapters. Because the pull side has only a single possible visitor (the main engine), and the button activities and the main engine activities are interleaved, not concurrent, everything on the pull side (buttons and the main engine) may be collapsed onto a single timeline, thus greatly simplifying scenario diagrams, without losing information.

In this figure, the convention is adopted of indicating an attempted visit that has not yet been satisfied by drawing the visit thread parallel to the host timeline until the visit can be satisfied. This shows waiting in a very graphic manner. However, the shape of the visit thread between timelines is not intended to be significant. Any shape that does not actually touch the host timeline will do to indicate waiting. In fact, in the semaphore examples that immediately follow, waiting is indicated by drawing the visit thread diagonally between its point of origin on the visitor's timeline and the point on the host's timeline where the visit can be satisfied.

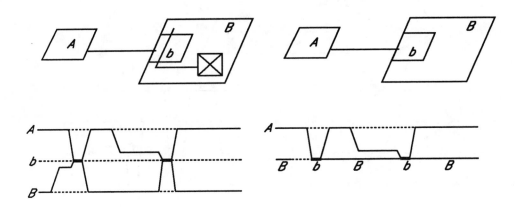

Figure 4.15: A NOTATIONAL SHORTHAND FOR VISIT SCENARIOS

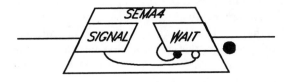

Figure 4.16: A SEMAPHORE ABSTRACTION

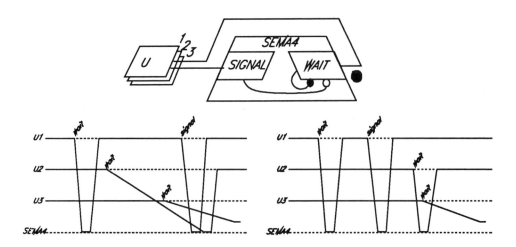

Figure 4.17: A SEMAPHORE AS A TEST-AND-SET FLAG WITH NON-BUSY WAITING

4.6.3 A BINARY SEMAPHORE

Figure 4.16 shows a semaphore as a reactor with a **SIGNAL** button and a **WAIT** button, with the latter marked as a waiting place. Figure 4.17 shows how such a semaphore may be used as the test-and-set flag was used in Chapter 3, to get permission to do something by first visiting **WAIT**, and then to notify that it is done by visiting **SIGNAL**. The shadow users in this figure indicate only that there is more than one user, not that the users are all identical; they are only identical in their use of the semaphore (later, in Chapters 5 and 10, this kind of representation will be used in conjunction with a template icon to indicate that multiple identical instances are installed from the same template, but without the template icon, the meaning is as here). The difference from the test-and-set flag is that repeated visits to **WAIT** are not necessary; the visitor always returns eventually from **WAIT** with implied permission. The return will be immediate if **WAIT** is open, or delayed if it is closed, until it is opened again. With this interpretation, **WAIT** must be open initially (corresponding to a test-and-set flag with an initial value of **0**). If semaphores are used only for permission granting in this way, then there will never be multiple signals arriving between waits (because the only possible visitor to **SIGNAL** is the one that was earlier released from **WAIT**), but there may be multiple waits arriving between signals. Such a semaphore is known as a binary semaphore, because it has only two possible internal states, **WAIT**-closed and **WAIT**-open.

IMPLEMENTATION IMPLICATIONS: The scheduling logic required by the binary semaphore interpretation of Figure 4.17 may be implemented in a very simple Ada task, as shown in Figure 4.6.3. Apart from the issue of the efficiency of a semaphore implemented as a task, this semaphore works fine for the

```
task body BinarySemaphore is
 openWAIT: boolean:=FALSE;
  begin
  loop
    select
      when openWAIT =>
        accept WAIT do
          openWAIT:=FALSE;
        end;
    or
        accept SIGNAL do
          openWAIT:=TRUE;
        end;
    end select;
  end loop;
end BinarySemaphore;
```

Figure 4.18: A BINARY SEMAPHORE IN ADA

permission-granting problem, in which there are only multiple waiters, but never multiple signallers. Because the value of **openWAIT** is **TRUE** initially, **WAIT** begins open. Later, if there are callers at **WAIT** when a **SIGNAL** occurs, then **SIGNAL**'s opening of **WAIT** will allow one to proceed to a rendezvous after the **SIGNAL** rendezvous is ended; during the ensuing **WAIT** rendezvous, **WAIT** will be immediately closed again, to prevent any more **WAIT** callers from proceeding. If there are no callers at **WAIT** when the **SIGNAL** occurs, then the result will be an open **WAIT** entry for the next caller. However, note that the program will lose extra signals that occur while the **WAIT** queue is empty, because multiple opens of **WAIT** will not make it "more" open. This is not a problem if the semaphore is used correctly for mutual exclusion, as illustrated here, because such extra signals will never occur.

A problem with all of the Ada implementations of semaphores discussed in this section is that they are inefficient relative to the usual intent of such mechanisms, namely quick interaction without task switching most of the time. Each interaction with a semaphore task always requires two task context switches, even for cases where no waiting is required, such as visiting **WAIT** when it is open. One might expect that Ada compilers would routinely optimize such situations, but this is not yet common at the time of this writing.

4.6.4 A COUNTING SEMAPHORE

Figure 4.19 shows behavioural requirements for the case where multiple signals are possible at any time. The assumption is that **WAIT** is closed initially. If there are visitors in the

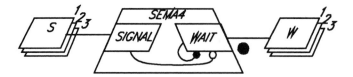

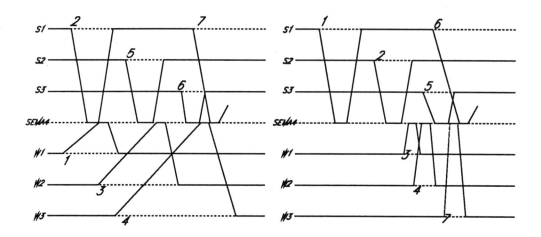

Figure 4.19: USING A COUNTING SEMAPHORE FOR SIGNALLING

WAIT queue, each **SIGNAL** opens **WAIT** to one of them, allowing its visit to **WAIT** to be completed. If there are no visitors in the **WAIT** queue, each **SIGNAL** stores up credit for one future visitor to complete its visit to **WAIT**. The implication is that credit is stored up by counting, so this type of semaphore is called a counting semaphore.

IMPLEMENTATION IMPLICATIONS:

Figure 4.6.4 provides the code for a counting semaphore that will do the job. The way of writing entry-opening and entry-closing actions in this program, and in ensuing programs that extend this one, is intended to exhibit a path to automating the generation of program skeletons from structure charts, rather than to suggest a desirable Ada programming style. This style may be a bit too verbose for ordinary programming.

The conventional way of opening and closing entries in selective accept statements is to make variable changes that have side effects on expressions in **when** statements associated with the select alternatives. The problem with this from our perspective is that control actions are hidden in the program text as variable changes. In this particular program, there are no variable changes other than those having control effects, but in more general programs there could be. In the conventional style of programming, they are not distinguished at the places where they occur. In the style of programming shown in the figure, control actions are explicitly identified where they occur by calls to functions that change boolean guard variables.

This particular program could be changed to shorter equivalent one by removing the variable declaration for **openWAIT** and the call to **controlWAIT**, and renaming the function **openWAIT**. One could even go further and remove the boolean function entirely, putting the expression it contains directly in the **when** statement.

The path to automation suggested by the program as given is as follows. Named waiting places in a structure chart map directly to boolean functions with the same names. Waiting condition annotations on the charts provide information for forming the bodies of the functions (either as comments to assist a programmer to write details, or semi-automatically if the annotations are properly formalized). The designer points to places in the structure chart where opening and closing actions are to take place, and the workbench places calls to the appropriate functions in the generated text at these places. The designer, or a programmer, completes details of the generated program skeletons, under the control of the workbench. A source level optimizer might then translate the result into more conventional Ada style.

4.6.5 CONTROLLING THE EFFECTS OF INDETERMINISM

However, we are not out of the behavioural woods yet! Figure 4.21 shows that anomalous temporal behaviour is possible with the counting semaphore during a period of congestion, due to indeterminism in the process of choosing among visitors in the queues of more than one open gate button. Assuming the choice is random (the only safe assumption when designing for Ada), new signallers may be chosen over currently-queued waiters simply because the **SIGNAL** queue is picked at random. (The presence of currently-queued waiters is indicated by the **WAIT** button being open *and* its queue being occupied.) The problem only arises if buttons always have separate queues; an interpretation that would have a single queue for all the buttons of a choice frame (like the single queue for all the service wickets in a bank) would not have this problem. This is because a single queue would be ordered on global time of arrival, with the consequence for this semaphore problem that new signallers would be behind currently-queued waiters in the single queue, and could therefore not be serviced before them as shown in the figure.

A solution suggested by Figure 4.22 is to assign priorities to gate buttons. The general intent of the priority assignment is to ensure that an occupied queue of an open, higher priority gate button is cleared out before lower priority open buttons are serviced. Specifically for this problem, the priority assignment ensures that currently-queued waiters are cleared out before new signallers are serviced, thus making the anomalous temporal behaviour of Figure 4.21 impossible.

We could leave it at that, assuming that appropriate priority mechanisms will be available in the implementation technology.

```
task body CountingSemaphore is
  COUNTER: integer:=0;
  openWAIT: boolean:=FALSE; -- GUARD VARIABLE
  function controlWAIT return boolean is -- CONTROL FUNCTION
    begin
     return COUNTER>0;
    end controlWAIT;
  begin
   loop
     select
       when openWAIT =>
         accept WAIT do
           COUNTER:=COUNTER-1;
           openWAIT:=controlWAIT;
         end;
     or
         accept SIGNAL do
           COUNTER:=COUNTER+1;
           openWAIT:=controlWAIT;
         end;
     end select;
   end loop;
 end CountingSemaphore;
```

Figure 4.20: A COUNTING SEMAPHORE IN ADA

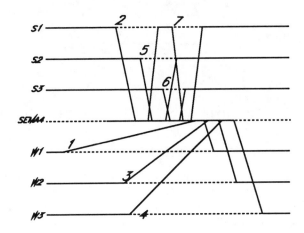

Figure 4.21: ANOMALOUS TEMPORAL BEHAVIOUR OF A SEMAPHORE

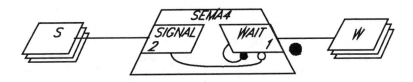

Figure 4.22: PRIORITY INTENT IN A SEMAPHORE REACTOR

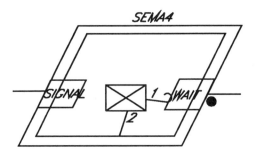

Figure 4.23: PRIORITY MACHINERY IN A SEMAPHORE ACTOR

IMPLEMENTATION IMPLICATIONS:

Unfortunately, Ada provides neither a common queue for all the entries of a selective accept, nor a way of declaratively prioritizing these entries. Priority must be programmed. We can design appropriate priority machinery at the MachineChart level, as illustrated by Figure 4.23. Higher priority of **WAIT** is ensured by always checking it first, using a balking pull, before pulling the choice covering both buttons. Note that because this machinery requires decision making by the main engine, the robot is an actor, violating the intent that a semaphore is passive in nature.

Figure 4.24 maps Figure 4.23 to an active Ada task. Note that an accept body for **WAIT** appears twice in the task body. Because of the mapping from a structure chart, the body has the same code in each place, but there is no constraint in Ada that forces it to have the same code. Creative programmers who push this feature of Ada to the limit can create tasks that are very difficult to understand from the outside, and maybe even from the inside.

There is also another way of doing it in Ada that leaves the task passive, but is a bit tricky, and has the disadvantage of being generally unsafe in situations where callers may time out. The solution is a purely programming one, not easily distinguished in a design diagram, except by textual annotation. It is illustrated in Figure 4.25. It uses Ada's **count** attribute of entry queues to test the number of tasks in the **WAIT** queue, and to close the **SIGNAL** entry if both this number is greater than zero, and the **WAIT** entry is open. The problem with safety arises because testing the count attribute of an entry requires one implicit call to the run time system, and accepting an entry requires another; the two implicit calls are not indivisible, making it possible for a task that is in a queue that has just been tested to leave the queue before the entry acceptance call is made, due to a timer interrupt being processed by the run time system in between the calls. This kind of problem is not necessarily unique to Ada;

it would arise with any real time executive that allowed tasks to make explicit calls to test the number of tasks in a queue, and then to make subsequent calls to effect scheduling decisions based on the assumption that the number will not have changed in the meantime.

Remember that the program structure shown in both these cases follows from Figure 4.6.4, and is intended to demonstrate the form that might be generated from pictures with the help of a workbench.

4.6.6   THE IMPORTANCE OF WAITING PLACE MARKERS

Figure 4.26 gives an example of how waiting place markers provide checks on internal machinery. Suppose the designer of the internal machinery of a counting semaphore, being aware of the anomalous temporal behaviour problem of Figure 4.21, tries to avoid it by performing alternate pulls of first **SIGNAL** and then **WAIT**, as illustrated by Figure 4.26. (Note that the numerical annotations in this figure indicate order, not priority. They would only mean priority if the buttons were joined by a choice frame, as before). Somewhat surprisingly, because there is no internal counter, this does give the required temporal behaviour property of a counting semaphore that signals are not lost; this is because they are stored up in the **SIGNAL** queue. The new internal machinery prevents the earlier anomalous temporal behaviour of new signallers getting ahead of old waiters, but replaces it with a new form of anomalous behaviour by making the **SIGNAL** button an unintended waiting place. The implication, as shown in the figure, is that both buttons should be marked as waiting places; but this was not the original intent.

However, we do not care that **SIGNAL** is a waiting place if the semaphore in Figure 4.26 is used for mutual exclusion, because there will never be a signaller when **SIGNAL** is closed; in other words, the semaphore will satisfy the scenarios of Figure 4.17. In fact, there is no need to mark **SIGNAL** as a waiting place because it will never be seen as one. This is like the philosopher's concern about the meaning of a tree falling in a forest if no one sees it. Do interfaces need to be marked with waiting places that will never be seen as such, given the correct visit protocol is followed? The answer is a tentative no; if the visit protocol is clearly given by a scenario, or other means, as part of the interface definition, then there is no need to obscure the diagram with meaningless markings; on the other hand, if the the interface may be used in unexpected ways, then the markings are needed.

4.6.7   CONCLUDING REMARKS

Semaphores were used in this section primarily as vehicles for delving deeply at the design level into behavioural properties of concurrent systems employing non-busy waiting, and for showing mappings to implementations. The point was not so much the semaphores themselves, as their behavioural properties in terms of waiting, choice, indeterminism, and races. The Ada programs developed for semaphores were presented more to illustrate the mapping process itself, and the way in which a workbench could assist it, and to illustrate some properties of Ada in relation to the visual notation, than to give Ada programs that would be useful in their own right.

```
task body PrioritySemaphore is
  COUNTER: integer:=0;
  openWAIT: boolean:=FALSE;
  function controlWAIT return BOOLEAN is
    begin
      return COUNTER>0;
    end controlWAIT;
  begin
   loop
     loop  -- CLEAR OUT HIGH PRIORITY FIRST
       select
         when openWAIT =>
           accept WAIT do
             COUNTER:=COUNTER-1;
             openWAIT:=controlWAIT;
           end;
       else
         exit;
       end select;
     end loop;
     select -- THEN ACCEPT ALL COMERS
       when openWAIT =>
         accept WAIT do
           COUNTER:=COUNTER-1;
           openWAIT:=controlWAIT;
         end;
     or
         accept SIGNAL do
           COUNTER:=COUNTER+1;
           openWAIT:=controlWAIT;
         end;
     end select;
   end loop;
  end PrioritySemaphore;
```

Figure 4.24: EXPLICIT PRIORITY CONTROL BY A SEMAPHORE TASK MAINLINE

```
task body TrickySemaphore is
  COUNTER: integer:=0;
  openWAIT: boolean:=FALSE;
  openSIGNAL: boolean:=TRUE;
  function controlWAIT return BOOLEAN is
   begin
     return COUNTER>0;
   end controlWAIT;
  function controlSIGNAL return BOOLEAN is
   begin
     return not(openWAIT and WAIT'count<>0);
   end controlSIGNAL;
  begin
   loop
     select
       when openWAIT =>
         accept WAIT do
           COUNTER:=COUNTER-1;
             openWAIT:=controlWAIT;
             openSIGNAL:=controlSIGNAL;
           end;
     or
       when openSIGNAL =>
         accept SIGNAL do
           COUNTER:=COUNTER+1;
             openWAIT:=controlWAIT;
             openSIGNAL:=controlSIGNAL;
           end;
     end select;
   end loop;
end TrickySemaphore;
```

Figure 4.25: A TRICKY ADA PROGRAM FOR THE PRIORITIZED SEMAPHORE

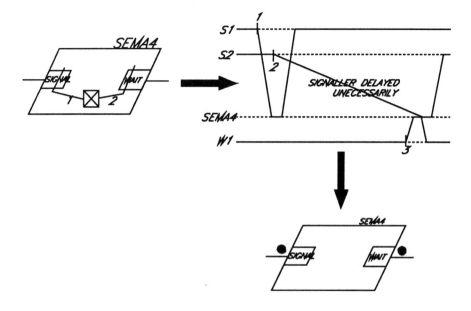

Figure 4.26: A SEMAPHORE THAT ALTERNATES SERVICING OF WAIT AND SIGNAL

The efforts devoted in this section to getting semaphore machinery right are not important in themselves if semaphores (or other, similar multitasking objects) are provided by real time executives. Then they are foreign machines, with internal mechanisms outside the control of the designer of the system that uses them. In any case, when semaphores are foreign machines, the problem of choosing between queues illustrated by these examples is unlikely to arise, because it is unlikely that different services of the executive, like **wait** or **signal**, would have separate queues. Tasks waiting for an executive are likely to be placed in a single queue for the executive as a whole, ordered by task priority first, and time of arrival second.

Semaphores are, however, important examples of components of *glue structures*. Recall from Chapter 1 that a glue structure binds peer concurrent machines (robots) together, by providing the machinery to support the protocols by means of which they may interact. Glue structures containing semaphores, or other, similar intermediate machinery, may be used to provide indirect communication between peer robots, either because direct communication would bind them too tightly together, or because direct communication is not available in the target implementation technology. Semaphore glue structures may be used to provide mutual exclusion or event signalling between peer robots, as the examples of this section have illustrated. The material of this section also illustrates the difference between an interface and a glue structure. Glue structures contain machinery, the components of which themselves have interfaces.

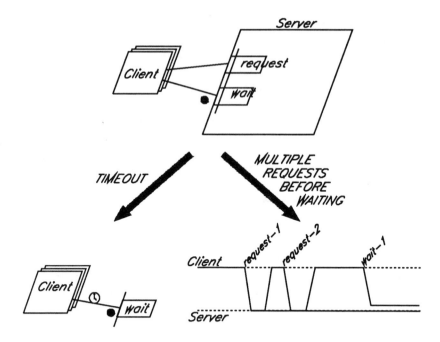

Figure 4.27: A SERVER WITH A REQUEST-WAIT LINEAR INTERFACE

4.7   A CLIENT-SERVER PROBLEM AS AN EXAMPLE OF WAITING PLACES

4.7.1   INTRODUCTION

Continuing with the exploration of waiting in concurrent systems, suppose, as shown in Figure 4.27, that an *active* server may provide services via attached gate buttons. The active server is a larger component than a semaphore that bundles together in one protected place any objects required to support the service (not shown in the figure) as well as buttons that support the transfer of events particular to the service. The idea here is that clients can request a service, return later to wait for results (or to pick them up immediately if they are available), and in the meantime go about their own business. The server processes transactions for possibly many clients, one at a time; in general, transaction processing may require activity outside the meetings with the clients themselves, so the server is shown as an actor.

The chart of Figure 4.27 is an example of how to indicate temporal behaviour at the interface level by a *linear interface structure*, so called because interaction points are strung linearly along both the interface and the time axis. Here the linear interface structure arises from the essential nature of the problem (clients want to **request** first and return to **wait** later). Later we shall see how such structures may naturally arise as a result of the choice of interaction mechanism even when clients do not need to do something else

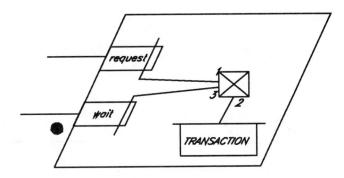

Figure 4.28: SOLUTION 1 (INCORRECT) : SERVER ALTERNATES REQUEST AND WAIT

between requesting and waiting.

What makes the ensuing discussion of this problem interesting is that clients are not assumed to be always well behaved: they may make a second request before getting the answer from the first one; or give up on waiting for the answer and then make another request later. The question is, how do the different ways available in MachineCharts for giving the server control over these interactions affect temporal behaviour? The answers in the ensuing discussion give further insight both into the notation itself and into its use for design.

For simplicity, parameters are not shown, but should be assumed to be needed.

The purpose of this example is to help the reader to visualize temporal behaviour in structure, by giving some examples of designs that have unsatisfactory temporal behaviour, and showing scenarios for them.

4.7.2 TEMPORAL BEHAVIOUR PROBLEMS AND SOLUTIONS FOR A SINGLE CLIENT

To make things simple initially, transaction processing will not be treated as concurrent with the server, but as internal to it, performed by an internal work button. This is suitable for a single client, but not for multiple clients. The final solution will then be generalized for multiple clients.

Figure 4.28 provides a naive internal structure for the server that does *not* give the desired outside temporal behaviour, even for single clients. The alternate servicing of **request** and **wait** introduces pathologies into the temporal behaviour that result in deadlock.

Figure 4.29 shows an example of the temporal behaviour created by the internal structure of Figure 4.28. With luck it will operate normally. However, if a client times out, or makes a double request before waiting, deadlock will occur, with the server stuck at **wait** and the client stuck at **request**.

Figure 4.30 makes an effort at patching up the deadlock problem by using a balking pull

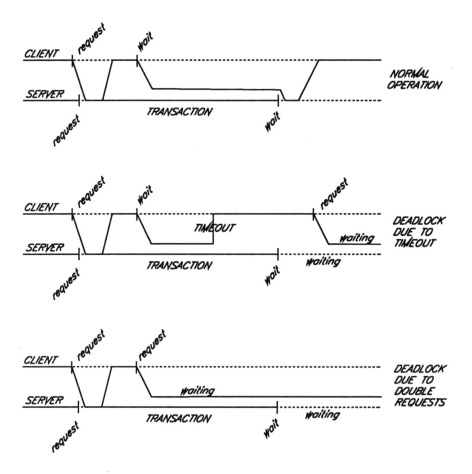

Figure 4.29: VISIT SCENARIOS FOR SOLUTION 1

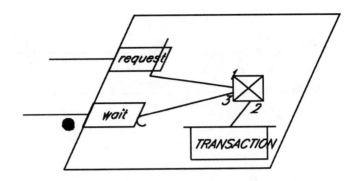

Figure 4.30: SOLUTION 2 (INCORRECT) : SERVER TRIES TO GIVE PRIORITY TO REQUESTS

internally on the **wait** button, with the idea of avoiding the server becoming stuck there. It does not attempt to solve the problem of **request** being an implicit waiting place.

Figure 4.31 shows that the patch-up effort of Figure 4.30 still does not work correctly. The timeout problem is fixed, but now there is a new deadlock possibility, due to a critical race. If the client gets to **wait** before the server engine pulls it, then everything works fine. However, if it arrives late, then deadlock occurs.

Figure 4.32 finally fixes the deadlock and critical race problems for a single client by grouping **request** and **wait** in a choice frame. Note that **TRANSACTION** opens **wait** when its work is completed.

Figure 4.33 shows the correct temporal behaviour of Figure 4.32 in the single client case.

IMPLEMENTATION IMPLICATIONS: Ada code for these solutions is given in Figures 4.34, 4.35, 4.36, and 4.37.

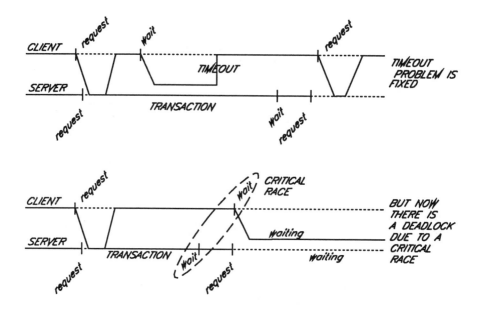

Figure 4.31: VISIT SCENARIOS FOR SOLUTION 2

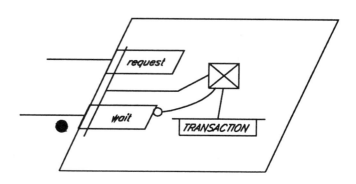

Figure 4.32: SOLUTION 3 (ALMOST CORRECT) : SERVER TREATS REQUEST AND WAIT EQUALLY

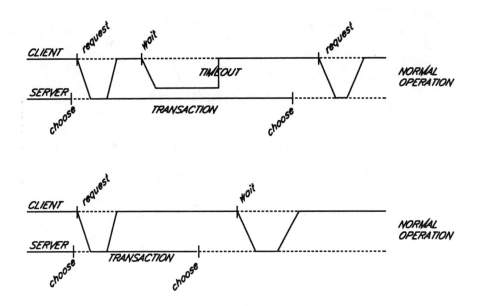

Figure 4.33: VISIT SCENARIOS FOR SOLUTION 3

```
task body wellbehavedCLIENT is
  loop
    ...
    server.REQUEST(...);--INITIATE TRANSACTION
      ...
    server.WAIT(...);--WAIT FOR RESULT
      ...
  end loop;
end wellbehavedCLIENT;

task body illbehavedCLIENT is
  loop
    ...
    server.REQUEST(...);--INITIATE TRANSACTION
    server.REQUEST(...);--AND ANOTHER ONE
      ...
    server.WAIT(...);--WAIT FOR 1ST RESULT
      ...
    select
      server.WAIT(...);--WAIT FOR 2ND RESULT
    or
      delay(timeout); CLEANUP(...);
    end select;
      ...
  end loop;
end illbehavedCLIENT;
```

(corresponding to Figure 4.27)

Figure 4.34: WELL BEHAVED AND OTHER CLIENTS IN ADA

```
task body SERVER is
  ...
  loop
    accept REQUEST(...) do ...;
    TRANSACTION ...
    accept WAIT(...) do ...;
  end loop;
  ...
end SERVER;
```

(corresponding to Figure 4.28)

Figure 4.35: SOLUTION 1: SERVER ALTERNATES REQUEST AND WAIT

```
task body SERVER is
  ...
  loop
    accept REQUEST(...) do ...;
    TRANSACTION;
    select
      accept WAIT(...) do ...;
    else
      null;
    end select
  end loop;
  ...
end SERVER;
```

(corresponding to Figure 4.30)

Figure 4.36: SOLUTION 2: SERVER GIVES PRIORITY TO REQUESTS

```
task body SERVER is
  ...
  loop
    select
      accept REQUEST(...) do ...;
      TRANSACTION
    or
      when DONE =>
          accept WAIT(...) do ...;
    end select
  end loop;
  ...
end SERVER;
```

(corresponding to Figure 4.32)

Figure 4.37: SOLUTION 3: SERVER TREATS REQUEST AND WAIT EQUALLY

4.7.3 GENERALIZING TO MULTIPLE CLIENTS

Solution 3 gives incorrect temporal behaviour for multiple clients, as shown in Figure 4.38. There is a critical race between clients to get to **wait** after visiting **request**. If they get there in the wrong order, as shown in the figure, then the results of one client's transaction will be delivered to another.

Solution 4 in Figure 4.39 fixes the critical race problem by providing an array of **wait** buttons, giving each client a unique waiting place (the array notation is simply a convenience — equally good would a set of buttons labelled **wait1, wait2, ...**). An assumption is that some identifier will be passed between servers and clients, either from clients before a meeting, or from the server after a meeting, that will enable clients to identify which **wait** button to visit; the assumption is that the **open** operation indicated by the arrow opens a particular button.

The disadvantage of this solution is that there must be enough **wait** buttons built in to the interface of the server to satisfy all possible clients that might have transactions going on concurrently. However, in spite of this disadvantage, the figure provides a standard mechanism for avoiding certain kinds of critical races. As will be shown in Chapters 5 and 8, this mechanism may be easily mapped into other, more flexible, mechanisms; it may be regarded as a kind of idiom for these other mechanisms, that can be drawn more simply in diagrams.

> IMPLEMENTATION IMPLICATIONS: A gate button array may be implemented by an entry family in Ada.

However, Solution 4 still does not fully provide for multiple clients; it fails to provide concurrent processing of transactions, effectively making **request** into an implicit waiting place.

Finally, Solution 5 in Figure 4.40 solves the complete problem correctly for multiple servers, by providing separate concurrent processing of transactions, with reporting of results back by means of a new button, **report** (note that this raises a new issue of making sure that no deadlock can occur due to mutual visits to **TRANSACTION** and **report** — such issues are discussed further in Chapter 8).

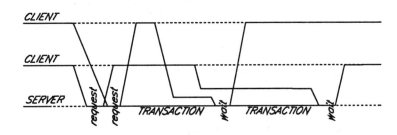

Figure 4.38: TEMPORAL BEHAVIOUR OF SOLUTION 3 IS INCORRECT FOR MULTIPLE CLIENTS

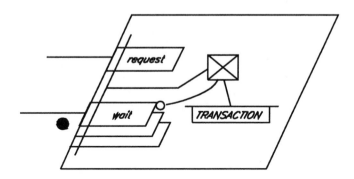

Figure 4.39: SOLUTION 4: AN ALMOST-CORRECT SOLUTION FOR MULTIPLE CLIENTS

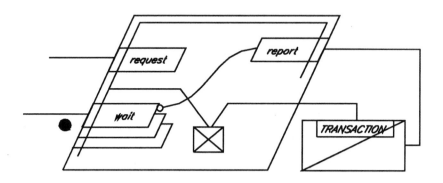

Figure 4.40: SOLUTION 5: A CORRECT SOLUTION FOR MULTIPLE CLIENTS

4.8 TEMPORAL IMPLICATIONS OF INTERNAL STRUCTURES

As illustrated earlier by Figure 4.4, internal structures of machines may be quite rich. This section gives a quick overview of some temporal implications of internal structures of robots.

A robot may have many engines available to do its internal work: all of its gate button engines, and its single main engine. These engines may do work associated with meetings either during or after the meetings. Figure 4.41 shows how to represent these two possibilities:

- A work button may be visited during meetings. This possibility is indicated by a finger with its tail touching the body of a gate button and its head touching the face of an internal work button.

- A work button may be visited after a specific meeting. In this case it is always visited by the main engine, with there being a choice of whether to visit it or not, depending on the meeting that just took place. A visually clearer way of showing this is to indicate the association of the work button with a particular gate button, by drawing a finger with its tail offset outside the body of the gate button and pointing at the work button; however, the implication is still that the main engine performs the visit.

  IMPLEMENTATION IMPLICATIONS: The second alternative might be programmed explicitly by placing a case statement in the agenda of the main engine, to select which work button to visit following which rendezvous. However, this may be done more directly in Ada, when using selective accept statements, by placing each work item following the appropriate critical section in the selective accept statement.

Figure 4.42 shows an even more complex internal structure for a robot, using combinations of several of the visual mechanisms introduced so far. An (optional) convention is shown in this figure of offsetting tails of fingers inside gate buttons to provide strong visual emphasis that visits via such fingers are made by the button engine, in direct contrast to fingers with tails offset outside the gate button. Comments on the figure show how it implies a variety of temporal behaviour patterns.

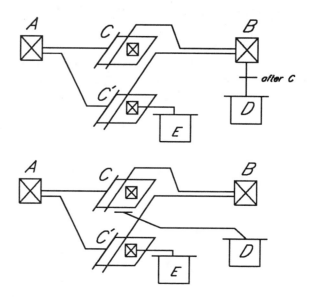

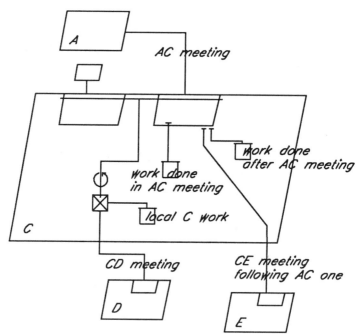

Figure 4.41: DOING WORK AFTER A MEETING

Figure 4.42:   SOME WAYS IN WHICH STRUCTURE MAY IMPLY TEMPORAL BEHAVIOUR

4.9 REPRESENTING THE COUPLING OF HARDWARE AND SOFTWARE

Given that this is a system design notation, rather than specifically a software design notation, no unique icons for hardware are provided. As shown in Figure 4.43, a hardware device that sends interrupts to software is conveniently represented as a box containing an actor (the interrupt source) and a device buffer. Then an interrupt path is appropriately represented as a push finger leading from a hardware robot to a software button representing the interrupt service routine (ISR); and, in the other direction, a push finger connecting a software source to a button of a hardware box represents access to a device register. The interlock on the ISR button represents the interrupt being implicitly disabled until the lowest level of servicing is finished (this is implicit in the notation, because the hardware robot generating the interrupt cannot continue until interlock is released by the button). The internal details on the hardware side would not normally be shown in a software design diagram.

As illustrated by Part I of Figure 4.43, a very simple structure has the ISR button as a gate button on a handler robot. This tightly locks the interrupting hardware robot to a handling software robot.

> IMPLEMENTATION IMPLICATIONS: As shown in Figure 4.44 and Figure 4.45, this nicely represents the Ada view of interrupts as described in the Ada reference manual, where a task entry is the interrupt service routine.

As illustrated by Part II of Figure 4.43, the ISR may also be represented as a detached work button that allows hardware to interact quickly with software via a sequence of interrupts to complete a transaction (such as moving a string of characters into a buffer) before involving any software robots. Not until it services the last interrupt of the transaction does the ISR button notify an associated software robot by pushing a shared gate button. This way is operationally different from the first only if the ISR button does not visit the associated robot on every interrupt.

> IMPLEMENTATION IMPLICATIONS: This way nicely represents the situation with many real time executives, which enable an interrupt handling procedure to be loosely coupled to a handler task, instead of tightly coupled.

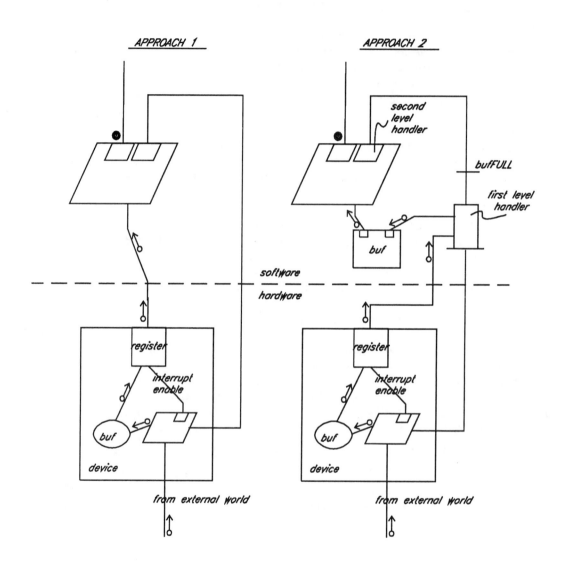

Figure 4.43: HARDWARE-SOFTWARE INTERACTIONS

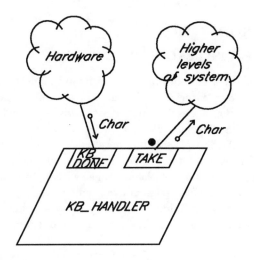

Figure 4.44: AN INTERRUPT HANDLER BUTTON

```
task KB-HANDLER is
  entry TAKE(CH: out CHAR);
  entry KB-DONE;
end KB-HANDLER;
task body KB-HANDLER is
  BUF,DBR:CHAR;
  for DBR use at 8#177462#;
  begin
    loop
      accept KB-DONE do BUF:=DBR; end;
      accept TAKE(CH:out CHAR) do CH:=BUF;end;
    end loop
end KB-HANDLER;
```

Figure 4.45: ADA INTERRUPT HANDLER CODE

4.10   ADDITIONAL ASPECTS OF THE NOTATION

4.10.1   INTRODUCTION

4.10.2   SELF-VISITING STRUCTURES

Self-visiting structures are ones in which visits are made from *inside* a machine to buttons on the machine's own interface. Because, in the subset notation, buttons are attached to interfaces with the face edge out, paths for visits to such buttons from inside must be shown by projecting fingers that have their sources inside and that point at the button from the outside. At first glance, this may seem an awkward convention, perhaps even an annoying one (for example, to Ada programmers, who may freely call exported procedures of a package from the body of the package, without declaring that this is being done). However, it is a very useful design convention that helps in the visualization of temporal behaviour. One views a machine differently, from a behavioural viewpoint, if one knows that its interface buttons are visited only from the outside, or from both the inside and the outside.

Figure 4.46 shows how self-visiting structures may imply useful or pathological temporal behaviour. A box self-visiting one of its buttons simply indicates use of an internal component that happens to be exposed outside. If the self-visit is from the box's engine, then it is obviously an initialization action. If it is from another place in the box, then it is simply normal use of an available button during normal operation. If the button actually visits itself, then every visit gets independent use of the engine's agenda.

However, as illustrated by the figure, self visits must be avoided with robots and gate buttons, because of the danger of deadlock. For example, a robot which may both pull and push one of its own attached gate buttons must choose one or the other at any particular time; if it chooses pushing, the result is deadlock, because there is now no engine available to exercise the required pull.

4.10.3   CONVENTIONS AND ERRORS

Figure 4.47 shows conventions associated with merging and splitting fingers in structure charts:

- Fingers that cross without connecting are indicated by looping the crossing line explicitly over the crossed line, in the manner often used in electrical wiring diagrams. This means that no special marker has to be used to indicate connections (such as a filled circle, which could be confused with a waiting place).

- Merging and splitting of fingers is just a drawing convenience that avoids having to draw multiple lines extending over long distances in a diagram.

- Parameters associated with merged and split fingers do not have to be repeated on all paths. For drawing convenience, if certain parameters are used on certain paths and treated as dummies on others, they may be shown next to the path on which they are used, but the assumption is that all parameters belong to all paths.

Figure 4.48 shows some icon combinations that are meaningless.

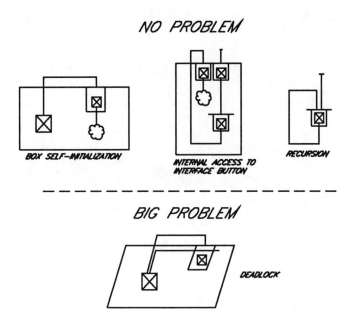

Figure 4.46: SELF-VISITING STRUCTURES

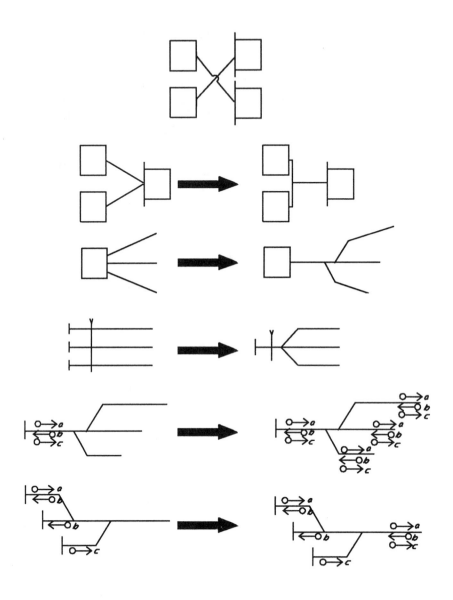

Figure 4.47: CONVENTIONS ASSOCIATED WITH CROSSING, MERGING AND SPLITTING FINGERS

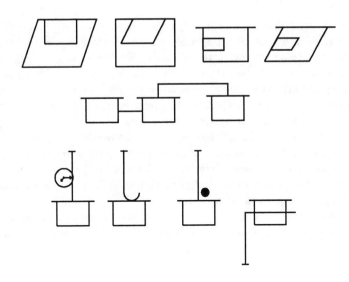

Figure 4.48: SOME MEANINGLESS ICON COMBINATIONS

- Buttons cannot be attached to incompatibly shaped black boxes.

- Fingers between buttons cannot go from face to face, or body to body (who would be the visitor?).

- Fingers with behavioural implications other than simple push cannot be associated with work buttons.

- Buttons cannot be attached to buttons (buttons have simple interfaces).

4.10.4 MACHINE CHARTS LANGUAGE (MCL)

There is obviously a requirement for programming-like textual fragments to appear in various places in MachineCharts designs (e.g., on flows to indicate data types, associated with buttons to indicate waiting conditions, associated with fingers to indicate alternatives to timeouts and balks, associated with engines to specify primitive agendas, on state machine transitions to indicate enabling conditions, events and actions): a MachineCharts language is required. In this book, a mix of natural language comments, programming-like annotations and, sometimes short program fragments in our reference programming language, Ada, takes the place of a formal MCL. However, to mobilize MachineCharts for temporal behaviour animation in a CAD system above the level of particular implementation technologies requires a simple, self contained MCL; as this is being written, one is under development in the author's research laboratory (Appendix A provides an overview).

4.11   CONCLUSIONS

A deliberate effort has been made with this notation to satisfy the KISS principle (Keep It Simple, Stupid!), by not inventing a plethora of icons to represent different machine idioms, but rather to rely on conveying the idioms by interface cues, naming conventions, scenarios, and, where necessary, flattened diagrams showing internals. That the notation is relatively simple may not at first glance be obvious, when one counts the number of icons for the first time. However, the core of the notation resides in a few simple icons with common sense semantics. The rest are declarative annotations.

As one uses the notation, the urge to invent new icons to represent often used idioms expressible only with combination of other icons is hard to resist. In some cases while writing this book the urge has proved irresistible (for example, special icons have been invented to represent reactors, abstract controller machines (ACMs) and asynchronous interactions, all of which can be expressed without them).

However, where does one stop? Too much of this can lead to icon explosion and diagrams which no one but the icon inventors can understand. The notation tries to strike a reasonable balance.

Chapter 5

STRETCHING AND EXTENDING THE SUBSET NOTATION

5.1 INTRODUCTION

This chapter stretches and extends the notation in several directions to give it greater expressivity. Some of these directions provide more expressivity than does our reference implementation technology, Ada; others increase its ability to express mechanisms that are not only in Ada, but also in other important implementation technologies. However, all of the material of this chapter is of relevance to architectural design, whether it is targeted for Ada, or for other implementation technologies.

Section 5.2 stretches the *TIME*-domain properties of the subset notation, without adding new icons, by using the existing icons in ways that give interesting and useful new forms of glue structures and interfaces. Some of the new forms are not directly representable in Ada, although some of them are directly representable in other implementation technologies. However, the temporal behaviour they embody is generally useful and examples of their mapping to the subset notation are given that will be of direct interest to Ada readers. The forms resulting from these mappings are accessible without having to stretch the notation first, but the stretched notation provides a unifying conceptual framework.

Section 5.3 is on structural forms that provide ways of handling abnormal events that are handled in software implementation technologies by mechanisms like exceptions. These forms are directly mappable to Ada, and Ada examples are given.

Section 5.4 is on structural forms to represent reuseable components and dynamic structures. These forms are directly mappable to Ada; however, Ada examples are left until Chapter 10, which treats principles and practice of componentry in a comprehensive fashion.

5.2 STRETCHING THE TIME-DOMAIN PROPERTIES OF THE NOTATION

5.2.1 INTRODUCTION

This section shows how the icons of the subset notation may be used to represent more general forms for glue structures and interfaces than we have seen yet. Some of these are not directly supported by our reference implementation technology, Ada. Others are. However, the ones that are not may be mapped to ones that are. And some of the ones that are not directly supported by Ada are supported by other technologies. The reasons for investigating such forms are as follows:

- They provide a unifying conceptual framework to help the designer think about mechanisms that are not straightforward to implement with some technologies, but that must be implemented in them anyway.

- They provide more natural representations of mechanisms found in some implementation technologies other than Ada, and perhaps in future versions of Ada.

Given that the book uses Ada for its examples, the forms that do not map directly to Ada are not used in an extensive way in the rest of the book to draw design diagrams, but they do provide a conceptual background to discussions of how to solve particular problems, and the examples given of mappings to the subset notation provide a path to Ada.

5.2.2 SYNCHRONOUS GLUE STRUCTURES WITH DETACHED GATE BUTTONS

INTRODUCTION

We have grown used to thinking of gate buttons as meeting places attached to robots. However, there are certain constraints on the ability of the notation to express meeting behaviour with attached gate buttons. Allowing gate buttons to be detached, like work buttons, removes these constraints, as will now be shown.

Many diagrams have been drawn up to now showing only engines meeting at gate buttons, leaving the reader to imagine an assumed robot on the pull side to which the buttons are attached that forms a home for the pulling engine. Now these diagrams may be viewed as also possibly representing detached buttons, with robots on both the pull and push sides providing homes for the pulling and pushing engines, but without the gate buttons being attached to either.

ANONYMOUS VISITOR AND ANONYMOUS HOST PARADIGMS

Recall from Figure 4.11 of Chapter 4 (and subsequent examples in that chapter) that gate buttons may be waiting places on the push or pull sides, but that the attached button model allows only the robot on the pull side to wait on that side, whereas it allows many robots to wait on the push side. Also recall from later figures in Chapter 4, like Figure 4.28, that pull-side waiting may be used by a server to wait for requests, and push-side waiting by clients to wait for answers. With this in mind, turn to Figure 5.1, which shows detached gate buttons for the first time. These detached buttons form synchronous glue structures between peer robots (like the semaphores of Chapter 4 formed asynchronous ones).

- **(Anonymous Visitor)** This glue structure introduces no new ideas (it could equally well be represented by pull-side attachment of buttons to robots, as before); however, it sets the stage.

  - Suppose a server host **H** may wait for requests at two functionally identical gate buttons, **S1** and **S2**, that "belong" to visiting clients **V1** and **V2**, in the sense that only **Vi** pushes **Si**. **H** waits on the pull side of these buttons for requests from either client. We can agree, given the background of Chapter 4, that this is not a sensible solution to a client-server problem, because it forces the server host **H** to wait specifically for a request from one or the other of the visiting clients **V1**, or **V2**, possibly causing it to wait in one place while there is a visitor at the other.

  - It is an easy matter to combine **S1** and **S2** into a single button **S** to eliminate this problem; the effect is to allow the server host to wait for a visit from whichever client arrives first. In effect, the visiting clients have become anonymous (at least until they actually meet with the server). Although this diagram has been drawn with detached buttons, the reader will recognize that attached buttons would have done just as well, so there is nothing new here.

- **(Anonymous Host)** Turning the anonymous visitor glue structure around produces something new that cannot be expressed with the old model of buttons attached to robots on the pull side.

  - Suppose different server hosts **H1** and **H2** may offer identical services to a single visiting client **V**, by means of different, but functionally identical, buttons **S1** and **S2** that "belong" to **H1** and **H2** in the sense that only **Hi** pulls **Si**. **S1** and **S2** are push-side waiting places, because the clients must wait for a server to become available before a request can be transferred to it. Now we have the complement of the above problem, with the visiting client being forced to pick a particular place to wait, instead of waiting for whichever host becomes available first.

  - Combining the services into a single button eliminates the problem; it has the effect of making the hosts anonymous. The reader will recognize that the resultant structure is not one that can be easily mapped into a model in which buttons are attached to robots on the pull side. Yet it represents an approach that is as natural as the anonymous visitor approach, for a complementary problem.

IMPLEMENTATION IMPLICATIONS: The anonymous visitor model is supported by Ada, and by many other multitasking technologies. The anonymous host model is not supported by Ada, nor by other common multitasking technologies, but is a useful design abstraction.

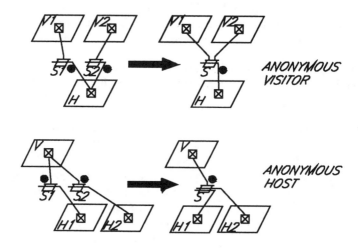

Figure 5.1: ANONYMOUS VISITOR AND ANONYMOUS HOST MODELS

CONCURRENT MEETINGS AND UNCOMMITTED WAITING

Experimenting further with the detached button model, Figure 5.2 gives new glue structures with even more general properties, suggesting two new interaction paradigms: *concurrent meetings* and *uncommitted waiting*, as follows:

- I. This simply shows that detached buttons may be joined by choice frames, to set the stage for the next two structures.

- II. (*Concurrent Meetings*) This structure supports concurrent, non-interfering meetings *at the same button* between pairs of anonymous visitors and anonymous hosts, on a first-come-first-served basis. In contrast, everything we have seen up to now restricts concurrent meetings to different buttons pulled by different hosts. The requirement that gate buttons provide mutual exclusion is still satisfied, because the meetings are non-interfering. This structure provides a powerful design level abstraction for matching clients with servers when there are many of each.

    IMPLEMENTATION IMPLICATIONS: This structure would be implicitly available in any implementation technology that supported both the anonymous host and anonymous server models (as we have seen, current implementation technologies lack direct support for the anonymous host model).

- III. (*Uncommitted Waiting*) This structure implies postponement of commitment to whether the next meeting will be the result of a push or a pull until the meeting actually occurs. It does this by including both push and pull of detached buttons in the same choice frame, implying that the first push or pull that can be satisfied will be. The buttons need to be detached so that pulls can be shown externally to the robot doing the pulling. In contrast, everything we have seen up to now requires commitment to where to wait *before* the meeting occurs, which may be characterized as *Committed Waiting*.

> IMPLEMENTATION IMPLICATIONS: The committed waiting model represents typical, practical multitasking technologies, including Ada. The uncommitted waiting model is not common in practice. In Ada, it would require a select with both call and accept alternatives (which is not available now, but has been proposed for Ada-9X). In other multitasking technologies it would imply something similar, such as the selection of the first to be satisfied of either a sendwait or a receive in a sendwait-receive-reply messaging technology.

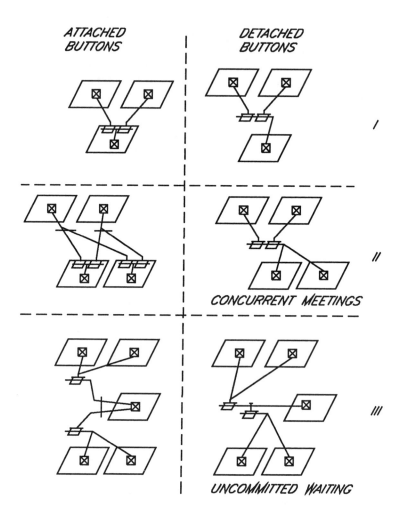

Figure 5.2: ADVANCED DETACHED BUTTON STRUCTURES

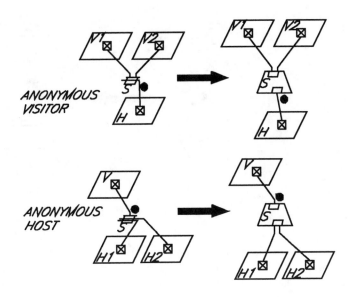

Figure 5.3: BUTTONS VS. ROBOTS AS MEETING PLACES FOR THE ANONYMOUS MODELS

5.2.3 MAPPING DETACHED-BUTTON GLUE STRUCTURES INTO ROBOT-BASED ONES

In general, the temporal behaviour implied by using detached buttons may be captured in the subset notation of Chapter 4 by mapping the detached-button glue structures to ones containing intermediary robots, somewhat like the semaphore robots of Chapter 4. This section gives some examples of simple mappings that provide useful, simple, standard glue structures. However, these simple mappings are not general; later examples will illustrate more general mappings.

Figure 5.3 revisits the anonymous host and visitor models of Figure 5.1 to show that the detached buttons that form waiting places in these models may be transformed into reactors that seem to achieve the same waiting place effect. In this figure, the detached S button is transformed into a reactor S with two buttons, one for push and the other for pull, with the waiting place being at one or the other of these buttons, depending on which model is being emulated. Although not shown in the figure, we might name the buttons on this reactor **push** and **pull**; then visiting **push** has the same purpose as pushing the original detached button, and visiting **pull** as pulling it. However, there is a difference; this structure does not provide a meeting between a visitor and a host. Instead, the reactor is used as a place to transfer information from one to the other *asynchronously*.

Thus we have mapped a synchronous glue structure into an asynchronous one that

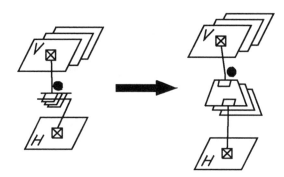

Figure 5.4: BUTTONS VS. ROBOTS AS UNIQUE WAITING PLACES

in general will not have the same temporal behaviour properties. However, there is one circumstance in which the temporal behaviour properties will be the same. If there is *always* a visitor at the waiting-place button when the non-waiting one that opens it is visited, then a synchronous effect is achieved between peers, provided either that all buttons have a common queue, or the waiting-place button has higher priority (as in the semaphore examples of Chapter 4). Because we expect waiting places to have visitors waiting when they are opened, this is an important circumstance.

This kind of thinking may be extended. For example, recall that button arrays were used in Chapter 4 to provide unique waiting places (e.g., Figure 4.40). Now imagine such a button array as detached, as shown on the left in Figure 5.4, and follow the mapping pattern of Figure 5.3 to give the result on the right in Figure 5.4 (**V** corresponds to the client and **H** to the server). The unique waiting places in this glue structure are provided by an array of reactors. Although this new structure will not in general have the same temporal behaviour properties as the original, for the same reasons as for Figure 5.3, the difference should normally be unimportant if waiting places always have visitors waiting when they are opened. The advantage of this structure over the one in Figure 4.40 is that these reactors may be installed dynamically when they are needed, using the methods to follow in Section 5.4 and Chapter 10, eliminating the problem of having to provide a fixed number of attached buttons to accommodate the maximum possible number of visiting clients.

Continuing with this kind of thinking, why not transform all of the attached buttons of our previous designs into glue structures containing intermediary robots (keeping in mind in doing so that an underlying assumption is that waiting places always have visitors waiting when they are opened)? Let us try it with Figure 4.40, with the result shown in Figure 5.5. The glue structure in this figure with separate **request** and **report** robots cannot provide the same temporal behavior as the original, because of the problem of the server having too many places to wait, and having to pick one (this comes about because a choice frame cannot be stretched across two robots). To get the same first-come-first-served behaviour between **request** and **report**, one would have to combine the **request** and **report** robots into a

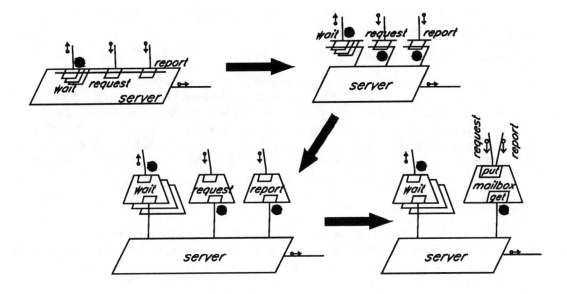

Figure 5.5: ATTACHED BUTTONS VS. REACTOR-BASED GLUE STRUCTURES

single robot that would give the effect of the original choice frame for these two buttons. As shown, an appropriate robot is a **mailbox** that gives the server only one place to wait for any input, and peers only one place to which to send input. The temporal behaviour of this transformed design will be effectively the same as the original provided waiting places always have visitors when they are opened, and provided that the meaning of the button array in the top left hand corner of the diagram is that the server opens a particular member of the array when a particular report arrives (this is the intended meaning). The loss of the synchronicity of the original **request** and **report** buttons is not practically important for the client-server problem if these assumptions hold (note that this loss of synchronicity may be avoided using the style of examples given later in this chapter (e.g., Figure 5.14)).

Why do any of this? An important answer is that it helps to make design thinking portable. Mappings that preserve temporal behaviour between widely different structural forms enable us to think one way and implement another, if we wish, or to think in the way that is most natural for a particular implementation technology, without losing the design thinking for other technologies.

IMPLEMENTATION IMPLICATIONS: Glue structures like the semaphore ones of Chapter 4 and like those of Figure 5.5 are examples of how one designs for target implementation technologies based on real time executives. They are not generally required for implementation technologies like Ada, although they may be used for particular purposes.

5.2.4   STRETCHING THE MEANING OF INTERFACES: WARM VS. COLD WAITING

INTRODUCTION

We have grown used to thinking of buttons as waiting places where visitors remain anonymous while they are waiting, even to the extent of any information they are carrying with them being unavailable until a meeting actually takes place. Readers from climates like the author's that have cold winters will immediately understand a characterization of this as *cold waiting*, implying that visitors are left outside in the cold while they are waiting. All the waiting examples so far in this book have been of cold waiting; this model is indicated by a waiting place marker *outside* a gate button.

WARM WAITING

In contrast to cold waiting, there is another model of waiting that may be characterized as *warm waiting*, implying that waiters come inside where it is warm before waiting; this model is indicated by a waiting place marker *inside* a gate button. The meaning is that push-visitors no longer remain anonymous, but may pass information about who they are or why they are waiting, before actually being forced to wait. In effect, there is an extended meeting at the button that has a preamble to pass information in to the meeting, a waiting phase, and a postamble to get information from the meeting. *During the waiting phase*, other meetings may occur at the same or different gate buttons, with the same host. Mutual exclusion is preserved because only one meeting at a time may be in a non-waiting phase. The result may be a whole series of overlapped, pairwise meetings that may be visualized as a form of multi-party meeting. Note particularly that this is a different model from the concurrent meeting model introduced above, because in that model there are no waiting phases, and the meetings are with different hosts.

MULTI-PARTY MEETINGS

The effect of N-way meetings may be achieved by carefully orchestrating sequences of 2-way meetings, but sometimes the orchestration can become messy (recall the orchestration required to avoid critical races in the client server example of Chapter 4). N-way meetings can provide simpler solutions to messy orchestration problems.

Figure 5.6 illustrates in a general way what is meant by an N-way meeting, *given that all visitors are ready to meet* (e.g., **C** is ready to meet with **A** and **B**, when the need for such a meeting is discovered during the **AB** meeting); this sidesteps for the moment the issue of where and how to wait for a meeting to begin or end. Highlights of Figure 5.6 are as follows:

- In a *2-way* meeting, there is activity at the meeting place for the duration of the meeting, and when the meeting ends, both visitors leave (e.g., Ada rendezvous). In the figure, **A** and **B** come together in a meeting, and when the meeting is over, both leave.

- In an *N-way nested* meeting, visitors arrive in any order and leave in the reverse order (e.g., Ada nested rendezvous). In the figure, visitors **A** and **B** discover during their

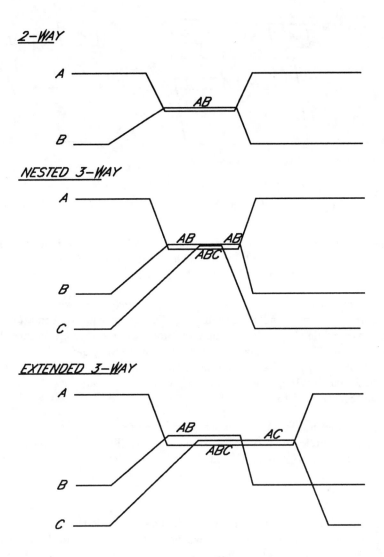

Figure 5.6: N-WAY MEETINGS

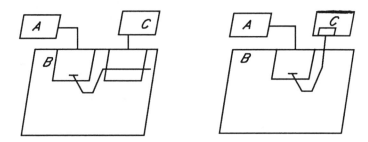

Figure 5.7: STRUCTURES FOR NESTED N-WAY MEETINGS

meeting that they need information from **C**, who is invited to join the meeting briefly to deliver it. **C**, who is ready, delivers the information and leaves immediately. The information is digested for **A** and/or **B**, following which both leave.

- In an *N-way extended* meeting, visitors arrive in any order and leave in any order. In the figure, visitors **A** and **B** are joined by **C**, who provides information that enables **B** to leave, while **C**, in turn, exchanges information with **A**, enabling them both to leave. The implication is that if **C** came to the meeting before **B**, it would still have to wait for **B** to arrive before handing over its information, instead of just depositing it with **A** and leaving; then the meeting would be nested; however, the point is that it is not constrained to be nested.

- Figure 5.6 does not illustrate a more constrained form of N-way meeting called N-way rendezvous that requires complete synchronicity. This form of meeting occurs only when all parties are ready for it, and then is indivisible and conceptually instantaneous. It is sometimes used for formal specification of temporal behaviour, but will not be explored further here.

How does all of this relate to warm waiting? The answer is that all parties in an N-way meeting must visit a warm waiting place, which may or may not be the same gate button; if different parties visit different gate buttons, then the gate buttons must be able to release waiters at other gate buttons. If ordering of visits can be guaranteed such that parties waiting for information can always be guaranteed to be present when a visitor brings it, then not all buttons need to be warm waiting ones, as will be shown.

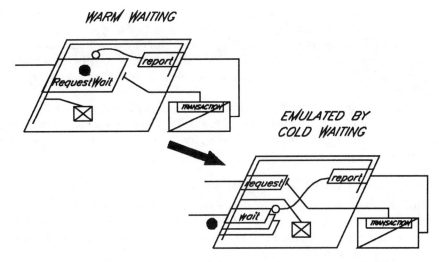

Figure 5.8: THE MEANING OF THE WARM WAITING IDIOM

EMULATING WARM WAITING BY NESTING

Limited forms of warm waiting may be represented using nested structures, as illustrated by Figure 5.7, which shows two ways of achieving the 3-way nested meeting Figure 5.6. While it is practical sometimes to map warm waiting into nesting, representing general extended meetings using nested structures is impractical, because the nestings would have to be in all possible ways relative to each other: the necessary structures are impossible to draw, and ugly to program.

MAPPING FROM WARM TO COLD WAITING MODELS

Warm waiting can be emulated using cold waiting, as we may now understand was illustrated by the client-server example of Chapter 4 (Figure 4.40). That example used a pair of gate buttons, a no-wait one called **request** to pass requests to the server, and a cold-wait one called **wait** to wait for results to be returned from the server (actually an array of such buttons). In effect, **request** and **wait** together emulate warm waiting, with the former providing the preamble, the latter the postamble, and the period between leaving one and meeting at the other the waiting period. The split between requesting and waiting was needed because other meetings had to be possible after a request was passed to the server, but before a result was available; specifically, with other clients at **request**, and with reporters of results at **report**. Results might even come back at **report** in a different order from that in which requests were made, meaning that visitors at **wait** would have to be serviced in any arbitrary order, relative to the order of requests (the array makes this possible, as well as eliminating the possibility of critical races).

As shown by Figure 5.8, a warm waiting solution to the client-server problem would replace **request** and **wait** by a single button, say **RequestWait**, that would pass in the request and then wait for the result from **report**, in what the client would see as a single visit. This provides a general 3-way meeting between the client, the server, and the reporter of results, in the sense of Case II of Figure 5.6, provided that clients are guaranteed always to be at **RequestWait** when results arrive. Otherwise, **report** does not require its visitors to wait for clients; it would do so if it were made into a warm waiting place; then **RequestWait** and **report** would be mutual warm waiting places, guaranteeing 3-way meetings always.

Rather than viewing Figure 4.40 as an emulation of warm waiting, we should now view warm waiting as an idiom, the meaning of which may be expressed by the mapping of Figure 5.8.

If the inflexibility of having to provide a fixed number of places to wait is untenable in an implementation, then the structure on the right in Figure 5.8 may also be regarded as an idiom, that has a further mapping into a glue structure that removes this inflexibility, shown earlier in Figure 5.4.

IMPLEMENTATION IMPLICATIONS:

Cold waiting models any mechanism where a waiting condition is imposed before any interaction can take place; it includes Ada's guarded entry mechanism. Warm waiting models mechanisms where a waiting condition may be imposed during an interaction.

Ada provides a limited form of warm waiting, via nested rendezvous. Nested rendezvous are not general; they require rendezvous to end in last-in-first-out order. Figure 5.8 shows by example how to map a general warm-waiting structure to a cold-waiting one that can be directly implemented in Ada. From an Ada perspective, one can regard either version in this figure as the design, with the difference being that the one on the left is an idiom, and the one on the right is directly implementable.

Sendwait-receive-reply technologies provide a general form of warm waiting, because replies can be sent at any time. If Ada could terminate an explicit rendezvous among a set of nested ones, the same effect would be achieved. Monitors, as in Concurrent Pascal, provide general warm waiting places in passive components.

5.2.5   AN ALLOCATOR EXAMPLE

Understanding is always deepened by looking at different examples, so here is an example that gives a different twist to the client-server problem, bringing in both detached gate buttons and warm waiting.

Suppose a set of servers provides service to a set of clients. All the servers have identical interfaces and perform identical services, so any available one will do for a client, except that servers have non-unique identifiers associated with them that split them into subsets. A client provides the subset identifier (henceforth called simply **sid**) as an indication that any server in that subset will do. This subsetting of otherwise identical servers might be appropriate, for example, if servers provided access to different computer networks or data bases. The problem is to match available servers to desiring clients and to provide a mechanism for clients and servers to wait until this can happen. Figure 5.9 shows some possible approaches to representing this problem and its solution.

Case I of Figure 5.9 combines the anonymous visitor and anonymous host paradigms, both to state the requirement, and to offer a path to its satisfaction. The servers within subsets are anonymous hosts. The clients are anonymous visitors. The detached **use** button is a warm waiting place where a client may wait for an appropriately identified server, or vice-versa. The requirement to pass in the desired **sid** makes it necessary that this be a warm waiting place, otherwise the cold waiting place of the original anonymous host diagram of Figure 5.1 would suffice. One could stop here and say the rest is detail.

Case II of Figure 5.9 maps the client-server meeting implied by Case I into an orchestrated sequence of 2-way meetings to achieve the same effect. The warm-waiting aspect of the detached **use** button of Case I is mapped into a passive **allocator** robot, and the **client-server** interaction aspect into an attached **use** button on each client. The **avail** button is needed to enable newly available servers to tell the allocator they are free. Because the client must interact later with an allocated server, a server identifier is required, called here **uid** because it identifies the place where the **use** button may be visited (the way in which **uid** is used to identify the place to visit is an implementation detail). A server visiting **avail** either releases a waiting client, or provides information that will enable later clients to be allocated a server immediately. The servers wait in their own places for allocated clients.

The temporal behaviour of this design is illustrated by Figure 5.10 and by Case II of Figure 5.11, which should be compared with each other, because they are alternate ways of expressing the same thing; the former shows visit threads directly on the structure chart; the latter shows them by means of a separate timing diagram (note that a workbench could draw the latter from a tracing of the former performed with a mouse). Both show the case where clients are waiting at **askwait** when servers visit. Note how clients may be released in any order (here the order is that in which they arrived); specifically, the order is not Last-In-First-Out, as it would have to be for nested meetings.

Case III of Figure 5.9 maps the design of Case II into one that employs only cold waiting, following the pattern of Figure 5.8. This is a linear interface structure that requires double visits by clients (on **sign_in** and **wait**) to achieve the effect of the extended **askwait** meeting in Case II. The parameter **uid** is shown as being returned on both visits, because if a server is immediately available, the second visit is not required (the implication is that some invalid

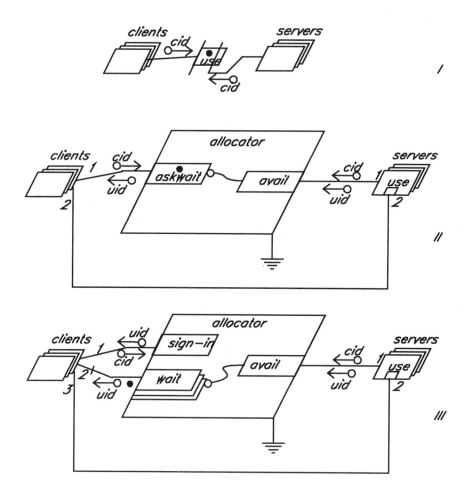

Figure 5.9: AN ALLOCATOR PROBLEM

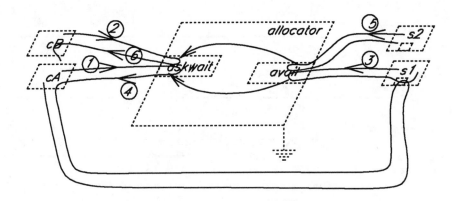

Figure 5.10: VISIT THREADS FOR ALLOCATOR CASE II

value indicates there is no server immediately available). There must be at least as many **wait** buttons as there are classes of servers; there may have to be even more than this, to avoid critical races in which clients race for the **wait** button for a particular class of server (if the order in which clients wait is important).

The temporal behaviour of this design is illustrated by Case III of Figure 5.11. Note how the implicit waiting of the warm waiting model is converted into explicit waiting by the client, by means of a double visit. The extra overhead of the double visit is not very significant from a performance viewpoint if waiting occurs only rarely, or the service provided is lengthy compared to the setup overhead, both of which should hold true in any sensible allocator system.

Different forms for client-server problems are explored further in Chapter 8, from the perspective of critical races.

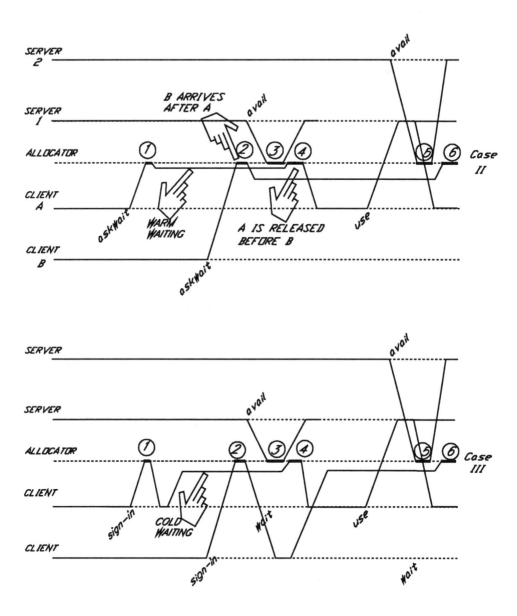

Figure 5.11: VISIT SCENARIOS FOR ALLOCATOR CASES II AND III

5.2.6 A MESSAGING EXAMPLE

The concept of a sendwait-receive-reply message protocol has been mentioned several times in this book. Let us now explore different structural forms for it, as a further example of the use of detached buttons and warm waiting.

Figure 5.12 provides examples of how message protocols may be mechanized by various patterns of cold and warm waiting at detached gate buttons. The fact that the buttons are detached not only provides greater generality, but also helps in seeing where the waiting is taking place. Note that the naming convention for buttons indicates the nature of the button from the push side; it is essential to have a standard naming convention like this if diagrams are to be understandable.

- Structures I and II accomplish the same purpose with different visit patterns; both transfer a message from a sender to a receiver.

- I. A waiting receive may be represented from the receiver's viewpoint by a **RCV** button that is pushed to receive and pulled to send, with cold waiting on the push (receive) side. If the button is attached to the pulling robot (the sender here), then there can only be a single sender; a detached button enables this structure to support multiple senders.

- II. A non-waiting send may be represented from the sender's viewpoint by a **SND** button that is pushed to send and pulled to receive, with cold waiting on the pull (receive) side. If the button is attached to the pulling robot (the receiver here), then there can only be a single receiver; a detached button enables this structure to support multiple receivers.

- III. Structures I and II may be combined to give Structure III, which effects a sendwait-receive-reply protocol. The sendwait is effected by first pushing **SND** and then pushing **RCV**. The receive is effected by pulling **SND**. The reply is effected by pulling **RCV**. The resulting structure is somewhat complex and has the undesirable property that a sender may get the wrong reply if there are many senders trying simultaneously to do a sendwait, because of critical races between robots visiting **SND** and **RCV**.

- IV: Structure IV embodies the same sendwait-receive-protocol more compactly, and without the critical race problem, by using warm waiting. A single **SENDWAIT** button is pushed both to send a message and wait for the answer, and pulled to receive the message. Warm waiting allows the sender to wait until there is a reply. There is no assumption of particular temporal ordering of replies relative to sends. An early send might get a late reply or vice versa. The reply is effected by opening **SENDWAIT** to release a particular waiting sender.

  IMPLEMENTATION IMPLICATIONS: If the last send always gets the first reply, then Ada can implement warm waiting by nesting accepts (however, last-message-in-gets-first-reply is a very restrictive message protocol).

Figure 5.13 shows the temporal behaviour implied by structures III and IV of Figure 5.12.

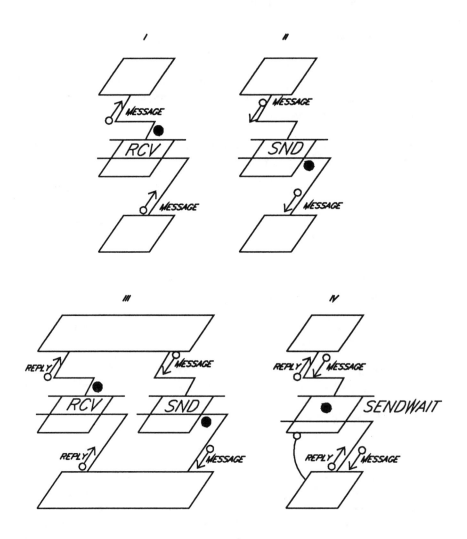

Figure 5.12: PROTOCOLS IN STRUCTURE

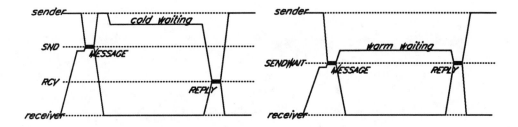

Figure 5.13: SCENARIOS FOR THE SENDWAIT-RECEIVE-REPLY STRUCTURES

Figure 5.14 shows how to build a general structure with the semantics of sendwait-receive-reply using a reactor **grv** (standing for generalized rendezvous) that provides a generalized meeting place, not just a waiting place. Robot **A** is the host of the meeting; it admits new participants by means of **admit** and releases them by means of **release**. The other robots are participants, who may join and leave the meeting as required; they join by means of **sign-in** and wait for information brought by other participants by means of **wait**. The parameter **rv-id** identifies which **wait** button will be used for a reply. Putting this structure in a box with a **sendwait-receive-reply** interface provides the implied service. Drawing of visit threads or scenarios is left to the reader.

> IMPLEMENTATION IMPLICATIONS: This is not necessarily a recommendation to build sendwait-receive-reply in an Ada program in this way and then use it as a general purpose mechanism (although it would be nice if the language supported it directly). When sendwait-receive-reply is not available, one may be better off to design specific structures for specific problems, as was illustrated by the earlier allocator example.

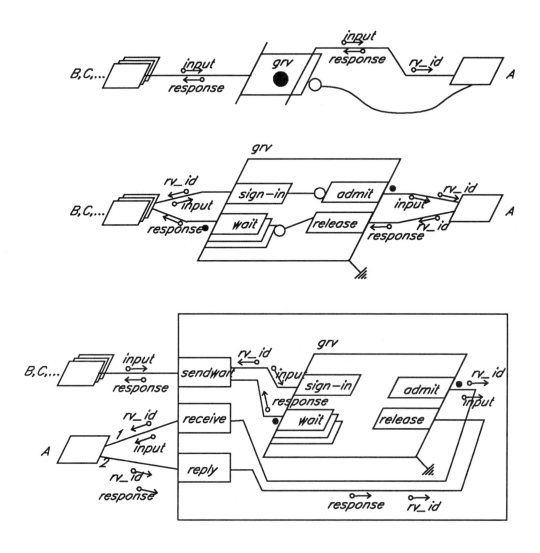

Figure 5.14: A SENDWAIT-RECEIVE-REPLY STRUCTURE

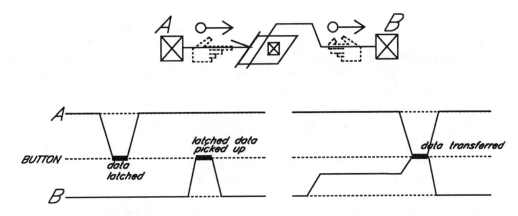

Figure 5.15: SEMANTICS OF THE GATE-JAB

5.2.7 ASYNCHRONISM WITH JABS

INTRODUCTION

As has been shown above, and in earlier chapters, asynchronism between peers may be effected by means of asynchronous glue structures. However, sometimes it is more natural to think directly in asynchronous terms, perhaps to sketch ideas quickly, or to represent a design in a manner that is more directly in line with an intended asynchronous implementation technology.

Recall that Figure 3.2 of Chapter 3 introduced a finger icon called a *jab* for this purpose. The term *jab* is intended to imply a momentary interaction, in contrast to the term *push*, which implies a sustained one. By implication, a gate button pointed at by a jab is *latching*, in the sense that hardware engineers use the term; i.e., values passed to the button by means of the jab are held at the button for pickup, while the jab visitor continues on its way, whether or not there is a pending pull. Latching is a familiar term to hardware engineers, but may not be familiar to software engineers: it means transforming a transient signal into a sustained one that may be examined by another component at any time. The pull on the gate button is still required to unlatch the information, or to wait for it to arrive, so there is nothing different about the pull.

THE DECOUPLING EFFECT OF GATE-JABS

In effect, the jab decouples the visits to the gate button, as illustrated by Figure 5.15. The effect is that only the host (pull visitor) ever waits, and then only if it specifically selects a particular button to pull, to the exclusion of all others, and there is nothing there to pick up. This is asynchronous, in the sense of avoiding coupling of visits, although note that this does not imply the total absence of interlocks, because even a jab is interlocked with the gate button for the duration of the jab interaction, thereby providing mutual exclusion protection.

Note that the implicit semantics of diagrams has now become more complicated, because many jabs might result in many items being sent but not picked up. This is not the same problem as sending many data items via a sequence of meetings, because each meeting guarantees that the item is picked up. In general, asynchronous interactions raise problems of this kind. Users of the jab icon must therefore state assumptions underlying its use regarding overwriting or queuing of transferred data.

GATE-JABS INTO ASYNCHRONOUS GLUE STRUCTURES

To emphasize that the gate-jab is in the nice but not necessary category, Figure 5.16 shows how to replace it, by introducing a reactor with buttons named, say, **JAB** and **PULL**, that provide the operations suggested by their names, and then replacing the jab finger with a push finger to **JAB**, and the pull finger with a push finger to **PULL**. This is just an asynchronous glue structure of a kind we have seen several times before.

IMPLEMENTATION IMPLICATIONS:

- If the objective is simply to indicate intent, then the jab does it nicely, whether the intended implementation technology supports asynchronous interactions or not.

- If the objective is to capture implementation organization relative to a particular implementation technology, then it depends on the technology. Asynchronous technologies without intermediaries are represented well by the jab. Asynchronous technologies with passive intermediaries can be satisfactorily represented without the jab, as can synchronous technologies (like Ada) that can only fake asynchronism by providing active intermediary tasks constrained by programming to behave passively.

EXAMPLES

The mappings of Figures 5.3 and 5.4 really correspond to that of Figure 5.16, and should therefore be redrawn with jab fingers pointing at the non-waiting places if we want to show the most general interpretation. However, as was explained in relation to these figures, the asynchronism has no effect if there is always a pending visitor at a waiting place when another button opens it.

One may represent a private semaphore waited on by only a single robot by a **signal** button attached to the robot with a jab finger pointing at it, or by a separate passive semaphore robot, as illustrated by Figure 5.17. The same trick may be used for other kinds of intermediaries, such as private mailboxes, as also illustrated in the figure. The choice is between more cluttered diagrams with more explicit display of semantics, and less cluttered diagrams with less explicit display of semantics.

The decoupling represented by gate-jabs is useful to represent not only asynchronous interactions in software, but also in hardware. A detached gate button may be associated with a hardware component that provides latched output for access by outsiders. In fact, as illustrated by Figure 5.18, the button could be attached with pull side out to the component that provides the output, the concept being that visitors pull it to get data. If timing is such that latched data is always waiting, then interacting machines never have to wait.

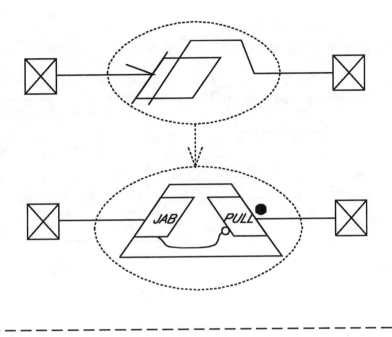

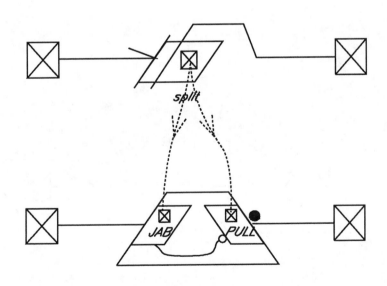

Figure 5.16: A JAB ROBOT

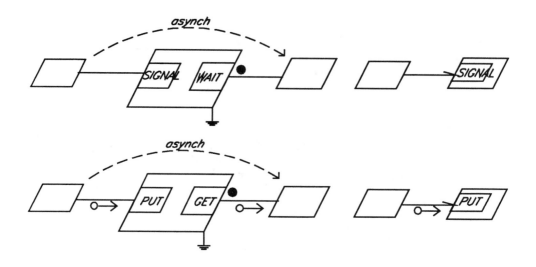

Figure 5.17: ALTERNATE NOTATIONS FOR ASYNCHRONISM

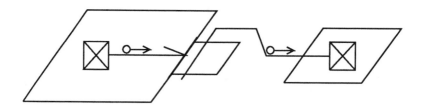

Figure 5.18: REPRESENTING LATCHED OUTPUT OF A COMPONENT

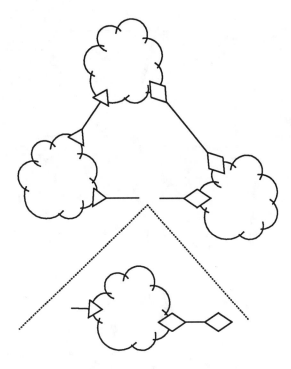

Figure 5.19: REVISITING THE CONCEPT OF CHANNELS

5.2.8 CHANNELS, INTERFACES AND GLUE STRUCTURES

Channels were introduced in Chapter 3 as placeholders for "wires" connecting interfaces. We have added considerably to the connection possibilities since then, and the concept needs to be revisited.

A glue structure is a collapsed structure, in the sense of Figure 4.6; it is a robot structure that is independent of how it may be bundled into a channel or a box.

A concern of later chapters (e.g., Chapters 6 and 7) is the appropriate bundling of glue structures. To lay the groundwork for such concerns, let us examine the relationship of the detached button glue structures we have seen in this chapter to channels. In general, channels may be used as placeholders not only for finger-button connections involving attached buttons, as before, but also for ones involving detached buttons (actual or emulated). Indeed, channels may have any sort of structure at all. They are "connection-boxes" that serve as placeholders for connection structures ranging from "wires" (visit paths provided by fingers) to complete machinery of any kind, including detached gate buttons.

Figure 5.19 revisits the concept of channels, showing that some patterns imply internal channel structure. In particular a channel that is itself the target of visits must have internal structure.

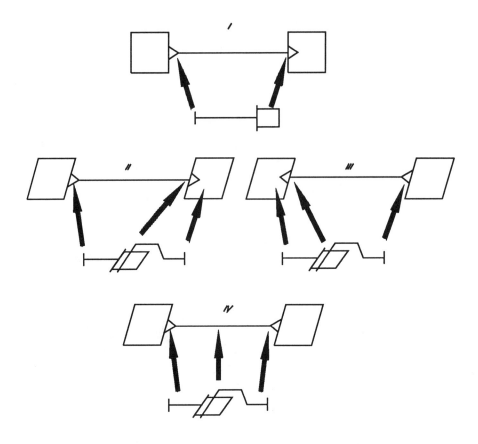

Figure 5.20: DIFFERENT POSSIBLE CHANNEL INTERPRETATIONS OF BUTTONS AND FINGERS

Figure 5.20 shows how attached and detached buttons may be viewed in channel terms. In cases I - III, buttons are directly *attached* to the connected machines, providing the perspective that there is a client end and a server end to the channel, which itself simply provides "wiring". Case I is simple and obvious. Cases II and III provide an interesting contrast. One has gate buttons attached in the ordinary way; the other has them attached "backwards". The latter case is useful for representing latching outputs, as was shown in Figure 5.18. In Case IV, the channel itself is viewed as a server that may contain not only "wiring" but also *detached* buttons serving as intermediaries between connected machines.

The channel concept, as described so far, indicates only visit direction between end points, and hides details. However, it might be advantageous to invent special channel icons to represent different styles of glue structure that give different styles of interaction. For example, special channel icons might be used to indicate multi-way meetings via detached buttons, like those represented by some of the earlier figures of this chapter. However, this is only raised as a possibility here, which will not be explored further in this book.

Channels and glue structures will be reexamined in the case studies of Chapters 6 and 7.

5.3   ALARMS

5.3.1   INTRODUCTION

This section extends the notation to cover special handling of "unusual" events, such as are typically implemented with exceptions. Most of this section maps directly to Ada, or to other implementation technologies with exceptions. Except for some Ada examples in Chapter 10 that include exceptions incidentally, this material is not used in the rest of the book.

The term alarm is used here to indicate an "unusual" event, to be handled by mechanisms outside of the button model of interactions. There is a certain arbitrariness from a design perspective in separating events into "usual" and "unusual" categories that require different methods of propagating and handling. Why not map all events into the button model of interactions, without introducing additional mechanisms? The answer is that implementation technologies often provide separate mechanisms (e.g., Ada exceptions); implementors may have no choice about using them, or may choose to use them deliberately, as a matter of style. Leaving the ability to express them out of a design notation weakens a designer's ability to indicate where they should, and should not, be used.

Two kinds of alarms may be identified:

- Reactive alarms are propagated to a visitor after a visit is abnormally terminated due to some unusual error occurring during the visit.

- Proactive alarms are autonomously propagated, without a visit from the destination being in progress. An example would be terminating a robot that is off doing work that is no longer required, because the operational state of the system that triggered the work has changed.

IMPLEMENTATION IMPLICATIONS:

Reactive alarms model exceptions. Run time systems and real time executives may raise exceptions. Ada libraries provide components that raise exceptions. Some Ada programmers may use exceptions as the normal way of handling all errors (whether this is a good practice, or not, is not at issue here). Without the ability to express exceptions in a design notation, one is not able to capture the fine structure of practical Ada programs.

Proactive alarms model mechanisms in multitasking technologies that enable signals to be sent to other tasks in a *whole-task* fashion, for example to terminate their operation. A proactive alarm models a graceful mechanism that allows the terminated task to clean up before terminating. Ada can only do it crudely, using the **abort** statement.

Implying that a design notation for unusual events is needed is easier than inventing a good one. A problem is that the mechanisms they need to model, in particular, exception propagating and handling mechanisms, as exemplified by Ada, are quite deliberately cross-grained relative to the mechanisms that handle normal operation, in order to keep exception handling code separate from normal operating code.

In MachineChart terms, the cross-grained nature may be simply stated: reactive alarms are bound to the head end of a normal visit path, but not to the tail end. This is because they are raised at the head end, but may be handled somewhere other than at the tail end, further back in a chain of visit paths, thus bypassing intermediate stages of the chain. If we want to convey this cross-grained nature accurately, we need a cross-grained connection structure.

5.3.2 REPRESENTING ALARMS IN STRUCTURE CHARTS

THE JAB CONNECTION APPROACH

The jab connection approach expresses alarm paths as connections drawn with jab fingers. Jab fingers projecting from machines indicate alarms raised there. Paths for alarms between machines are indicated by jab fingers drawn from one machine to another machine as a whole (not to one of its buttons). Jab fingers pointing at machines indicate reactive alarms are handled there. When alarms are drawn between machines in this *whole-machine* way, the implicit structural source is an internal engine in the source machine and the implicit structural destination is an internal engine in the destination machine. The implication at the destination end is that there is a handler agenda associated with the engine, to process the alarm, that is separate from the engine's normal agenda. Jabs may also be drawn from an engine to itself to indicate there is a local handler. Alarm jabs are paths for visits, but the visits have new semantics:

- Alarm visits are asynchronous; they only serve to transfer the alarm event; no parameters are passed; no meetings result.

- The effect of an alarm visit at its destination is to trigger operation of the handler agenda.

- The effect of an alarm visit at its source is termination of the normal operating agenda if

  - the alarm is reactive (in other words, raised during an interaction with another machine, in which case the destination had better be that machine, or a machine further back in a chain of visit paths), or

  - the destination is a handler associated with the engine that raised the alarm.

- The effect of an alarm visit at its source is nil if the alarm is proactive (in other words, raised autonomously against some other machine, as opposed to reactively).

Some examples of how to draw reactive alarms using the jab connection approach are given, for the simple case of detached buttons, in Figure 5.21.

- Button A (with no reactive alarm on its interface) raises and handles an alarm internally.

- Button B sends a reactive alarm to a visiting engine that has a handler for it.

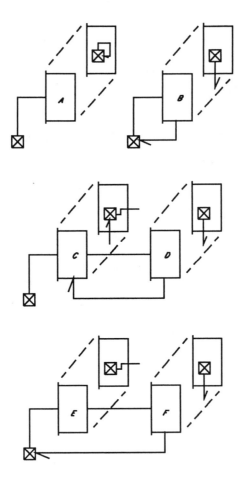

Figure 5.21: SIMPLE ALARMS IN JAB CONNECTION FORM

- Button D sends a reactive alarm to a visiting machine, Button C, where there is a handler for it.

- Button F sends a reactive alarm that bypasses an intermediate machine in the visiting path, Button E, that has no handler for it. This example shows the cross-grained nature of the jab connection approach. It visually indicates where the handler is, by bypassing intermediate places where there is no handler.

Figure 5.22 shows how an outgoing alarm may be part of a more structured interface that may be wired into some context. There is nothing in the interface structure to say whether the jab is proactive or reactive, but the internal structure shows it. Again, this figure shows how the jab connection indicates where there is a handler.

These figures clearly illustrate the crossgrained nature of the jab connection approach: the jab connection structure may be quite different from the normal connection structure.

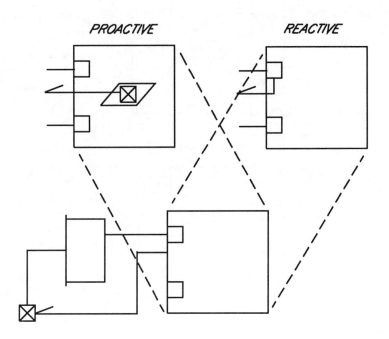

Figure 5.22: JABS FROM INTERFACES MAY BE REACTIVE OR PROACTIVE

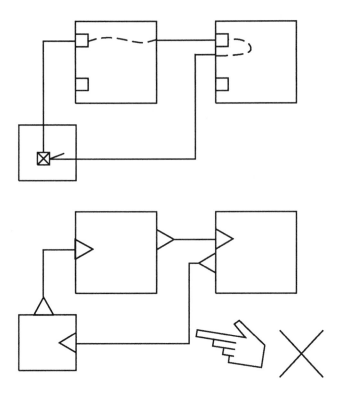

Figure 5.23: THE CROSS-GRAINED NATURE OF JAB CONNECTIONS

Figure 5.23 further illustrates this cross grained nature, by showing how it may be inappropriate sometimes to include jab connections in channels. One might think that the jab in this figure could be included in a uni-directional channel in the direction of the jab. However, a uni-directional channel implies proactive visits in the channel direction. The alarm jab indicates a reactive visit caused by a proactive visit over another channel. We would need to extend the channel concept to include channels that are related in this way. The result would be messier than leaving channels out of the picture. But channels are clean structural concepts. It is the cross-grained jab connections that introduce the messiness.

Figure 5.24 shows in a structure chart a reactive alarm between two robots and indicates with a scenario the asynchronous nature of the alarm mechanism in this case. The current meeting is abandoned and both robots abandon their normal agendas to handle the alarm independently without further interaction with each other (the cross hatched parts of their timelines). After doing so, each may independently terminate operation, or continue operating, as appropriate. The notation provides no way other than text of distinguishing the latter two cases.

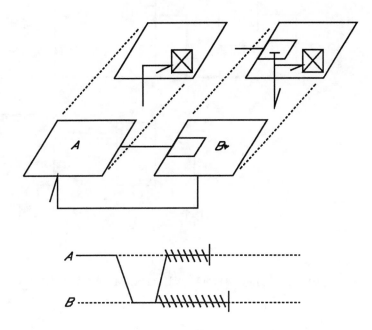

Figure 5.24: ALARMS INVOLVING ROBOTS

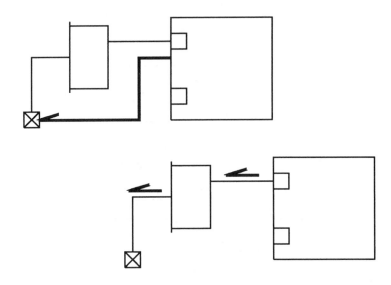

Figure 5.25: REPRESENTING REACTIVE ALARMS AS JAB CONNECTIONS OR JAB PARAMETERS

THE JAB PARAMETER APPROACH

Figure 5.25 shows how a jab connection structure may be represented by an ordinary connection structure, without any cross-grained messiness, with jabs indicated as parameters rather than connections. However, this approach fails to separate alarms from normal processing structures, because the alarm jab must be shown for every segment of every visit path that triggers the alarm, even though its handling is independent of particular visit paths. However, an advantage is that the commitment to whether a jab parameter is simply an error parameter, or something more, may be deferred until design of the insides of the machines at either end. It is left as an exercise for the reader to redraw the earlier jab connection figures in jab parameter form.

5.3.3   REPRESENTING ALARM HANDLERS

Whether the jab connection or the jab parameter approach is used externally between machines, the implication internally is the same; there must be a handler at the destination end. Figure 5.26 shows some ways of visually representing alarm handlers. The most uncluttered representation is one that assumes a segment of the engine pointed at by jabs represents an alarm handler (or the set of all alarm handlers for all jabs). The visual representation may be no more detailed than this, or it may be elaborated by showing handlers as separate components.

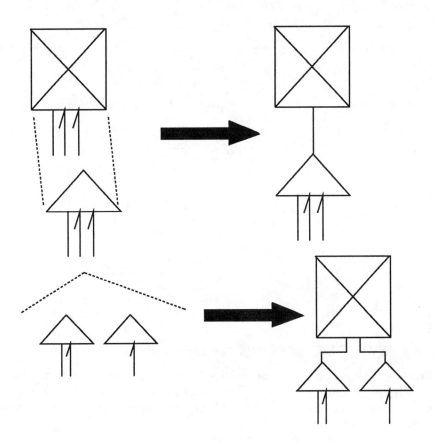

Figure 5.26: ALARM HANDLERS

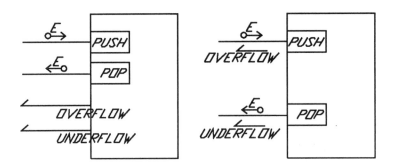

Figure 5.27: INTERFACE OF A STACK WITH ALARMS

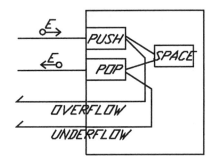

Figure 5.28: INTERNAL STRUCTURE OF A STACK WITH ALARMS

5.3.4   IMPLEMENTATION EXAMPLES

Here are some examples of how alarm structures, expressed in jab connection form, may be mapped into Ada programs. These examples are intended only to illustrate how the notation may be mapped into Ada and not necessarily to indicate recommended ways of handling errors in Ada.

Figure 5.27 and Figure 5.28 show a stack subsystem with external alarms; Figure 5.29 gives the corresponding Ada code.

Figure 5.30 illustrates handling of operator errors by iteration and recursion. Figure 5.31 and Figure 5.32 give corresponding Ada code. Note how the iterative version uses a block structure not directly represented in the diagram. The need for it is informally implied, but a human has to see it.

A few figures follow that indicate some alarm patterns that may be represented by jab connections. These all map easily to Ada; we leave the details to the reader.

Figure 5.33 shows how the same alarm from different places may be handled in one place.

Figure 5.34 and Figure 5.35 show how an alarm may be propagated onwards, so that it is handled in different contexts.

```
package STACK is
  procedure PUSH(E: in ELEM);
  procedure POP(E: out ELEM);
  OVERFLOW,UNDERFLOW:exception;
end STACK;

package body STACK is
  SPACE:array(1..SIZE) of ELEM;
  INDEX:INTEGER range 0..SIZE:=0;
  procedure PUSH(E: in ELEM) is
  begin
    if INDEX = SIZE then
      raise OVERFLOW;
    end if;
    INDEX:=INDEX + 1;
    SPACE(INDEX):=E;
  end PUSH;
  procedure POP(E: out ELEM) is
  begin
    if INDEX = 0 then
      raise UNDERFLOW;
    end if;
    E:=SPACE(INDEX);
    INDEX:=INDEX - 1;
  end POP;
end STACK;
```

Figure 5.29: ADA CODE FOR THE STACK WITH ALARMS

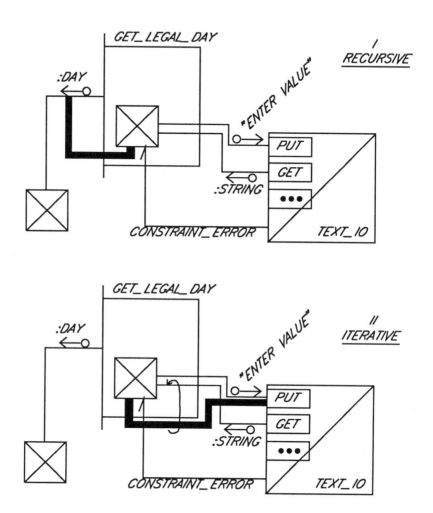

Figure 5.30: RECURSIVE AND ITERATIVE ALARM HANDLING IN AN IO EXAMPLE

```
with TEXT_IO;
procedure MAIN is
   type DAY IS(MON,TUE,WED,THU,FRI,SAT,SUN);
   W:DAY;
   function GET_LEGAL_DAY return DAY is
     TMP : STRING(1..3);
     LOC : DAY;
   begin
     TEXT_IO.PUT("ENTER VALUE");
     return DAY'VALUE(TEXT_IO.GET(TMP));
   exception
     when CONSTRAINT_ERROR  =>
        return GET_LEGAL_DAY;
   end GET_LEGAL_DAY;
begin
   W:=GET_LEGAL_DAY;
end MAIN;
```

Figure 5.31: RECURSIVE EXCEPTION HANDLING IN THE IO EXAMPLE

```
with TEXT_IO;
procedure MAIN is
  type DAY IS(MON,TUE,WED,THU,FRI,SAT,SUN);
  W:DAY;
  function GET_LEGAL_DAY return DAY is
    TMP : STRING(1..3);
    LOC : DAY;
  begin
    TEXT_IO.PUT("ENTER VALUE");
    loop
      begin
        return DAY'VALUE(TEXT_IO.GET(TMP));
        exit;
      exception
        when CONSTRAINT_ERROR  =>
          TEXT_IO.PUT("ENTER VALUE");
      end;
    end loop;
  end GET_LEGAL_DAY;
begin
  W:=GET_LEGAL_DAY;
end MAIN;
```

Figure 5.32: ITERATIVE EXCEPTION HANDLING IN THE IO EXAMPLE

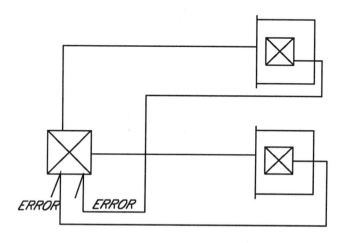

Figure 5.33: THE SAME ALARM FROM DIFFERENT PLACES

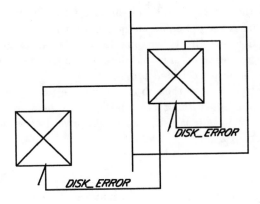

Figure 5.34: AN EXAMPLE OF ALARM RE-RAISING

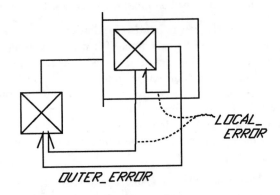

Figure 5.35: A SECOND EXAMPLE OF ALARM RE-RAISING

5.4 REUSEABLE COMPONENTS AND DYNAMIC STRUCTURES

5.4.1 INTRODUCTION

This section extends the subset notation in the direction of providing more expressiveness for structure. It touches on reuseable components and dynamic structures. All of the examples of this section are directly mappable to Ada, although it is possible to draw sensible, innocent-appearing structures that do not map to Ada at all, although they would be quite natural ones in object oriented programming.

A comprehensive treatment of the subject of reuseable components and dynamic structures is given in Chapter 10, so this section just gives a quick overview of the main ideas. It is introduced here, because it is used in straightforward ways in a few examples in the chapters before Chapter 10.

5.4.2 NOTATION

Figure 5.36 shows structure chart icons for reuseable components and dynamic architectures.

- Template: The template icon symbolizes a set of plans for constructing a component (think of it as a partially unrolled blueprint). It is used as an annotation in structure charts to distinguish machines that are installed instances of templates, and to indicate their origin. This annotation approach makes it easy for designers to choose whether to sketch components and interactions first, postponing identification of reuseable components until later, or to commit to reuseable components from the start, whichever is most appropriate for the problem at hand. Templates are outside diagram hierarchies like that of earlier Figure 4.4. They are distinguished from other diagrams by using the template icon as a visual frame for the entire diagram, or as an annotation in a corner. Templates are not just ordinary detailed diagrams, but rather contain manufacturing instructions for components in instance diagrams. Parts customizable for different instances are shown in template diagrams in dotted outline.

- Install: The *install* arrow indicates installation of an instance from a template. It may or may not originate at a machine. If it does not, then static installation is implied (in other words the instance is installed when its enclosing machine is installed); otherwise dynamic installation is implied by the machine at the tail of the arrow. Statically installed instances are "wired in place". Dynamically installed instances are shown as if they were wired in place, but may actually be passed around from place to place. A template icon is always associated with an install arrow, to indicate the source of the instance. Customizing parameters for instances are shown next to the install arrow.

- Remove: This icon indicates explicit removal of an installed instance. However, it is not the only way of removing such an instance (other ways are discussed in Chapter 10).

- Instance: There is normally no need for a special icon to indicate an instance of a template in a place. An instance is just shown as an ordinary machine, in the place where it is installed, that repeats the visual interface structure of the template (so that the interaction patterns can be visualized in the place where it is installed). Instances installed from templates do not have detailed diagrams underneath in the place where they are installed (details are underneath the template). However, a special icon is needed to show the flow of instances from place to place. The icon is unidirectional or bidirectional, according to whether the instance is simply passed from place to place, without modification, or is modified in a place. The instance icon shown here does not identify the kind of machine that is being moved; if desired, machine icons with attached arrows may be used for instance flows, instead. Instances that are passed around may remain fixed in the place they were installed, where they may be interacted with from elsewhere, or they may appear transiently in different places, perhaps placed in stores, perhaps visited by local machinery, or perhaps themselves performing visits to local machinery; distinguishing these cases is necessary during design.

- Replication: Multiple shadow machines shown installed from a template indicate replication from the template; in other words, multiple instances of the same template. (Without a template, they simply indicate informally that there may be many machines of this general kind in some place). The number of instances is indicated by naming or by some other textual annotation. Connection patterns drawn for the shadowed machine may be inferred to be repeated for the shadows. Connections among shadow machines may be indicated by channels, with details given elsewhere, or by drawing a diagram in which the shadow machines are shown side by side with explicit connections shown.

5.4.3 DYNAMIC INSTANCES

Figure 5.37 gives an example showing how to draw and conceptualize the installation and flow of dynamic instances. The figure indicates that an instance **A** of template **T** is installed by an engine and then passed to some other part of the system (symbolized by the cloud), which subsequently may interact with it. The instance is shown being interacted with in the place where it was installed, indicating that there may be widespread distribution of it to many places in the rest of the system, and consequent shared use. The double headed instance icon is used to indicate that the interacting with the instance may cause changes to its internal state.

5.4.4 SOME TYPICAL STRUCTURES WITH TEMPLATES

Figure 5.38 is intended to give a quick impression of the nature of designs using templates. It may be skipped on first reading; it contains many, sometimes tricky, implementation implications. Chapter 10 gives the details.

- Part I shows robot-in-a-button idiom which might be used to implement a client waiting protocol. Here the robot instance is statically installed in place when the button is pushed and remains in place holding up termination of the button's engine until some synchronization with another part of the system is completed. Note that

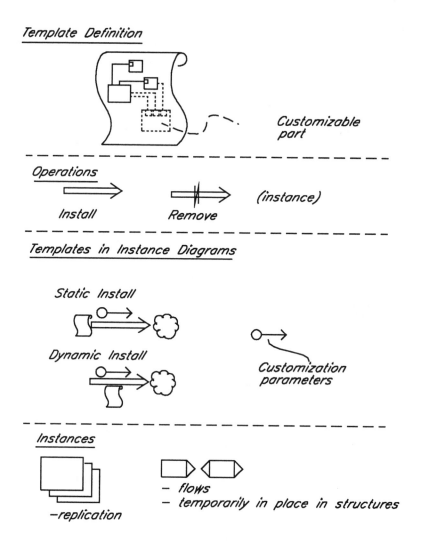

Figure 5.36: STRUCTURE CHART ICONS FOR REUSEABLE COMPONENTS AND DYNAMIC ARCHITECTURES

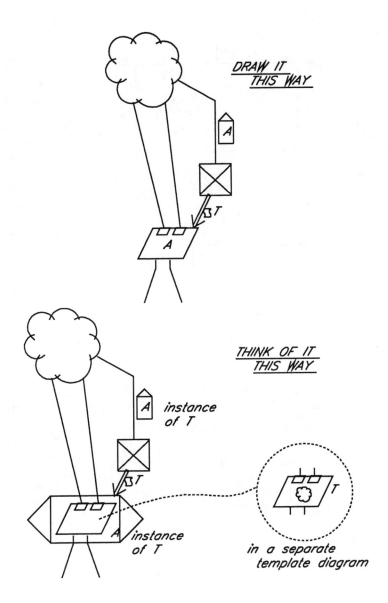

Figure 5.37: CONVENTIONS FOR TEMPLATE INSTANCES

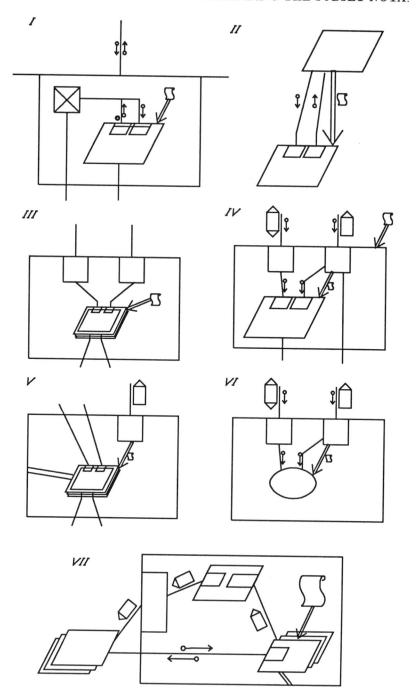

Figure 5.38: REUSEABLE COMPONENTS AND DYNAMIC ARCHITECTURES

words like static and dynamic are slippery here; the robot is statically installed in a dynamic context, that of the button.

- Part II illustrates dynamic installation and use of one robot by another.

- Part III illustrates a robot pool idiom, in which a pool of robots is statically installed and used as required by clients without being directly visible to them.

- Parts IV and VI show visual idioms for *type managers* for active and passive components, which support operations to install, interact with and remove instances, but do not actually store any instances; the drawing of an instance internally is for purposes of showing the operations that may be performed on *any instance*. Here, the intent is that instance flows literally move the instances from place to place, making them unavailable in the previous place.

- Part V shows a robot pool idiom in which the robots are used directly, in place, in the pool location. The expose icon not only makes the robots instances accessible outside, but also locks them in place. With this constraint, the instances flowing from place to place are aliases which provide access to the locked-in-place instances.

- Part VII shows a similar pool idiom, except the instances are statically installed and a dispatcher allocates clients to them (this might be visualized in terms of customers of a bank getting teller instances from a dispatcher and then interacting with them directly).

IMPLEMENTATION IMPLICATIONS:

Certain forms of templates may be interpreted as indicating the underlying intent of programming language concepts like "type", "generic", "class" and "instance" in languages like Ada and the various object oriented programming languages. There is deliberately no representation for the concept of *pointer*, or *access type* (these are regarded as implementation details, not design abstractions).

Programming interpretations of these simple diagrams in our reference programming language, Ada, can be surprisingly complex, but enough clues are present in the diagrams to infer appropriate, if not necessarily unique, interpretations, guided by programming rules and idioms. Ada examples are provided in Chapter 10.

Concepts like dynamically installing a machine from a template may also be interpreted in object oriented programming terms; for example, sending a message to a class (template) to install an instance of itself.

5.5   CONCLUSIONS

This chapter has provided some extensions to the subset notation that add considerably to its power of expression.

New models of temporal behaviour have been introduced that provide a framework for thinking, a starting point for mapping to more elaborate designs represented in the subset notation, and, in some cases, a means of representing designs in a way that is more directly aligned with particular implementation technologies. These models form a background to discussions in the rest of the book, particularly in Chapter 8.

Alarms have been included to extend the expressiveness of the notation relative to implementation technologies, but there is a price to be paid for using them: implied behaviour can become complex to the extent that confidence in correct behaviour can probably only be obtained by appealing to the implementation technology, particularly if they are combined with dynamic structures. It seems to the author to be better to do most of the design thinking without alarms, and to add them later, as guides to implementors. The notation has been specifically designed to facilitate this add-on approach. Alarms are not touched on again in the book, except for incidental inclusion in some examples in Chapter 10.

Templates and dynamic structures have been introduced as a means of expressing reuseability. They are used from time to time in following chapters, but are not covered again in detail until Chapter 10.

Part III

CASE STUDIES IN SYSTEM DESIGN

Chapter 6

A CASE STUDY: THE GAME OF LIFE

6.1 INTRODUCTION

Up till now, the method and notation have been illustrated only on fragments of systems, not complete systems. This chapter aims to give the reader a feeling for how they may be applied to a complete design problem. The problem — to design a system to "play" the game of **LIFE** — is very simple, but elaborations of it lead to some quite general issues. The "game" has tokens being born and dying on the cells of a grid, according to some birth and death rules. Two versions of a system to play the game are explored, one sequential, and the other concurrent. In the sequential version, the cells are passive storage places for tokens, to which a central controller applies the birth and death rules globally. In the concurrent version, the cells are autonomous components in their own right, that communicate their states to each other, and that apply the birth and death rules in light of the states of neighbouring cells.

This treatment of the same problem from both a sequential and a concurrent perspective aims to highlight both the similarities and the differences between designing sequential and concurrent systems. A particular point to be made is that, although components and interfaces may be expressed in the same style from both perspectives, concurrent systems require deeper thinking about underlying temporal behaviour before committing to concrete interfaces, and interfaces that are perfectly acceptable for sequential systems may give performance problems for concurrent ones.

The concurrent version of the system is a model of a concurrent system of a quite general kind that requires symmetrical communication among subsystems. Exploring this requirement leads to the definition of a set of canonical glue structures that will be useful throughout the rest of the book.

Along the way, the case study touches on other issues, such as reuseability, and dynamic structures.

6.1.1 REQUIREMENTS AND APPROACH

The game of **LIFE** has tokens appearing and disappearing on the cells of a rectangular board through a series of generations (representing "life" being "born" and "dying"). A human player sets up the desired initial token patterns and controls the number of generations to be played, which thereafter evolve on a time scale and in a manner totally under the control of the system.

The idea of the birth and death rules is that each cell needs some, but not too many, living neighbours for it to continue living or have new life, where a neighbour is a cell in one of eight adjacent positions. The following set of arbitrary rules produces interesting patterns: a living cell continues life only if it has 2 or 3 alive neighbours; a dead cell gains new life only if it has exactly 3 alive neighbours.

However, the actual birth and death rules are in the *WORK* domain, and are therefore outside the scope of our treatment of the problem. All we need to be concerned about relative to these rules is that there is a place to apply them, with an interface that enables them to be applied. As appropriate for the Architectural Design process, the case study focuses on the *TIME* and *PLACE* domains.

For the sequential version, the main *TIME*-domain concerns center around the interactions between the human player and the system to establish the dimensions of the board, the initial token patterns, and the number of generations to be played, and that enable play to be continued from some stopping point, perhaps with modified token patterns. Actually playing the game is more in the *WORK* domain than the *TIME* domain. Therefore the main Architectural Design concerns associated with playing the game are in the *PLACE* domain.

The situation is quite different with the concurrent version. *TIME*-domain concerns now extend into the actual playing of the game, because of the fact that cells operate concurrently and must communicate with each other.

Accordingly, our approach to solving this problem is to begin by focusing on the player-system interactions, and later to widen the scope to include interactions required by concurrent cells, both among themselves and with the rest of the system. The requirements are developed as part of the preliminary design process.

The overall design process is generally that of Figure 3.1 of Chapter 3, except that we do not number the steps as was done there (as was pointed out there, the process may have more or fewer steps, or the steps may be shuffled, so designing by numbers is not appropriate). However, the reader will be able to recognize particular steps by the names of the diagram types.

6.2 PRELIMINARY DESIGN OF THE SEQUENTIAL VERSION

6.2.1 ABSTRACT STRUCTURE CHART

Figure 6.1 is an *abstract structure chart* showing a trial partitioning into subsystems and events. The **player** box is the internal analogue of the human player; it will emerge as the only active subsystem for the sequential version. The **life** box hides the rules and detailed control of the game. The **board** box hides the details of how the board is represented and displayed. The **dshell** (standing for "dialogue shell") box maps the details of interactions between the human player and the machine into abstract events. This figure illustrates how diagrams at this early stage of design need to be textually commented to indicate intent (functionality of boxes, nature of what they hide, nature of interactions) because at this stage the names are not enough. As detail accumulates during design, the comments become formally redundant, but are still useful as reminders. The details of the events have not yet been filled in.

> IMPLEMENTATION IMPLICATIONS: The **io** box might be supplied by built-in services of a programming language, like Ada's TextIO package or Modula-2's InOut module.

Let us focus on the **dshell-player-life** interfaces and interactions centered around **player**. Figure 6.2 shows some details of events flowing into and out of the **player** box. These events are deliberately free of commitment to being supported in a particular way, either in the human-system interaction (e.g., mouse positioning vs. keystrokes, pretty graphics vs. teletype-style text, menu selection vs. text entry, multiple window vs. full screen, etc.), or by specific interface mechanisms within the system. For the moment, the **display** event will do as a placeholder for all events that update the board during the setup phase.

This figure contains an example of an arbitrary event decision, with no particular rationale behind it, made here to show that such arbitrary decisions may have to be made at this stage of design, as part of the process of experimentation with design alternatives. The arbitrary decision is that there will be only one type of data event, an integer, to cover all numerical data entered by the human operator, including specifying board sizes, cell coordinates, and the number of generations to be played. As a consequence, for example, two successive data events are required to give a cell coordinate. If this decision is carried through to the concrete interface level, by requiring a visit per event, then **dshell** would be required to transform the mouse position into two successive events to give to **player**; on the other hand, two successive integers entered from the keyboard would simply be passed on as two successive events.

6.2.2 AN EVENT SCENARIO FOR PLAYER

Continuing with the events centered around **player**, Figure 6.3 gives an event scenario embracing **player**, **life** and **dshell**. One scenario is not enough to explore the interactions thoroughly, but serves here only to illustrate the nature of scenarios for this particular problem. For example, this scenario does not show how the help event **h** is processed.

Drawing such scenarios is time consuming and not very interesting if all we want to do is design a sequential system to solve this problem; a list of events presented in textual form, in sequence, on a page would do just as well (perhaps better, because it would be missing all the visual clutter). However, the point of the exercise here is not to constrain ourselves to sequential thinking. Even so, one scenario will do to make the point, so we shall now move on to state machines to capture the temporal logic of the problem.

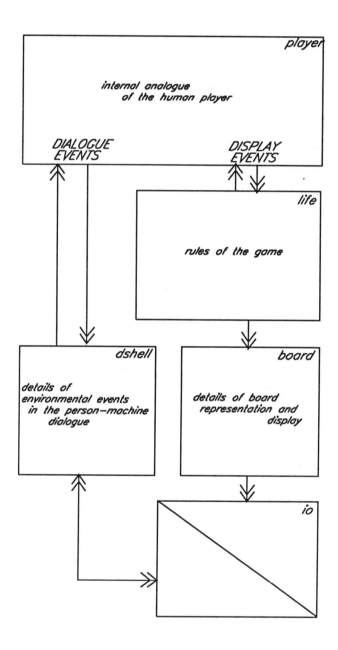

Figure 6.1: A PARTITIONING OF THE LIFE SYSTEM

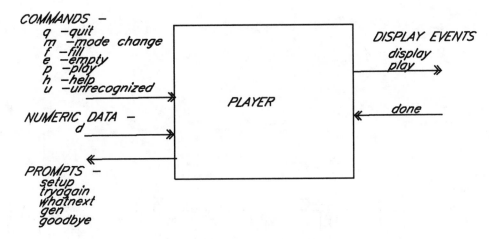

Figure 6.2: EVENTS AT THE PLAYER SUBSYSTEM

6.2.3 AN ABSTRACT STATE MACHINE FOR PLAYER

Figure 6.4 gives a state transition diagram of an abstract state machine that captures the temporal logic of which Figure 6.3 is a manifestation.

Here are explanations of the key points of Figure 6.4:

- The machine begins in the **idl** state.

- The states **da1, da2,** and **da3** are needed as a result of the decision that data events are restricted to single integers; these states pick up the first data event of an expected pair (two dimensions of the board in the case of **da1**, and two cell coordinates in the cases of **da2** and **da3**).

- The states **up1** and **up2** are update states, in which cells are initialized with tokens (in the case of **da1**), or with the absence of tokens (in the case of **da2**). The **m** (change mode) event toggles between these two modes of update.

- The **rdy** state is the one from which play is initiated.

- Handling of the **h** (help) event is independent of state; the same help information will be given in every state (via the **tryagain** event). This is a bad decision from a human interface viewpoint, made here to keep things simple.

- There is no **playing** state; the **p** (play) event triggers a transition back to an update state. Thus the **done** event has not been incorporated in the state machine. This illustrates the point that, because state machines are not conceived as the drivers of temporal behaviour in MachineChart designs, they do not have to include all events in the system, but only the ones that have complicated, conditional scheduling logic associated with them that we may wish to hide in an ACM. There is no requirement

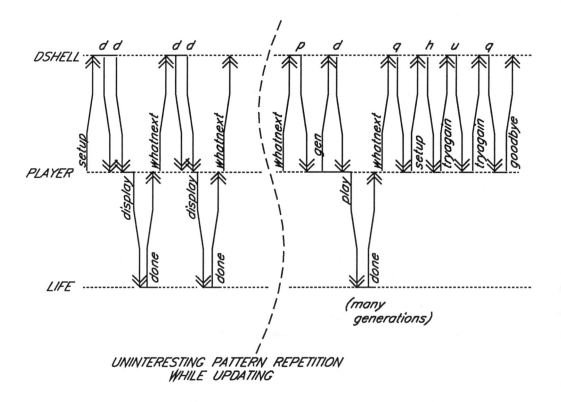

Figure 6.3: AN INTERACTION PROTOCOL SCENARIO FOR LIFE

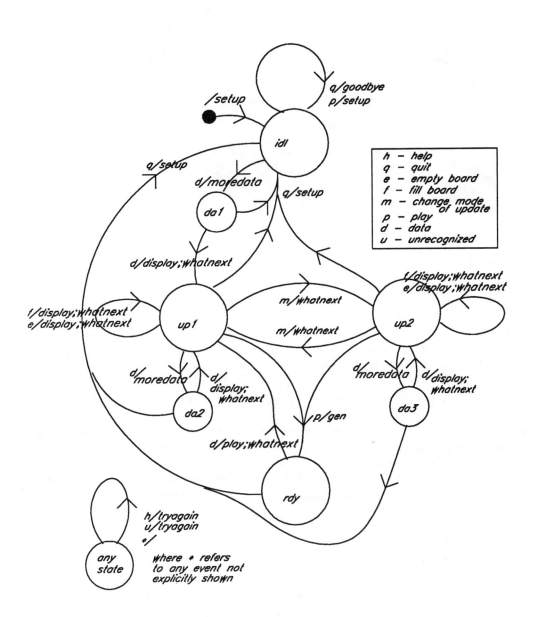

Figure 6.4: AN ABSTRACT STATE MACHINE FOR PLAYER

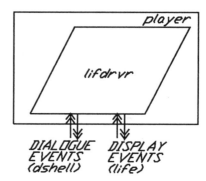

Figure 6.5: RECURSIVE DECOMPOSITION OF THE PLAYER SUBSYSTEM

to have a state machine in every component, the actions of which become the events of state machines in other components. The thinking behind leaving out **done** event is that it is not really needed: one simply arranges that the state machine will not be given any more events until concrete machinery recognizes the **done** event; it is always a good idea to simplify state machines as much as possible.

6.2.4   A ROBOT IN THE PLAYER BOX

Figure 6.5 recursively decomposes the **player** subsystem in terms of black boxes and events. It shows that the **player** box is just a container for a **lifdrvr** robot that drives the system. This illustrates the point made earlier that, depending on structure, boxes can become effectively any kind of machine; here a box is effectively a robot. In such a simple case, the robot might be promoted up a level, to replace the box, but in more general cases, this might not be desirable. A workbench for designing with this notation might support marking boxes that contain concurrent machinery in the manner of Figure 4.10, to distinguish them from simpler boxes; however, in this book, we rely only on looking inside.

  Lifdrvr will be the only robot in the sequential version of the system.

> IMPLEMENTATION IMPLICATIONS: In Ada, the **player** subsystem would map into a package with an internal task. Leaving the mainline of the main procedure null would give all the control to the task, providing a satisfactory implementation of a sequential program. Tasking may be made invisible for Ada sequential programming by putting all the control in the mainline of the main procedure, but representing this in MachineCharts directly for this design requires erasing the outlines of the **player** box and **lifdrvr** robot, leaving only the engine of the robot as the driver. This can be done, but why bother? The

representation as it is is perfectly adequate, and provides a consistent view of sequential and concurrent systems (as will be shown later).

6.3 DETAILED OUTSIDE DESIGN OF THE SEQUENTIAL VERSION

6.3.1 CHANNEL STRUCTURE FOR THE ENTIRE SYSTEM

A channel structure for the entire system is shown in Figure 6.6, that commits to undirectional visits. This commitment implies, for example, that both **dshell** and **life** provide buttons for **player** to visit, but that the reverse is not true. It accommodates **player** as the only active subsystem, by virtue of the fact that no one visits it, while not absolutely requiring the other subsystems to be passive. This figure is not an alternative to Figure 6.1, but rather a supplement to it, providing a different perspective on the system, to be used as a starting point for detailed design.

Note that the decisions made in this chart may not be the best ones for the concurrent version. Let us proceed this way now, and look at the consequences for the concurrent version later.

6.3.2 CONCRETE INTERFACES IN THE PLAYER-LIFE-BOARD RELATIONSHIP

The next step is the elaboration of the channel details in terms of buttons and fingers. One way of doing this is by drawing detailed structure charts on a port-by-port basis.

Figure 6.7 shows a possible button structure for the **dshell** port on the **player-dshell** channel.

- The **say** button provides a means of visiting **dshell** to deliver a prompt ("say" implies "say the words to the operator that are implied by this prompt identifier"). The visit, along with its parameter, is the abstract event.

- The **decodeinput** button provides a means of visiting **dshell** to get input events, which are returned in a pair of parameters, one indicating the nature of the event, and the other providing a numeric value, in the case of a data event. The visit itself is not an abstract event in earlier terms; it is simply a means of getting an abstract event; the end of the visit marks the occurrence of the abstract event.

Visits to **say** and **decodevent** would follow each other, to deliver a prompt first and then get a response. Another approach would be to have a single button, with the prompt delivered by the visit and the response by the return from the visit. Thus mapping of abstract events into buttons and fingers can take place in many ways.

In the approach of Figure 6.7, an input error appears as an unrecognized event in response to visiting the **decode-event** button, thus committing the internal design of dshell and **player** to handle errors as part of normal operation.

Figure 6.8 shows how the **life** port of the **player-life** channel might be arranged (as with **dshell**, other button configurations are possible).

- The **create** button is visited to generate a new board of given dimensions.

- The **fill**, **clear**, **placetoken**, and **removetoken** buttons are visited to initialize the board with a pattern of tokens.

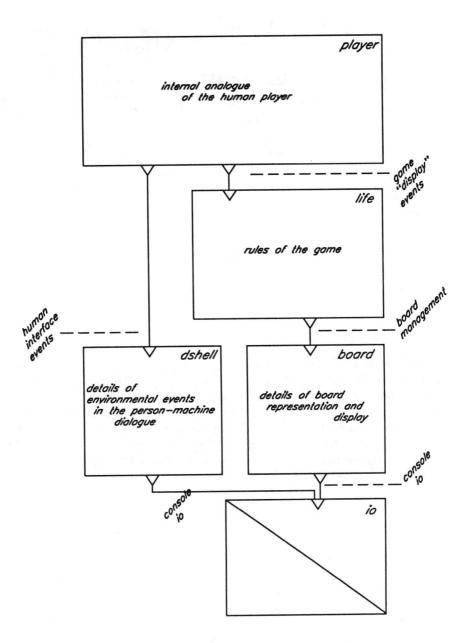

Figure 6.6: A STRUCTURE FOR THE LIFE SYSTEM EXPRESSED WITH CHANNELS

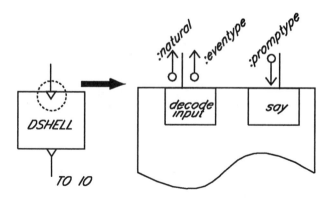

Figure 6.7: A POSSIBLE PORT STRUCTURE FOR THE DSHELL SUBSYSTEM

- The **play** button is visited to play a given number of generations of the game.

6.3.3   A VISIT SCENARIO FOR PLAYER, DSHELL, AND LIFE

Figure 6.9 gives a visit scenario that (when compared with Figure 6.3) shows the relationship between events and visits. This scenario is a rather elaborate way of explaining that things happen in the order shown. Drawing a waveform shape to give this information is overkill for a sequential system; however, we are trying to break away from sequential thinking, and get used to thinking of interactions in waveform terms, because it is very helpful to do so with concurrent systems. This diagram should be viewed as a step in that direction, not necessarily as a recommended way of expressing temporal behaviour of sequential systems. Note that the **done** event maps into a return from a visit.

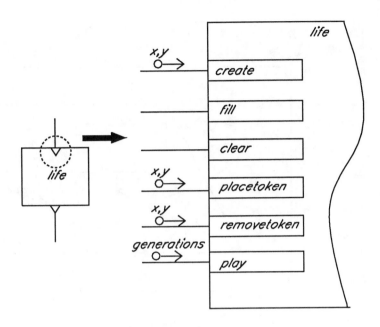

Figure 6.8: A POSSIBLE PORT STRUCTURE FOR THE LIFE SUBSYSTEM

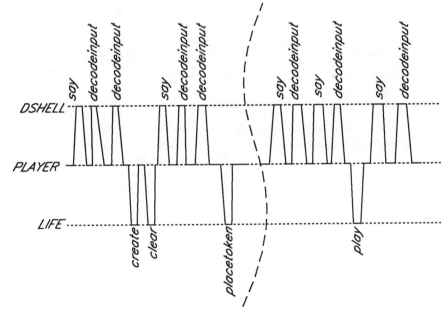

Figure 6.9: A LIFE VISIT SCENARIO

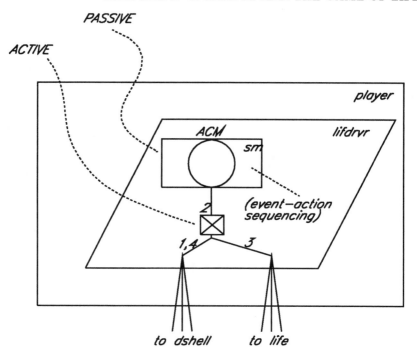

Figure 6.10: INTERNAL STRUCTURE OF THE PLAYER SUBSYSTEM

6.4 DETAILED INSIDE DESIGN OF PLAYER IN THE SEQUENTIAL VERSION

6.4.1 INTERNAL MACHINERY

Figure 6.10 begins detailed design corresponding to Figure 6.5, showing two levels of decomposition in a single flattened chart. The **lifdrvr** robot is proactive, so its agenda is concerned only with making visits. It uses the **sm** ACM to tell it what to do next.

6.4.2 ENGINE AGENDA

In principle an agenda can be written knowing only the events from Figure 6.2 and the possible places to visit from Figures 6.7 and 6.8, , leaving all the complex details of choosing what to do next to the ACM. All that is left for the agenda is a loop that alternates visits with case statements.

The engine simply cycles around, first accessing **dshell** to get an input event, then accessing **sm** to determine what output event is required, and performing visits according to the result. Thus the agenda of the engine is concerned neither with the details of the abstract events and actions (which are hidden in **dshell** and **life**) nor with the sequencing rules (which are hidden in **sm**).

IMPLEMENTATION IMPLICATIONS: An agenda for the engine of the **lifdrvr** robot of Figure 6.10 is given as an Ada program fragment in Figure 6.11. Internal details of the **sm** ACM are given later. The **nop** action is a default value for the action parameter when no action is required. The earlier **display** placeholder has been replaced by specific display actions. Each display action is really a compound action, consisting of **display**, followed by **whatnext**. We could configure the ACM to return compound actions for more general cases, but do not need to do so for this particular case. There is no exit from the loop, so a program incorporating this fragment would never terminate.

```
dshell.say (dshell.help);
dshell.say (dshell.setup);
action := sm.nop;
loop
  dshell.decodeinput(event, n);
  action := sm.DecodeEvent(event);
  case action is
    when sm.nop =>
        null;
    when sm.tryagain =>
        dshell.say (dshell.tryagain);
    when sm.goodbye =>
        dshell.say (dshell.goodbye);
    when sm.moredata =>
        nsav := n;
    when sm.whatnext =>
        dshell.say (dshell.whatnext);
    when sm.gen =>
        dshell.say (dshell.gen);
    when sm.setup =>
        life.boardsize (nsav, n);              -- DISPLAY
        life.clear;
        dshell.say (dshell.whatnext);
    when sm.doplace =>                          -- DISPLAY
        life.placetoken (nsav, n);
        dshell.say (dshell.whatnext);
    when sm.doremove =>                         -- DISPLAY
        life.removetoken (nsav, n);
        dshell.say (dshell.whatnext);
    when sm.dofill =>                           -- DISPLAY
        life.fill;
        dshell.say (dshell.whatnext);
    when sm.doempty =>                          -- DISPLAY
        life.clear;
        dshell.say(dshell.whatnext);
    when sm.doplay =>                           -- PLAY
        life.play (n);
        dshell.say (dshell.whatnext);
    when others =>
        null;
  end case;
end loop;
```

Figure 6.11: AN ACM-BASED AGENDA FOR LIFDRVR

6.4.3 ABSTRACT CONTROLLER MACHINE

The **sm** ACM simply encapsulates the abstract state machine of Figure 6.4.

> IMPLEMENTATION IMPLICATIONS: A fragment of an Ada program to implement the ACM following the style developed in Chapter 3 is given in Figure 6.12. The concept is that code like this would be produced automatically by a workbench from an entered state transition diagram, properly fleshed out with the details required for code generation. Note that a better initialization mechanism for the state table is available in Ada's **aggregate** mechanism, but this is not an Ada programming book, so we do not always seek to illustrate programming features of Ada that have no direct counterpart in the visual notation.

```
package sm is
  type ActionType is
    (nop, goodbye, moredata, setup, tryagain,  whatnext,  gen,
      dosetup, doplace, doremove, dofill, doempty, doplay) ;
  function DecodeEvent(event:in dshell.EventType) return ActionType ;
end sm;
package body sm is
  type
    StateType is ( idl,up1,up2,da1,da2,da3,rdy ) ;
  type EntryType is
    record
      sta : StateType ;
      act : ActionType ;
    end record;
  tabl    : array  (dshell.EventType, StateType) of EntryType ;
  action : ActionType ;
  state  : StateType ;
  procedure InitTabl is
   begin
   tabl ( q , idl ) . sta := idl ;      tabl ( q , idl ) . act := goodbye ;
   tabl ( d , idl ) . sta := da1 ;      tabl ( d , idl ) . act := moredata ;
   tabl ( m , idl ) . sta := idl ;      tabl ( m , idl ) . act := tryagain ;
   tabl ( f , idl ) . sta := idl ;      tabl ( f , idl ) . act := tryagain ;
   -- etc.
   tabl ( q , da1 ) . sta := idl ;      tabl ( q , da1 ) . act := setup ;
   tabl ( d , da1 ) . sta := up1 ;      tabl ( d , da1 ) . act := dosetup ;
   tabl ( m , da1 ) . sta := da1 ;      tabl ( m , da1 ) . act := tryagain ;
   tabl ( f , da1 ) . sta := da1 ;      tabl ( f , da1 ) . act := tryagain ;
   -- etc. etc.
   end InitTabl ;
  function DecodeEvent ( event : in dshell.EventType ) return ActionType is
   begin
      action := tabl ( event , state ) . act ;
      state := tabl ( event , state ) . sta ;
      return action ;
    end DecodeEvent ;
  begin
    InitTabl ;
    state  := idl ;
end sm ;
```

Figure 6.12: AN ADA PACKAGE FOR THE LIFE ACM

6.5 REUSEABILITY ISSUES

6.5.1 INTRODUCTION

We have designed this system so far with an eye to modularity, but not yet to reuseability. This is all right for a quick first pass, but one should always design with an eye to reuseability. Of all the subsystems in Figure 6.6, the **board** box is most obvious candidate for reuseability, because it might be reuseable for many different games. Just to get a feeling for reuseability issues, without going into detail, here are some alternative ways of making this box reuseable.

6.5.2 A STORE MANAGER APPROACH FOR THE BOARD SUBSYSTEM

Figure 6.13 shows a **board** machine interface that will support the game of life (as shown by its relationship to the **life** box) and that has enough generality that it could conceivably be copied for other games. However, it has a 2-board feature (revealed by the button **newold**, described below) that is special for the game of life and that might be redundant for other games. Because **board** stores game boards internally, it is characterized as a store manager machine.

The button **newold** is intended to be used by **life** to copy the new generation to an old board for the next round; **yestoken** is used to check on the status of neighbouring cells on the old board; and updates and displays via the remaining buttons are conducted on the new board.

6.5.3 A TYPE MANAGER APPROACH FOR THE BOARD SUBSYSTEM

A better approach to reuseability of the **board** box might be to make it type manager that can support as many game boards as users want to create and store in their own contexts, and that provides only the machinery for creating instances of game boards and the operations for manipulating them, without itself storing anything. This is exactly the concept of an abstract data type in programming. With such an approach for this particular problem, the **life** box would be responsible for storing the new and old game boards and would only use the **board** box to create, operate on, and destroy them. For a different problem, one game board might be sufficient. Details will not be given here, but Chapter 10 has detailed examples of this concept (although not for this particular problem).

6.5.4 BOARD TYPE MANAGERS FROM REUSEABLE TEMPLATES

So far, the only way of reusing the designs for the **board** box is for the human designer to copy them to another place, with change of names as necessary to ensure uniqueness. However, this loses their common origin and does not provide a framework for propagating later changes to all instances.

A better way is to provide a **board-support** template from which instances can be installed, as illustrated by the **board** instance in Figure 6.14.

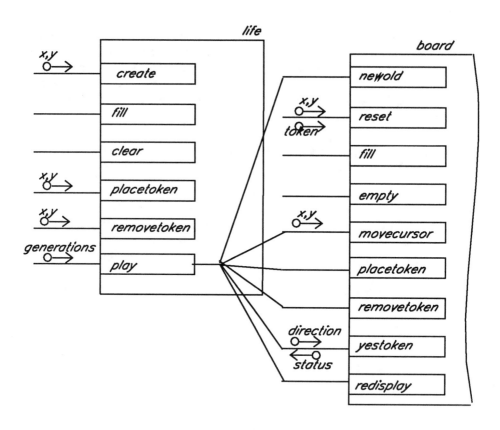

Figure 6.13: A BOARD STORE MANAGER AND ITS INTERACTION WITH LIFE

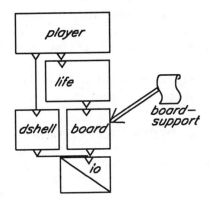

Figure 6.14: A BOARD INSTANCE INSTALLED FROM A REUSEABLE TEMPLATE

The implication is that there are no details "underneath" the particular in-place instance named **board**. The use of annotation to indicate this, rather than change of form of the instance (such as showing it in dotted outline), enables the decision on one-of machines vs. instances of templates to be made at any time in the design process before or after the instance has been drawn in-place, without affecting any of the drawing already completed. The name associated with the template icon in Figure 6.14 identifies the template diagram where its internal details are drawn. In general, although not used here, the notation allows customization of installed instances. Details are given in Chapter 10 (although not for this example).

IMPLEMENTATION IMPLICATIONS:

A store manager maps to an Ada package with internal data that is manipulated by procedures named in the specification.

A type manager maps to an Ada package that provides private types (possibly, although not necessarily, access variables). Instances of these types may be declared by the user of the package and passed to its procedures for manipulation.

A box template maps to an Ada generic package that is installed and customized at compile time.

6.6 A RETURN TO PRELIMINARY DESIGN FOR THE CONCURRENT VERSION

6.6.1 INTRODUCTION

Now we loosen the earlier constraints on temporal behaviour of the system to allow each cell to be an active robot that controls its own change of state and display of token, with the only constraint being that neighbouring cells do not get more than a generation ahead of each other.

This changes the fundamental nature of the problem from one of centralized control to one of distributed control, thereby introducing a whole new set of issues.

6.6.2 COMMUNICATING CELLS

Figure 6.15 illustrates the pattern of cell robots and event interchanges implied by allowing concurrency. Is this a requirements diagram? Or is it a design diagram? The distinction here, as is often the case with *TIME*-intensive systems, is not clear cut. One person's requirements diagram may be another person's design diagram. In fact this diagram could have been used as a starting point for expressing the requirements for the sequential version, adding only the constraint that displays of status changes (but not necessarily the status changes themselves) be synchronized across the board.

Each cell follows the agenda suggested by the scenario of Figure 6.16, with display of the cell occurring at the time of the status change. It must inform its neighbours of its own current status and wait to discover its neighbours' current status before changing its own status to the next generation (the term "broadcasting" in the figure is not meant to imply a mechanism for information exchange, but only that all neighbours must be advised).

The cells are autonomous robots with completely symmetrical communication requirements with respect to each other. The inherent indeterminism in such a configuration gives rise to races among robots which may be critical (cause erroneous behaviour). Scenarios help in answering what-if questions about such matters. For example, are the cases in Figure 6.17 correct or incorrect?

Figure 6.18 answers this question by showing interactions among three neighbouring cells. A neighbour's status report may arrive at a cell in generation N from a neighbour in generation N+1 (Case A of Figure 6.17), but not vice versa (Case B of Figure 6.17), because this would indicate the a cell has jumped to the next generation without waiting to receive all of the current generation status reports from its neighbours, in violation of the protocol implied by Figure 6.16. Note how the scenario of Figure 6.18 illustrates a ripple effect.

Figure 6.19 refines the earlier **player-life** scenario for the sequential version. New events are installing the cell robots, giving them initial conditions, starting them all playing, and discovering when they have all terminated play. As shown, all cells must be installed before any can be started, otherwise play interactions among cells might result in attempts to communicate with ones that are not yet installed. The figure does not completely resolve the problem of coordinating termination. As shown, there is a need for a gathering point for termination events; it might be in **player**, or in **life**, to free **player** from the details. We shall return to this point later.

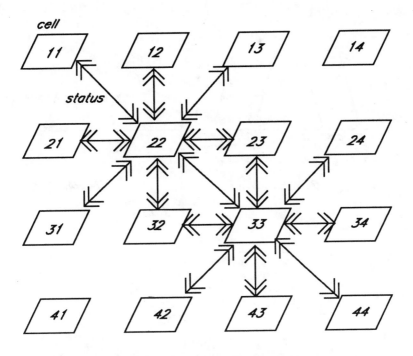

Figure 6.15: CONCURRENT CELLS

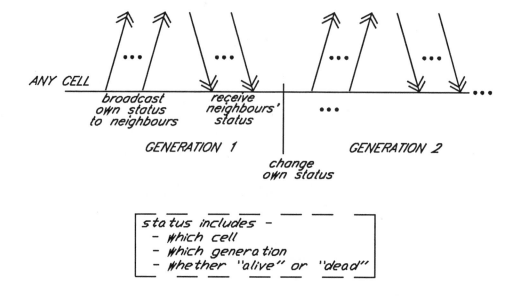

Figure 6.16: BEHAVIOUR GENERATED BY CELL AGENDAS

Figure 6.20 gives a state machine describing cell behaviour which is relatively uninteresting in its own terms, but which helps to illustrate a point about coordination among state machines in MachineCharts designs, namely that the coordination is not direct. Let us assume that cells will have ACMs incorporating this state machine, just like **lifdrvr** (Figure 6.10) has an ACM incorporating the state machine of Figure 6.4 (although we shall not proceed with the details here). If this is so, how can the two ACMs be coordinated, given there are no events in the state machine of Figure 6.4 that are triggered directly by actions of cell state machines? The answer is that coordination is provided through concrete machinery surrounding the ACMs that has not been designed yet for this system.

This machinery must leave the state machine in Figure 6.4 in state **up1** with no events being sent to it while the cells are proceeding with their interactions. Only when the cells are finished will further events be sent to it. In the sequential system this synchronization happens automatically because of the interlock on **play** interactions with **life**. In the concurrent system it must be explicitly arranged.

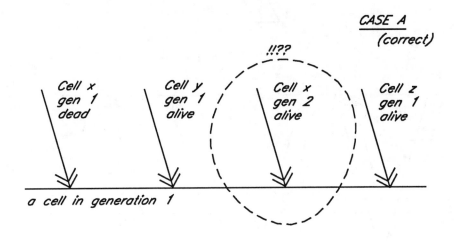

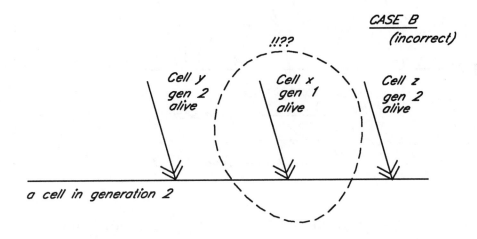

Figure 6.17: ASKING WHAT-IF QUESTIONS ABOUT BEHAVIOUR

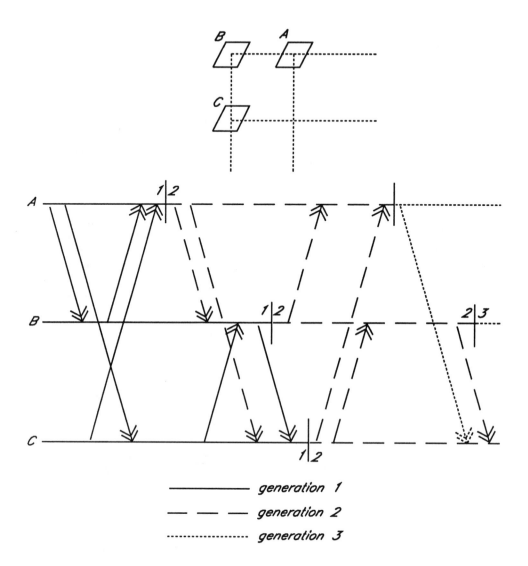

Figure 6.18: ANSWERING WHAT-IF QUESTIONS ABOUT BEHAVIOUR

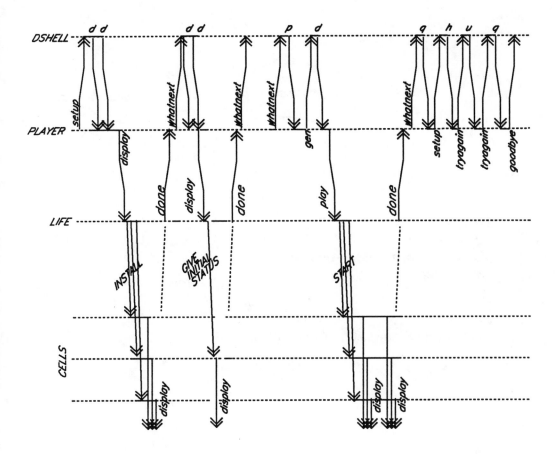

Figure 6.19: AN EXPANDED SYSTEM SCENARIO

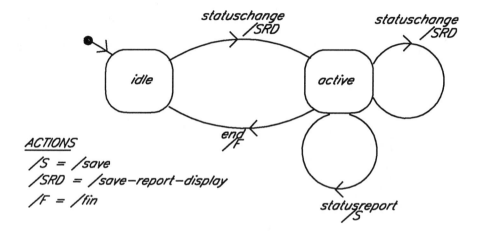

Figure 6.20: A CELL STATE MACHINE

6.7   DETAILED OUTSIDE DESIGN OF THE CONCURRENT VERSION

6.7.1   SYSTEM LEVEL

Now turn back to the earlier system level structure of Figure 6.6. Is this structure still appropriate? The answer is maybe not. However, let us proceed with it anyway, retaining the same port structures for **player, dshell,** and **life,** and focus on the internal organization of **life** first; this means that we can assume the interface of Figure 6.8 for **life.** After working out the consequences of this decision, we can then reexamine it.

The events of Figure 6.19 are mapped into the buttons of the **life** interface as follows: **INSTALL** into the **create** button; **GIVE** into the appropriate update button (**fill, clear, placetoken, removetoken**), the implication being that these buttons give starting data to the cells; and **START** into the **play** button. In our first design pass, **DONE** is signalled by returning from a visit **play.**

6.7.2   LIFE SUBSYSTEM LEVEL

INTER-CELL

Figure 6.21 shows possible channel arrangements among cells internal to **life.** Channels need to be bidirectional and symmetrical for this problem. Ports need to be shared. These are very general requirements, and there are many ways of satisfying them. Canonical glue structures for this purpose are presented at the end of this chapter. For the moment, consider only one simple possibility.

Figure 6.22 shows a direct asynchronous channel represented using jabs. The cell robot participates in the button interaction by pulling its own **give-status** button at points in its agenda when it wants status information and jabbing someone else's to give status information in an asynchronous fashion.

Because of asynchronism, mutual interactions of the same kind at the same time over the channel are safe.

The canonical glue structures discussed at the end of this chapter essentially aim to achieve this safety with a variety of different mechanisms involving intermediaries. It will turn out that sometimes the intermediaries are more appropriately situated in the cells than in separate channels, so we must anticipate this possibility when we turn to the overall structure of the **life** subsystem.

INTRA-LIFE

Figure 6.23 provides a first pass at the internal structure of an active **life** subsystem with the same interface as before (which we recognize may not be the best one for this purpose). Anticipating that in general a cell may have some intermediary robots in it, in addition to the cell robot, the cells are drawn as boxes that may contain the necessary robots. Dynamic installation and removal of cells is necessary in order to be able to reconfigure the game for a different grid, so dynamic installation of the cell boxes is required.

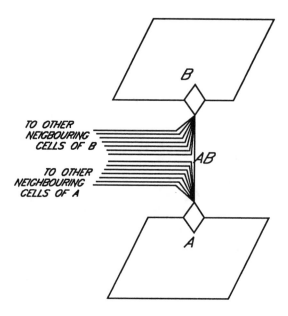

Figure 6.21: CHANNELS ARE SYMMETRIC IN THIS PROBLEM

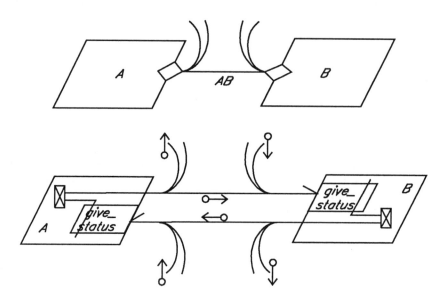

Figure 6.22: A DIRECT, ASYNCHRONOUS CHANNEL

IMPLEMENTATION IMPLICATIONS: Note that some implementation technologies, such as Ada or Modula-2, do not directly allow the equivalent of dynamically installed boxes, so the effect would have to be achieved by programming trickery. In Ada, for example, the effect could be achieved by placing the cell tasks in a record that represents the packaging intent of the box.

The gathering point for the individual cell **DONE** events is the **sync** robot. The reader should have seen enough of robot interfaces by now to recognize that the engine of this robot is intended to cyclically pull **done** until all cells are finished (it knows how many, because **create** told it, via **init**) and then opens **wait**, signifying play has finished.

A simpler (but unsatisfactory in this application) way of implementing the gathering point would be to nest the entire collection of cell robots in the **play** button, thus holding up termination of **play** until they all terminate (the assumption being that each cell robot would play a given number of generations and then terminate itself). However, this approach is unsatisfactory, because we do not want them to terminate; they must stay available to continue the game from where it was left off, if the human player requires it.

Each cell robot will be independently responsible for placing or removing its own tokens on the display board and displaying the result at each generation. No direct synchronization is required among cell robots themselves relative to display if the **board** box provides mutual exclusion protection. This may be accomplished by protecting it with a semaphore (hidden inside), or by making it into a reactor. Note that **life** no longer requires the **board** buttons **yestoken** or **newold**, because the cells interact among themselves to perform the work of **yestoken**, and each cell simply updates its own place on a single board.

We have only sketched this design in enough detail to convey the general idea; working out further details is left for the reader.

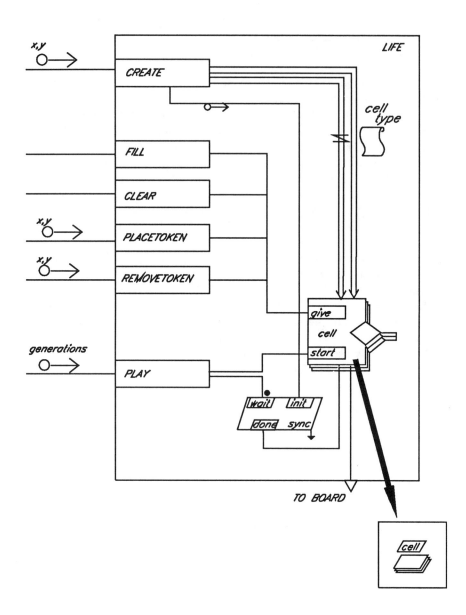

Figure 6.23: AN ACTIVE LIFE SUBSYSTEM

6.8 INTERFACES FOR CONCURRENT SYSTEMS

6.8.1 INTRODUCTION

Now let us return to the larger question of whether or not interfaces need to be approached differently for concurrent systems than for sequential ones. This issue was raised when we decided to use the same interface for **life** in both versions. Our ability to sketch a sensible design for the internal machinery of **life** in Figure 6.23 without changing the interface demonstrates that, at least in some cases, a different approach is not *necessary*. However, is a different approach *desirable*?

The reason we were able to get away with using the same interface is that we gave **player** nothing else to do while play is going on other than to wait for play to be finished. What if **player** had something else to do? It might, for example, be required to control several concurrent games at different stages of play on different screens.

Figure 6.24 addresses the interface question in this larger context in a somewhat stylized fashion, leaving out details that are peripheral to its point, which is that there are potentially bad consequences of making interface decisions in the same way for sequential and concurrent systems.

- I. An interface decision was made that **player** must visit a **play** button on **life** to cause play to happen.

- II. Hidden behind **play** is a waiting place (the **wait** button on **sync**).

- III. The waiting place behind **play** requires that a robot be available to wait. The only available robot in the **player** system is **lifdrvr**.

- IV. The **lifdrvr** robot may have other matters to attend to in its own place (as suggested above).

- V. If it does, then a special intermediary robot, called here **waiter**, must be added to the design to do the waiting on **lifdrvr**'s behalf; otherwise **lifdrvr** will not be able to attend to matters in its own place while play is proceeding. This requires changing **lifdrvr**'s interface so that **waiter** can report that play is done by visiting **done**, and also so that other events can be reported to **lifdrvr** by other buttons on its new interface. We now have a chain of interactions required to start play and report its completion, involving three robots: **lifdrvr**, **waiter**, and **sync**; this is inefficient.

- VI. A more appropriate approach may be to provide a notifier mechanism at the subsystem interface level by means of which **life** can report **done** directly to **player**.

- VII. This eliminates the need for the extra **waiter** robot, and perhaps even for the **sync** robot, although the latter would be at the cost of forcing **lifdrvr** to keep track of individual cell completions.

The effects of choosing the structure of **lifdrvr** shown in part VII of this figure ripple throughout the system, because the implication is that it gets all its events by waiting in its own place, rather than by waiting elsewhere, as the architecture of Figure 6.10 would

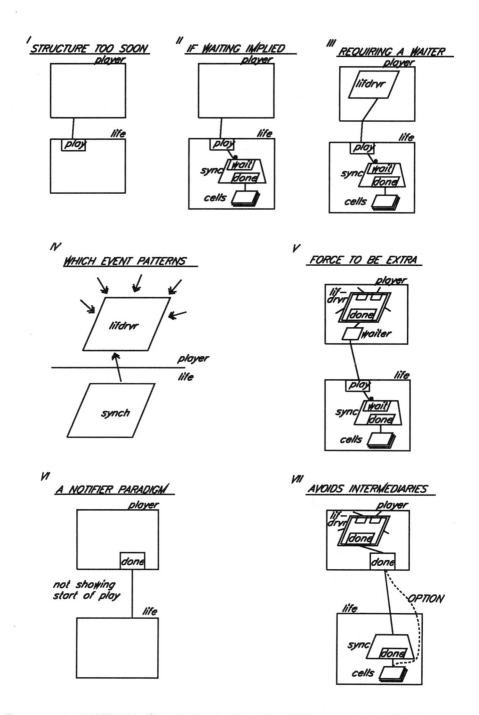

Figure 6.24: AVOIDING TOO EARLY COMMITMENT TO STRUCTURE

require. One consequence is that **dshell** in Figure 6.10 would need to be converted into a notifier. Another is that the plug-in **sm** box would be invoked by the button engines of **lifdrvr** to interpret events, rather than by lifdrvr's engine. The details can be worked out using notations already illustrated and methods already explained.

The lesson is that channels and interfaces should not be decided for concurrent systems until temporal behaviour is understood.

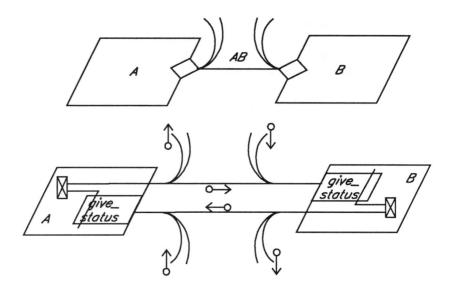

Figure 6.25: AN UNSAFE CHANNEL ORGANIZATION

6.9 CANONICAL GLUE STRUCTURES FOR SYMMETRICAL COMMUNICATION

6.9.1 INTRODUCTION

The problem requires a very general kind of symmetrical communication between the peer robots of a grid. Let us call the interaction structures that will support communication among peers, the *glue* that binds them together. Exploring the ways of configuring this glue so that the result accomplishes the purpose safely leads to a set of canonical glue structures that are of wider interest than just this case study. The canonical structures are expressed in several different forms: as channels, as cooperating robots, and as boxes.

6.9.2 AN UNSAFE GLUE STRUCTURE

Figure 6.25 shows an unsafe direct synchronous channel and Figure 6.26 illustrates graphically with scenarios why it is unsafe (deadlock).

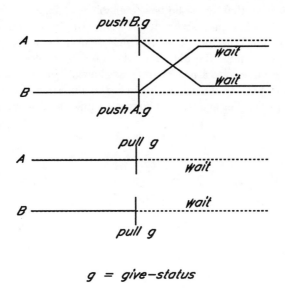

g = give-status

Figure 6.26: DEADLOCK WITH THE UNSAFE CHANNEL ORGANIZATION

6.9.3 A PASSIVE GLUE STRUCTURE

Figure 6.27 shows an indirect asynchronous channel which uses synchronous interactions with intermediate reactors that act as buffers to enable exchange of information safely in a symmetric manner. This diagram may be viewed as describing the semantics of Figure 6.22.

Figure 6.28 shows how the details of this design may be packaged in boxes. Each cell robot is a box which hides the details of the interaction mechanism. The inter-box interactions may be grouped into a new channel as shown. The combination of box **cellA**, box **cellB** and channel **AB'** looks very much like the combination of cell robot **A**, cell robot **B** and channel **AB** in an earlier figure. This suggests thinking of the boxes **cellA** and **cellB** as "multirobots".

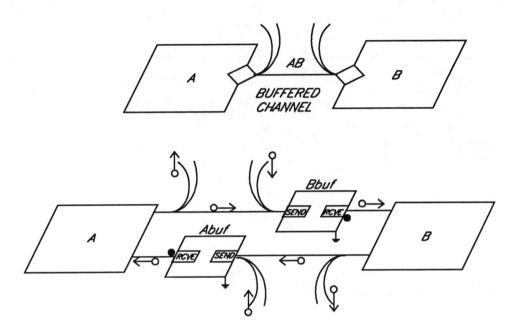

Figure 6.27: A BUFFERED CHANNEL

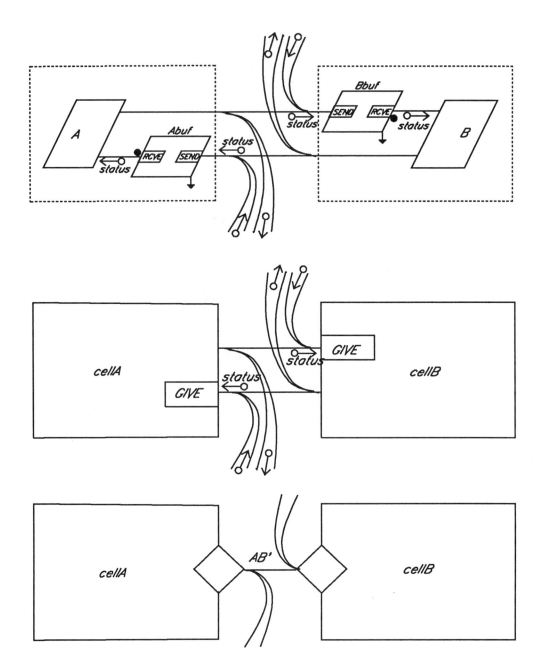

Figure 6.28: PACKAGING THE BUFFERED CHANNEL

6.9.4   AN ACTIVE GLUE STRUCTURE

Figure 6.29 shows that glue structures may contain active transporters. A choice is shown between transporters dedicated to single pairwise interactions (many transporters required) or ones capable of carrying status information to all neighbours (fewer transporters required). Transporters may be standard components described by templates that are useable in any design, with customization of sources, destinations and the type of information to be transferred; this approach is explored further in Chapter 10

Figure 6.30 shows some packaging choices for the active channel case. This is the first time a channel has been shown as mapped directly into a box. This may sometimes be appropriate when a channel is more than just a set of fingers and buttons on interacting machines, as it is with both Figure 6.27 and Figure 6.29. It did not make any sense in the former case to have a channel box between each pair of communicating robots because then reception buffers would be duplicated; this would not only be wasteful, but also incorrect, because it would force cell robots to pick one of many places to wait for input, not just one as in Figure 6.28. Figure 6.30 shows a channel box between each pair of neighbouring cells as one alternative; it is not incorrect here, but it is wasteful. The solution without a channel box is cleaner.

6.9.5   CONCLUSIONS

Glue structures to effect communication among peer subsystems may be detached from the subsystems, or included in the subsystems. A number of canonical glue structures have been identified, and their forms expressed visually both with and without channel icons. The result seems to indicate that greater representation flexibility is achieved by leaving channels as they were originally conceived, as placeholders for "connecting wires", rather than as containing machinery of their own. This approach was assumed in drawing Figure 6.23.

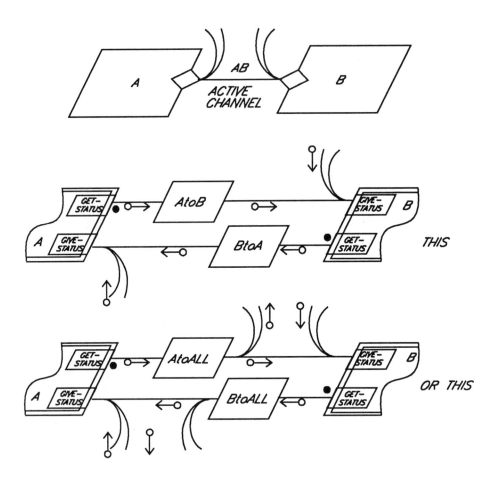

Figure 6.29: AN ACTIVE CHANNEL

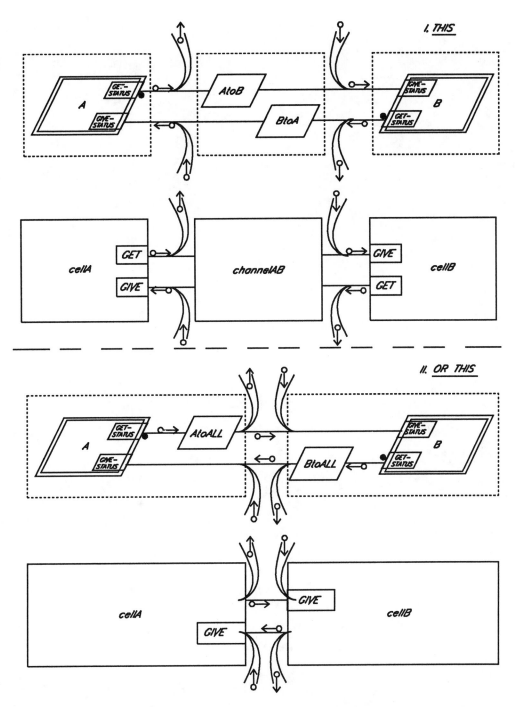

Figure 6.30: PACKAGING THE ACTIVE CHANNEL

Chapter 7

SYNTHESIZING FORM

7.1 INTRODUCTION

Between application requirements on the one hand and components on the other hand lies the problem of synthesizing system form. This chapter is concerned with this problem as it pertains only to the synthesis of the concurrency aspects of system form.

In a typical concurrent system, many forms will produce the required behaviour when implemented (although not necessarily adequate performance). We can be more positive about spotting forms that will fail to work correctly, or that are likely to perform badly, than about choosing the best among many alternatives that will work correctly. If this seems an unsatisfactory state of affairs, remember that it is not unique to the computer field, but is an unavoidable feature of engineering design synthesis.

The fact that it is hard to enunciate rules that will lead directly from requirements to appropriate forms means that it is all the more important to have means by which forms arrived at by inspiration, judgment, experience, copying, or whatever other means, can be evaluated quickly, so that bad forms can be rejected quickly. Graphical notations seem to expose the essential aspects of form that enable quick evaluations to be made. A workbench to support design drawing and quick behaviour animation would be a very powerful assistant.

Inexperienced designers tend to spend too much time worrying about performance details of parts of the system before they have an appreciation of how the parts fit together and where it is worth investing effort in performance improvement. A good pair of rules is:

- First get it right: Find a form that will have the right concurrent components waiting in the right places for the right events and doing the right things, without introducing any unacceptable behaviour patterns.

- Then make it fast: Identify the critical places where tuning must occur in the design or the implementation technology to make the performance meet requirements.

7.2   FIRST GET IT RIGHT

7.2.1   INTRODUCTION

Most of the material in this book so far has been concerned with getting it right. A number of canonical forms for parts of systems and for the glue structures that join the parts have been identified in various examples and case studies. The problem of choosing a system form that will get it right can be reduced to choosing appropriate parts and joining them together with appropriate glue structures. However, just saying this does not give any information on how to do it.

7.2.2   CANONICAL FORMS

Having some canonical forms in one's pocket for peer structures of robots and glue structures to join them helps to get it right.

A basic starting point is that there will be peer robots at the system edges to transport events in and out. These robots are the internal surrogates of concurrent objects in the world outside the system. Additional internal robots then arise for the following reasons:

- The problem has some additional aspects that are naturally concurrent.

- The system may be partitioned at some future time into concurrent sub-parts, and the design must pave the way.

- Appropriate glue structures require them.

Consider each of these points in relation to the game-of-life example of Chapter 6. One robot was required at the edge of the system to be the internal surrogate of the human player. Additional cell robots arose from the natural concurrency of the problem. Still more robots arose from the glue structures required to join the cell robots together and to join the set of cell robots to the player robot. The overall form of the solution to this problem was very general: a grid of robots communicating with each other in a highly regular manner via replicated glue structures, and with an outsider by means of an ad hoc glue structure. Experimenting with alternative forms for this system led to a number of canonical forms for glue structures including symmetrical buffer structures, symmetrical transporter structures, and asymmetrical notifier structures.

The kinds of canonical forms for glue structures that were derived for the game-of-life example apply to more than just grid structures for interacting peers, but also to other regular and irregular forms, such as trees, funnels, and networks that may be viewed as derived by pruning grids.

Protocols for using the glue structures may be implied by their visual form, as we have seen in many examples.

Regularity of form can have an important effect on understandability and verifiability of a design. In hardware, forms must be regular for physical production reasons. In software, forms are often irregular because there are no physical production reasons for them to be regular and because we give programmers freedom to make them irregular. Greater regularity could have significant benefits for software, not the least of which is that it leads to the possibility of design automation for software.

7.2.3 PIPELINES: AN EXAMPLE OF A CANONICAL FORM

We restrict our attention in this chapter to pipelines, on the twin premises that glue structures for pipelines apply also to other two-dimensional forms, and that performance problems with glue structures are likely to be severest with pipelines, because an event entering one end of a pipeline has to traverse all of the intervening nodes and glue structures to get out the other end.

Bidirectional pipelines, in which communication in the two directions is coupled at the nodes often arise naturally in communications applications (e.g., because of acknowledgements going one way for earlier messages sent the other way). Such coupling is accomplished simply and naturally by providing each node with a robot manager through which all communication in both directions must pass.

The two canonical forms for pipeline shown in Figure 7.1 and Figure 7.2 are a result of combining this active manager model with different glue structures for bidirectional communication. These figures are intended only to indicate style and not detail; in particular, there is no intent to limit waiting places on manager robots to one in each of the up and down directions, or to limit buffers to one per manager; more waiting places or buffers allows interaction patterns to be more clearly understood from the figures. Furthermore, the decision on whether the manager is an actor or a reactor has not yet been made.

Also shown in these figures are different ways of containing the robots of these forms in boxes with interfaces that hide the details. Although our concern in this chapter is not so much with containment structure as with the underlying robot structure, it is interesting to note the properties of the different containment structures:

- Figure 7.1(a) shows that a bidirectional pipeline may be formed by cascading top-access boxes. Figure 7.1(b) shows that this limits the range of possible glue structures to ones with active transporters. In particular, note how the only transporter that can be removed is the downward going one, making it impossible to effect an upward-going notifier paradigm (in a communications system in which *up* is the *reception* direction, this is a significant drawback).

- Figure 7.2 shows that a bidirectional pipeline formed by cascading boxes with both top and bottom access is more flexible. In particular, note how a notifier paradigm may be effected by replacing the upward going transporter with a direct connection between the two managers.

If the entire pipeline is a system, then the reasons for the existence of the robots in these figures may be articulated as follows, in terms of the factors giving rise to robots in Section 7.2:

- The manager robots may be viewed as arising both from natural concurrency in the problem, and from the designer's foresight that the nodes of the pipeline might be physically separate, concurrent components in some future implementation.

- The buffer and transport robots in these figures are part of the glue structures required to join the managers.

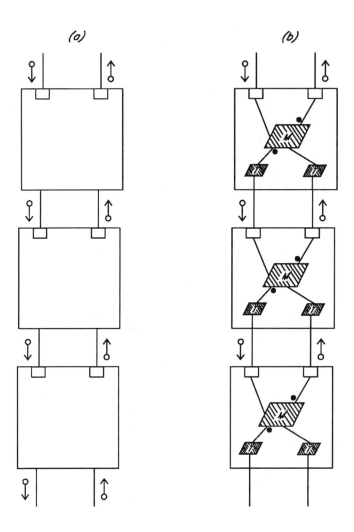

Figure 7.1: A BIDIRECTIONAL PIPELINE WITH TOP-DOWN ACCESS

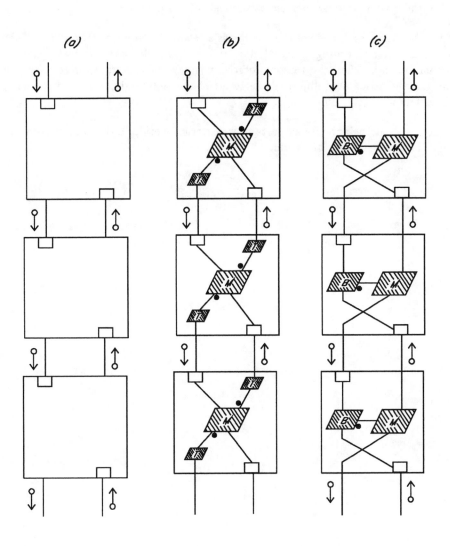

Figure 7.2: A BIDIRECTIONAL PIPELINE WITH TOP AND BOTTOM ACCESS

- The only robots that could be surrogates of concurrent components in the external world of the system are transporters at the ends of the pipeline.

If, on the other hand, each node of the pipeline is a separate system, as it would be if the foresight of its designer regarding eventual allocation of the nodes onto separate physical processors came to pass, then the reasons for the existence of the transporter robots in these figures may be articulated differently in terms of the factors giving rise to robots in Section 7.2, as follows:

- Each node sees its neighbours as parts of its external world, so the transporters are the internal surrogates of this world.

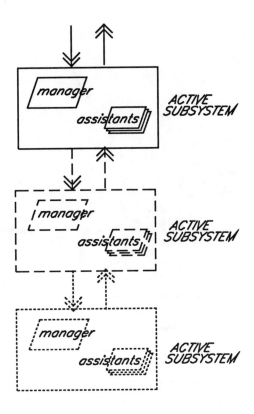

Figure 7.3: IN-PLACE CONCURRENCY

7.3 THEN MAKE IT FAST

7.3.1 INTRODUCTION

Consider how to make pipelines fast. Real performance depends on implementation factors such as processing horsepower, physical allocation of software to processors, and interprocessor communication bandwidth. However, "making it fast" does not necessarily have to wait until implementation, although it does need an understanding of what the implementation technology will be. Let us now examine factors in the design of pipelines that can contribute to "making it fast".

7.3.2 STYLES OF PIPELINE

Two extreme forms for pipelines are characterized in a stylized fashion by Figures 7.3 and 7.4:

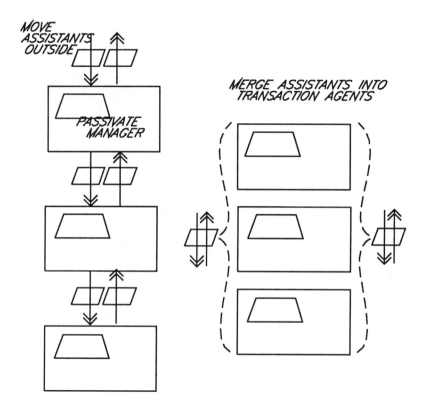

Figure 7.4: TRANSACTION CONCURRENCY

- *In-place concurrency*: The style of Figure 7.3 shows managers as actors, assisted in their own subsystems by actor assistants, some of which are assumed to be part of the glue structure for joining managers. This provides the highest level of bureaucracy possible for a pipeline, because an event coming in at one end of the pipeline has to make its way through a chain of actors before any effects will be felt at the other end. Without knowing anything about how this is likely to be implemented in a multitasking system, one can draw on experience with human bureaucracies to infer that this may be inefficient.

- *Transaction concurrency*: Figure 7.4 shows how to move towards a style of transaction concurrency in two stages from the bureaucratic style of Figure 7.3:

  - In the first stage, managers and any non-transporter assistants are combined into a single reactor manager per subsystem, and the glue structures are formed of transporters outside the subsystems.

  - In the second stage, transporter-based glue structures, in which transporters move items between subsystems, are merged into transaction-based glue structures, in which *transactors* (transaction agents) take responsibility for transactions that thread through different subsystems.

The transporters with arrows through them in Figure 7.4 are not new icons of the notation, but stylized representations used only in this figure to suggest the difference between a conventional transporter that moves events in one direction only and a transactor that may move events in both directions, and, in doing so, zig-zig its way from node to node.

A transactor shepherds an incoming event through the system, following up all of its immediate repercussions in either direction, until there is nothing more to do. As it moves through the system, if "wears the hat" of each subsystem it visits, thus performing the function of the original active manager with respect to making things happen ("wearing the hat" of a subsystem means acting through its interface buttons). Transactors are viewed as being at the edges of the system, where environmental events occur; however, events arriving there must include not only those from the environment, but also ones that follow consequentially from visits by transactors, such as timeouts. Machinery not shown in the figure is required to make this happen.

There is obvious tension between the two styles: in-place concurrency provides a nice model for cooperating active subsystems which leads easily to distributed implementations, but tends to result in implicit bureaucratic overhead accumulating in transactions that must pass through many subsystems; transaction concurrency reduces the implicit bureaucratic overhead, but does not provide the same nice model of cooperating active subsystems and therefore does not lead as naturally to distributed implementations.

Does reducing implicit bureaucratic overhead produce a significant performance improvement for multitasking software implementations? Remember that in implemention terms, what we mean here is reducing the amount of task context switching. The answer depends strongly on the implementation technology. If the run time system is a general purpose operating system like Unix without real time enhancements then the answer is almost certainly yes. However, if the run time system is an efficient real time executive that has underlying response mechanisms that are fast enough to deal with the application, then the answer may not be so obvious, even if every robot in the pipeline is interpreted as a fully concurrent task.

We have experimented with an efficient real time executive at Carleton and found that pipelines implemented by the in-place concurrency approach with active managers and transporters interacting via rendezvous are not necessarily slower than pipelines implemented by the transaction approach, at least for multiprocessor implementations. We have heard that others have had similar experiences. Much seems to depend on the efficiency of the rendezvous mechanism and the extent to which the implicit overhead eliminated by the transaction approach must be replaced by explicit overhead that needs to be programmed into every task to check what it is supposed to be doing at any time. A positive advantage of the in-place concurrency approach is that no such explicit overhead is required and that there is therefore a single place for performance tuning: the run time system.

The message is, don't automatically assume that "getting it right" is incompatible with "making it fast". First get it right and then check the consequences for performance.

If it turns out that there is a significant performance improvement to be achieved by transaction concurrency, the in-place concurrency style may still be a good starting point, because it is so regular and therefore can be systematically mapped into the other style (perhaps at some time in the future with automated assistance).

To summarize, there are two approaches to performance tuning at the design level for multitasking software, neither of which it is safe to assume will be best in all circumstances, but the first of which is obviously preferable if it will do the job:

- run time system tuning (which includes buying faster hardware or a better compiler or executive, not just tinkering with the ones you have); and

- transformation of designs that are too inefficient with available run time systems.

7.4   A CASE STUDY IN DESIGN TRANSFORMATION: REMOTE RENDEZVOUS

7.4.1   INTRODUCTION

This case study illustrates the transformation of a design from a bureaucratic in-place concurrency style, in stages, towards a design that approaches the transaction concurrency style. The tools used to analyze the behaviour and performance of the design are visit threading and scenario analysis. The process may be called "visual prototyping", because it effectively "executes" the design visually.

7.4.2   THE PROBLEM

Figures 7.5, 7.6, 7.7, 7.8, and 7.9 set the stage. Figure 7.5 shows robots representing software tasks interacting directly via rendezvous supported by an underlying run time system. Figure 7.6 shows how the same interactions may take place in a distributed environment if the run time systems support them. In the absence of run time support, one is faced with the situation in Figure 7.7, which is the context of this case study; local communications software must explicitly arrange for remote rendezvous in a non-transparent fashion. Figure 7.8 partitions the problem: the **RR** box is intended to support remote rendezvous through use of messaging facilities provided by an underlying **COMM** box which is given; Figure 7.9 provides details of the given communication service.

The remote rendezvous problem is intended here only as an easy-to-describe representative of a range of distributed system problems, rather than as a problem of particular importance in its own right; the point of the following exercise is not to present new solutions to this problem, but rather to demonstrate how alternative solutions to problems such as this may be explored in a common sense fashion.

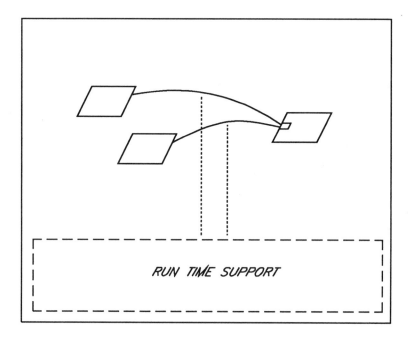

Figure 7.5: ROBOTS MODELLING TASKS IN A MULTITASKING SYSTEM

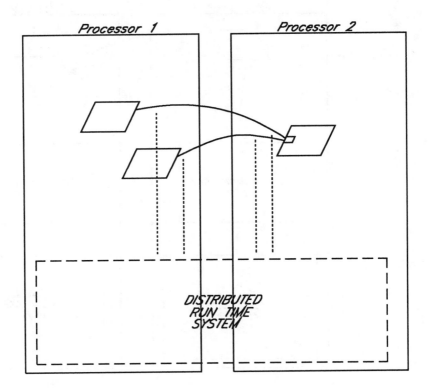

Figure 7.6: TRANSPARENT MULTIPROCESSING WITH THE SAME TASKS

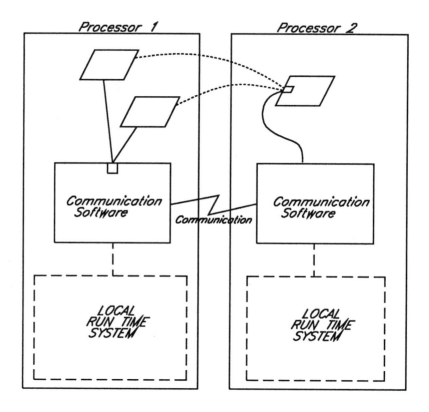

Figure 7.7: NON-TRANSPARENT MULTIPROCESSING WITH THE SAME TASKS

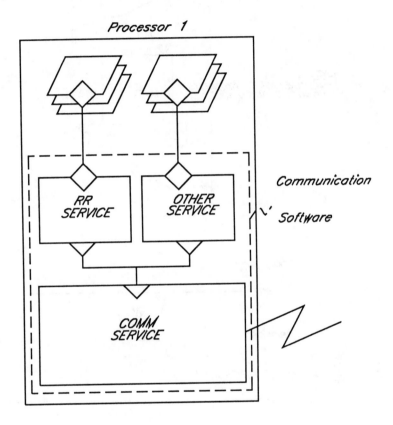

Figure 7.8: USE OF A COMMUNICATIONS SERVICE IN NON-TRANSPARENT MULTIPROCESSING

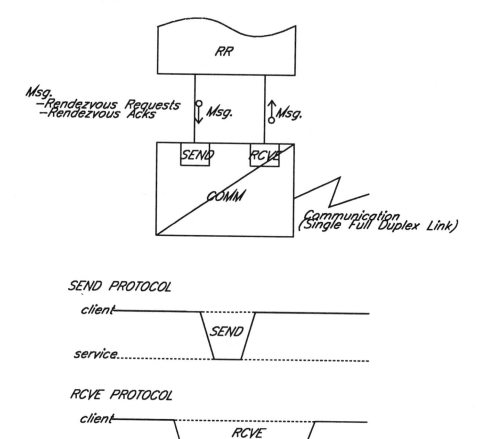

Figure 7.9: ASSUMED DETAILS OF USE OF COMM BY RR

7.4.3 DESIGN 1 : ACTIVE BUREAUCRACY

STRUCTURE

Figure 7.10 shows a first cut at a design for **RR** following the in-place concurrency style.

Before examining the properties of this design, notice some notational conventions in these figures. Although they show a sending side and a receiving side, this is only for purposes of illustration; both sides may send and receive concurrently (this is an example of the use of *overlays* to highlight particular aspects of a system under design, while suppressing details not of concern to these aspects). The dotted **fwd** and **ack** arrows in the structure diagram are annotations indicating sequencing.

This first trial design makes **RR** an active subsystem. This is a logical approach, because **RR** is at the intersection of a number of concurrent activities, which it must control: local **SEND** requests and remote messages received via **COMM's** receive service may arrive unpredictably, possibly while local rendezvous are in progress; in general, it may be necessary for **RR** to spontaneously generate its own internal activities, such as timing out on failing to receive acks (not illustrated here). Furthermore, an active subsystem approach make sense if the possibility exists of splitting local operations among different processors, with low end communications up to an including **COMM** handled by one processor and high end communications above **COMM** handled by another.

An active manager (here **RR_MGR**) is naturally in charge of an active subsystem. Obviously it must be available as much as possible of the time to respond to requests and messages. However, the statement of the problem provides it with many places to wait (in its own place for rendezvous requests, at **COMM** for incoming messages, at local clients for rendezvous completions); if it waits exclusively at one place it may unduly delay processing of events at other places and it cannot wait in many places at once. Therefore it needs assistants (**NOTIFIER** and the **PARTNERs**). A real bureaucracy has emerged!

Note that the **NOTIFIER** solution shown here would work only if **RR** is the only user of **COMM**; if many different services used **COMM**, as suggested by Figure 7.8, then a central notifier would be required outside **RR** to distribute incoming messages to the right subsystems.

7.4.4 PIECING TOGETHER TEMPORAL BEHAVIOUR

Figure 7.11 shows how one sees temporal behaviour from outside the subsystems. Clients visit **FWD** and return with the remote rendezvous accomplished. The **RR** subsystem visits **SEND** to ask for messages to be sent and leaves with sending in progress. It also visits **RCVE** to wait for messages from **COMM**. Recall that the protocol for using **SEND** and **RCVE** was shown in Figure 7.9.

Figure 7.12 shows how one sees temporal behaviour from outside the manager robot. A 2-visit pattern is required to **SEND** a remote rendezvous request and then **WAIT** for an acknowledgment. The **RR_MGR** is itself an actor that visits elsewhere after a meeting at **SEND**. A visit at **PUT** opens **WAIT**. There are also other visit threads not shown associated with other functions of the manager.

This illustrates a property of recursive decomposition. We may understand interface behaviours associated with a subsystem and its internal components, but we still have to

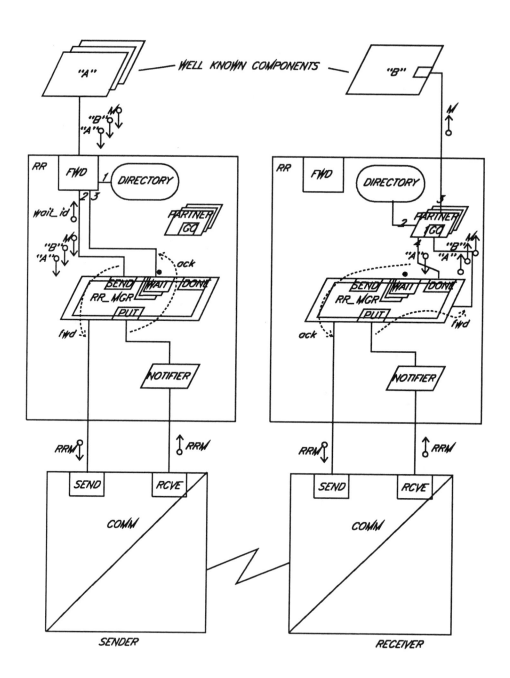

Figure 7.10: DESIGN 1 FOR THE RR SUBSYSTEM - STRUCTURE

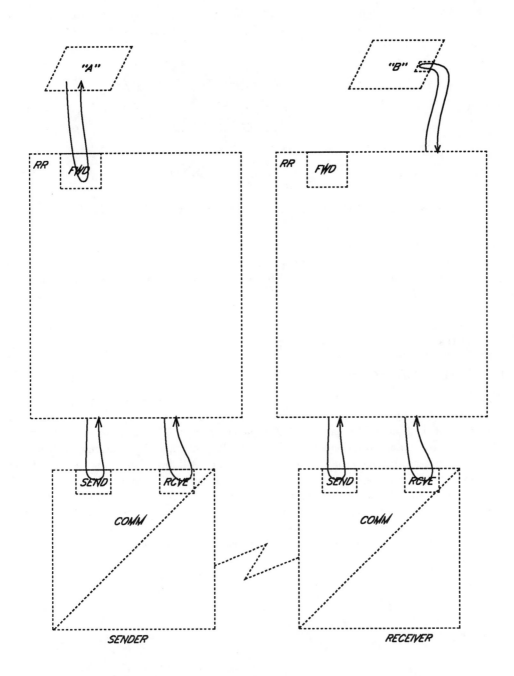

Figure 7.11: DESIGN 1: RR INTERFACE VISIT THREADS

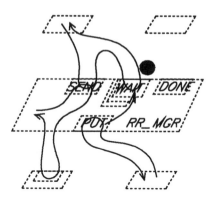

Figure 7.12: DESIGN 1: MANAGER INTERFACE VISIT THREADS

piece together the behaviours to make sure that the overall behaviour is correct. From a different perspective, we may have an expectation of overall behaviour that we must ensure is consistent with the possible individual behaviours of components. Figure 7.13 gives an example of how behaviour can be pieced together. Figure 7.14, shows the same behaviour as that in Figure 7.13, except linearized in scenario form.

All of this behaviour information is test information created before agendas have been specified that may be used to test agendas.

7.4.5 PERFORMANCE

From Figures 7.13 and 7.14, it is apparent that the bureaucracy in **RR** results in the same kinds of annoying delays caused by bureaucracies in the human world; clients must hand over work to active bureaucratic intermediaries, who in turn must hand it over to other active ones, and so on, possibly through a long chain of interactions, each link of which adds overhead; the overhead-producing links of the interaction chain are circled and numbered in the figure for comparison with later designs (only meetings are so highlighted, on the assumption that they will dominate the overhead picture). Cumulative delays can be substantial when a single transaction (such as a single remote rendezvous in this example) requires many such links. In this particular example, matters may be even worse than suggested by the scenario, because **COMM** is itself an active subsystem which may have an internal bureaucracy.

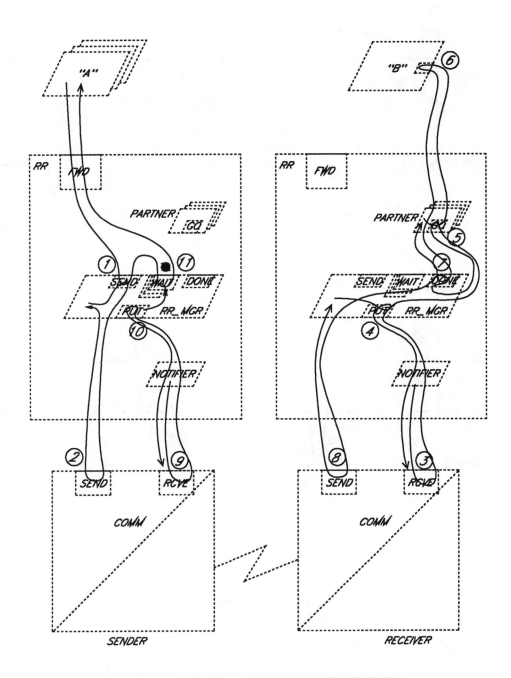

Figure 7.13: DESIGN 1: SYSTEM VISIT THREADS

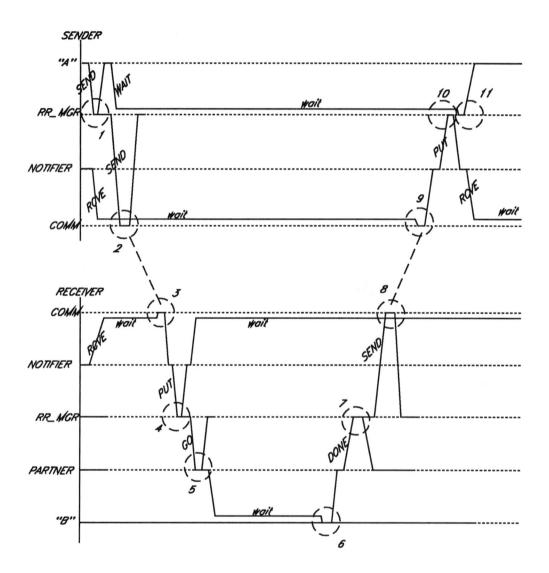

Figure 7.14: DESIGN 1: VISIT SCENARIO

7.4.6   DESIGN 2 :   A "SNEAKY" BYPASS OF PART OF THE BUREAUCRACY

A careless "quick fix" to get the **RR_MGR** off the critical path is illustrated by Figures 7.15 and 7.16. Requests from clients via **FWD** on the sending side "sneak by" the **RR_MGR** and **SEND** their requests directly to **COMM** before going back to the **RR_MGR** to **SIGN_IN**; similarly, **PARTNER**s on the receiving side "sneak by" **RR_MGR** to send acks. However, as illustrated by Figures 7.17, 7.18, and 7.19, this "quick fix" opens up possibilities for critical races which make it unworkable. The problem illustrated by Figure 7.18 of having no place available to wait for an ack after starting the action which will eventually result in an ack is obviously likely to occur and critical. The problem illustrated by Figure 7.19 of an ack arriving before sign-in is pathological and fairly unlikely to occur, but would be disastrous if it did, because there would be no waiting place for the ack to open.

The problem of having no place available to wait for an ack is caused by the interface of **RR_MGR** providing only a fixed number of places to wait. The solution hinted at by Figure 7.17 of making waiting places and partners dynamic is not possible with the fixed interface of this architecture, but a slight change in viewpoint provides a workable solution illustrated later (fourth trial design).

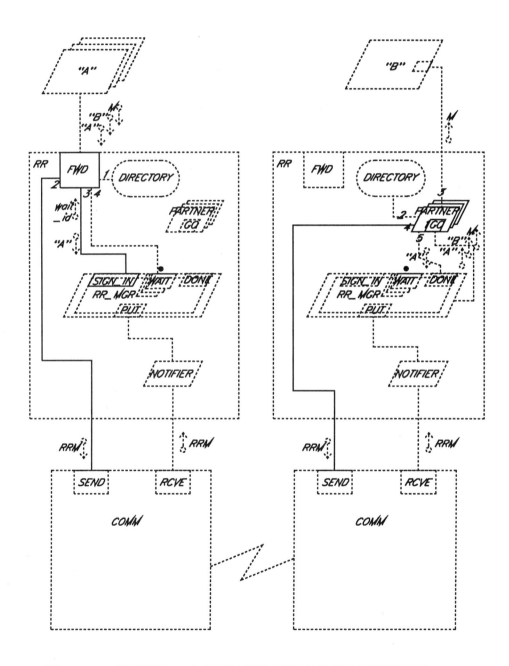

Figure 7.15: DESIGN 2 - A "SNEAKY" BUREAUCRACY-BYPASS

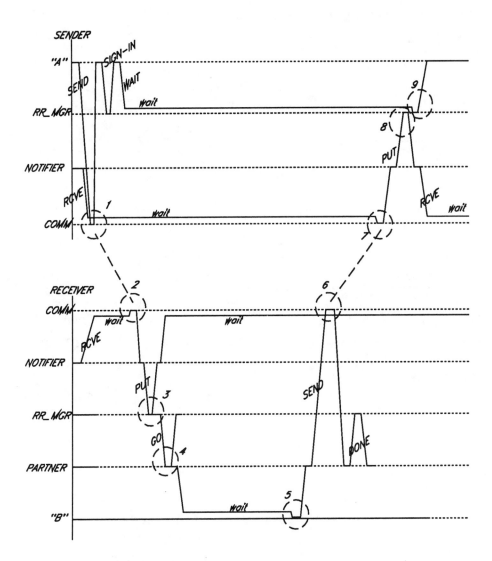

Figure 7.16: THE BYPASS SPEEDS THINGS UP

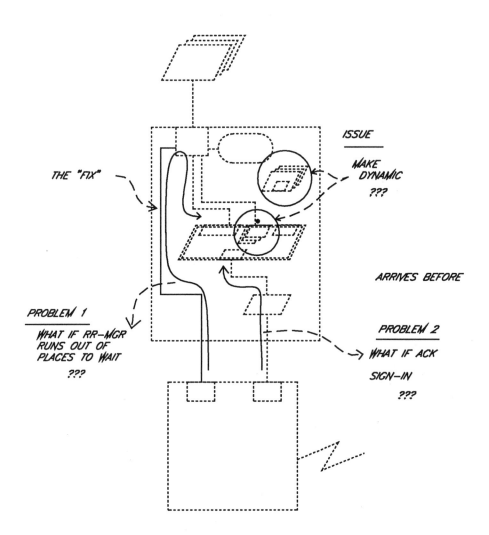

Figure 7.17: PROBLEMS WITH DESIGN 2

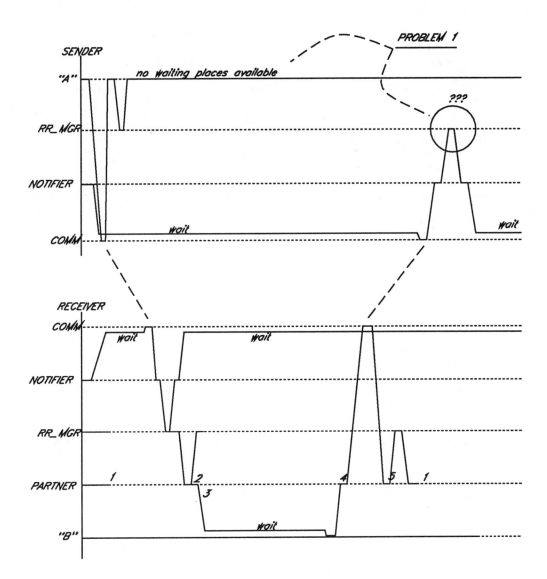

Figure 7.18: A LIKELY CRITICAL RACE IN DESIGN 2

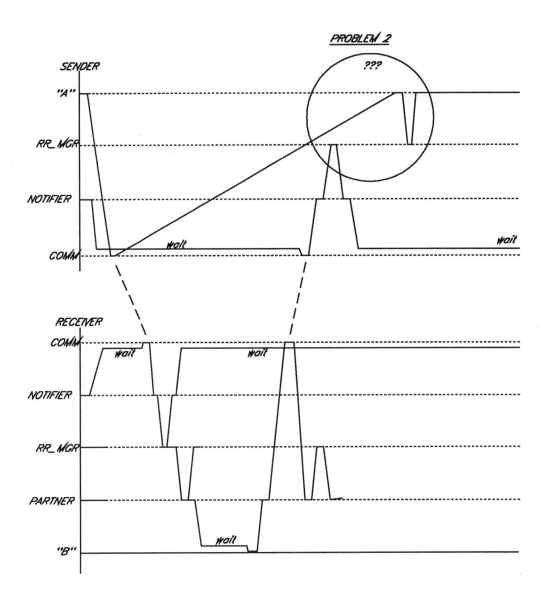

Figure 7.19: AN UNLIKELY BUT POSSIBLE CRITICAL RACE IN DESIGN 2

7.4.7   DESIGN 3 : MORE EFFICIENT BUREAUCRACY

Rather than sneaking by the bureaucracy, we can try to make its bottleneck (the manager) more efficient by making it passive as shown by Figure 7.20. Previously the manager autonomously performed interactions, as shown by the scenario of Figure 7.14 (e.g., **SEND** to **COMM** *after* completion of servicing of its own **SEND**). Now it must perform such interactions before interlocks are released, as shown by the scenario of Figure 7.21. This makes the critical interaction chain slightly more efficient because each interaction does not have to complete before the next one can be started. However, there is also another efficiency benefit which is probably more important.

Run time efficiency is now under the control of the implementor. If in a software implementation the manager robot is implemented as a task whether or not it is passive, then nothing much has been gained. However, if the passive manager is implemented not as a task, but as a protected passive object (sometimes called a monitor) then a considerable improvement in efficiency is likely to result, because the interactions with the manager do not involve task context switching, except as required to enforce mutual exclusion in the (presumably relatively infrequent) situations where more than one task is trying to access it simultaneously. This second implementation alternative is not available for the active manager.

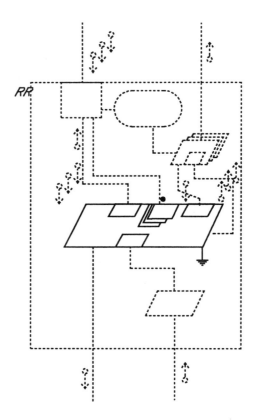

Figure 7.20: DESIGN 3 - PARTIALLY PASSIVATING THE BUREAUCRACY

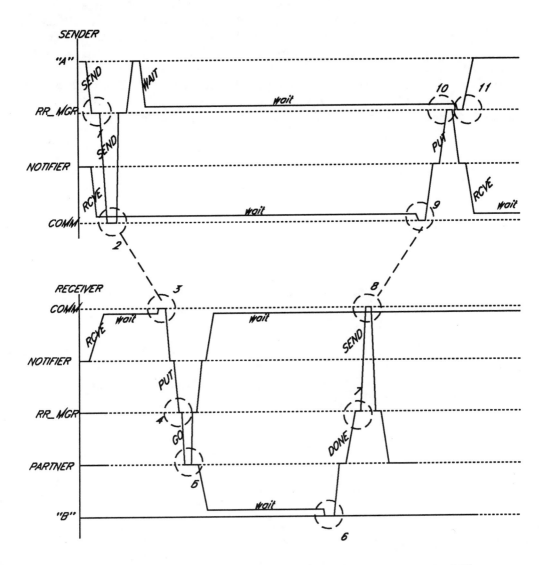

Figure 7.21: DESIGN 3 IMPROVES PERFORMANCE OVER DESIGN 1

7.4.8   DESIGN 4 : PARTIALLY ELIMINATING THE BUREAUCRACY

Figure 7.22 eliminates both the bureaucracy and the constraint of a fixed number of places to wait for acks, at the cost of having no central input-output coordinating point inside the **RR** box which is independent of clients (this cost is acceptable for this problem but would not be for a protocol which included, for example, timeout and retransmission). As shown by the chain of circled interactions in Figure 7.23, performance has apparently been improved. However, note that all is not necessarily gravy, because dynamic installs may be slower than rendezvous in some implementation technologies. Therefore the reduction in the number of rendezvous may be counterbalanced by an increase in the time required to set up a dynamic waiter, which is on the critical path, because taking it off the critical path would result in a similar situation to Figure 7.19. The arrangement of Figure 7.22 with the sequencing illustrated by Figure 7.23 ensures that a robot to wait for the **ACK** is in place before triggering the interaction chain which is expected to produce the **ACK** eventually.

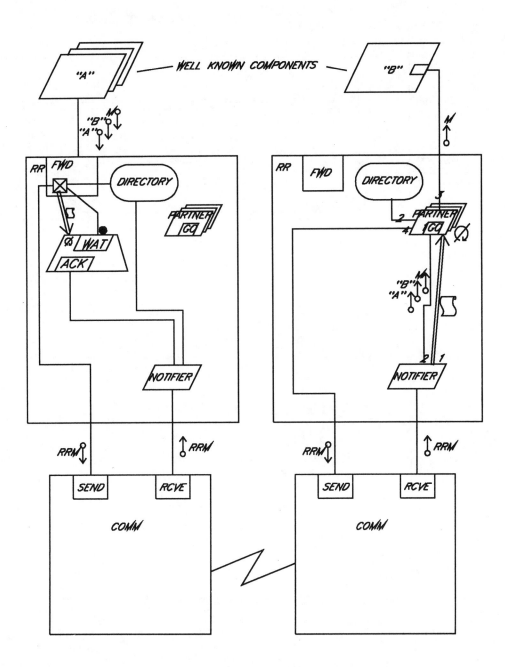

Figure 7.22: DESIGN 4 - PARTIALLY ELIMINATING THE BUREAUCRACY

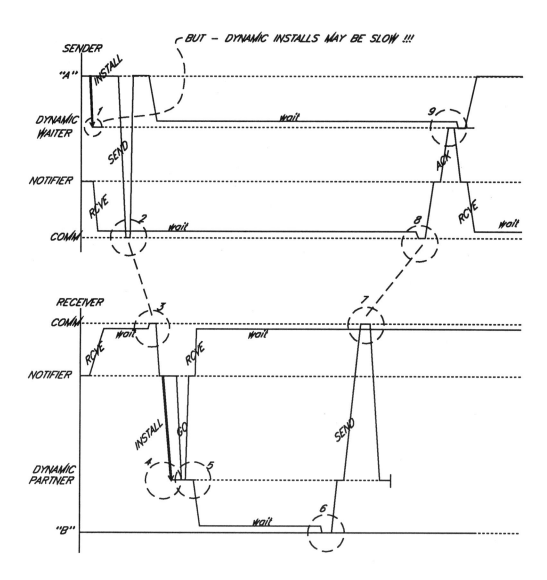

Figure 7.23: IMPROVED PERFORMANCE WITH DESIGN 4

7.4.9 DESIGN 5 : A VARIANT OF DESIGN 3

Going back to the third trial design (Figures 7.20,7.21), Let us now suppose that notification of arriving "mail" will come autonomously to **RR** from outside, either because **COMM's** receive service provides active notification directly (Figure 7.24 - a change of the initial assumptions), or because an external robot is given the responsibility of performing required notifications (Figure 7.25). Then the **NOTIFIER** robot in **RR** can be transformed into a **NOTIFIER** button attached to **RR's** interface, as shown in both figures.

Figure 7.25 is purely a structural change without behavioural ramifications. However, Figure 7.24 is more efficient, as shown by the scenario of Figure 7.26 (compare with Figure 7.14).

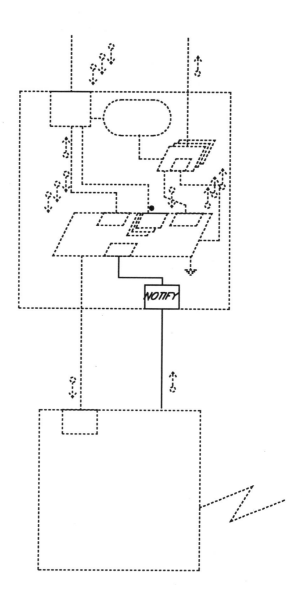

Figure 7.24: DESIGN 5 - A PERFORMANCE-ENHANCING IMPROVEMENT OF DE-SIGN 3

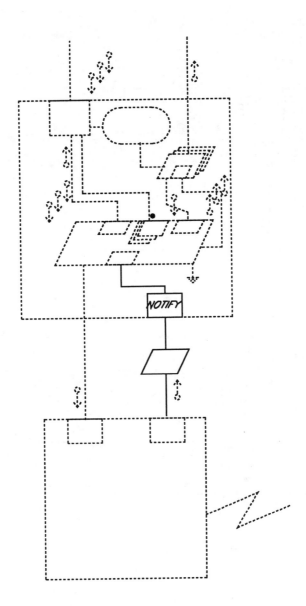

Figure 7.25: A COSMETIC CHANGE TO DESIGN 3

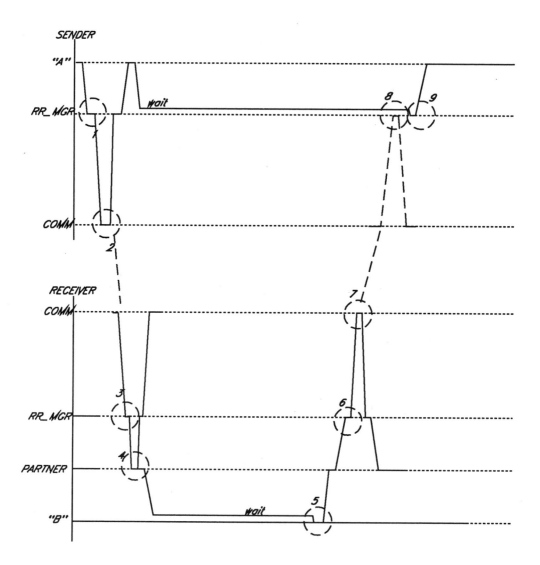

Figure 7.26: PERFORMANCE OF DESIGN 5

7.4.10   DESIGN 6 : A VARIANT OF DESIGN 4

The fourth trial design (Figures 7.22,7.23) can similarly be made more efficient by getting rid of the **NOTIFIER**, as shown in Figure 7.27, with the performance results shown in the scenario of Figure 7.28 (compare with Figure 7.23).

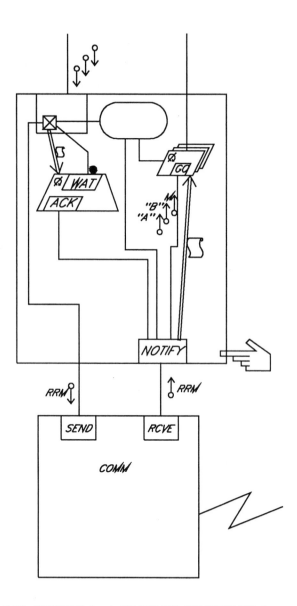

Figure 7.27: DESIGN 6 - A VARIANT OF DESIGN 4

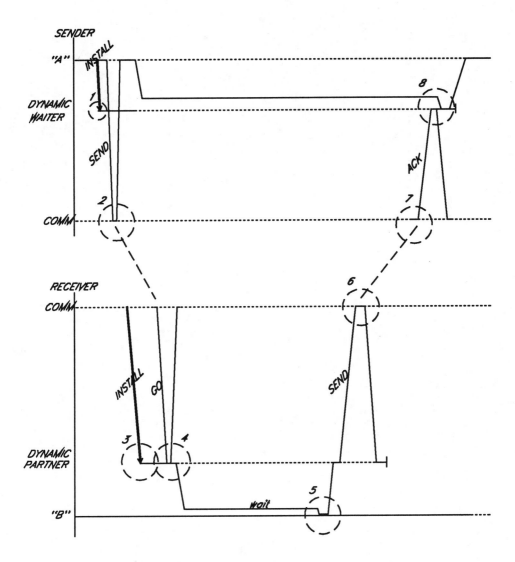

Figure 7.28: PERFORMANCE OF DESIGN 6

Part IV

EXERCISING THE NOTATION ON TIME-INTENSIVE PROBLEMS

Chapter 8

ISSUES IN TIME-INTENSIVE SYSTEMS

8.1 INTRODUCTION

This chapter explores temporal behaviour issues at the interface level, with particular focus on issues that are important in *TIME*-intensive systems. It continues the exploration of topics that were only introduced briefly in the foundation chapters, including busy-waiting, non-busy waiting, deadlocks, protocols, flow control, critical races, priority, real time, and timeout. One objective is to show how properties of temporal behaviour may be recognized and specified at the interface level; in other words, the chapter aims to help the reader to develop a critic's and designer's "eye" for suitable form in interfaces and their interconnections.

8.2 BUSY-WAITING

8.2.1 INTRODUCTION

Let us begin with a form of waiting that we dismissed as bad in Chapter 3, namely busy-waiting, or polling. Polling is sometimes introduced into designs because the requirements seem to demand too many places to wait for events, or because other mechanisms are perceived as not satisfying the requirements. However, problems can usually be transformed into a form that eliminates these concerns, as will be shown here.

First, what is polling? Loosely speaking it is repetitive testing of some condition. But what does repetitive mean?: periodic?; at some rate determined only by how fast a program can execute a loop? And what does testing mean?: with the cooperation of the component being polled (because it returns a parameter, as in the control flag example of Chapter 3)?; without the cooperation of the component being polled (using balking)? All of these are practical possibilities.

Basically, the bad form of polling is looping and testing at an uncontrolled rate in an asynchronous system. How the testing is done may be an issue in trying to optimize polling, but it is not an issue in deciding whether to use it or not. Polling is not an issue in periodic systems.

Now let us examine some examples.

8.2.2   A TRACK DISPLAY PROBLEM

Consider a track display problem illustrated by Figure 8.1.

- I. The problem is to show on a screen the track of a sequence of point positions **PP** that arrive sporadically from an input device. The result is a sequence of display positions **DP** on the screen, some resulting directly from inputs, and the others from estimates that are made in between inputs.

- II. A first pass at an interface-level design has a **TRACK_DISPLAY** robot with a single **UPDATE** button, visited from the measurement source, and a **DISPLAY_MGR** visited by **TRACK_DISPLAY** box.

- III. This interface forces a polling solution, in which the engine of **TRACK_DISPLAY** polls **UPDATE**, calculating and displaying an estimated position on every unsuccessful cycle, without any constraint on the rate at which estimated positions are displayed other than the speed of the calculation and display. This might be thought necessary because otherwise **TRACK_DISPLAY** could be stuck at **UPDATE** without being able to display estimated positions; this is certainly so if one is not allowed to introduce real time into the solution of the problem.

- IV and V. It is hard to imagine this problem being practical without being able to control the rate of display of estimated positions. In the these solutions, the first of which requires visits from a clock to **TICK**, and the second of which simply times out on waiting for visits to **UPDATE**, estimated positions are displayed at a controlled rate, without polling.

    IMPLEMENTATION IMPLICATIONS: The track display example has been used in the Ada community to show how Ada has a "polling bias"; this seems so for this problem only if artificial constraints are imposed on its solution. For Ada readers, skeleton code for solutions *III*, *IV* and *V* is given in Figure 8.2, Figure 8.3, and Figure 8.4, showing how the figures are interpreted in Ada terms.

8.2.3   A FIRE ALARM PROBLEM

Figure 8.5 and Figure 8.6 describe a fire alarm problem that leads naturally to a proactive solution that looks superficially like polling but is not; it is an appropriate use of balking (the alarm processor does not keep trying *call* until it gets through but only tries once and then goes somewhere else). However, extending the look of Figure 8.6 just a bit makes it a polling solution, as is shown in the next example.

    IMPLEMENTATION IMPLICATIONS: For Ada readers, Figure 8.7 shows how the balking interaction is programmed.

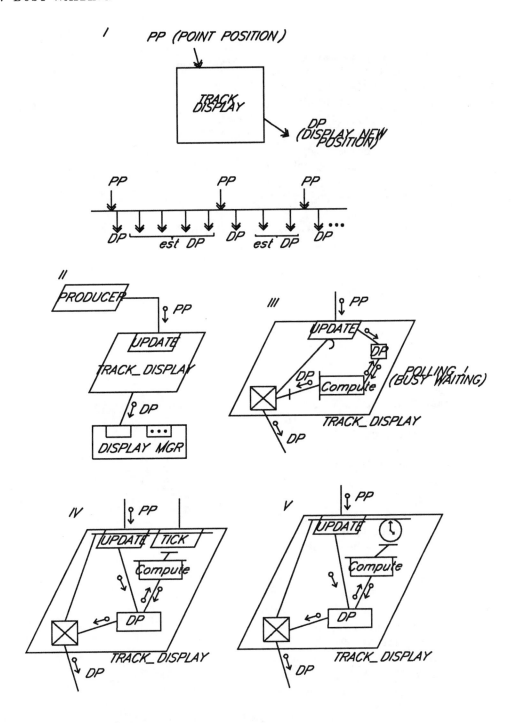

Figure 8.1: A TRACK DISPLAY PROBLEM

```
task TRACK_DISPLAY is
        entry UPDATE (PP:...);
end TRACK_DISPLAY;
task body TRACK_DISPLAY is
        DP:...;
        loop
          select
            accept UPDATE(PP:...) do
            --save PP as DP
            end UPDATE
          else
            --Compute new estimated DP
          end select;
          --display DP
        endloop;
end TRACK_DISPLAY;
```

Figure 8.2: ADA REACTIVE POLLING SOLUTION (III)

```
task TRACK_DISPLAY is
   entry UPDATE (PP:...);
   entry TICK;
end TRACK_DISPLAY
task body TRACK_DISPLAY is
  DP:...
  loop
    select
      accept UPDATE(PP:...) do
      -- save PP as DP
      end UPDATE
    or
      accept TICK
      -- compute new estimated DP
    end select
    -- display DP
  end loop;
end TRACK_DISPLAY;
```

Figure 8.3: ADA PERIODIC SOLUTION (IV)

```
task TRACK_DISPLAY is
   entry UPDATE (PP:...);
end TRACK_DISPLAY
task body TRACK_DISPLAY is
  DP:...
  loop
    select
      accept UPDATE(PP:...) do
      -- save PP as DP
      end UPDATE
    or
      delay(TIM};
      -- compute new estimated DP
    end select
    -- display DP
  end loop;
end TRACK_DISPLAY;
```

Figure 8.4: ADA TIMEOUT SOLUTION (V)

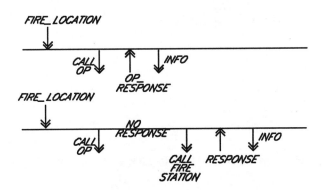

Figure 8.5: A FIRE ALARM PROBLEM

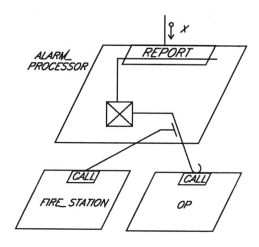

Figure 8.6: A PROACTIVE ALARM PROCESSOR

```
loop
  accept REPORT (X:LOCATION);
    select
     OPERATOR.CALL (INFO:...);
    else
     FIRE_STATION.CALL (INFO:...);
    endselect
end loop
```

Figure 8.7: AN ADA PROGRAM FOR THE PROACTIVE ALARM PROCESSOR

8.2.4 POLLING AND THE ANONYMOUS HOST PARADIGM

Figure 8.8 and Figure 8.9 provide a slight generalization of the fire alarm problem that can lead naturally to a polling solution. What we have here is a problem crying out for support for the anonymous host model of interactions. If this is not available and turning the problem around to make it reactive is unacceptable, then there are two alternatives: the proactive polling solution of Figure 8.9 (undesirable); or an asynchronous solution using an intermediary (we have seen a number of these in the book, so one will not be repeated here).

IMPLEMENTATION IMPLICATIONS: For Ada readers, Figure 8.10 shows how the proactive polling solution would be implemented in Ada.

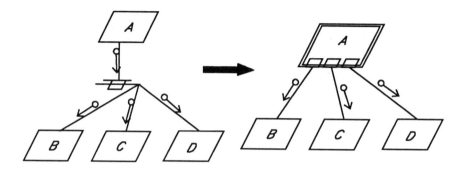

Figure 8.8: PROACTIVE VS. REACTIVE SOLUTIONS

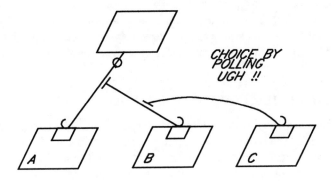

Figure 8.9: PROACTIVITY WITHOUT ANONYMOUS SERVERS LEADS TO POLLING

```
loop
  select
    A.a
  else
    select
      B.b
    else
      select
        C.c
      else
        null;
      end select;
    end select;
  end select;
end loop
```

Figure 8.10: AN UNDESIRABLE ADA PARADIGM: PROACTIVE POLLING

8.3   NON-BUSY WAITING

8.3.1   INTRODUCTION

Non-busy waiting normally requires picking a particular place to wait; in trying to solve this problem, a designer may perceive too many places to wait, and in consequence think that polling is necessary. (If the designer can assume an uncommitted waiting model (Chapter 5) that does not require picking specific places to wait, then this problem goes away). Let us consider how to design structures that will provide only one place to wait for each robot that must wait for events.

8.3.2   THE RULE OF ONE PLACE TO WAIT

Suppose that we divide robots into two classes with respect to events: sources and sinks, leaving aside for the moment the possibility that a robot might be both. Figure 8.11 identifies possible waiting structures in a general way, in terms of source and sink relationships. The figure omits buttons and internal pull structures, and shows only single fingers connecting robots. Markers indicate waiting places; a waiting place marker inside a robot indicates it waits in its own place; one outside a robot indicates its visitors wait. Sinks may wait in their own places or elsewhere; sources only wait in their own places, although they may visit elsewhere.

The ensuing discussion assumes that event patterns are unpredictable relative to the life cycles of the sinks. The opposite extreme would be to have event patterns tied to their life cycles in such a way that a sink's presence at one place would make it impossible for an event to occur at another, which might happen only as a consequence of the particular character of a particular part of a particular system, but would never be safe to assume in general.

A general rule is: do not provide active event sinks with many different places to wait for events with unpredictable arrival times. In other words, if a sink must wait for many possible events from many different sources, any of which might arrive at any time, the events should be funneled to one place. In this light, here is an analysis of the cases represented by this diagram (note that this analysis is independent of whether or not interactions at non-waiting places are synchronous, except as specifically indicated):

- *A-I*: This is a bad structure in general, because it requires the sink either to visit all of its many sources in turn to check for events (thus violating the non-busy waiting rule) or to select one place to wait at a particular time and risk the possibility of being stuck there while events are arriving elsewhere.

- *B-I*: This is desirable structure for the sink because it waits in its own place to be visited by many sources bringing events. To the sink, this is not essentially different from having only a single source of events. However, this may not be a good structure for sources, particularly if the interactions are synchronous and sinks cause delays, say due to latency of a busy sink, or because a sink is exercising brute force flow control (as discussed later).

- *A-II*: This is a desirable structure for the source (again because of own-place waiting). It is good for the sinks also, provided the events they are waiting for all come from the

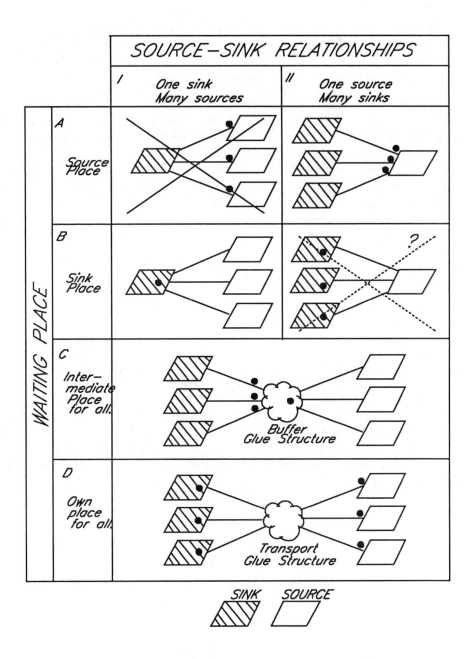

Figure 8.11: A CLASSIFICATION OF WAITING STRUCTURES FOR A PARTICULAR MODEL

single source shown. Otherwise, the problem of missing events at their home places arises.

- *B-II:* This may be a poor structure, because it takes sources away from the places where they get events, leaving them at the mercy of congestion and latency at sinks. If congestion is unlikely, and sinks are always guaranteed to be waiting when the visit is made, then there is nothing wrong with it.

- *C:* This structure combines the good structures of *B-I* and *A-II* as one way of satisfying the requirements of both. The central place becomes a source for visiting sinks and a sink for visiting sources. This solution resolves the latency problem by ensuring that visitors are not trying to meet with busy hosts. In fact, this solution has eliminated synchronism as an issue, because the central place is passive. However, it has also eliminated the desirable property of *own-place waiting*. This structure may be effected in the anonymous server model by placing a buffer robot in the intermediate place, with attached gate buttons for delivery and pickup. In the more general anonymous host model, the intermediate place could be a set of shared, detached, gate buttons.

- *C:* This structure combines the bad structures of *A-I* and *B-II* in a way that removes their bad properties while retaining the desirable property of *own-place waiting* provided by *A-II* and *B-I*. There is no free lunch: active transporters are required. This solution also eliminates synchronism as an issue, because the transporters are not bothered by latency delays.

What if a robot can be both a source and a sink? Then nothing really new is introduced. A strategy of combining the good solutions of Figure 8.11 would combine Solution A-II for events sourced at the robot with Solution B-I for events sunk at the robot, leading to a model in which a robot is always visited and never visits; in other words, sources visit it to give it events, and sinks visit it to wait for events. This requires a transport mechanism between robots, as shown in Solution *D*. The buffer solution of Solution *C* would also work. The discussions above about the advantages and disadvantages of these solutions still apply.

Recall that we saw canonical forms for transporter and buffer structures suitable for Solutions *C* and *D* in Chapter 6.

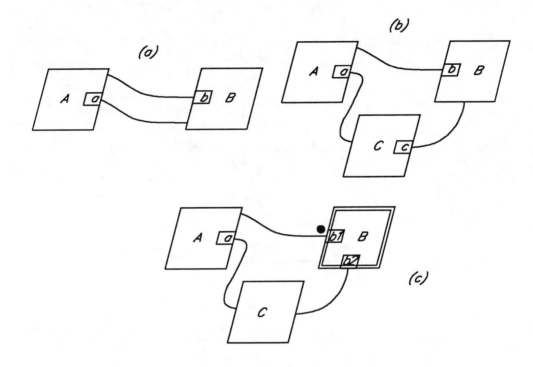

Figure 8.12: UNSAFE INTERACTION STRUCTURES

8.3.3 MUTUAL WAITING AND DEADLOCK

Deadlock is a complex issue with many ramifications. In this chapter, we are concerned with spotting visit patterns that can lead to mutual waiting at different places, without any possibility of the wait being satisfied. This form of deadlock may be called *structural deadlock*, because it arises from the connection and waiting structure of a system. Systems following the *committed waiting* model, in which all interactions are synchronous, like Ada, are particularly prone to this form of deadlock.

The canonical glue structures of Chapter 6 are free of structural deadlock. But what of less regular structures?

Figure 8.12 gives some examples of deadlock prone glue structures (presumably the interactions would also transfer information left out of these sketches). Temporal orderings leading to deadlock are shown in Figure 8.13. The sources of the deadlock are as follows:

- (a) A direct visit cycle in a structure chart.

- (b) An indirect visit cycle in a structure chart.

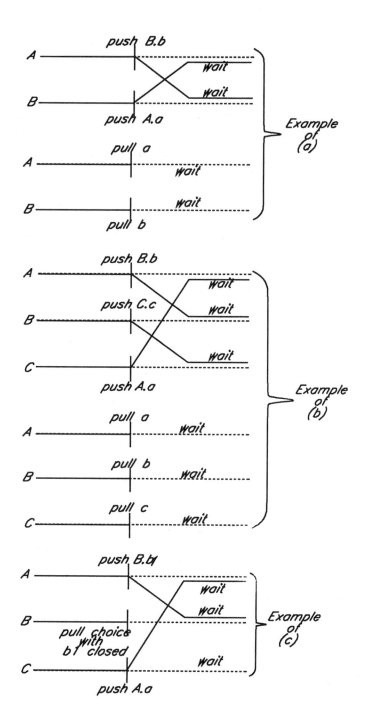

Figure 8.13: DEADLOCK SCENARIOS

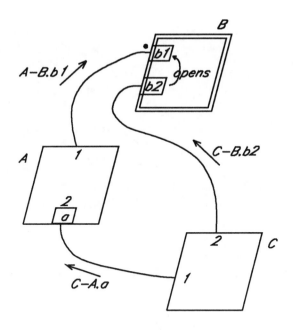

Figure 8.14: IDENTIFYING VISIT DEPENDENCY

- (c) A structure without apparent cycles that violates the principle of *one place to wait* by setting up a mixed waiting pattern, combining *other place waiting* (A waiting at B.b1) and *own place waiting* (A waiting at A.a). This is a very bad design because C, which supplies events that A waits for in its own place, also is the only possible supplier of events to change the waiting condition at B.b1 where A also waits. Note how deadlock in this example is independent of whether or not the waiting place B.b1 uses cold or warm waiting; in either case A will have to wait until the condition can be cleared by another interaction that can ever occur.

For cases where bad designs are not so obvious, Figure 8.14 and Figure 8.15 give a way of spotting hidden dependencies that might lead to deadlock. First give the visits names and directions; then draw a visit dependency graph showing which visits enable which other ones to be satisfied. A cycle in the latter graph may be unsafe, depending on the temporal ordering constraints or lack thereof imposed by the engine agendas. Analysis methods for deadlock are available in the literature that go deeper than this, but that is not our purpose here.

A lesson from this example is that irregular structures should be avoided.

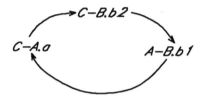

Figure 8.15: A VISIT DEPENDENCY GRAPH

8.3.4 CANONICAL GLUE STRUCTURES SUMMARIZED

Figure 8.16 summarizes canonical glue structures that provide safe waiting mechanisms for mutual delivery of events. In each case **M1** and **M2** are the peers; any other robots are intermediaries in glue structures. This figure summarizes the material on this subject in Chapter 6, and provides specific machinery for satisfying the requirements of Figure 8.11.

DIRECT INTERACTIONS

The direct glue structures are not general.

The configuration of Figure 8.16(a) is safe if the mutual visits are carefully ordered; one robot must make the first push, the other the first pull, and thereafter each robot's pushes and pulls must alternate. However, it is a very restrictive configuration, suitable only for particularly simple client-server relationships, not general peer-to-peer ones.

The configuration of Figure 8.16(b) illustrates a way of making a direct structure chart cycles safe, by using a balking visit in one direction. This concept is simple but requires additional logic to decide what to do if the visit fails and when and how often to try it again. The overall system is conceptually more complex.

The configuration of Figure 8.16(c) is appropriate where there is a client-server relationship in which all items generated by the server are a responses to earlier visits by the client. However, it is unsatisfactory for general peer-to-peer relationships, because the visitor picking up items must either poll, or wait (polling is unsatisfactory because it does not follow the recommended waiting paradigm, and waiting is unsatisfactory because waiting in one place holds up action in another).

TRANSPORTER SOLUTIONS

Figure 8.16(d) has a transporter in one direction. However, the remaining direct connection puts one of the peers at the mercy of the other's congestion or latency. This structure has the advantage over the next one of using fewer robots but the disadvantage of providing an asymmetric solution to what was posed as a symmetric problem (however, it is appropriate for asymmetric client-server interactions).

The solution of Figure 8.16(e) uses two transporters, one in each direction, each of which place-waits for items to transport. This solution is flexible because neither of the peers is at the mercy of the other's congestion or latency.

Figure 8.16(f) mimics a solution one often sees in human organizations for batched transport of items, where immediate delivery is not of concern but transport costs are of concern. A single transporter performs both pickup and delivery of batches of items in both directions, on a cyclic basis, without place-waiting. For low levels of interaction activity, this approach suffers from transport latency. For high levels of interaction activity in both directions, this solution may work as well as any other transporter solution. However, it seems unlikely that the transport cost factor that leads to the adoption of such solutions in the physical world would come into play in a computer system, unless the system were physically distributed and batched communication provided economies of scale.

Transporter solutions have great flexibility, but suffer from two disadvantages in certain circumstances:

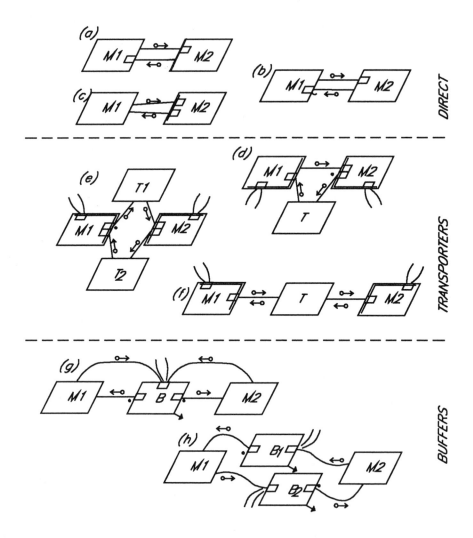

Figure 8.16: SAFE GLUE STRUCTURES

- the number of transporters required is proportional to the number of pairs of interacting peers, which could be high if each robot interacts with many others (although this can be reduced if some cases, as desribed in Chapter 6);

- there may be a need for internal buffering of items in the sender or target robots, if interaction activity is high.

BUFFER SOLUTIONS

Buffer configurations avoid these disadvantages, at a possible cost of some loss of flexibility. Figures 8.16(g) and 8.16(h) illustrate the possible approaches. Note that the fingers coming from other than **M1** and **M2** are important to the solution, because they provide other sources of visits that prevent what could otherwise be pairwise deadlock caused by **M1** and **M2** both waiting at their buffers, with nobody left to send. System-wide deadlock is still possible if everybody waits at their buffers at the same time, without anything being in the buffers; there must be at least one proactive robot in the system to ensure this does not happen (e.g., one that delivers events into the system from outside).

Possible loss of flexibility arises from a desire to keep processing logic particular to an application problem separate from transfer logic needed to get items from place to place. Attached buttons with waiting places provide a screening mechanism in the place where the application processing is performed that is easily tailored to the application; this power is missing from a separate, general purpose buffer (of course, the buffer could be provided with application-specific screening, but this now splits application logic among several different places, which is not modular).

DISCUSSION

In terms of efficiency, both transporter and buffer approaches require the same number of visits to transfer data between a pair of primary robots.

> IMPLEMENTATION IMPLICATIONS: However, this is somewhat misleading for a multitasking interpretation: the number of task context switches may be higher for the transporter approach, because the buffer approach may be able to eliminate some context switching due to buffers being passive.

Multi-way glue structures among many robots may be handled by piecing together pairwise glue structures from Figure 8.16 in a consistent fashion.

To be avoided are ad-hoc combinations of different forms of glue structures. Such combinations could contain hidden deadlocks due to pernicious combinations of interaction patterns, even when cycles are not present in the structure chart. An example of this kind of deadlock was given in Figure 8.12(c).

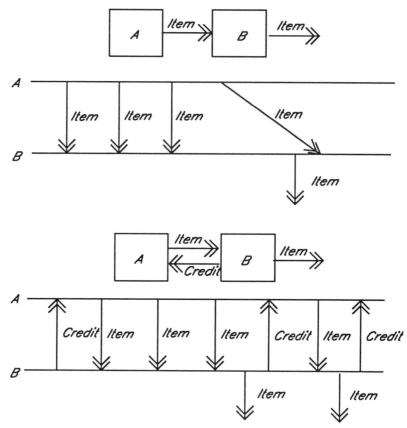

Figure 8.17: THE NATURE OF FLOW CONTROL

8.4   FLOW CONTROL

8.4.1   INTRODUCTION

When items must flow from place to place in a system, the possibility exists that sinks may sometimes be temporarily overtaxed, due to storage or other limitations; then some form of flow control must be exercised by the sinks. Figure 8.17 illustrates the nature of the problem, showing how a sink's ability to continue receiving items may depend on other factors, such as the successful transfer of (perhaps) consequential outgoing items from itself to some other place. Item transfer from its sources may need to be held up in the meantime. Two possibilities exist: one is the brute force blockage of a transfers that may have already started (as shown at the top of the figure); the other is some form of protocol that ensures items are not held or transferred when they are not wanted by the sink (as shown at the bottom of the figure).

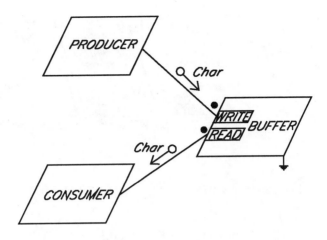

Figure 8.18: BRUTE FORCE FLOW CONTROL

8.4.2 A SIMPLE EXAMPLE

Figure 8.18 illustrates use of a buffer to smooth fluctuations in production and consumption of items between a producer and a consumer. It shows two styles of item transfer between sources and sinks, one in the direction of a visit, and the other in the reverse direction, with brute force flow control exercised on both of them.

The producer is a source that visits a sink (the buffer) to deposit items (characters) via a **WRITE** gate-button; the buffer exercises brute force flow control by closing the button.

The consumer is a sink that visits a source (the buffer) to pick up items held by it via a **READ** gate-button; the consumer exercises brute force flow control indirectly, by not picking up items as quickly as they are produced. This eventually reflects back to the producer through the imposition of brute force flow control on it by the buffer when its internal storage is full.

The **READ** interaction is naturally synchronous, whether or not the **WRITE** one is. If the **WRITE** one is synchronous, as it is here, then the producer is stopped cold by the imposition of flow control, which is a bit drastic if it has anything else to do.

Scenarios are left for the reader.

Rather than stopping a visiting source cold without warning, as is done here, one might wish to allow it to continue. This would be possible if the buffer stopped the flow by refusing to accept items from the visiting source during a normal deposit interaction, leaving the source with the responsibility of repeatedly retrying until the item is acceptable. However, this ties up not only processing resources (through polling), but also system resources (space to hold items that cannot be accepted at the sink). In this case the system resources are not large (space for one character), but one might have much larger items, such as screen windows, or even entire files, without changing the logic of this example at all.

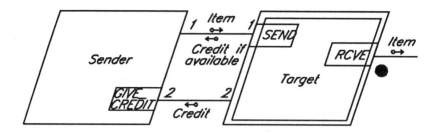

Figure 8.19: DIRECT 2-WAY INTERACTION ON CREDIT

8.4.3   OTHER, LESS DRASTIC POSSIBILITIES

Giving warning of impending flow control is not going to work in general, because a race could easily take place between the warning arriving at the source and the source producing an item for the sink (this race might result in deadlock, as illustrated by the earlier, general discussion of deadlock). One needs prior agreement between sources and sinks that items may be produced and transferred.

A way of doing this is with a credit protocol. Sinks tell sources in advance how many items may be accumulated for pickup. The sink stops accumulation or transfer action when the credit runs out and does not start again until items are picked up or more credit becomes available. In its simplest form, credit would take the form of a count of the number of acceptable items.

The following figures illustrate some different ways of doing this. Only brief textual explanations of each are given; the reader should be able to infer from previous discussions and examples not only the motivation for trying these different ways but also details of visit scenarios and appropriate code. In other words, these examples illustrate earlier material in ways that do not need long-winded explanation. In these figures, the sink is called *target* and the source is called *sender*. Note how the figures illustrate that a protocol may be implicit in the glue structure, or hidden in underlying message sequences, or some mix of the two. Making it explicit in the glue structure is a desirable approach for visual prototyping.

2-WAY INTERACTION

Figure 8.19 has the sink visiting the source to give credit after credit has run out. To avoid a race resulting in deadlock, this visit must take place only when the sink knows that the source is not going to send anything. The parameters in the figure suggest how this may be accomplished, because the intended protocol is implicit in the glue structure. Sinks must know their sources, either statically as shown here, or dynamically as discussed in a later chapter.

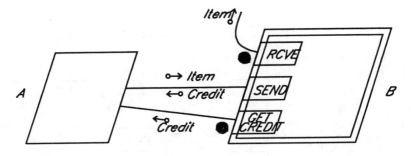

Figure 8.20: A LINEAR INTERFACE STRUCTURE FOR CREDIT

ONE-WAY INTERACTION WITH A LINEAR INTERFACE

Alternatively, a *linear interface structure* may be used that allows the source to visit the sink at its own convenience to get credit after it has run out, as shown by Figure 8.20. This has the disadvantage mentioned of not providing *own-place-waiting* for the source (a transporter could be used to resolve this if it is important). This is a more specific example of a client-server interaction of the kind discussed in Chapter 4, except that here we assume the client will not behave badly. Again, the intended protocol is implicit in the glue structure.

HIDING THE DETAILS OF A LINEAR INTERFACE STRUCTURE

The details can be hidden by packaging as shown in Figure 8.21. A result is that that senders can no longer do anything in between the disappearance of credit and its reinstatement. Superficially, it appears we are back to brute force flow control, implying that the simpler structure of the earlier buffer example would do the job just as well. However there is a subtle, but important difference here. This approach is only brute force relative to the sender, not to the items being transferred. It ensures that items are never hanging around unable to be absorbed, thus avoiding the problem of tying up resources (apart from the sender itself) unecessarily.

COMPRESSING A LINEAR STRUCTURE

If there is no need for a visitor to an interface with a linear interface structure to do something else between making a request and waiting for it to be completed, then one may compress the linear structure by using *warm waiting* at the request place, instead of having a separate button purely for waiting as in all the flow control examples up till now. The consequences of this idea for this example are shown in Figure 8.22 (the request place is **SEND** and the separate waiting place missing is the earlier **GET_CREDIT**). This accomplishes the external purpose of Figure 8.21 using a more compact interaction mechanism. The waiting marker would be annotated to indicate the condition for releasing the sender; this condition would be changed by arrival of a receiver.

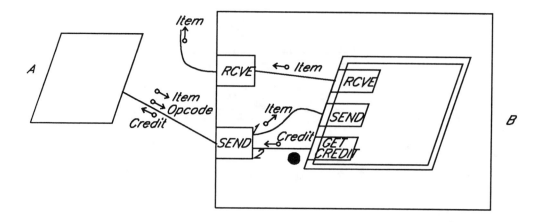

Figure 8.21: HIDING THE DETAILS

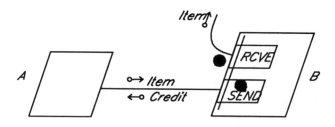

Figure 8.22: A COMPRESSED LINEAR STRUCTURE

IMPLEMENTATION IMPLICATIONS: This mechanism is not available in many implementation technologies (e.g., Ada), in which case the earlier representation should be used, or this one interpreted in terms of it. This illustrates a theme that reappears over and over again in this book: that design ideas are expressible in many forms and that it is not always appropriate to insist that the form matches available implementation technology, provided it can be easily mapped into a form that does; Figure 8.21 may be viewed as the mapping of Figure 8.22 that is appropriate for Ada.

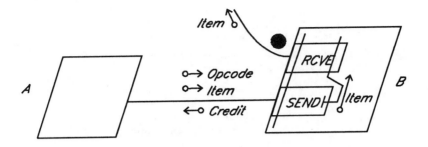

Figure 8.23: A NONLINEAR INTERFACE STRUCTURE

EMULATING A COMPRESSED, LINEAR STRUCTURE WITH A NONLINEAR ONE

The weaker mechanism of nesting meetings in other meetings may be used to emulate the compressed solution just described, as illustrated by Figure 8.23. A pull of a button during a meeting resulting from a push on another button results eventually in a nested meeting, in which termination of the first one is deferred until the second one finishes. In the meantime, the first visitor is experiencing warm waiting. This is the LIFO-meeting model identified earlier. This approach may not work for more general problems, as was shown in Chapter 5.

> IMPLEMENTATION IMPLICATIONS: Nesting is the only way of accomplishing warm waiting directly in Ada. Figure 8.24 shows how.

A BUFFER STRUCTURE BASED ON MESSAGING

In the examples up till now, the flow control protocol has been implicit in the glue structure. A completely different approach that hides the protocol is illustrated by Figure 8.25. This approach uses buffers as the only points of interaction, following configuration (h) of Figure 8.16. The buffers are owned by the sender and target, in the sense that each is the only one that waits to **GET** from its own buffer. Anyone may **PUT** messages in an owned buffer, but not **GET** from it. The flows of item and credit messages shown are just specific examples of messages; more than just item messages may be sent to the target via its **PUT**; more than just credit messages may be sent to the sender via its **PUT**. In fact the whole structure is so entirely application independent that it reveals nothing about what is going on. A separate description of the protocol (not given here) would be required by scenario and/or operational specification.

```
task body SOURCE is
...
begin
  loop
    select
      when ITEM_AVAILABLE =>
        accept RCVE (item:  out ...) do
          -- OUTPUT ITEM
        end;
    or
        accept SEND (item: in ...; credit: out ...) do
          -- INPUT ITEM
          if credit=0 then
            accept RCVE(item: out ...) do
              -- OUTPUT ITEM
            end;
          else -- STORE ITEM AND DECREMENT CREDIT
          end if;
        end;
    end select;
  end loop;
```

Figure 8.24: WARM WAITING BY NESTED RENDEZVOUS IN ADA

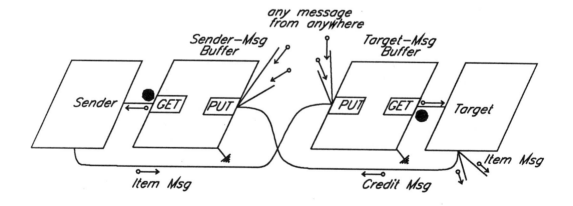

Figure 8.25: A BUFFER STRUCTURE HIDES THE PROTOCOL

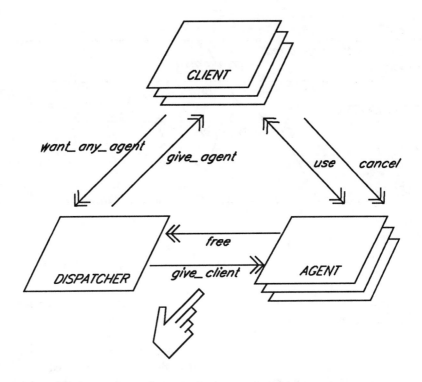

Figure 8.26: PATTERN 1: EVENT FLOWS IN AN AGENT POOL PROBLEM

8.5 CRITICAL RACES AND THEIR AVOIDANCE

8.5.1 THE NATURE OF CRITICAL RACES

Races abound in concurrent systems. Critical races cause errors and must be avoided. The purpose of this section is to show visual ways of reasoning about critical races, as a step in helping the reader to develop an eye for spotting the possibility of them in structure charts. The discussion centers around a problem where a dispatcher controls access by clients to a pool of agents. Recall from the client-server problem of Chapter 4 and the allocator problem of Chapter 5 that critical races can easily occur in such problems when the performance of some purposeful activity requires multiple visits by multiple visitors to the same places.

Critical races may be encouraged by race-prone event patterns in the preliminary design. They may be avoided by designing proper machinery when such patterns exist, or by avoiding such patterns in the first place, as will now be explained.

8.5.2 RACE-PRONE EVENT PATTERNS

Figure 8.26 shows a particular structural pattern of event flows that is prone to critical races. The part of this pattern causing the problem is agents needing to be informed by the

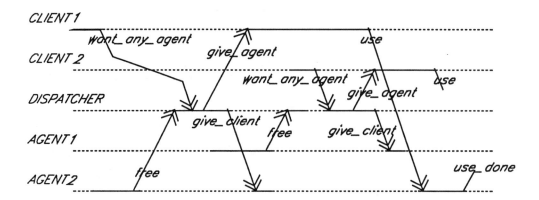

Figure 8.27: PATTERN 1 EVENT SCENARIO

dispatcher that they have been allocated — by means of the **give-client** event — before beginning interactions with clients (perhaps to provide advance information that will enable, for example, agents to check the credentials of clients later, or to perform preparatory work to get ready for clients, such as establishing communication connections). Why this pattern is prone to critical races will become clear as designs are developed.

Figure 8.27 gives an example of intended temporal event sequences for Pattern 1. All the ensuing designs identified as 1-A, 1-B, etc., refer to Pattern 1 (a second pattern is treated later).

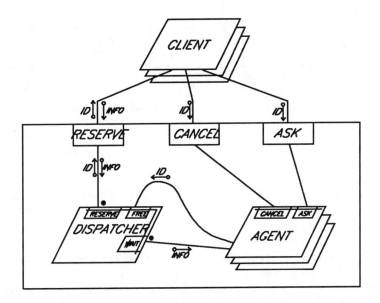

Figure 8.28: DESIGN 1-A: A PLAUSIBLE-LOOKING FIRST PASS

8.5.3 DESIGN 1-A

Figure 8.28 is a flattened structure chart, showing two structure charts in the same diagram: a partial client level chart, and an internal chart for the allocation subsystem. Note that in neither chart has design proceeded beyond the detailed outside design stage. The inside chart shows a plausible looking design to solve the allocation problem. The significant points to observe are that **free** event in Figure 8.26 has been mapped to a visit by an agent to **FREE**, with an agent-identification parameter going in the direction of the visit, and the **give-client** event to a return by the agent from a visit to **WAIT**, with a returned parameter giving advance information. **WAIT** is a cold waiting place where agents wait to be allocated to clients.

Figure 8.29 shows how Design 1-A is intended to work. Figure 8.30 and Figure 8.31 show that it cannot be guaranteed to work properly, due to a critical race that mixes up clients and agents, such that agent 2 is waiting for client 1 at its own place, while client 1 is waiting for agent 1 at agent1's place.

The two figures show alternate ways of visualizing the problem. Figure 8.31 shows

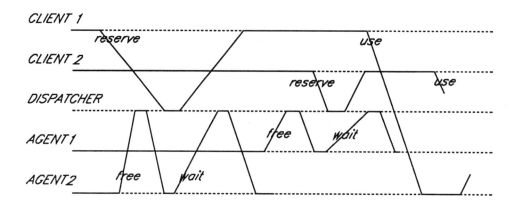

Figure 8.29: DESIGN 1-A: VISIT SCENARIO SHOWING EXPECTED BEHAVIOUR

how one tends to think about it while drawing or observing structure, and to explain it to colleagues in design reviews. However, drawing visit threads on structures in this way can make diagrams incomprehensible if extended patterns need to be examined. Figure 8.31 shows how to record extended patterns.

The pattern revealed by these figures looks like deadlock but in fact is not because a later client will get things moving again. However, there is a mysterious and unnecessary wait for service by the first client, and the ensuing meetings by clients with agents will be the wrong way round (meaning that agents will have advance information for the wrong clients).

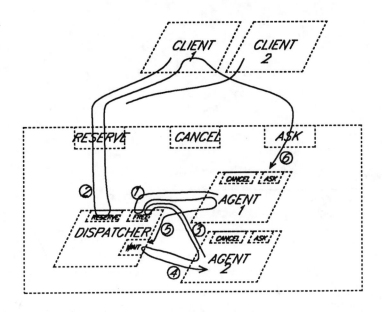

Figure 8.30: DESIGN 1-A: AN EXAMPLE OF RACING VISIT THREADS

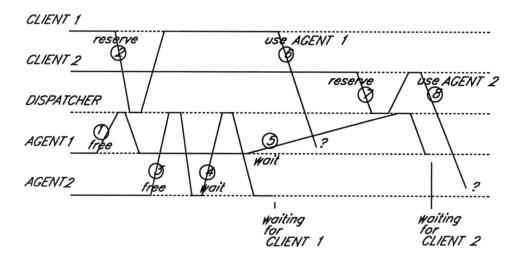

Figure 8.31: DESIGN 1-A: A CRITICAL RACE

8.5.4 DESIGN 1-B

The problem with design 1-A is that it makes an incorrect assumption that agents will always arrive at **WAIT** in the same order they left **FREE**. We know from Chapters 4 and 5 that a conceptual solution to this problem is that shown in Figure 8.32; it gets rid of the critical race by providing individual waiting places for agents.

8.5.5 DESIGN 1-C

Figure 8.33 eliminates the critical race by bringing the dispatcher, the agent and the client together in a 3-way, nested meeting. With this solution, the dispatcher waits for a client first at **RESERVE** and then, while still interlocked with the client, waits for an available agent at **FREE**, taking the first agent to come along. This is satisfactory only if *any* agent will do. Reciprocally, agents wait for clients. The solution is a mapping of the warm waiting concept of Chapter 5.

Note that the ability to use nesting here depends on a particular characteristic of the problem: the dispatcher has a pivotal place where a visitor must arrive before there is any need to look elsewhere for visitors, namely the **RESERVE** button. This is not a characteristic of waiting problems in general.

8.5.6 DESIGN 1-D

Figure 8.34 shows another nonlinear solution that has, however, more interactions, making it less attractive from a structural viewpoint. However, it is also more flexible, because the dispatcher can reserve whichever free agent it desires.

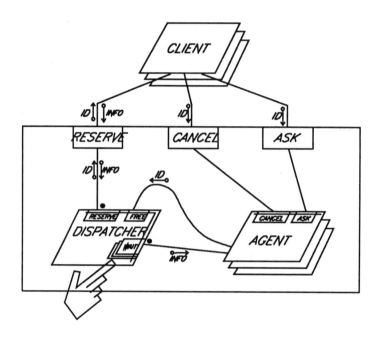

Figure 8.32: DESIGN 1-B: SPECIFIC WAITING PLACES ELIMINATE CRITICAL RACE

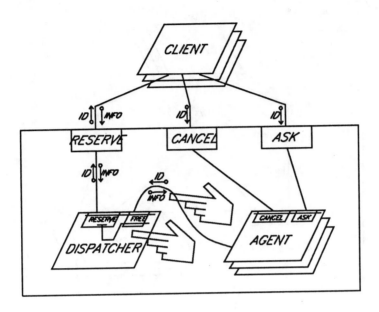

Figure 8.33: DESIGN 1-C: A NONLINEAR, RACE-FREE SOLUTION

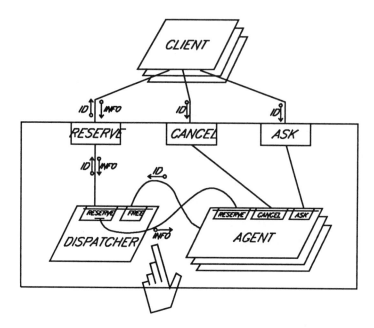

Figure 8.34: DESIGN 1-D: A LESS RESTRICTIVE BUT BUSIER NONLINEAR SOLU-
TION

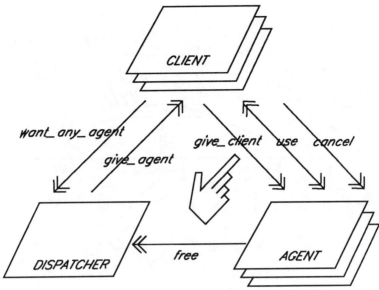

Figure 8.35: PATTERN 2: CLIENT-AGENT EVENT FLOWS

8.5.7 RACE-FREE EVENT PATTERNS

Figure 8.35 shows a different pattern of client-agent-dispatcher event flows in which the constraint that the dispatcher must tell the agent it has been allocated is removed. With this design, any advance information required by an agent must be handed over directly by the client.

Design 2-A: Figure 8.36 hides from clients the fact that the allocation pattern has been changed. However, internally, the **RESERVE** button on the allocation box visits the agent's **RESERVE** button on behalf of the client to effect the new pattern.

Design 2-B: Figure 8.37 doesn't hide the new allocation pattern from clients. In fact, it offers an entirely new design, following a notifier paradigm, in which clients wait in their own places for the **give-agent** event; in other words, the **give-agent** event is mapped into a visit from the dispatcher to the client. This visit is made possible by the client "sending itself" to the dispatcher, using the instance flow notation of Chapter 5 (this would imply that client instances are installed from a template, but this is not shown). Chapter 10 has more on such structures.

There is a need to return the identification of the allocated agent to the client in two places, to cover the two possibilities that an agent may be available immediately (eliminating the need for the notification at **GO**), or not until later. If an agent is not available immediately, the identification returned by **RESERVE** will have a special value.

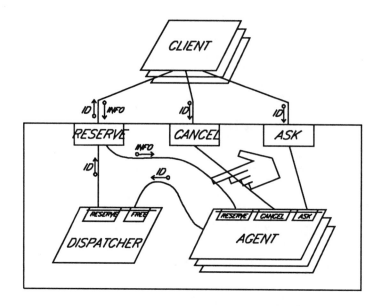

Figure 8.36: DESIGN 2-A: A LINEAR, RACE-FREE SOLUTION

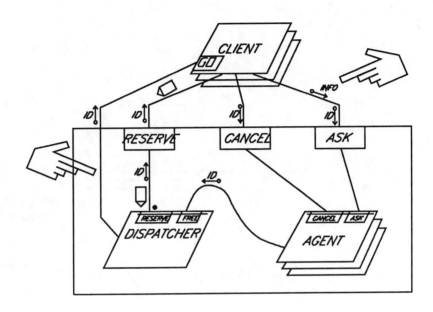

Figure 8.37: DESIGN 2-B: A LINEAR, RACE-FREE SOLUTION WITH NOTIFICATION

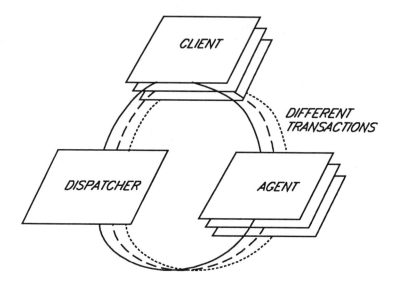

Figure 8.38: TRANSACTIONS IN THE AGENT POOL PROBLEM

8.5.8 REMARKS

The aim with this example has been to show how to use the notation to spot and correct potential critical races at the design level, before machinery inside components has been designed. Basically, critical races may arise if multiple transactions involving multiple actors are taking place concurrently, where each transaction involves the same set of interactions among the actors (perhaps only partially ordered). The informal meaning of the term "transaction" is illustrated, for this particular problem, in Figure 8.38. The lines between actors in this figure mean only that they must interact. The union of the interaction lines that binds a specific set of robots to accomplishing a specific application purpose identifies a transaction. If there is more than one transaction associated with a particular robot, there is a possibility of a critical race, because of the possibility of mixing up transactions at critical interaction points. (Note that the use of the term transaction here is consistent with its use in common practice, where it implies the accomplishment of some application purpose that may involve multiple components and interactions).

To spot the possibility of a critical race, look for places where a party to one transaction might be mistaken for a party to another one in a way that would cause errors (such as giving advance information for one client to a different agent than the one to which the client has already been allocated). This requires knowledge of how the components process interactions relative to the objectives of each transaction, and seems therefore to require knowledge of internal machinery and agendas. Such knowledge is required for formal analysis, but a designer who understands the intended temporal behaviour of a system can spot the critical race possibilities from the outside, by looking for places where agendas might make assumptions about ordering of interactions, either inadvertently, or because there is no other choice.

When critical interactions causing critical races are identified, the solutions are to coalesce or eliminate interactions (e.g., Design 1-C), or to provide machinery for distinguishing interactions belonging to different transactions (e.g., Design 1-B), as was illustrated by the various designs of this case study.

8.6　PRIORITY

8.6.1　INTRODUCTION

Static priorities in MachineCharts are identified by integers attached to robots (indicating relative priorities of different robots) or to buttons (indicating relative priorities of different buttons on a particular robot's interface). The problem of remembering whether small or large numbers indicate high priorities is a universally annoying one. Smaller numbers for high priorities have a common sense appeal (**1** means first, **2** means second, and so forth), so that is how they are represented in MachineCharts.

8.6.2　BUTTON PRIORITY

We have already seen examples of priority allocation to buttons, and of unsafe and safe machinery for enforcing it, in Chapter 4, in association with two examples, line-to-character conversion, and semaphores. This section continues with some further discussion of issues.

8.6.3　ROBOT PRIORITY

TWO DIFFERENT MODELS

Remember that MachineCharts assumes robots are fully concurrent, so assigning priority to them has no meaning in the sense of positioning them in a ready to run queue (the concept of a ready to run queue is in the implementation technology, not MachineCharts).

There are a number of possible models of priority that one might assume for MachineCharts. The first and simplest is that the priority of a visiting robot determines its position in the queue of any button it visits. A more powerful model might allow a high priority visiting robot to preempt a current lower priority meeting, resuming it later. Whatever model of priority is assumed, there are two ways of working with robot priority in MachineChart design:

- Give all robots the same priority and design the glue structures so priority of service is provided by explicit control where it is needed, rather than by implicit semantics everywhere.

   IMPLEMENTATION IMPLICATIONS: This is the way one has to do it for Ada, because the Ada priority model only prioritizes tasks relative to the ready to run queue of a single processor. Ada does not prioritize tasks in entry queues, which are FIFO. One may assign priorities to robots for Ada design, simply to indicate this is the implementation intent for the corresponding tasks, but one must specifically design priority queuing mechanisms where they are required.

- Assign priorities to robots and assume deeper MachineChart priority semantics.

   IMPLEMENTATION IMPLICATIONS: This is a useful approach when designing for implementation technologies where run time system semantics support priorities in the manner desired. It may be appropriate to assume different MachineChart priority semantics to match the intended implementation technology, enabling designs to be as simple as possible. However, then one loses independence of implementation technology. Care must be taken to state the assumed priority semantics for designs clearly, so that simple designs that assume deep priority semantics can be mapped into more complicated designs for implementation technologies that do not provide support.

PRIORITY INVERSION

As an illustration of how sensible MachineChart designs can have pathologies when implementation technologies don't support the obvious interpretation, consider the structure of Figure 8.39. The three robots run concurrently, in principle. *HIGH* should be able to interact with *LOW* without concern for what *MEDIUM* is up to. One might expect a run time system to guarantee this by ensuring that *LOW's* priority is dynamically raised when it is visited by *HIGH*.

IMPLEMENTATION IMPLICATIONS: Correct operation of this example is not guaranteed if the run time system treats *MEDIUM* as the highest priority ready to run task at the time *HIGH* calls *LOW*, as as illustrated by the timing diagram at the bottom of the figure (note that this is not a MachineChart scenario, because it shows interleaving of tasks on the same processor not concurrent operation of robots); this is called priority inversion. Ada run time systems that do not raise the priority of tasks according to the priority of tasks in their entry queues will cause priority inversion.

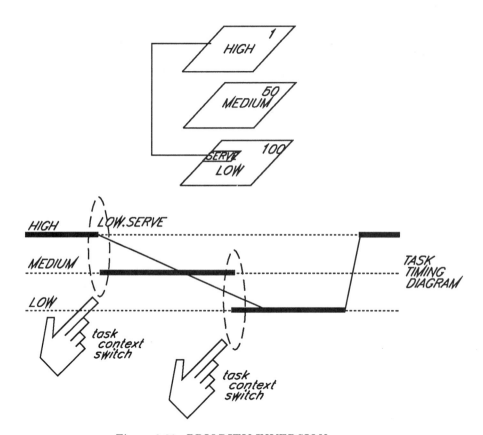

Figure 8.39: PRIORITY INVERSION

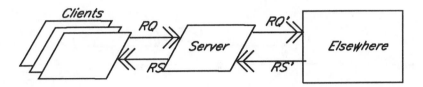

Figure 8.40: A TIMEOUT PROBLEM

8.7 TIMEOUT

8.7.1 INTRODUCTION

Here follows an example illustrating some practical ramifications of using timeout in a design. The framework for discussion is a client-server problem in which clients are only willing to wait so long for service. Timeout was discussed in a preliminary way in relation to a client-server problem in Chapter 4, and it has been referred to elsewhere in relation to the safety of certain Ada methods of achieving button priority, but the intent here is to explore the timeout problem in more depth, to give insights into the many ways it can be handled, and the pathologies of some of them.

Figure 8.40 and Figure 8.41 set the stage; results may take too long to arrive, or fail to arrive. In these figures, **RQ** stands for request, and **RS** for result. As shown in Figure 8.41, timeouts may have to be cancelled when they are no longer required, and stale results arriving after timeouts have occurred may have to be discarded. The responsibilities for these matters may be given to the client or the server, or shared between them.

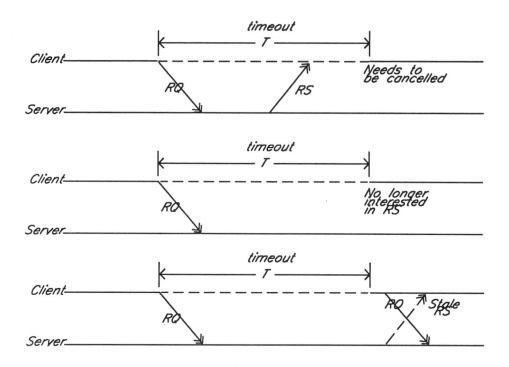

Figure 8.41: TIMEOUT EVENT SCENARIOS

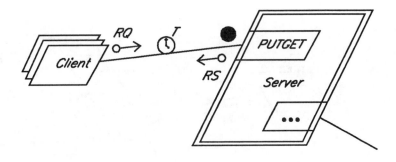

Figure 8.42: DESIGN 1 IS BASICALLY FLAWED

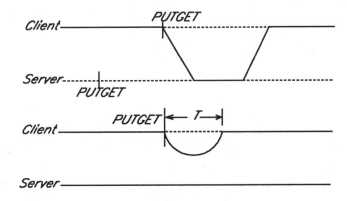

Figure 8.43: HOW DESIGN 1 DOES NOT WORK

8.7.2 DESIGN 1

Design 1 (Figure 8.42, 8.43) is so basically flawed that it would be ludicrous to include it as a design alternative, except that it serves to reemphasize some points about the notation. **PUTGET** cannot be used as a place to both put the request and get the result, because it is a cold waiting place. Furthermore, timeout is supposed to be on waiting for a result from the server, not on waiting for a first meeting with the server, as the mechanism in the figure would do (as soon as the meeting starts, the timeout is implicitly cancelled).

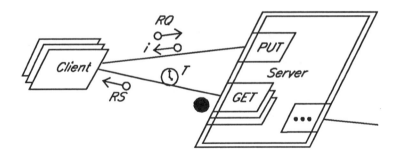

Figure 8.44: DESIGN 2 STRUCTURE

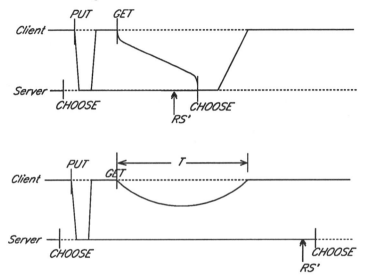

Figure 8.45: SIMPLE BEHAVIOUR OF DESIGN 2

8.7.3   DESIGN 2

Design 2 (Figure 8.44, 8.45, 8.46) is essentially the the client-server design of Chapter 4 (Figure 4.40) repeated here for comparison with the other approaches. In this case, the client does not provide a parameter that can be used to identify a waiting place, so the server must provide the parameter (**i** here).

Figure 8.45 shows how this design is expected to work without timeout, and Figure 8.46 shows the need for "timestamping" (i.e., uniquely identifying) requests, so that stale results can be distinguished from good ones after timeout has occurred. With this design, discarding stale results is the responsibility of the server, during a **GET** meeting with the client, forcing the client to perform another visit to **GET** to wait for a desired result.

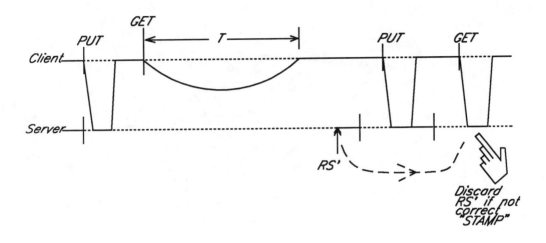

Figure 8.46: DESIGN 2 MUST UNIQUELY IDENTIFY RESULTS

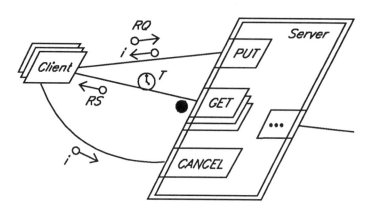

Figure 8.47: DESIGN 3 STRUCTURE

8.7.4   DESIGN 3

Design 3 (Figure 8.47, 8.48) tries to forestall the need for the second **GET** required by Design 2 by providing an explicit **CANCEL** button on the server that enables cancelling a previous request after a timeout. The desired behaviour is shown in Figure 8.48. Providing an explicit cancel operation eliminates the need for timestamping, if the client obeys the rules and does not try to get a new result before cancelling an old one. However, the interface is more complex, and nothing really has been saved from a temporal behaviour viewpoint, because the visit now required to **CANCEL** replaces the second visit to **GET** required by Design 2.

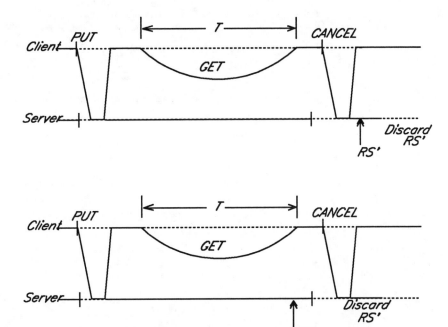

Figure 8.48: BEHAVIOUR OF DESIGN 3

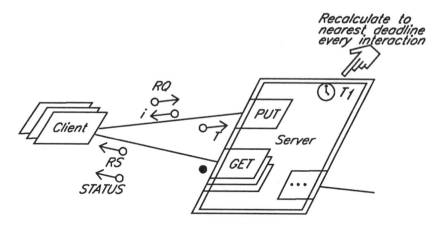

Figure 8.49: DESIGN 4 STRUCTURE

8.7.5   DESIGN 4

Design 4 (Figure 8.49) places the responsibility for timing out on the server, instead of the client. This eliminates the need for timestamping or cancelling in client-server interactions, but requires the server to recalculate deadlines every time it processes an interaction.

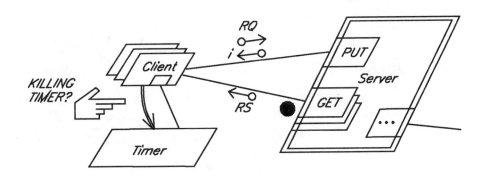

Figure 8.50: DESIGN 5 STRUCTURE

8.7.6   DESIGNS 5 AND 6

Designs 5 and 6 (Figures 8.50, 8.51, 8.52) are not good ones, because of races between timers to time out, clients to cancel timers, and servers to produce results before timeout. The designs as drawn in Figures 8.50 and 8.51 are incomplete, because they do not show timer initialization or cancellation; Figure 8.52 shows some possibilities. Design 5 matches up with Design 2, and Design 6 with Design 3, with the timer robot providing timeout instead of the previous mechanism. Drawing scenarios to illustrate the possibilities is left to the reader.

Timer cancellation is a big source of trouble in these designs, as hinted at by Figure 8.52. The dynamic installation and removal tricks of this figure are covered in more detail in Chapter 10. The timer may be cancelled by asking it to **KILL** itself.

- In Design 5 (Part I of the figure), this could result in deadlock, because of a race between the timer visiting the client to report timeout, and the client visiting the timer to cancel it, unless the **KILL** visit is balking as shown in Part I (recall that this is one of the approaches to avoid deadlock given in Figure 8.16).

- In Design 6 (Part II of the figure), the visit to **KILL** could encounter an already dead timer, because the convention here would be that the timer would terminate after visiting **CANCEL** at the server. Again, a balking visit to **KILL** is appropriate.

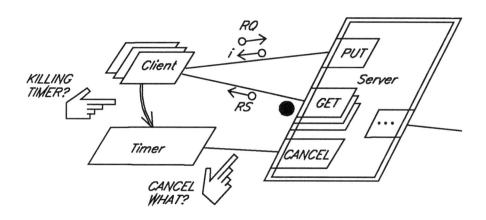

Figure 8.51: DESIGN 6 STRUCTURE

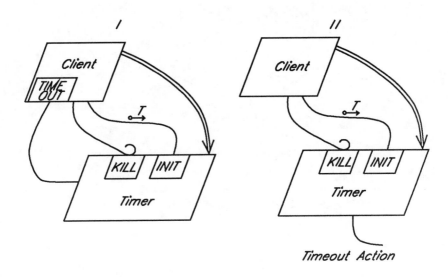

Figure 8.52: TIMER ISSUES IN DESIGNS 5 AND

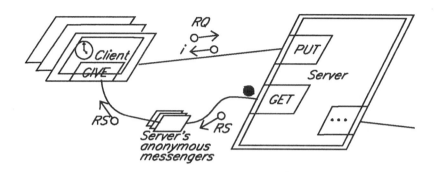

Figure 8.53: DESIGN 7 STRUCTURE

8.7.7   DESIGNS 7 AND 8

Finally, Designs 7 and 8 (Figures 8.53, 8.54) show an underlying configuration that was identified in Figure 8.11 as a poor one: a single source (the server) delivers events to a number of different sinks (the clients). These designs provide different fixes for the problem. With either design, clients time out in their own places, waiting for visits at **GIVE**. Without the extra machinery shown in the figures, the configuration has the problem that servers could end up stuck at **GIVE** because clients have timed out and are performing some alternate action.

Design 7 (Figure 8.53) is essentially configuration (d) of Figure 8.16. There is a transporter for each client that delivers the results for the server. This eliminates the problem of the server having to leave its own place, to possibly get stuck at a client's place. However, there is now a new problem. After a client times out, a transporter may arrive at **GIVE** with a stale result. If so, the client will now have to wait at **GIVE** again while the transporter goes through another **GET-GIVE** cycle, introducing unnecessary latency into the delivery and pickup of results. If timeouts are rare occurrences, perhaps this can be tolerated, but perhaps not, depending on the application requirements.

Observe that Design 7 in effect turns Design 2 around, by replacing the fixed number of designated waiting places at the server for clients with a pool of messengers that deliver results to clients. An advantage of this approach is that the messengers of the pool can be installed dynamically, avoiding the need to know how many waiting places there must be in advance. Recall from Chapter 5 that another approach with the same advantage is to use a pool of detached reactors as waiting places.

Design 8 (Figure 8.54) is essentially configuration (b) of Figure 8.16. It solves the problem in a different way, by having the server balk on visits to the client to deliver results. However, a new problem is that the server cannot assume that an unsatisfied visit means it can throw away a stale result; the client might not have timed out, but just be busy interacting with other visitors. This leaves the server with the problem of deciding when to try re-delivery.

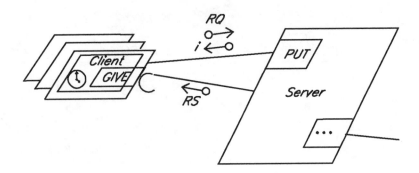

Figure 8.54: DESIGN 8 STRUCTURE

8.7.8 RULES OF THUMB

We may extract some rules of thumb from this case study:

- Do not distribute timeout control.

- Do not complicate timeout problems by adding unnecessary concurrency to them in the form of active timers that may artificially create critical races.

  IMPLEMENTATION IMPLICATIONS: The only circumstance in which an active timer might be justified is when the basic waiting mechanism does not provide for timeout. Then an active timer may be necessary to supply timeout events; and then one must deal with the race conditions that arise.

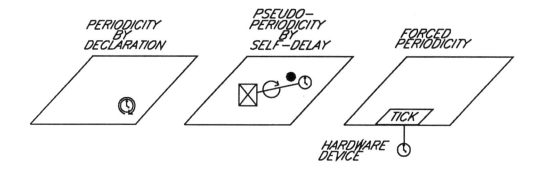

Figure 8.55: WAYS OF REPRESENTING PERIODICITY

8.8   REAL TIME

8.8.1   INTRODUCTION

So far, our only concern with time has been in relation to timeouts, where accurate timing is not usually important. This section aims to expose some issues associated with real time, and to relate them to the notation.

8.8.2   THE PROBLEM OF FUZZY TIME

A periodic robot and ways of representing how it might work are shown in Figure 8.55.

> IMPLEMENTATION IMPLICATIONS: As illustrated by Figure 8.56, self-delay does not work very well as a practical way of achieving periodicity in multitasking systems because of slippage and jitter. Driving a periodic component from an external clock is the only practical way of achieving true periodicity (a single scheduler may drive many such periodic components at different time scales).

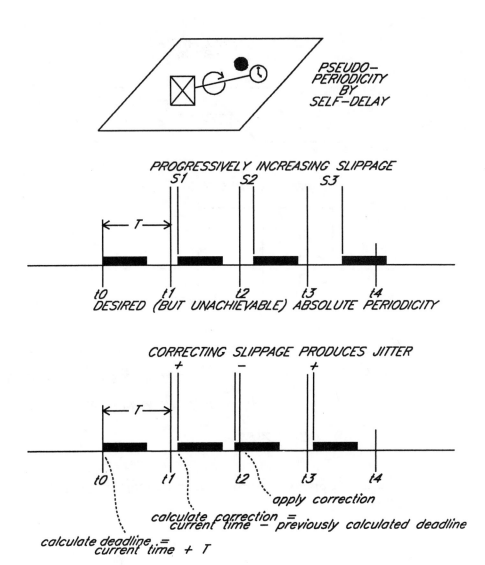

Figure 8.56: SLIPPAGE AND JITTER IN SELF-DELAY

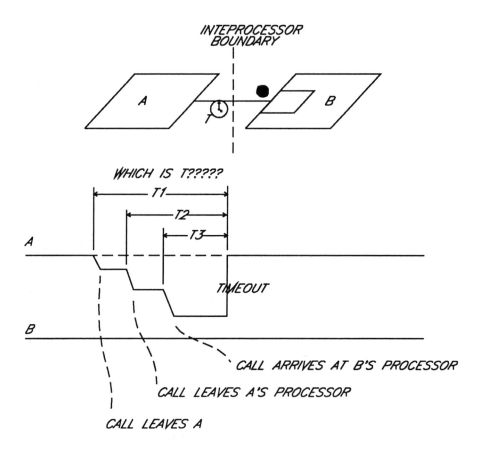

Figure 8.57: FUZZY TIMEOUT IN DISTRIBUTED SYSTEMS

Timers may be associated with push and pull fingers and with choice frames to provide timeout on waiting for interactions.

> IMPLEMENTATION IMPLICATIONS: Remember that timeout periods have a certain inevitable fuzziness in multitasking and multiprocessing systems. Timeout is like self-delay in having slippage associated with multitasking overhead. Figure 8.57 shows how there may also be fuzziness due to multiprocessing. Different implementation technologies may place different interpretations on timeout in relation to this diagram. From this point of view, Ada is not a single implementation technology, because the language reference manual does not specify any particular interpretation.

8.8.3   THE DIFFERENCE BETWEEN SOFT AND HARD REAL TIME

In computerspeak, the term *real time* is so overused that to indicate we are serious about it we must call it *hard real time* (thus suggesting that the normal use of the phrase implies *soft real time*). Soft real time is concerned with providing mechanisms for timeouts, and with arranging matters such that during periods of high load or overload, responses to urgent events are adequately fast. Hard real time is concerned with guaranteeing periodicity, or response time by a deadline.

Do the methods of this book have anything to do with hard real time? The answer is that they can be used to express intent, but must be mapped to hard real time technology to realize it, and there are no examples of how to do that in the book (the book gives only multitasking software examples, expressed using Ada, and multitasking is essentially a soft real time technology).

Chapter 9

A CASE STUDY: READERS-WRITERS

9.1 INTRODUCTION

This chapter provides an extended case study showing how insight into temporal behaviour guides the choice of structural form. It does so painstakingly for a particular problem, by revealing a little bit about temporal behaviour using scenarios and state machines, drawing structure charts to represent a solution, and then showing flaws in the solution that lead in turn to more scenarios, state machines and structure charts. An experienced designer might do much of this mentally, and go much more directly to a suitable solution; the many figures in this chapter aim to illustrate this thinking process, not to suggest that such large numbers of diagrams should be drawn for practical problems.

The chapter also contains several examples of the use of abstract state machines (ASMs) and abstract controller machines (ACMs).

The design path followed in this chapter is generally that of Figure 3.43 of Chapter 3.

9.2 STATEMENT OF THE PROBLEM

The problem is to control access to a resource by a number of *readers*, who may safely access the resource concurrently, and *writers*, who must have exclusive access to the resource. We don't care about the nature of the resource, but only about the method of controlling access to it (the resource may, for example, be a data buffer, or a file). It would be too restrictive to enforce complete mutual exclusion by allowing only one reader or writer at a time access to the resource, because who may have permission to use it at any time depends on the access history, not just on whether or not the resource is currently being used. Furthermore there are subtle problems of starvation that may require interleaving of permission in judicious ways; for example, many busy readers should not be allowed to starve a waiting writer; however, if there are many busy writers, perhaps they should not be allowed to starve waiting readers either. The problem is *TIME*-intensive because correct sequencing of access to the resource is the dominant design concern, not what work is actually being done while the resource is being accessed. It is easy to invent solutions that apparently solve the

355

problem but have unacceptable behaviour from some point of view.

Figure 9.1 sets the stage. With reference to this figure, the following are the givens of the problem:

- a set of concurrent readers and a set of concurrent writers, all of which are actors,

- a reading activity for each reader and a writing activity for each writer performable on a shared, passive resource (whether by the readers and writers directly or by an agent is unspecified at this stage),

- events Want-R and Want-W sourced, respectively, at readers and writers, that indicate a desire to perform an activity and are expected eventually to result in its performance.

Specifically excluded from the givens are:

- the sinks for the Want-R and Want-R events,

- the sources and sinks for the implicit Grant and Fin events that signal the start and end of activities,

- the nature of the interaction with the resource.

These exclusions postpone commitment to the structural place where reading and writing are controlled (it may be a central place, or control may be distributed among readers and writers).

To constrain the range of possible solutions, the only solutions considered in this chapter are ones with attached gate buttons on robots. Chapter 5 showed how to think about and use the more general case. Recall that attached gate buttons adequately represent a wide variety of mechanisms in current implementation technologies.

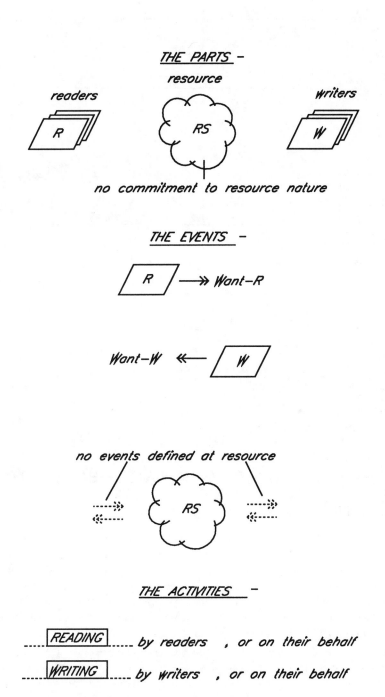

Figure 9.1: GENERAL NATURE OF THE READERS-WRITERS PROBLEM

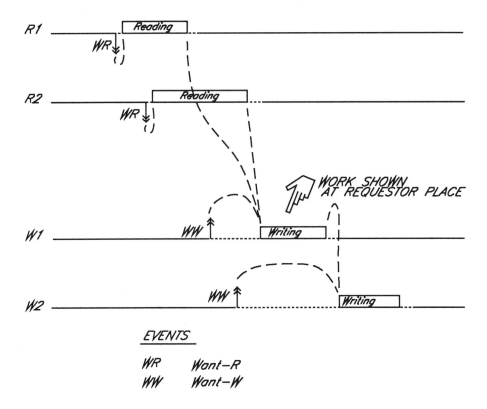

Figure 9.2: MIXED ACTIVITY-EVENT SCENARIO: PATTERN 1

9.3 HOW TO APPROACH EARLY SCENARIOS

9.3.1 INTRODUCTION

Figures 9.2 and 9.3 show semantically equivalent mixed scenarios with an appropriate lack of commitment to secondary events (recall from Chapter 3 that a mixed scenario is one that shows work activities explicitly, but not starting and ending events for them, and that placing work activities on timelines in such scenarios does not have the effect of making a commitment to where the work is done). At this uncommitted stage, it does not matter whether reading and writing activities are shown taking place on the reader and writer timelines (Figure 9.2), or not (Figure 9.3).

Figures 9.4 and 9.5 show that when the secondary events are included, making the scenarios into complete event scenarios (the work activities are still in these figures, for reference, but are actually redundant), the diagrams become more cluttered, and they also imply more commitment. The additional commitment is shown by the structure chart insets in these diagrams. For example, in the pattern of Figure 9.4 the Fin events must be

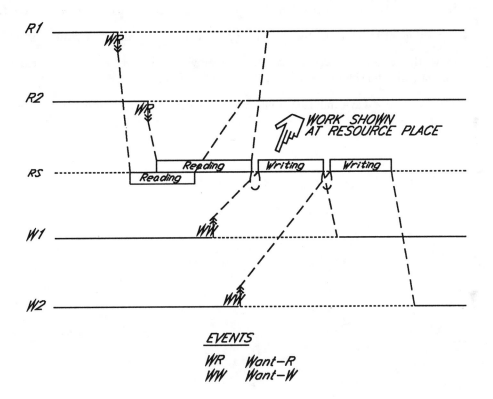

Figure 9.3: MIXED ACTIVITY-EVENT SCENARIO: PATTERN 2

sourced on the reader and writer timelines, whereas in the pattern of Figure 9.5, they must be sourced on the resource timeline; during early behaviour exploration such commitments should be deferred.

The dashed lines in these figures show the following intra-timeline and inter-timeline cause-effect relationships:

- A reading effect is caused directly by a read request if there are only readers active.

- A write request while readers are active has no direct effect, but eventually results in a writing activity (the event is not lost) when other causes are taken into account.

- A writing effect is caused by a previous write request and all active readers finishing.

- A writing effect may also be caused by a previous write request and the currently active writer finishing.

- Causes do not have immediate effects: there is latency due to event transfer and decision making.

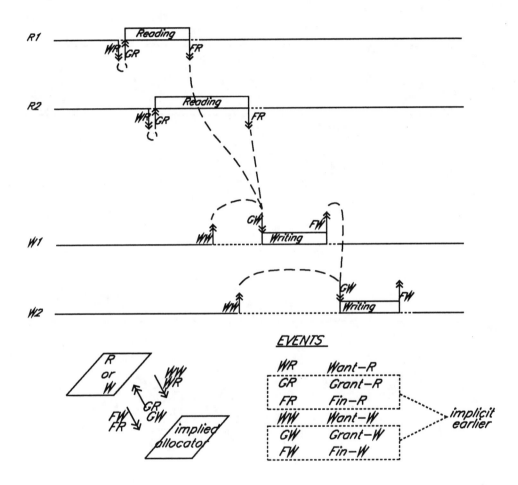

Figure 9.4: COMPLETE EVENT SCENARIO: PATTERN 1

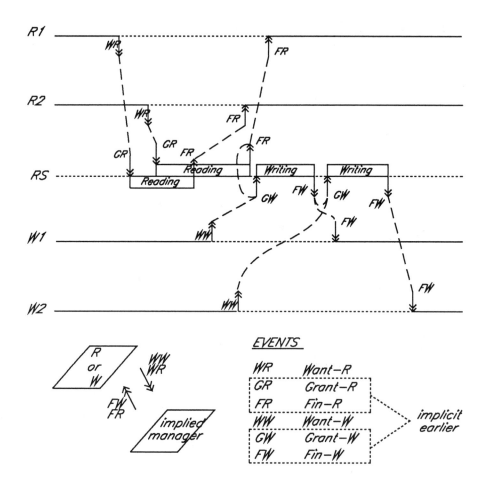

Figure 9.5: COMPLETE EVENT SCENARIO: PATTERN 2

9.4 STARVE PRELIMINARY DESIGN

9.4.1 INTRODUCTION

The first case study — called STARVE — develops a very simple design that has the unsatisfactory property of potentially starving both readers and writers. More satisfactory designs will be developed later. This one just sets the stage.

9.4.2 STARVE SCENARIOS

Steps 1 and 2 of the process of Figure 3.43 have already been almost completed. The earlier Figure 9.2 illustrates the following properties and constraints:

- Readers may be overlapped.

- Readers, *once started*, lock out writers.

- Want-W events that occur while readers are active may be safely queued until all current readers finish, because they have no effect until then.

- Want-W events are satisfied in the order in which they occurred, implying that if they are queued, they must be queued in FIFO order (thus we are implicitly assuming a queued event model).

- Writers are not overlapped.

Continuing with Step 2, Figure 9.6 repeats this scenario, showing how states may be found in it by inspection: there is no activity in the IDLE state; the READING state exists while there is any reading activity (whether due to one or many readers); the WRITING state persists only for one writing activity, because writers are not overlapped; the IDLE state intervenes between the termination of the READING or WRITING states and any subsequent READING or WRITING state (a different possible interpretation, in which the WRITING state persists as long as there are outstanding writers, is explored later).

9.4.3 STARVE ABSTRACT STATE MACHINES

Step 3 of the process of Figure 3.43 develops a state machine to generate earlier scenarios automatically and to provide a means of generating other scenarios; Figure 9.7 does the job for STARVE. Note that the implicit Grant and Fin events are shown as actions and events, respectively, without any structural commitment. The boolean variable LAST is an implied auxiliary variable needed to keep track of whether or not there are more readers active (a workbench would enable transitions to be annotated with action details expressing this).

This state machine represents desired readers-writers behaviour in the abstract (as will be shown later, the behaviour is unsatisfactory, but pretend for the moment that you do not know this yet).

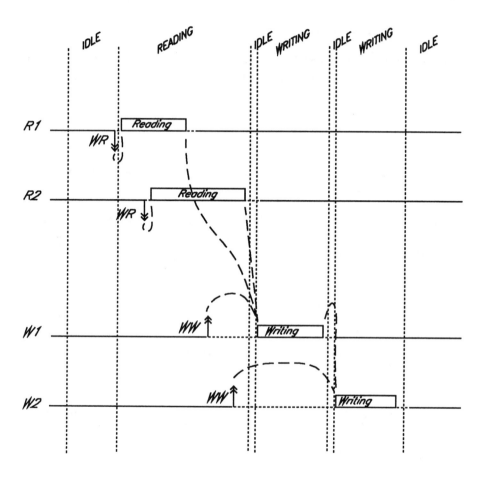

Figure 9.6: FINDING STATES IN SCENARIOS

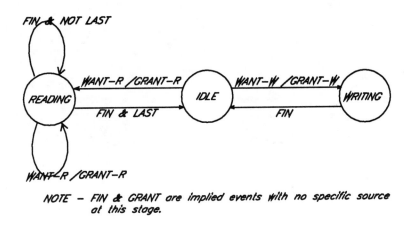

Figure 9.7: STARVE STATE MACHINE DERIVED FROM SCENARIOS SO FAR

9.4.4 PRELIMINARY GLUE STRUCTURE AND EVENT FLOW PATTERNS

Step 4 of the process of Figure 3.43 decides on whether or not intermediate machinery will be required in the glue structure joining readers and writers, without yet committing to the details. Alternatives and a particular choice are indicated by Figure 9.8. This is a *TIME*-domain step, because the decision is about robots in the glue structure, and finding robots is in the *TIME*-domain. The choice made in the figure is to require an allocator robot in the glue structure.

Step 5 of the process of Figure 3.43 decides on event patterns among components. The details of Figure 9.9 are the direct consequence of earlier decisions; this figure simply shows consequences, not new decisions. How the events are moved between components is still undecided.

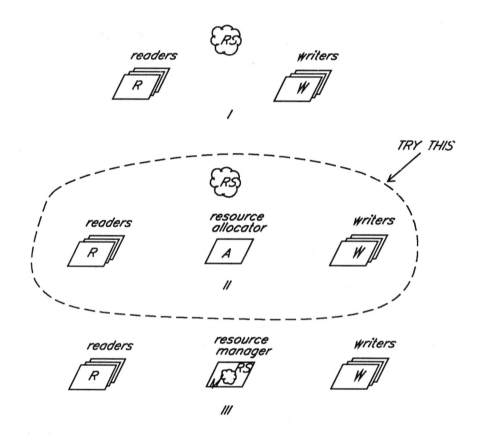

Figure 9.8: CHOOSING THE NATURE OF THE GLUE STRUCTURE

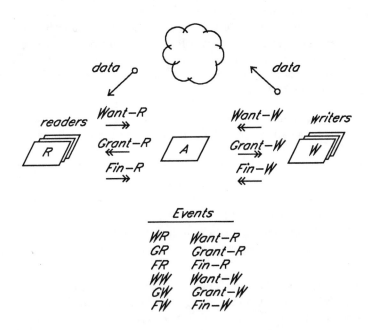

Figure 9.9: DECIDING ON FLOW PATTERNS

9.5   A FIRST PASS AT DETAILED DESIGN OF STARVE

9.5.1   STARVE CHANNELS

Step 6 of the process of Figure 3.43 makes the first detailed design commitment in terms of channels between readers and writers. Figure 9.10 shows alternatives and a particular choice. The choice is determined by where waiting is required:

- *I*: Without central control, this problem becomes like the concurrent life game of Chapter 6, with every party sending status reports to other parties and waiting for status reports from other parties, except here the other parties are not constrained to subsets of the whole. The status reports would contain information about who is reading and writing and would be part of a protocol to transfer not only information, but also permission to read or write. This approach would be necessary if readers and writers are physically distributed and central control is not allowed by the requirements of the problem. Later we shall reexamine this possibility, but for the moment, assume central control is allowed.

- *II, III, IV*: The sources of primary events are the readers and writers. The sink for these events is the allocator. Therefore, following the guidelines of Chapter 8:

  - *II*: Bidirectional channels make sense if readers or writers need to do other things while waiting for permission to read or write. This structure allows them to visit the center to report requests to the waiting allocator, but to wait in their own places for notification of permission.

  - *III*: Unidirectional channels radiating from the center do not make any sense because the source of the primary events is the readers and writers, not the central place.

  - *IV*: Unidirectional channels pointing towards the center make sense if the readers and writers cannot do anything else while they are waiting for permission to proceed. This structure requires the readers to visit the central place to make requests (the primary events) and to wait there for permission (the secondary events). This one has been chosen here because it seems to fit the nature of the problem. The implication is that the allocator is a reactor.

Step 7 of the process of Figure 3.43 is omitted here; it would simply elaborate obvious scenario details to show concrete protocols (visit scenarios) including all flow elements of Figure 9.9 (this step is illustrated in later studies).

9.5.2   STARVE-1 INTERFACE

Step 8 of the process of Figure 3.43 decides on interfaces. The analysis of temporal behaviour so far has revealed that reading events have no effect while writing is in progress and writing events have no effect while reading is in progress. Furthermore, the requirement that readers and writers wait for permission after making a request without doing anything else means that they can queue with their requests. So we need two waiting places, one for readers

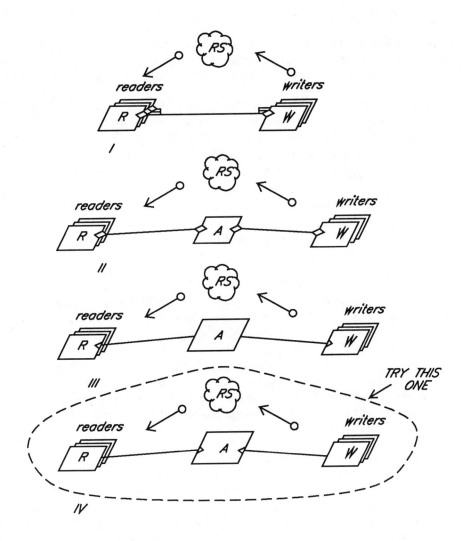

Figure 9.10: CHOOSING CHANNEL STRUCTURE

and one for writers, each of which can simply be closed when reading or writing permission cannot be granted immediately.

The interface of Figure 9.11 for the allocator follows directly. The way in which the events are mapped to the buttons is shown in the lower part of the figure.

9.5.3 STARVE-1 AGENDAS

Jumping to Step 10 of the process of Figure 3.43, we must now decide on internal agendas. One approach is to plug the state machine of Figure 9.7 into the allocator structure, using an ACM, following the approach of Figures 3.40 and 6.10, as shown in Figure 9.12.

> IMPLEMENTATION IMPLICATIONS: The ACM would be a package of the form of Figures 3.42 and 6.12, with a specification declaring

```
type EVENT_TYPE is (WANT_R,WANT_W,FIN);
type ACTION_TYPE is (NOP,OPEN,GRANT_R,GRANT_W);
```

> The actions are those of Figure 9.7, except for NOP and OPEN: NOP (standing for "no operation") indicates that no action is required; OPEN is associated with the transitions that return to the IDLE state in Figure 9.7 (it indicates that the allocator is to be open to all events). Figure 9.13 gives the body of an Ada allocator task that uses this ACM to control its behaviour. Note that this task is programmed with all entry code inside the critical sections, to conform to the design requirement that it is a reactor. A body for the ACM package is given in Figure 9.14. In it, the state machine is encoded in the DECODE procedure, instead of in a table in the body of the package as with earlier examples, mainly because it enables the program to fit on one page (note that the code assumes that only events that are appropriate for the current state will be passed to the ACM — a practical program would have an error action or parameter to be returned if this did not happen). All of this code is extremely regular in structure and invites mechanical generation from diagrams; only PERFORM must be hand-crafted.

A more direct approach is to transform the state machine into an explicit rendezvous state machine as shown in Figure 9.15; here, this is just an interpreted copy of the earlier state machine of Figure 9.7, but later we shall see that in general rendezvous state machines may need additional transitions and states. A rendezvous state machine is one in which the transitions are rendezvous, the states control opening and closing of waiting buttons, and the actions are performed during the associated rendezvous (actions do not include other rendezvous).

> IMPLEMENTATION IMPLICATIONS: Figure 9.16 shows an Ada program for the allocator following the rendezvous state machine model. Although the code is obviously smaller and tighter, the state machine is bound to the specific concrete interface of this task.

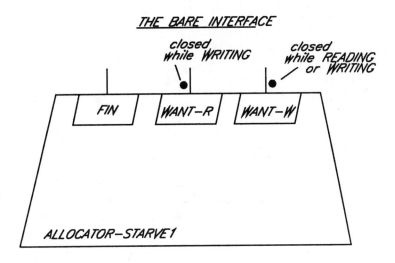

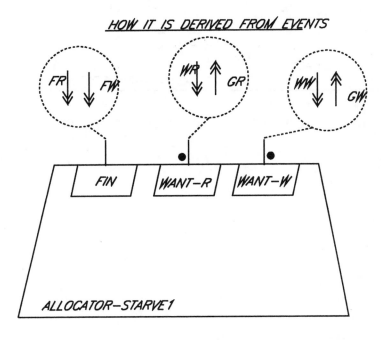

Figure 9.11: STARVE-1 ALLOCATOR INTERFACE

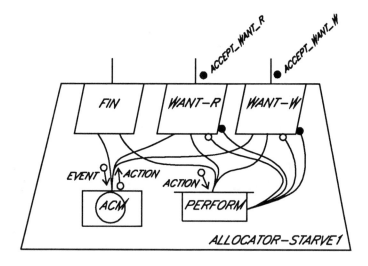

Figure 9.12: AN ACM-DRIVEN ALLOCATOR FOR STARVE-1

```
task body ALLOCATOR is
     ACCEPT_WANT_W : BOOLEAN := TRUE; -- GUARD
     ACCEPT_WANT_R : BOOLEAN := TRUE; -- GUARD
     ACTION: ACM.ACTION_TYPE;
     procedure PERFORM (ACTION: in ACM.ACTION_TYPE) is
       begin
         case ACTION is
           when ACM.NOP      => null;
           when ACM.OPEN     => ACCEPT_WANT_R := TRUE;
                                ACCEPT_WANT_W := TRUE;
           when ACM.GRANT_R  => ACCEPT_WANT_W := FALSE;
           when ACM.GRANT_W  => ACCEPT_WANT_R := FALSE;
                                ACCEPT_WANT_W := FALSE;

         end case;
       end PERFORM;
   begin
     loop
       select
         when ACCEPT_WANT_W =>
           accept WANT_W do
             ACM.DECODE(ACM.WANT_W,ACTION);
             PERFORM(ACTION); end;
       or
         when ACCEPT_WANT_R =>
           accept WANT_R do
             ACM.DECODE(ACM.WANT_R,ACTION);
             PERFORM(ACTION); end;
       or
           accept FIN do
             ACM.DECODE(ACM.FIN,ACTION);
             PERFORM(ACTION); end;
       end select;
     end loop;
 end ALLOCATOR;
```

Figure 9.13: ADA ALLOCATOR TASK FOR STARVE-1 USING AN ACM

```
package ACM is
   type EVENT_TYPE is (WANT_R,WANT_W,FIN);
   type ACTION_TYPE is (NOP,OPEN,GRANT_R,GRANT_W);
   procedure DECODE(EVENT: in EVENT_TYPE; ACTION: out  ACTION_TYPE);
end ACM;

package body ACM is
   type STATE_TYPE is (IDLE, READING, WRITING);
   STATE: STATE_TYPE := IDLE;
   READERS: integer:=0;
   procedure DECODE(EVENT: in EVENT_TYPE; ACTION: out  ACTION_TYPE) is
     begin
       case EVENT is
         when FIN =>
           if (READERS=1) and (STATE=READING) then
             READERS := 0; ACTION := OPEN; STATE := IDLE;
           elsif (READERS > 1) and (STATE = READING) then
             READERS := READERS - 1; ACTION := NOP;
           elsif STATE = WRITING then
             ACTION := OPEN; STATE := IDLE;
           end if;
         when WANT_R =>
           if (STATE = IDLE) or (STATE = READING) then
             READERS := READERS + 1; ACTION := NOP; STATE := READING;
           end if;
         when WANT_W =>
           if STATE = IDLE then
             ACTION := GRANT_W; STATE := WRITING;
           end if;
       end case;
     end DECODE;
end ACM;
```

Figure 9.14: THE STARVE-1 ACM

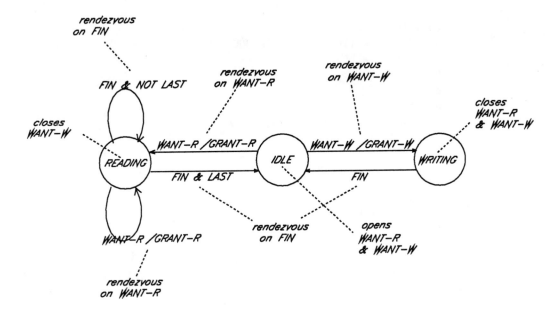

Figure 9.15: A RENDEZVOUS STATE MACHINE FOR STARVE-1

```
task body ALLOCATOR is
type STATETYPE is (IDLE, READING, WRITING);
STATE:STATETYPE:=IDLE;
READERS: integer:=0;
  loop
    select
      when STATE = IDLE => accept WANT_W
        do STATE: = WRITING;end;
    or
      when STATE /= WRITING =>
        accept WANT_R
        do case STATE is
          when IDLE    => STATE:=READING;READERS:=READERS + 1;
          when READING => READERS:=READERS + 1;
          end case;
        end;
    or
        accept FIN
        do case STATE is
          when READING => READERS:=READERS - 1;
                          if READERS = 0 then
                           STATE:=IDLE;end if;
          when WRITING => STATE:=IDLE;
          end;
    end select;
  end loop;
end ALLOCATOR;
```

Figure 9.16: A DIRECT IMPLEMENTATION OF THE RENDEZVOUS STATE MA-CHINE FOR STARVE-1

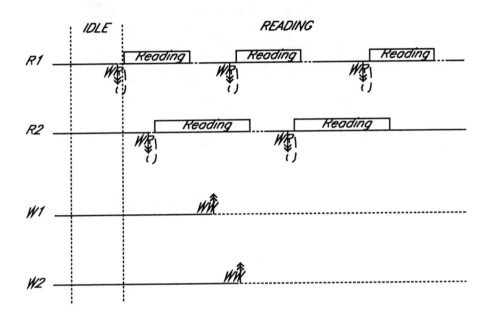

Figure 9.17: STARVE-1: WHAT IF READERS OVERLAP?

9.6 REVISITING STARVE

9.6.1 STARVE-1: A BASICALLY FLAWED STARTING POINT

All is not well with the STARVE-1 solution, as shown by Figure 9.17; once readers get started, they may STARVE writers forever by overlapping read activities. Pursuing this case as if we did not realize there was a problem has enabled us to discuss representation and method issues without worrying about application subtleties. Little can be done about this form of writer starvation in the framework of the design that emerged from this process. The issue is explored further in the next design study (READSTARVE).

9.6.2 STARVE-2: PRIORITIZING THE STARVE-1 INTERFACE

There is a form of transient writer starvation in the STARVE-1 that we can do something about (although as a general rule it it not worth partly fixing a bad design, to do so here illustrates a point). What if there are both many readers and many writers waiting at the end of a write activity? Assuming that we want circumstances to unfold in a more orderly manner than just random choice, we need a choice rule. Let us assume the choice we want in these circumstances is always a writer; in general, this may not be the case

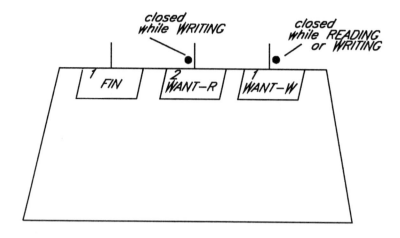

Figure 9.18: STARVE-2: PRIORITIZING THE STARVE-1 INTERFACE

(there may be high priority readers needing information, even if it is not completely up to date), however let us for the moment proceed with it. Without a choice rule, readers might accidentally starve writers temporarily, even when reading is not overlapped, simply because of indeterminism in the choice.

One solution is to give the Want-W button higher priority, as shown in Figure 9.18, in a manner similar to the prioritized *WAIT* button of the semaphore of Chapter 4. Another solution is given in the next section.

> IMPLEMENTATION IMPLICATIONS: As discussed in Chapter 4, such prioritization cannot simply be declared in Ada, but must be programmed; Figure 9.19 does it for the earlier ACM program following the weak prioritization approach described there (this assumes writers will never balk or time out).

```
loop
  select
    when ACCEPT_WANT_W =>
      accept WANT_W do
        ACM.DECODE(WANT_W,ACTION);
        PERFORM(ACTION);
      end;
  or
    when ACCEPT_WANT_R and WANT_W'COUNT=0 =>
      accept WANT_R do
        ACM.DECODE(WANT_R,ACTION);
        RESULT := PERFORM(ACTION);
      end;
  or
      accept FIN do
        ACM.DECODE(FIN,ACTION);
        PERFORM(ACTION);
      end;
  end select;
end loop;
```

(compare with Figure 9.14)

Figure 9.19: STARVE-2: ADA ACM DRIVER

9.6.3   STARVE-3: A DIFFERENT STARVE STATE MACHINE

Another solution to the indeterminism problem is not to allow the circumstance where one has to choose indeterministically between readers and writers to occur. The source of this circumstance goes all the way back to the scenario of Figure 9.6, where a state transition back to idle was marked between writers. If the scenario is interpreted differently in state terms, as shown in Figure 9.20, then we end up with the different state machine shown in Figure 9.21. This machine has a satisfying symmetry between readers and writers.

The state machine of Figure 9.21 can easily be mapped into an ACM like that used in Figure 9.12, but the new ACM would not be compatible with the interface of the latter figure, because that interface is specifically designed to keep WANT-W closed while in the WRITING state, thus preventing discovery of WANT-W events while in that state. This point is further illustrated by Figure 9.22; we seem to require either an additional button or an extended rendezvous on the existing button; either changes the nature of the interface. Further exploration of this interface issue follows in the next design study (READSTARVE).

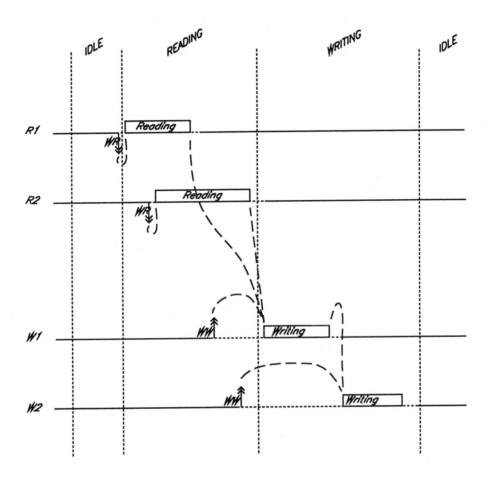

(compare with Figure 9.6)

Figure 9.20: STARVE-3: A DIFFERENT STATE SEQUENCE FROM THE SAME SCE-NARIO

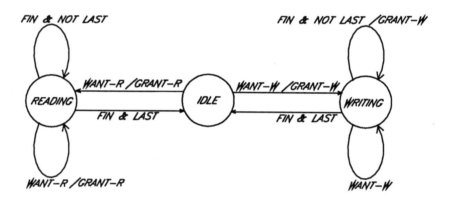

(compare with Figure 9.7)

Figure 9.21: STARVE-3: A DIFFERENT ABSTRACT STATE MACHINE

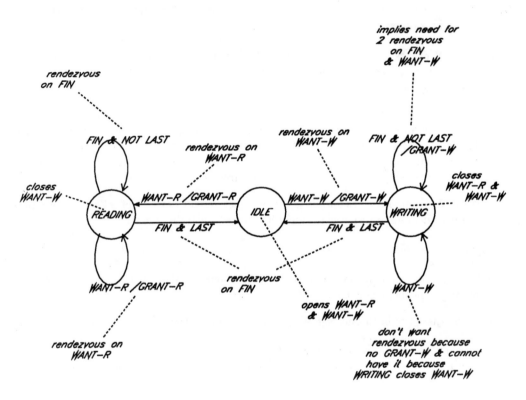

(compare with Figure 9.6)

Figure 9.22: STARVE-3: A NEW RENDEZVOUS STATE MACHINE

9.7 READSTARVE

9.7.1 INTRODUCTION

This design study is called READSTARVE because it eliminates writer starvation while retaining reader starvation. Several alternative designs called READSTARVE-1, READSTARVE-2, etc. are explored.

9.7.2 READSTARVE-1

READSTARVE-1 EARLY SCENARIOS

Going back to Step 2 of the process of Figure 3.43, Figure 9.23 expands our knowledge of the problem as follows:

- Want-W events occurring while readers are active must have an immediate effect, namely that subsequent Want-R events are to have no effect; therefore they cannot be safely queued until readers are finished.

- Want-R events occurring after a Want-W event will have no effect until all subsequent writers are finished; therefore they may safely be queued until that point (this could STARVE readers, but the implicit assumptions are that writers should have priority over readers and that they interact relatively infrequently with the resource, so the prospect of them starving readers is not a problem).

- Want-W events occurring while a writer is active will have no effect until the writer is finished; therefore they may safely be queued until this point.

Figure 9.24 emphasizes some constraints that have already been discussed:

- Deferred readers start in the same order as their Want-R events (again, we are assuming a queued event model).

- When there are both deferred Want-R and Want-W events, the latter take priority.

Figure 9.25 summarizes our scenario knowledge to this point and illustrates the way scenario information might be recorded for a problem like this in a design project.

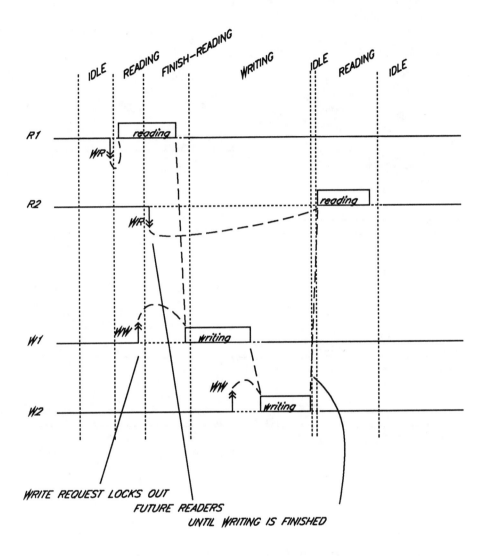

Figure 9.23: WHAT IF A WRITE REQUEST OCCURS WHILE READERS ARE ACTIVE?

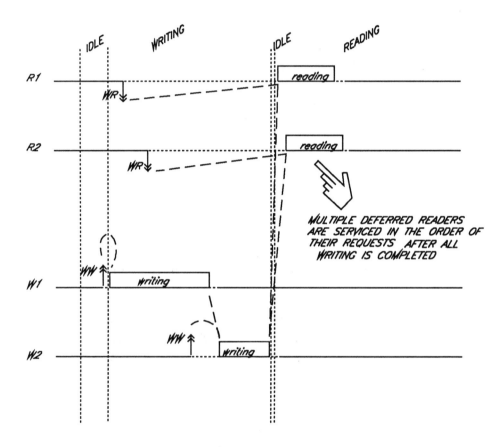

Figure 9.24: WHAT IF MULTIPLE READERS ARE DEFERRED?

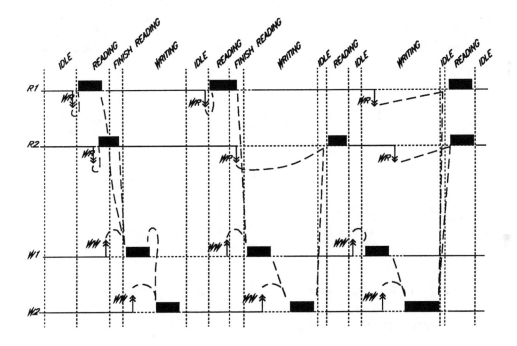

Figure 9.25: SUMMARY OF READSTARVE-1 SCENARIOS

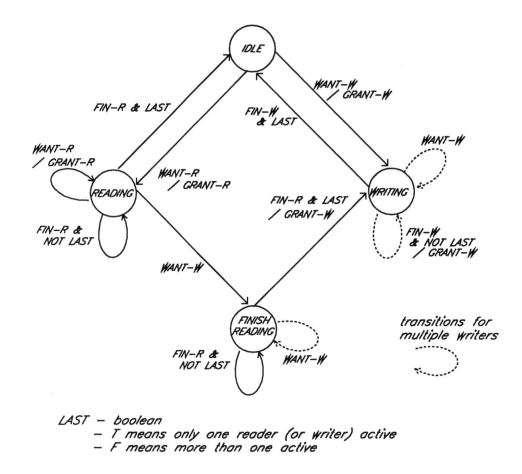

LAST — boolean
       — T means only one reader (or writer) active
       — F means more than one active

Figure 9.26: READSTARVE-1 STATE MACHINE

READSTARVE-1 STATE MACHINE

Revisiting Step 3 of the process of Figure 3.43 with this new knowledge produces the state machine of Figure 9.26. The dotted transitions are not needed if there is only one writer.

Steps 4-6 of the process of Figure 3.43 are assumed to be the same as before.

READSTARVE-1 DETAILED EVENT SCENARIOS

It is now interesting to show Step 7 of the process of Figure 3.43, because the want event and the grant action for writing are not always handled together, temporally, as they were in STARVE. The new scenarios showing this are Figures 9.27 and 9.28. There is really nothing new in these scenarios because they are implicit in what has gone before, but it is helpful to have them in front of us just to illustrate this point. Note that there is still no commitment to the detailed mechanism of event transfer.

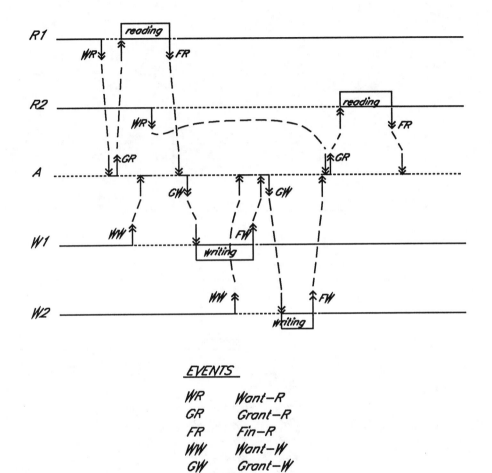

EVENTS

WR	Want-R
GR	Grant-R
FR	Fin-R
WW	Want-W
GW	Grant-W
FW	Fin-W

(compare with Figure 9.23)

Figure 9.27: FIRST DETAILED READSTARVE-1 EVENT SCENARIO

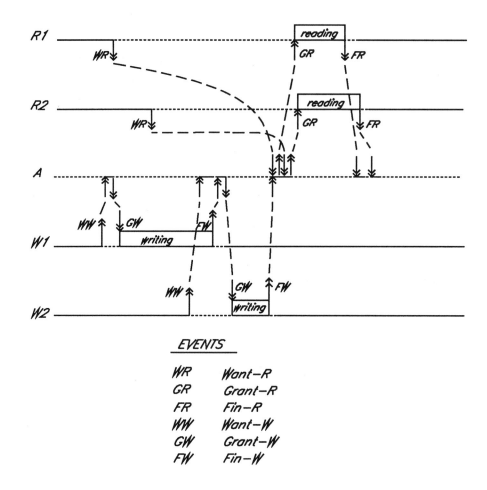

EVENTS

WR	Want-R
GR	Grant-R
FR	Fin-R
WW	Want-W
GW	Grant-W
FW	Fin-W

(compare with Figure 9.24)

Figure 9.28: SECOND DETAILED READSTARVE-1 EVENT SCENARIO

9.8 DETAILED INTERFACE AND INSIDE DESIGN OF READSTARVE-1

9.8.1 READSTARVE-1 INTERFACE

Revisiting Step 8 of the process of Figure 3.43, taking into account the new factor that the allocator cannot defer Want-W events until Grant-W is possible, as was done in STARVE, leads to the conclusion that the warm waiting mechanism of Chapter 5 is exactly what we need here. Mapping this to a cold waiting structure, following Chapter 5, yields Figure 9.29, in which a double visit is required by writers to report Want-W and wait for Grant-W. An array of Want-W buttons may be needed if critical races are to be avoided, as discussed several times before. Because the scenarios would be unchanged if Fin-R and Fin-W are replaced by a single Fin event, it is sufficient to have a single Fin button.

READSTARVE-1 TEMPORAL BEHAVIOUR

It is now interesting to show Step 9 of the process of Figure 3.43. Figure 9.30 shows a double visit corresponding to Figures 9.27 . Figure 9.31 shows an equivalent scenario representing the warm waiting approach from which the READSTARVE-1 interface was implicitly mapped. Figure 9.32 shows a double visit interaction corresponding to Figure 9.28.

Figures 9.33 and 9.34 show how behaviour would normally be explored initially by walking through schematic diagrams following visit threads and then transcribing only significant patterns into linearized scenarios for the record (a workbench might support the latter process automatically).

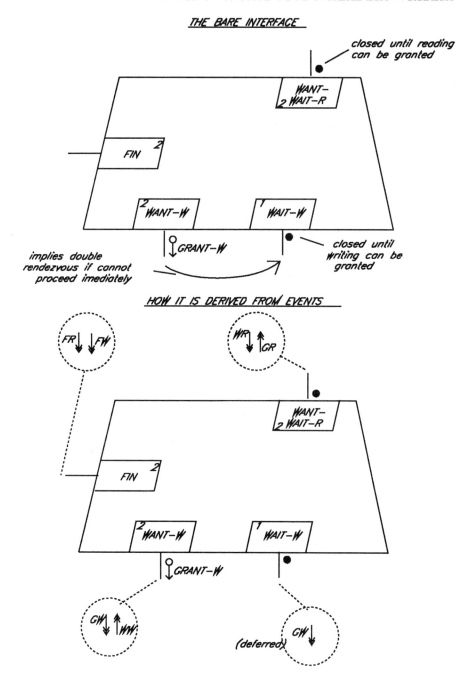

Figure 9.29: READSTARVE-1 ALLOCATOR LINEAR INTERFACE

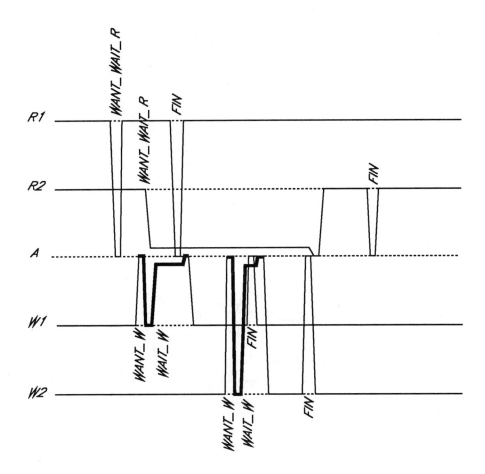

(corresponding to Figure 9.27)

Figure 9.30: READSTARVE-1 VISIT SCENARIO SHOWING DOUBLE RENDEZVOUS

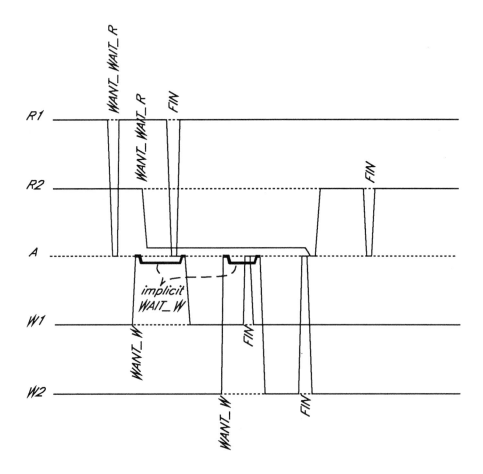

Figure 9.31: READSTARVE-1 VISIT SCENARIO SHOWING EXTENDED REN-DEZVOUS

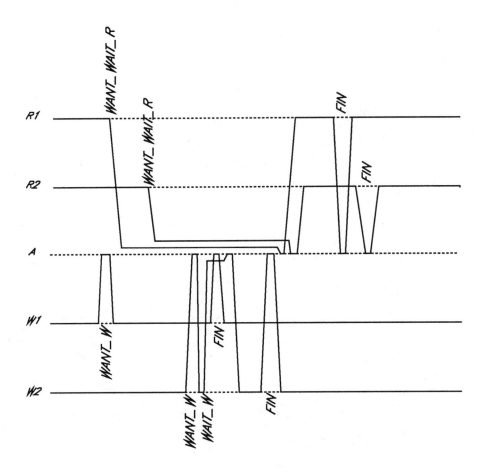

(corresponding to Figure 9.28)

Figure 9.32: ANOTHER READSTARVE-1 DOUBLE RENDEZVOUS VISIT SCENARIO

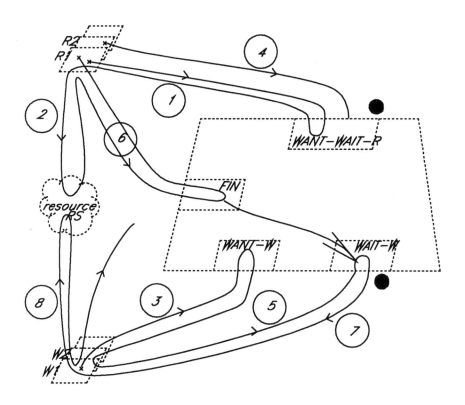

(corresponding to Figure 9.30)

Figure 9.33: THREADING VISITS THROUGH STRUCTURE

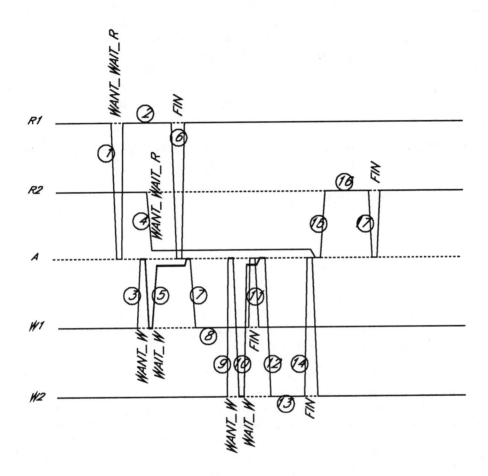

(annotated copy of Figure 9.30)

Figure 9.34: LINEARIZING THREADED SCENARIOS

READSTARVE-1 ACM

Figure 9.35 shows how an ACM to incorporate the state machine of Figure 9.26 may be plugged into this structure. Note how WAIT-W does not interact with the ACM. This is because a meeting at this button signifies that write permission has already been granted by opening the button; therefore all that happens is that the button closes itself again. This is of no interest to the ACM, which assumes that granting write permission implies that a writer becomes active, somehow. Thus, the concrete double-visit machinery for writers that is a property of this particular concrete interface is decoupled from the scheduling logic for granting permission. The same ACM may be used for other concrete interfaces (e.g., see Figures 9.46 and 9.47).

> IMPLEMENTATION IMPLICATIONS: Assume the ACM package has a specification that includes the following type definitions:

```
type EVENT_TYPE is (WANT_R,WANT_W,FIN);
type ACTION_TYPE is (NOP,OPEN,FINISH,GRANT_R,GRANT_W);
```

> All the events and actions are the same as for Figure 9.13 except that FINISH is a new action that is implicitly associated with transitions that have no actions in Figure 9.26, but that actually imply "allow the current reader or writer to finish, and therefore do not allow any readers or writers to start". Then an Ada program fragment for the body of the allocator in Figure 9.35, in the style of Figure 9.13, is given in Figure 9.36, omitting ACM details (the reader may fill in ACM details using Figure 9.14 as a guide).

As an illustration of the modularity of the ACM approach, consider the following issue. We know from previous examples that double-visits cause critical races when there are multiple double-visitors. Assuming that the ACM supports multiple writers, there could be critical races among them between WANT-W and WAIT-W. We know that such races can be avoided by expanding WAIT-W into an array of waiting places. Making WANT-W into a waiting place that is closed when writing is granted to one writer will also do it; the mechanism might be called *double cold waiting*. (Double cold waiting is not a general solution for critical races, which is why it was not mentioned before; it is not general, because it does not permit the visitor to the first waiting place to continue operating after posting a request, but before waiting for an answer.) The point is that changing the interface in either of these ways would not require any changes to the ACM, because the same underlying scheduling logic would still apply; only the details of PERFORM would require change.

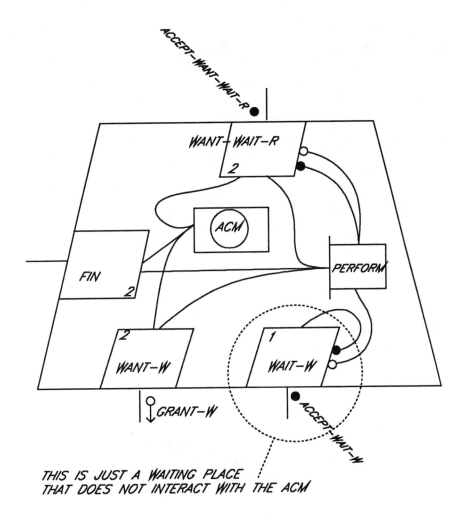

(compare with Figure 9.12)

Figure 9.35: PLUGGING IN AN ACM

```
...
   ACCEPT_WAIT_W: BOOLEAN := TRUE;
   ACCEPT_WANT_WAIT_R: BOOLEAN := TRUE;
   procedure PERFORM (ACTION: in ACM.ACTION_TYPE) is
     begin
       case ACTION is
         when ACM.NOP            => null;
         when ACM.GRANT_R        => null;
         when ACM.FINISH         => ACCEPT_WAIT_W := FALSE;
                                    ACCEPT_WANT_WAIT_R := FALSE;
         when ACM.GRANT_W        => ACCEPT_WAIT_W   :=  TRUE;
                                    ACCEPT_WANT_WAIT_R := FALSE;
         when ACM.OPEN           => ACCEPT_WAIT_W := TRUE;
                                    ACCEPT_WANT_WAIT_R := TRUE;

       end case;
     end PERFORM;
begin
  loop
    select
       accept WANT_W (grant: out BOOLEAN) do
         ACM.DECODE (WANT_W,ACTION);
         PERFORM(ACTION);
         if ACTION=ACM.GRANT_W then grant:=TRUE else grant:=FALSE; end if;
       end;
    or
      when ACCEPT_WAIT_W =>
        accept WAIT_W do
          -- no ACM call because ACM has already issued GRANT_W
          -- otherwise we would not be here
          ACCEPT_WAIT_W := FALSE;  end;
    or
      when ACCEPT_WANT_WAIT_R =>
        accept WANT_WAIT_R do
          ACM.DECODE(WANT_R,ACTION);
          PERFORM(ACTION); end;
    or
        accept FIN do
          ACM.DECODE(FIN,ACTION);
          PERFORM(ACTION); end;
    end select;
  end loop;
end;
```

Figure 9.36: ADA ACM DRIVER FOR READSTARVE-1

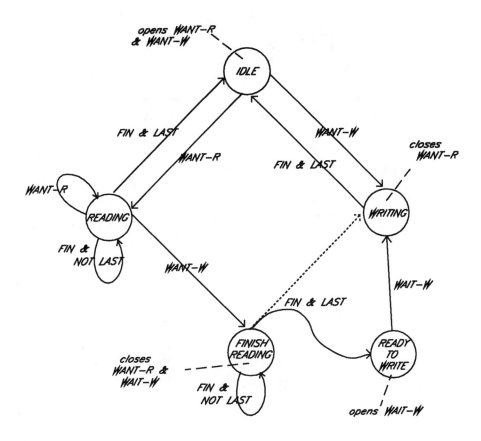

Figure 9.37: RENDEZVOUS STATE MACHINE FOR READSTARVE-1 (1 WRITER)

READSTARVE-1 RENDEZVOUS STATE MACHINE

Revisiting Step 10 of the process of Figure 3.43 shows how scenario state machines do not always translate directly into rendezvous state machines. Figure 9.37 shows that a new state is needed to control the deferment of the WAIT-W rendezvous until all readers are finished (for simplicity, the one-writer version of the state machine is shown).

> IMPLEMENTATION IMPLICATIONS: This may be translated into an Ada program along the lines of Figure 9.16 that has the state machine logic inextricably intertwined with the details of the interface, unlike the ACM approach.

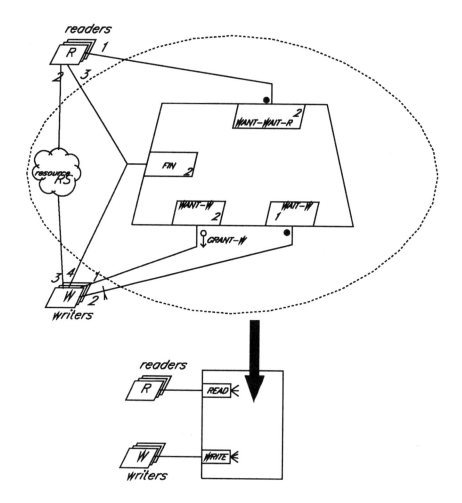

Figure 9.38: STRUCTURAL HIDING FOR READSTARVE-1

9.8.2   READSTARVE-1 STRUCTURAL HIDING

Figure 9.38 shows how structure can be added to hide details, following Step 12 of the process of Figure 3.43.

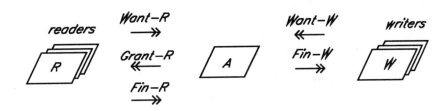

Figure 9.39: ASYMMETRIC EVENT FLOWS

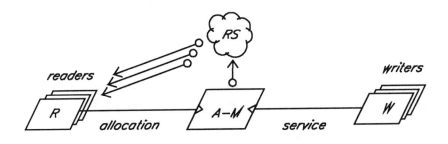

Figure 9.40: ASYMMETRIC CHANNEL STRUCTURE

9.8.3 READSTARVE-2: AN ASYMMETRIC SOLUTION

Observe that the asymmetry of the readers-writers relationship can be usefully captured in the interface structure: because readers cannot interfere with each other and may be overlapped, let them do their own reading; because writers cannot be allowed to overlap, hand over writing responsibility to a combined allocator - resource manager. The need for the double visit is thus eliminated.

Relative to the steps of Figure 3.43, Step 5 results in Figure 9.39 and Step 6 results in Figure 9.40. The scenarios of Step 7 are now quite different (Figures 9.41 and 9.42). Step 8 can produce an interface superficially like that of STARVE, without the double visit for writers (Figure 9.43) or one superficially like READSTARVE, with the double visit (Figure 9.44). The state machine of Figure 9.26 is still pluggable here using an ACM approach in the now familiar style. Details are left to the reader.

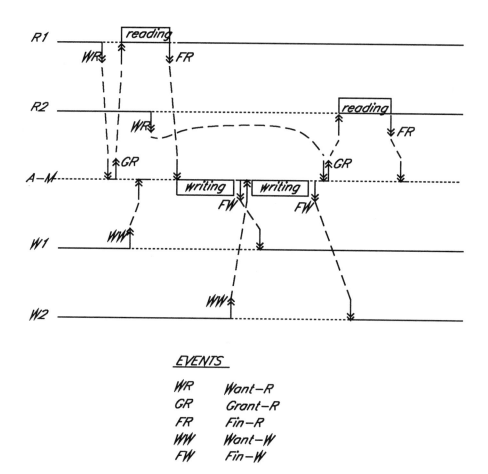

EVENTS

WR	Want-R
GR	Grant-R
FR	Fin-R
WW	Want-W
FW	Fin-W

(compare with Figure 9.27 for the symmetric case)

Figure 9.41: AN EVENT SCENARIO FOR THE ASYMMETRIC CASE

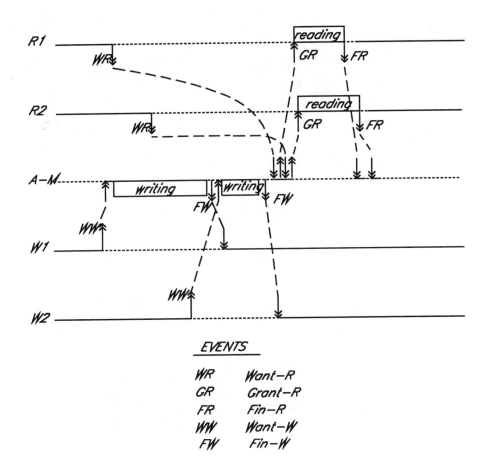

(compare with Figure 9.28 for the symmetric case)

Figure 9.42: A SECOND EVENT SCENARIO FOR THE ASYMMETRIC CASE

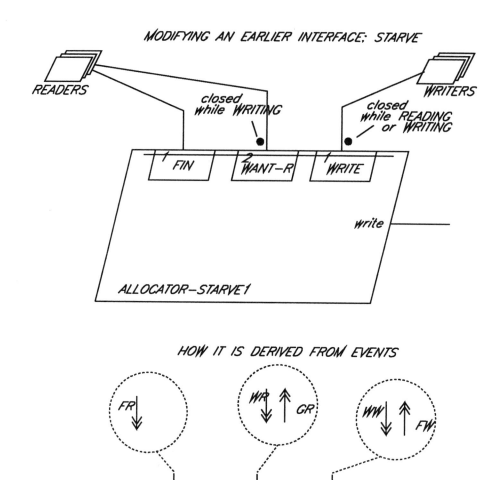

(a modified version of Figure 9.18)

Figure 9.43: MODIFYING THE STARVE INTERFACE FOR ASYMMETRICAL OPERATION

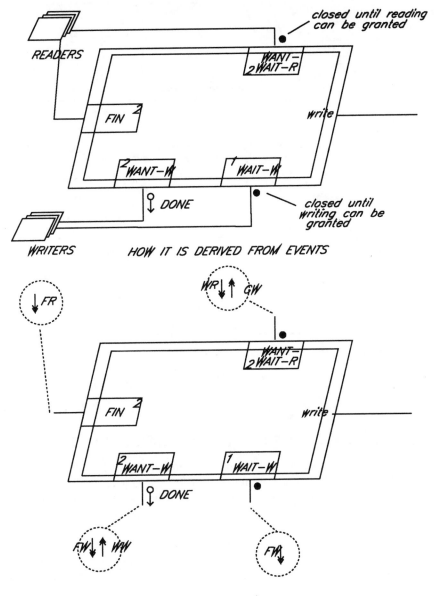

(a modified version of Figure 9.29)

Figure 9.44: MODIFYING THE READSTARVE-1 INTERFACE FOR ASYMMETRICAL OPERATION

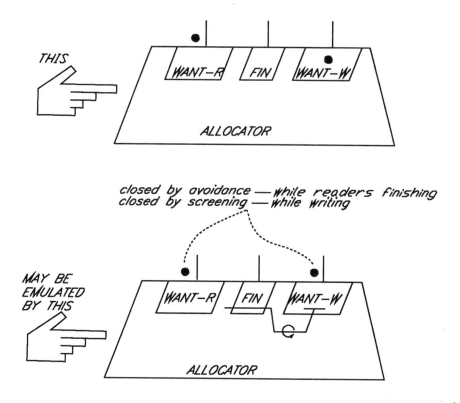

Figure 9.45: EMULATING WARM WAITING WITH NONLINEARITY

9.8.4 READSTARVE-3: A NONLINEAR SOLUTION

As discussed in Chapter 8 nonlinearity can be used in simple cases to emulate warm waiting when it is not available in the implementation technology and multiple-visit solutions are to be avoided. Figure 9.45 shows how for READSTARVE. Warm waiting is mapped to a combination of nesting and cold waiting that is somewhat complex at the interface level because it combines the screening and avoidance approaches to closing waiting places. In spite of this very different interface structure, the same ACM as used for Figure 9.35 may be used here. Figure 9.46 shows the new structure. A difference here is that every button uses the ACM, because there are no purely waiting-place buttons like WAIT-W in the earlier figure.

> IMPLEMENTATION IMPLICATIONS: Figure 9.47 gives an Ada driver for the ACM version. Without the ACM approach, the program has interface details and state machine logic intermixed, with the FINISH-READING state not explicitly represented, as illustrated by Figure 9.48.

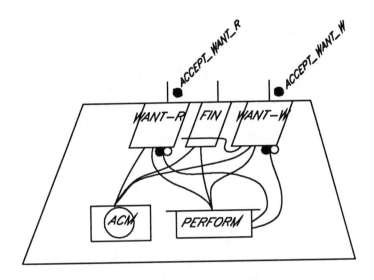

(compare with Figure 9.35)

Figure 9.46: PLUGGING THE EARLIER ACM INTO THE NONLINEAR STRUCTURE

```
...
ACCEPT_WANT_R: BOOLEAN := TRUE;
ACCEPT_WANT_W: BOOLEAN := TRUE;
procedure PERFORM (ACTION: ACM.ACTION_TYPE) is
  begin
    case ACTION is
      when ACM.NOP      => null;
      when ACM.GRANT_R  => null;
      when ACM.FINISH   => ACCEPT_WANT_W := FALSE;
                           ACCEPT_WANT_R := FALSE;
      when ACM.GRANT_W  => ACCEPT_WANT_W := FALSE;
                           ACCEPT_WANT_R := FALSE;
      when ACM.OPEN     => ACCEPT_WANT_W := TRUE;
                           ACCEPT_WANT_R := TRUE;
    end case;
  end PERFORM;
begin
  loop
    select
      when ACCEPT_WANT_W =>
       accept WANT_W do
         ACM.DECODE (ACM.WANT_W, ACTION);
         PERFORM(ACTION);
           while ACTION = FINISH
             loop
               accept(FIN);
               ACM.DECODE(ACM.FIN, ACTION);
               PERFORM(ACTION);
             end loop;
        end;
    or
      when ACCEPT_WANT_R =>
        accept WANT_R do
          ACM.DECODE(ACM.WANT_R, ACTION);
          PERFORM(ACTION);
        end;
    or
        accept FIN do
          ACM.DECODE(FIN, ACTION);
          PERFORM(ACTION);
    end select;
  end loop;
```

Figure 9.47: ADA ACM DRIVER FOR THE NONLINEAR STRUCTURE

```
select
  when STATE /= WRITING =>
    accept WANT_W do
     case STATE is
       when IDLE => STATE:=WRITING;
       when READING =>
         loop
           accept FIN;
           READERS:=READERS - 1;
           if READERS = 0 then STATE:=WRITING; exit; end if;
         end loop;
      end case;
    end WANT_W;
or
  when STATE /= WRITING =>
    accept WANT_R do
      case STATE is
        when IDLE => STATE:=READING;READERS:=READERS + 1;
        when READING => READERS:=READERS + 1;
      end case;
    end WANT_R;
or
    accept FIN do
    case STATE is
      when READING => READERS:=READERS - 1;
                      if READERS = 0 then
                        STATE:=IDLE;end if;
      when WRITING => STATE:=IDLE;
     end case;
    end FIN;
 end select;
```

Figure 9.48: A NONLINEAR ADA SOLUTION FOR READSTARVE-3

9.9   NOSTARVE

What if it is important to prevent not only writer starvation by readers but also reader starvation by writers? Figures 9.49 and 9.50 give Step 2 scenarios conveying the idea (introducing for the first time a negative scenario). Assuming the asymmetrical Step 6 channel structure of Figure 9.40 and without going through all of the other steps, a possible Step 8 interface is shown in Figure 9.51 that is capable of handling all of the interactions needed by means of double visits for both readers and writers; details of a an appropriate state machine and ACM are left as an exercise for the reader.

However, why not adapt the earlier asymmetrical READSTARVE structure of Figure 9.43 to the NOSTARVE requirement (recalling that this avoids double writer visits)?

> IMPLEMENTATION IMPLICATIONS: Figure 9.52 shows how an expert Ada programmer might write the internal logic of the allocator. The Ada code uses the trick of run time elaboration to capture the number of readers in the queue at the time writing is finished, which is then used in a guard to control the acceptance of all of them but no new ones. Obviously this program has not been mechanically derived by plugging a state machine into an ACM-based design. Figure 9.53 shows the program structure in MachineCharts. One clearly has to understand the internal program structure in detail to know what is going on. The ACM approach makes the logic less dependent on the skill of the programmer, because it specifies it visually in an orderly way before programs are written, and provides a mapping path to an implementation. We leave it as an exercise to the reader to show that the same ACM as before can still be used here (and of course works for more interface structures than this one).

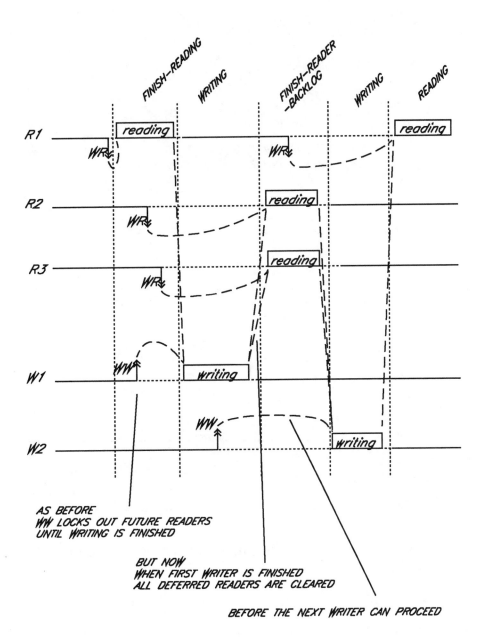

Figure 9.49: WHAT IF READERS SHOULD NOT BE STARVED?

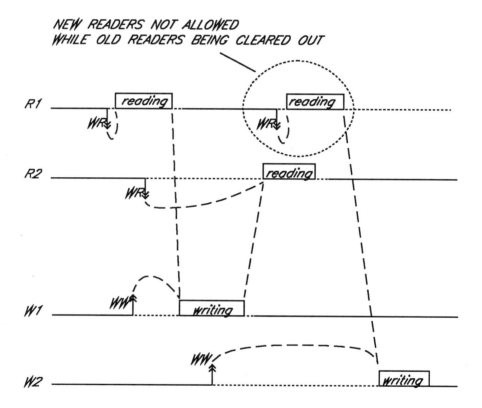

Figure 9.50: WHAT IF NEW READERS ARRIVE WHILE OLD ONES ARE BEING CLEARED?

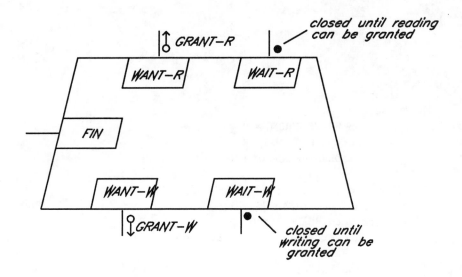

Figure 9.51: A GENERAL NOSTARVE LINEAR INTERFACE

```
loop
 select
   when WRITE'COUNT = 0 =>
     accept WANT_WAIT_R;
     READERS:=READERS + 1;
   or
     accept FIN-R;
     READERS:=READERS - 1;
   or when READERS = 0 =>
     accept WRITE(E : in ELEM) do
       VARIABLE:= E;
     end WRITE;
     declare
       COUNT:INTEGER:= WANT_WAIT_R'COUNT;--RUNTIME ELABORATION
     begin
       loop
         select
           when COUNT > 0 =>
             accept WANT_WAIT_R;
             READERS:=READERS + 1;
             COUNT:=COUNT - 1;
           else
             exit;
           end select;
         end loop;
     end;
   end select;
 end loop;
```

Figure 9.52: A DIRECT ADA APPROACH TO ASYMMETRIC NOSTARVE

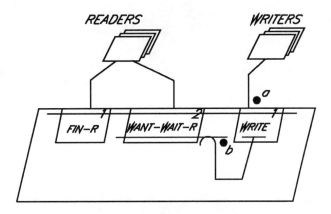

a − closed while readers active

b − closed after pending readers
    (but not new ones) cleared.

Figure 9.53: REPRESENTING THE ADA PROGRAM IN MACHINE CHARTS

9.10   OTHER APPROACHES

Some other approaches that might occur to the reader are shown in Figure 9.54. The approach of having all reading and writing done centrally by a resource manager robot suffers from the problem that readers cannot overlap their activities directly; a better solution that has the same interface effect is to provide resource manager box, like in Figure 9.38. The ring approach might be suitable for a distributed system, in which the resource was central to all nodes.

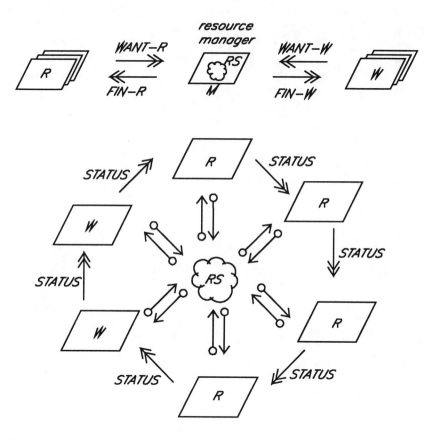

Figure 9.54: OTHER APPROACHES

Part V

COMPONENTRY

Chapter 10

PRINCIPLES AND PRACTICE OF COMPONENTRY

10.1 INTRODUCTION

Design may proceed from the top down or from the bottom up. When it proceeds from the top down, a process of recursive decomposition takes place that produces subsystems, subsubsystems, and so forth, to whatever depth of nesting is appropriate, that are tailored specifically to the application requirements. Real design does not seem to proceed this way. More likely, design ideas are reused, with a certain amount of cobbling together of components (or ideas for components) taking place from the bottom up, and a certain amount of new thinking taking place from the top down. The MachineCharts notation is intended to be suitable for either of these ways. In the top down approach, reuseable components may be identified for use in other designs after a design has been completed, or for use in other parts of the same design after the design of some subsystem has been completed. In either case, the notation identifies such components by adding icons and annotations to existing diagrams, without changing them. Given a design library of such components, they may be incorporated in new designs from the beginning.

Reuseability may take a number of forms. At the most basic level, one reuses well-known design idioms or structures, but redraws them every time in a new design context. At a more advanced level, a library of standard components would be available. Such a library would have template diagrams for installing instances of the component where desired, and timing diagrams for showing how to interact with it, like a hardware components manual. A key feature of reuseable components for concurrent systems is that they may be active.

Reuseable design ideas have appeared throughout the book, with particular emphasis on concurrent systems; they include ideas for organizing peer robots into cooperating teams, for designing their interfaces and internal structures, and for forming the glue structures that bind them together. These ideas are reuseable, even if templates for them are not in a library.

This chapter is concerned with representing reuseable components that may be stored in a library, following the foundation laid in Chapter 5. Both passive and active components are considered. Coverage includes definition, installation, distribution, and removal of components described by templates. Systems that dynamically restructure themselves by installing new components while they are running are also considered.

10.2 TEMPLATES

Recall from Chapter 5 that templates are "manufacturing instructions" for instances, and that instances are identified in the place where they are installed by pointing an install arrow at them, and associating a named template icon with the arrow.

Templates for machines (buttons, boxes, or robots) define *machine structures*, with parts that may be customized on installation shown in dotted outline. Instances appear in diagrams in-place as ordinary machines, and passed between places as appropriately named template-instance parameters (optionally, such parameters may take the shape of the machines they represent).

Stores implicitly have templates, but they are normally only named in diagrams (in the form of a type name prefixed by a colon), and not drawn; they define data structures, but not operations on them. The combination of a data structure definition with a type manager machine that provides operations on it defines an abstract data type (ADT); binding the data structure definition to the type manager is normally done implicitly by associating instance flow icons (identified by type name) with the buttons that operate on them; however, it may be made explicit, in cases where ambiguity might otherwise result, by drawing a template icon for the data structure definition as part of the type manager interface, bound to it by an expose icon to show that it is part of the interface. Flows of data values between machines are drawn differently, depending on whether they are ordinary instances of data structures, or instances of ADTs; the former are drawn as ordinary parameters, the latter as template-instance parameters.

Machine ADTs, in which the templates for the instances define machines rather than just data structures, are possible in the notation, but are better viewed as a way of implementing a more general abstraction (a dynamically installed machine) in a limited implementation technology, as will be shown.

> IMPLEMENTATION IMPLICATIONS:
>
> Ada templates for data structures and tasks are type definitions; instances of them *can* be installed and moved around dynamically, but *cannot* be customized on installation. Otherwise, Ada templates are generic definitions; instances *cannot* be installed and moved around dynamically, but *can* be customized on installation. The visual difference between ordinary parameters and template-instance parameters is a design-level one; all appear in an Ada program as ordinary parameters; the implication for an Ada program is that a **private** type definition is required in the specification of the Ada package that provides the operations on the instances (this may or may not be an access variable).
>
> The notation deliberately has no representation for pointers (access variables in Ada); using pointers is an implementation detail. And the concept of passing a template-instance from place to place is somewhat different from that of passing a pointer, because the default implication is that control over the instance goes along with it, unless specifically indicated otherwise.

10.3 BOXES

10.3.1 INTRODUCTION

For brevity, boxes will be treated as stand-ins for all passive components (active boxes with internal robots will be considered later). We can think of a detached push button as a degenerate box with only one attached button and no internal structure. We can think of an isolated store in a similar manner as a box containing an exposed store and nothing else (in fact, this is a good way to think about stores from a design point of view, because it encourages approaching data abstraction by hiding the stores and attaching buttons to provide operations on them).

> IMPLEMENTATION IMPLICATIONS: This ignores the fact that the Ada view of templates for data structures and packages is quite different; perversely, the Ada view of templates for tasks and data structures is the same, but is different from that for packages. For design conceptualization, it is best to stay above the Ada view and only map to that view for implementation.

10.3.2 BOX TEMPLATE DIAGRAMS

A stack is a convenient data abstraction that will do for illustrating the approach. Figure 10.1 gives template definition charts for one reuseable stack of the store-manager variety and two of the type-manager variety:

- STACK1 is a *store manager* that pushes items into and pops them from a single internal stack store. The nature of the items themselves is customizable. However, note that the the push and pop operators do not define the way in which the items may be used elsewhere, so the item is just an ordinary parameter of the STACK1 machine.

- STACK2 is a *type manager* that provides a template by means of which clients may make their own stack store instances. The STACK parameter is a data abstraction in MachineChart terms because it can only be manipulated by the operations of STACK2. In principle, the only aspect of the STACK template that is visible at the interface is its name.

- STACK3 is a *type manager* that provides create and destroy operations to make new, empty STACK instances and get rid of old ones.

> IMPLEMENTATION IMPLICATIONS: There is no significant conceptual difference between STACK3 and STACK2. In fact, one might say that STACK3 conveys the same concept in a more direct fashion. However STACK3 forces a pointer-based implementation in a program whereas STACK2 does not, so the two different representations are handy for program design. Figures 10.2, 10.3 and 10.4 give Ada generic definitions for STACK1, STACK2, and STACK3, respectively. The body for STACK2 is not given because it contains only procedures that would be identical to those of

those of STACK1. Only the parts of STACK3 that relate to CREATE and DESTROY are shown, because that is the only new stuff. STACK1 and STACK2 are adapted from the Ada reference manual.

10.3.3   BOX STATICS

Figure 10.5 illustrates how boxes may be statically installed from templates and used. Note particularly the difference between data flow and instance flow in the diagrams and how it relates to earlier explanations and diagrams. The alarm jabs are left dangling at this stage, indicating that decisions have not been made about where to put handlers (such decisions may be left until implementation).

IMPLEMENTATION IMPLICATIONS: Figures 10.6 and 10.7 provide Ada examples corresponding to this figure for STACK1 and STACK2 (STACK3 is not shown, because there is essentially nothing new to show).

10.3.4   BOX DYNAMICS

Figure 10.8 illustrates the idea of a box itself being a dynamic object, not just the operands of its buttons. The figure shows a box being dynamically installed from a template, passed around, used, and removed. Recall that the need for this kind of thing arose before in the game-of-life case study (Figure 6.23). There, the box was an active one, which is a more interesting case than the one shown in Figure 10.8. Detailed discussion of dynamic boxes is deferred until after robots are covered, in order that cases like that of Figure 6.23 may be included in the discussion.

IMPLEMENTATION IMPLICATIONS:

Dynamic installation and removal of boxes has no direct meaning, when boxes are interpreted as Ada packages. It may be emulated in Ada for store manager boxes (not illustrated in Figure 10.8) by transforming them into type managers. Simply remove the internal stores, make a type definition for them that treats them as one data structure, put this definition, along with a pointer to it, in the package specification as a private type, and then dynamically create instances as needed. Thus a single type manager package operating on different dynamically created instances of its types achieves much of the effect of dynamically created store manager boxes, each of which operates on different internal data. The only differences are that the type manager itself cannot be passed from place to place, or removed.

Dynamically installed store instances are represented in Ada by pointers to dynamically allocated memory. Pointers are deliberately not part of the notation. Removal in Ada is accomplished by releasing the pointer and leaving it up to the run time system to reclaim the storage. Direct deallocation of the storage itself may only be accomplished in an unchecked manner that may be error prone.

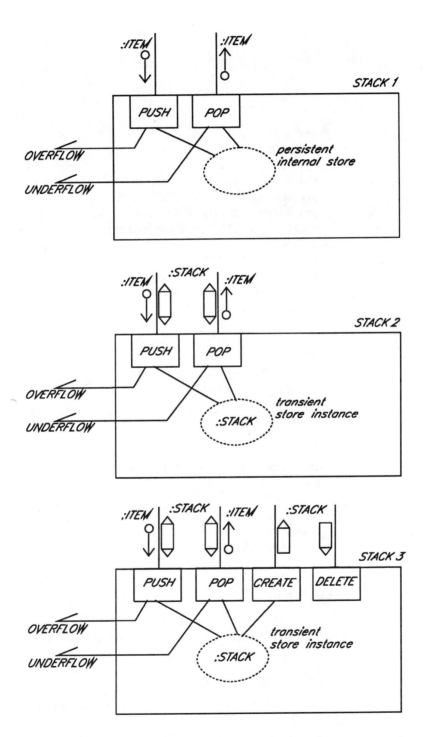

Figure 10.1: STACK MACHINE TEMPLATES

```ada
generic
  SIZE: POSITIVE;
  type ITEM is private;
package STACK is
  procedure PUSH(E: in ITEM);
  procedure POP(E: out ITEM);
  OVERFLOW, UNDERFLOW : exception;
end STACK;

package body STACK is
  type TABLE is array(POSITIVE range <>) of ITEM;
  SPACE : TABLE(1..SIZE);
  INDEX : NATURAL:=0;
  procedure PUSH(E: in ITEM) is
  begin
    if INDEX >= SIZE then
      raise OVERFLOW;
    endif;
    INDEX:=INDEX + 1;
    SPACE(INDEX) := E;
  end PUSH;
  procedure POP(E: out ITEM) is
  begin
    if INDEX = 0 then
      raise UNDERFLOW;
    endif;
    E := SPACE(INDEX);
    INDEX:=INDEX - 1;
  end POP;
end STACK;
```

Figure 10.2: ADA GENERIC STACK1 (SPEC AND BODY)

```
generic
  type ITEM is private;
package ON_STACKS is
  type STACK(SIZE:POSITIVE) is limited private;
  procedure PUSH(S: in out STACK; E: in ITEM);
  procedure POP(S: in out STACK; E: out ITEM);
  OVERFLOW, UNDERFLOW : exception;
private  -- USED BY CLIENTS ONLY FOR MANUFACTURE
  type TABLE is array (POSITIVE range <>) of ITEM;
  type STACK(SIZE:POSITIVE) is
    record
      SPACE : TABLE(1..SIZE);
      INDEX : NATURAL:=0;
    end  record;
end ON_STACKS;
```

Figure 10.3: ADA GENERIC STACK2 (SPEC ONLY)

```
generic
  type ITEM is private;
package MAKE_STACKS is
  type STACK is private;
  procedure CREATE(S: out STACK);
  procedure DESTROY(S: in STACK);
  procedure PUSH(S: in out STACK; E: in ITEM);
  procedure POP(S: in out STACK; E: out ITEM);
  OVERFLOW, UNDERFLOW : exception;
private
  type STACK_STRUCTURE(SIZE:POSITIVE);
  type STACK is access STACK_STRUCTURE;
end MAKE_STACKS;

package body MAKE_STACKS is
  type STACK_STRUCTURE(SIZE:POSITIVE);
    array (POSITIVE range <>) of ITEM;
  procedure CREATE(S: out STACK);
  begin
    S := new STACK_STRUCTURE(SIZE);
  end CREATE;
  procedure DESTROY(S: in out STACK);
  begin
    S:= null;
    -- BUT NOTE THIS DOES NOT DEALLOCATE STACK_STRUCTURE
  end DESTROY;
  -- INCOMPLETE
end MAKE_STACKS;
```

Figure 10.4: ADA GENERIC STACK3 (SPEC AND INCOMPLETE BODY)

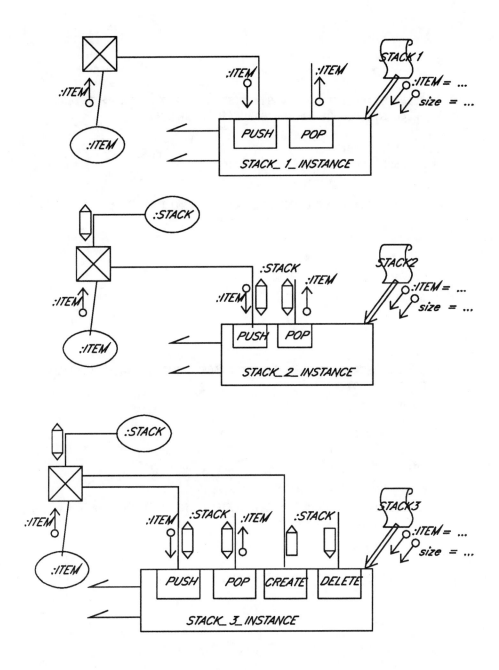

Figure 10.5: STATIC INSTALLATION AND USE OF STACK MACHINES

```
package STACK_INT is new STACK(SIZE => 200, ITEM => INTEGER);
package STACK_BOOL is new STACK(100, BOOLEAN);
...
STACK_INT.PUSH(N);
STACK_BOOL.PUSH(TRUE);
```

Figure 10.6: STACK1 STATIC INSTALLATION AND USE IN ADA

```
declare
 package STACK_REAL is new ON_STACKS(REAL); use STACK_REAL;
 S:STACK(100);
begin
   ...
  PUSH(S,2.54);
   ...
end;
```

Figure 10.7: STACK2 STATIC INSTALLATION AND USE IN ADA

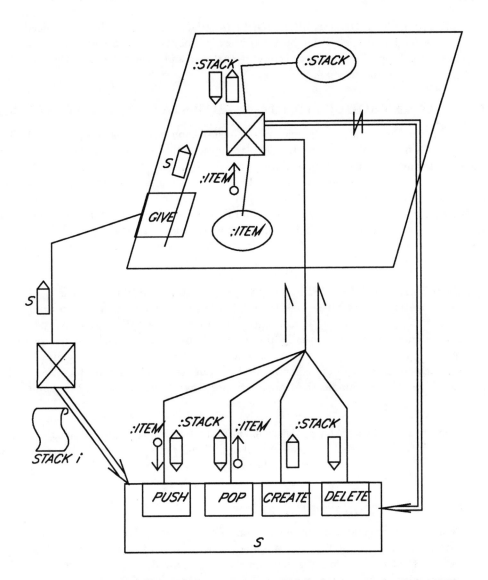

Figure 10.8: DYNAMIC INSTALLATION AND DISTRIBUTION OF BOXES

10.4   ROBOTS

10.4.1   ROBOT TEMPLATE DIAGRAMS

Robot template diagrams are similar in form to box template diagrams, including customization possibilities.

> IMPLEMENTATION IMPLICATIONS: In Ada, tasks cannot be customized from type definitions so this notation must be mapped into a combination of use of the type definition in the conventional way and then initializing the task through an initialization entry.

10.4.2   AN INTRODUCTION TO ROBOT STATICS AND DYNAMICS

Installation may be static or dynamic. Static installation has the same operational effect as designing a one-of robot in a particular place, except that using a template allows more than one instance to appear in that place.

However, static installation places may be dynamic themselves. Figure 10.9 illustrates static installation of a pool of robots in a dynamic place (the inside of a button). The way this is structured, no more than the number of robots in the static pool can ever run because the robots do not outlive the lifetime of the place where they are installed. A converse effect is that the button will not terminate until the robots have terminated (so the robots better not be indefinitely cyclic).

> IMPLEMENTATION IMPLICATIONS: Figure 10.10 shows how this may be implemented in Ada. The task type definition cannot be "with-ed" to bring it in from a file to where it is needed, as can be done with generic package specifications, but must actually appear in the program text. This is because instances of Ada task types are variables and their templates are type definitions that can no more be library components than can other variable type definitions. In this particular example, there are never more than 3 tasks running at the same time.

Figure 10.11 slightly transforms this problem so that the robots are dynamically installed outside the installing button. The robot pool is no longer of static size (its maximum size depends on how many times **A** visits **B**), because the robots can now outlive the place that installed them.

> IMPLEMENTATION IMPLICATIONS:
>
> Figure 10.12 gives an Ada implemention of Figure 10.9. The mapping of the structural aspect of the diagram into program declarations is not entirely obvious without some explanation; the diagram gives clues, not details. As we shall see, the MachineChart diagram expresses a common sense intent that is obscured in the Ada implementation.
>
> The template/instance machinery for the tasks is rather distributed in the program; the instances are represented by pointers (access variables), but the

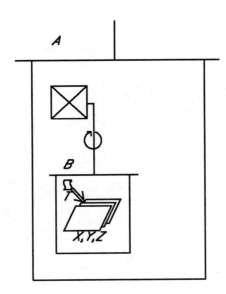

Figure 10.9: STATIC INSTALLATION OF ROBOTS IN A DYNAMIC PLACE

```
procedure A is
  task type T;
  task body T is ... end T;

  procedure B is
    X, Y, Z:T;
  begin
    null;
  end B;

begin
  for I in 1..10
  loop
    B;
  end loop;
end A;
```

Figure 10.10: TASKS STATICALLY INSTALLED IN A DYNAMIC PLACE

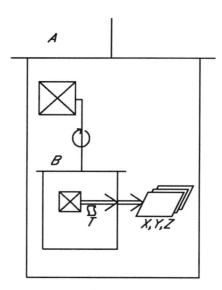

Figure 10.11: DYNAMIC INSTALLATION OF ROBOTS OUTSIDE THE INSTALLING PLACE

pointer type definition is in one place and the declarations that associate names with pointer instances are in another. The key rule in mapping to Ada is that the pointer type definition is placed in the text where the the task is intended to run. In this example, this is the place where the MachineChart diagram positions the corresponding robot. This place is outside the installing procedure here, so the installed tasks can run independently of their installer.

Naming is a bit counterintuitive, because the pointer instances are given names inside the installing place, whereas the tasks they point to actually outlive this place. In fact we may have the bizarre effect that the pointers are lost as ways of identifying the tasks if they are not returned as parameters by the installing procedure before it terminates. Clearly one must be careful about interpreting names in machine chart diagrams as task pointer names. There may be many tasks (X,Y,Z, ...) and only a few pointer variable names (P,Q,R). There is no place in this program example where it is meaningful to give a program component the names X,Y,Z, ...; to do this, the pointer variable declarations would have to be moved outside of the lower scope.

10.4.3   MOVING DYNAMIC INSTANCES AROUND

Given that we can dynamically install active instances, the next question is how may they be made dynamically available to other than the installer (i.e., distributed)? The common sense MachineChart concept illustrated by Figure 10.13 is that the instances are actually

```
procedure A is
  task type T;
  task body T is ... end T;

  type NAMET is access T;

  procedure B is
    P, Q, R: NAMET;
  begin
    P:= new T;
    Q:= new T;
    R:= new T;
  end B;

begin
  for I in 1..10
  loop
    B;
  end loop;
end A;
```

Figure 10.12: ADA PROGRAM FOR DYNAMICALLY INSTALLED TASKS

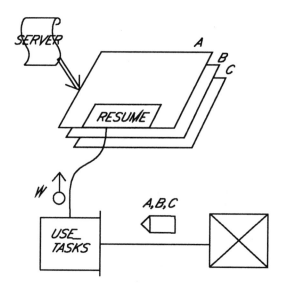

Figure 10.13: DISTRIBUTION OF STATICALLY INSTALLED ROBOTS

sent from place to place for this purpose; the concept in the figure is that the installing place's engine passes the instances to USE_TASKS for action. These are statically installed instances; however, the concept is the same for dynamically installed ones.

> IMPLEMENTATION IMPLICATIONS: Ada code for this example is provided in Figure 10.14. Note that in Ada tasks can only be **in** parameters, so if one wants to pass a task **out**, as suggested by some of the diagrams in this book, one must embed it in variable such as an array or a record (not illustrated here).

10.4.4   DYNAMIC REMOVAL OF ROBOTS

A difference between removal of boxes and robots is that robots can remove themselves (commit suicide) by terminating their agendas or by other means.

There are several cases where robots should not run forever, as discussed below:

- Robots installed in dynamic places should obviously not run forever. A way of indicating this is shown in Figure 10.15(a): the implication is that the suicide choice is taken when the robot has nothing else to do and the place in which it is installed is itself removed.

- A robot may be removed explicitly by politely asking it to commit suicide at a convenient time, as shown in Figure 10.15(b).

```
procedure MAIN is
  task type SERVER is
    entry RESUME(X:DATA);
  end SERVER;

  task body SERVER is seperate;

  A, B, C : SERVER;

  procedure UXE_TASKS(L: in SERVER) is
    W:DATA;
  begin
  --COMPUTE ALL KINDS OF DATA HERE
    W:= ........;
    L.RESUME(W);
  end USE_TASKS;

begin
  USE_TASKS(A);
  USE_TASKS(B);
  USE_TASKS(C);
end MAIN;
```

Figure 10.14: DISTRIBUTION OF STATICALLY INSTALLED TASKS IN ADA

- A robot may be removed directly without its consent, using the remove icon, as shown in Figure 10.15(c). The semantics of this approach depend very critically on the implementation technology; inadequate technology might cause matters to be left in an inconsistent state. Normally, this approach would be undesirable; however, there are practical situations where doing it might be desirable (such as a change of operational mode in which nothing the robot is doing is of any further significance, or the termination of a situation that has gotten out of control due to some error).

IMPLEMENTATION IMPLICATIONS:

Figure 10.16 shows how to implement the concept of Figure 10.15(a)in Ada; suicide is accomplished by a terminate alternative in the selective accept.

Figure 10.17 shows how to implement the concept of Figure 10.15(b)in Ada; suicide is accomplished by exiting the main loop and reaching the end of the agenda.

There is no graceful way in Ada of implementing the concept of Figure 10.16(c); one aborts the task without giving it any chance to clean up and takes the consequences. There used to be the concept of raising a tasking exception, that allowed cleanup before termination, and there is ongoing discussion about putting it back into the language.

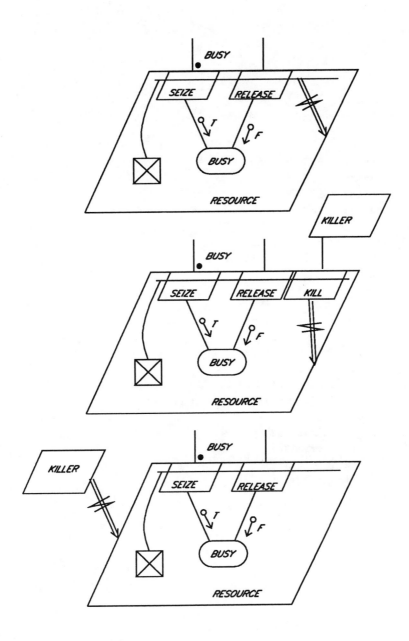

Figure 10.15: SUICIDE IN A DYNAMIC CONTEXT

```
task type RESOURCE is
  entry SEIZE;
  entry RELEASE;
end RESOURCE;

task body RESOURCE is
  BUSY :BOOLEAN := FALSE;
begin
  loop
    select
      when not BUSY =>
        accept SEIZE
          do BUSY:= TRUE; end SEIZE;
    or
      accept RELEASE
        do BUSY:= FALSE; end RELEASE;
    or
      when not busy =>
        terminate;
    end select;
  end loop;
end RESOURCE;
```

Figure 10.16: TASK SUICIDE IN A DYNAMIC CONTEXT

```
task type RESOURCE is
  entry SEIZE;
  entry RELEASE;
  entry KILL;
end RESOURCE;

task body RESOURCE is
  BUSY :BOOLEAN := FALSE;
begin
  loop
    select
      when not BUSY =>
        accept SEIZE
          do BUSY:= TRUE; end SEIZE;
    or
      accept RELEASE
        do BUSY:= FALSE; end RELEASE;
    or
      accept KILL
        do cleanup; exit; end KILL;
    end select;
  end loop;
end RESOURCE;
```

Figure 10.17: TASK SUICIDE BY EXTERNAL REQUEST

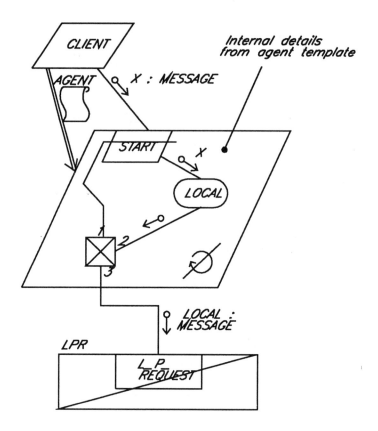

Figure 10.18: A PRINT AGENT FROM A TEMPLATE

10.5   THE ART OF COMPONENTRY

10.5.1   INTRODUCTION

This section provides several progressively more sophisticated examples of the art of componentry, showing first the ideas in MachineChart diagrams and then examples of their translation into implementations in our reference programming language, Ada.

10.5.2   PRINTER SUPPORT

THE BASIC IDEA

Figure 10.18 shows how a client might install a print agent from template whenever and wherever printing is called for, to avoid having itself to visit LPR and wait for printing to be done. The concept is that the agent template is stored in a library.

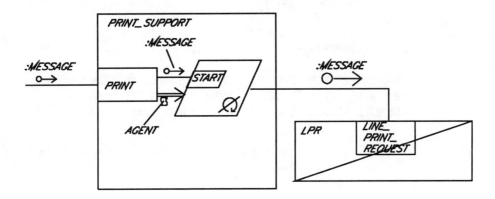

Figure 10.19: A PRINT SUPPORT SUBSYSTEM

A PRINT SUPPORT SUBSYSTEM

Now suppose we want to pave the way for a future general print service of which this agent provides only a simple example. Then it might be better to hide the agent in a print support subsystem as shown in Figure 10.19. Internally there is a dynamically installed instance of AGENT.

A full generalization, not explored in this example, would have PRINT-SUPPORT itself as a template for dynamically installable subsystem instances (as we have seen, this generalization is not directly implementable in Ada).

IMPLEMENTATION IMPLICATIONS:

Figure 10.20 gives the Ada specification for a package to implement Figure 10.19.

Figure 10.21 gives an Ada program for the body of the print support package. The Ada tasking machinery follows from earlier rules. This combination of packaging and tasking may seem excessively complicated if all we want is a dynamically installed print agent as the original Figure 10.18 suggested. However, it is the only way of getting the agent's definition into a library. An Ada designer can choose to indicate this possibility explicitly by drawing MachineCharts in the style of Figure 10.19. Or such matters can be left undecided at the level of Figure 10.18 until a design is complete. Then Figure 10.19 indicates the implicit interpretation of Figure 10.18 for the purpose of getting the agent's definition into a library. Alternatively, the Ada program may be viewed as providing the implicit interpretation of the earlier figure without the need for Figure 10.19.

For cases where figures like Figure 10.19 fall naturally out of the application requirements, this Ada example shows how to intepret them.

```
package PRINT_SUPPORT is
   type MESSAGE is .........;
 procedure PRINT(X:MESSAGE);
end PRINT_SUPPORT;

--PROCEDURE PRINT WILL DISPATCH A REQUEST TO LINE PRINTER
--BUT WILL NOT WAIT UNTIL ACTUAL PRINTING IS DONE.
--IT WILL RETURN TO CALLER AFTER AGENT STARTS.
```

Figure 10.20: ADA SPECIFICATION OF A SIMPLE PRINT SUPPORT MANAGER

```
with LPR
package body PRINT_SUPPORT is

  task type AGENT is
    entry START(X:in MESSAGE);
  end AGENT;

  type AGENT_PTR is access AGENT;

  task body AGENT is
    LOCAL:MESSAGE;
  begin
    accept START(X: in MESSAGE)
      do LOCAL:=X;
    end START;
    LPR.LINE_PRINT_REQUEST(LOCAL);
  end AGENT;

  procedure PRINT(X: in MESSAGE) is
    T:AGENT_PTR;
  begin
    T:=new AGENT;
    T.START(X);
  end PRINT;

end PRINT_SUPPORT;
```

Figure 10.21: ADA PRINT SUPPORT PACKAGE

```
generic
package PRINT_SUPPORT is
  type MESSAGE is .........;
  procedure PRINT(X:MESSAGE);
end PRINT_SUPPORT;

--PROCEDURE PRINT WILL DISPATCH A REQUEST TO LINE PRINTER
--BUT WILL NOT WAIT UNTIL ACTUAL PRINTING IS DONE.
--IT WILL RETURN TO CALLER AFTER AGENT STARTS.
```

Figure 10.22: CHANGING THE PRINT SUPPORT MANAGER TO A TEMPLATE

THE PRINT SUPPORT SUBSYSTEM AS A TEMPLATE

It would be a simple matter to change PRINT-SUPPORT in Figure 10.19 into an instance called, say PRINT-SUPPORT-INSTANCE, of a template called PRINT-SUPPORT, instead of as a designed-in-place component. All we would have to do is add an installed-from-template annotation like that in Figure 10.29 (the notation has been specifically designed to make such changes convenient).

IMPLEMENTATION IMPLICATIONS:

The corresponding Ada package specification would now look like Figure 10.22. This is a non-customizable generic that allows multiple reuse of the code.

DYNAMIC INSTALLATION

Following the lead of the original idea in Figure 10.18, we might want to install instances of the PRINT-SUPPORT template not only statically, but also dynamically, as illustrated by Figure 10.23. Note that this is a more general example than Figure 10.8, because the dynamically installed box is active. Extending the repertoire of box categories, we may now add *machine manager* to the earlier categories of store manager and type manager. A machine manager contains active internal machinery.

IMPLEMENTATION IMPLICATIONS: Dynamic installation of a machine manager as in Figure 10.23 is not directly possible in Ada, but the effect may be achieved in a similar fashion to that for a store manager, because Ada treats tasks as variables. Transform the dynamically installable machine manager box into a type manager package, the operands of which are instances of a private type declared in the specification that includes everything that was intended to be inside the box, including tasks representing the internal robots of the box. This works as long as there are no nested boxes. The result has the same constraints as mentioned before for the store manager case. Details are left for the reader.

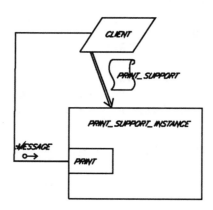

(compare with Figure 10.18)

Figure 10.23: A SENSIBLE DIAGRAM NOT IMPLEMENTABLE IN ADA

10.5.3 KEYBOARD MANAGER

INTRODUCTION

Transporter glue structures have emerged as canonical forms in this book, but so far have always been treated as custom structures in the place where they operate. A standard transporter part, customizable for use in particular places in designs, would be desirable. For example, it would be useful to be able to customize a transporter to deliver keyboard input obtained from a GET button on some IO subsystem to a client-defined place, to save the client from the possibility of having to wait at GET. Figure 10.24 conveys the basic idea first, and then shows some transformations of it. The first structure shows a transporter, called WATCHER, dynamically installed by a CLIENT, and customized on installation to notify WHO_TO_CALL when keyboard input arrives. The intermediate structure recognizes that, in general, one might want a dynamically installable keyboard management subsystem containing not only WATCHER, but also possibly other machinery as well (not shown). The final structure separates (somewhat awkwardly) the customization and dynamic installation into two parts: customization is done statically at the subsystem level, and affects only the KEYBOARD_WATCHER template; dynamic installation is performed only of WATCHER, through a CONTROL_KEYBOARD button of the installed instance of KEYBOARD_MANAGER; this structure indicates how it would have to be done in Ada to get a customizable keyboard watcher into a library.

A KEYBOARD MANAGER SUBSYSTEM

Let us continue to develop the final structure in Figure 10.24 (this will be of interest mainly to Ada readers). Figure 10.25 shows a way of drawing the KEYBOARD_MANAGER template; remember that the template is not an operational component itself, so the internal dynamic installation of an instance of WATCH_KEYBOARD is shown only to indicate what will happen in an instance of KEYBOARD_MANAGER. The dotted finger extending from the instance of WATCH_KEYBOARD to WHO_TO_CALL identifies WHO_TO_CALL as a customizable feature of KEYBOARD_MANAGER, not WATCH_KEYBOARD.

> IMPLEMENTATION IMPLICATIONS: Figure 10.26 gives a generic package specification for the keyboard manager in Figure 10.25, showing how to parameterize WHO-TO-CALL. Figure 10.27 gives the body details, including the watcher task type definition. Figure 10.28 gives the watcher task details.

INSTALLATION AND USE OF THE KEYBOARD MANAGER SUBSYSTEM

Figure 10.29 shows static installation and use of an instance of KEYBOARD-MANAGER. Dynamic installation along the lines of the earlier Figure 10.23 might also be desired, including the possibility of making the instance available in different places dynamically.

> IMPLEMENTATION IMPLICATIONS: MachineCharts allows dynamic installation, but Ada does not; Figure 10.29 matches what Ada can do. Figure 10.30

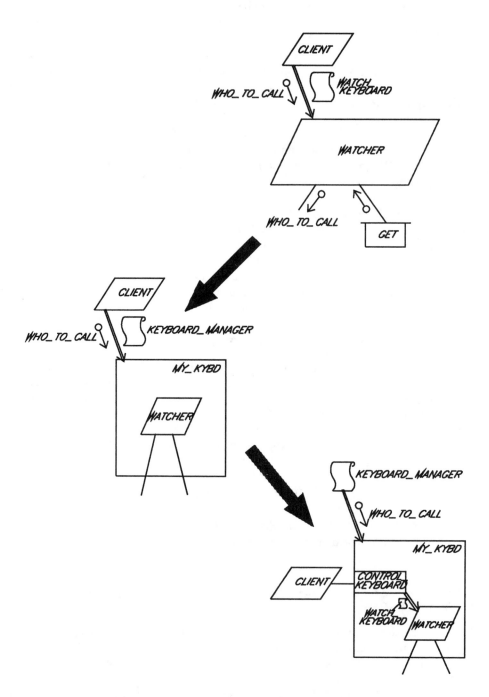

Figure 10.24: DYNAMIC INSTALLATION OF A KEYBOARD WATCHER

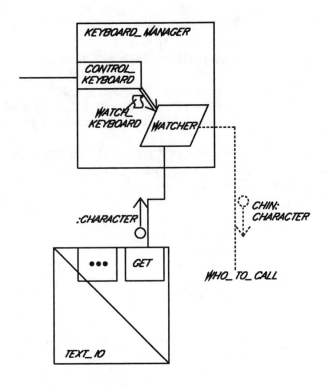

Figure 10.25: A KEYBOARD MANAGER TEMPLATE

```
generic
with procedure WHO_TO_CALL(CHIN: in CHARACTER);
package KEYBOARD_MANAGER is

  procedure CONTROL_KEYBOARD;

--MANAGES THE KEYBOARD AND GENERATES A CALL TO
--WHO_TO_CALL WHENEVER KEY IS PRESSED.

end KEYBOARD_MANAGER;
```

Figure 10.26: ADA SPECIFICATION OF A GENERIC KEYBOARD MANAGER

```
with TEXT_IO
package body KEYBOARD_MANAGER is

  task type WATCH_KEYBOARD;
  type NAME is access WATCH_KEYBOARD;
  task body WATCH_KEYBOARD is seperate;
--
--WATCH_KEYBOARD WILL MONITOR FOR KEYBOARD INPUT,
--AND CALL WHO_TO_CALL
--

  procedure CONTROL_KEYBOARD is
    WATCHER: NAME;
  begin
    WATCHER:= new WATCH_KEYBOARD;
  end CONTROL_KEYBOARD;
end KEYBOARD_MANAGER;
```

Figure 10.27: ADA BODY OF A GENERIC KEYBOARD MANAGER

```
seperate KEYBOARD_MANAGER
task body WATCH_KEYBOARD is
  LOC_CHAR:CHARACTER;
begin
  loop
    TEXT_IO.GET(LOC_CHAR);
    exit when LOC_CHAR = ASCII.ESC;
    WHO_TO_CALL (LOC_CHAR);
  end loop;
end WATCH_KEYBOARD;
```

Figure 10.28: ADA WATCH-KEYBOARD TASK TYPE DEFINITION

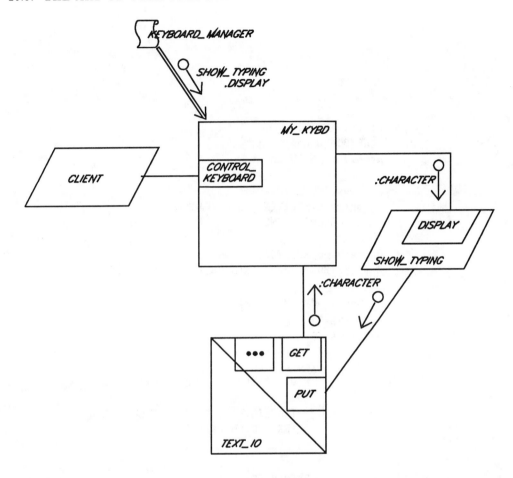

Figure 10.29: INSTALLING AND USING AN INSTANCE OF THE KEYBOARD-MANAGER TEMPLATE

gives a corresponding Ada program. As with the print support system, Figure 10.29 and Figure 10.30 can be regarded as interpretations for Ada implementations of the top or middle structures of Figure 10.24.

AN "ENHANCED" KEYBOARD MANAGER

The keyboard manager of Figure 10.25 is deficient in not providing a way to stop keyboard watching. Actually providing such a mechanism is tricky because there are too many places to wait. Figure 10.31 shows a naive attempt at enhancement for this purpose; internal details of WATCH-KEYBOARD are given in Figure 10.32. The problem is that this will not work. Once WATCH-KEYBOARD visits GET, it is stuck until a character arrives. After a character arrives it can check STOP, but in the meantime the client is stuck at STOP,

```
with TEXT_IO,
  KEYBOARD_MANAGER;
procedure MAIN is

  task SHOW_TYPING is
  entry DISPLAY(X: in CHARACTER);
  end SHOW_TYPING;

  package MY_KYBD is new
    KEYBOARD_MANAGER(SHOW_TYPING.DISPLAY);

  task body SHOW_TYPING is
    begin
      loop
        select
          accept
            DISPLAY(X: in CHARACTER)
          do
            TEXT_IO.PUT("INTERRUPT RECEIVED");
            TEXT_IO.PUT(X);
          end DISPLAY;
        or
          terminate;
        end select;
      end loop;
  end SHOW_TYPING;
  begin
    MY_KYBD.CONTROL_KEYBOARD;
    delay 100.0;
end MAIN;
```

Figure 10.30: ADA INSTANTIATION AND USE OF THE GENERIC KEYBOARD-MANAGER

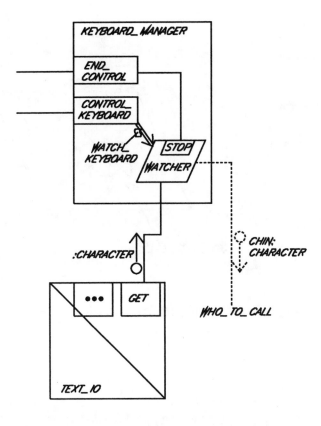

(compare with Figure 10.25)

Figure 10.31: AN "ENHANCED" KEYBOARD MANAGER TEMPLATE

waiting, unless the client itself balks or times out, in which case WATCH-KEYBOARD will not know that it is no longer wanted. One could require the transporter to balk or time out at GET, but then TEXT-IO would require modification, because it is meaningless to balk or time out on an immediate button such as GET. The nature of transporters is to wait where waiting is unavoidable as it is with GET; trying to interfere with this obviously causes problems. In fact there is no good solution to this problem without changing TEXT-IO.

The underlying cause of the problem is the nature of GET; one has to visit it and wait without any alternative. One should be able either to specify a timeout parameter on visits to GET, or to customize TEXT_IO as a notifier, so GET is not needed.

IMPLEMENTATION IMPLICATIONS: Figure 10.33 gives a new Ada specification; Figure 10.34 gives a corresponding package body. Figure 10.35 gives the WATCH-KEYBOARD task body.

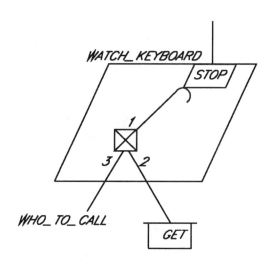

Figure 10.32: AN "ENHANCED" WATCH-KEYBOARD ROBOT

```
generic
with procedure WHO_TO_CALL(CHIN: in CHARACTER);
package KEYBOARD_MANAGER is

  procedure CONTROL_KEYBOARD;
  procedure END_CONTROL;

--MANAGES THE KEYBOARD AND GENERATES A CALL TO
--WHO_TO_CALL WHENEVER KEY IS PRESSED.
--
--THE USING PROGRAM NOW EXPLICITLY DECIDES ON A
--A CHARACTER BY CHARACTER BASIS WHETHER OR NOT TO
--TERMINATE THE MONITORING. THE USER MUST STILL BE
--SURE TO TERMINATE THE MONITORING
--PROCESS BEFORE ENDING THE PROGRAM.
--
end KEYBOARD_MANAGER;
```

Figure 10.33: NEW ADA GENERIC SPECIFICATION

```
with TEXT_IO
package body KEYBOARD_MANAGER is

  task type WATCH_KEYBOARD is
    entry STOP;
  end WATCH_KEYBOARD;

  type NAME is access WATCH_KEYBOARD;
  WATCHER: NAME;
--
--DECLARATION HERE FOR VISIBILITY FROM END_CONTROL
--
  task body WATCH_KEYBOARD is seperate;
--
--WATCH_KEYBOARD WILL MONITOR FOR INPUT,
--AND CALL WHO_TO_CALL
--STOP WILL EVENTUALLY STOP IT
--
  procedure CONTROL_KEYBOARD is
   begin
    WATCHER:= new WATCH_KEYBOARD;
   end CONTROL_KEYBOARD;

  procedure END_CONTROL is
   begin
    WATCHER.STOP;
   end END_CONTROL;
end KEYBOARD_MANAGER;
```

Figure 10.34: NEW ADA GENERIC BODY

```
seperate (KEYBOARD_MANAGER)
task body WATCH_KEYBOARD is
  LOC_CHAR:CHARACTER;
begin
  loop
    select
      accept STOP;
      exit;
    else
      null;
    end select;
    TEXT_IO.GET(LOC_CHAR);
    WHO_TO_CALL(LOC_CHAR);
  end loop;
end WATCH_KEYBOARD;
```

Figure 10.35: NEW ADA WATCH-KEYBOARD TASK TYPE DEFINITION

10.5.4   MOUSE MANAGER

Let us suppose we have a single-button mouse and that we arrange to use it in the following way. One click sets a timer going; the timer running out triggers user-defined action P1; a second click before the timer runs out triggers user-defined action P2. The idea is that the mouse user defines work buttons to perform P1 and P2, and then customizes a mouse manager subsystem to visit P1 and P2 when required. The mouse subsystem must provide a click handler that can trigger P1 or P2 and a position tracker that will provide the mouse position when it is needed by the user. This could be accomplished with a mouse manager template to be used in the manner of Figure 10.29, but let us try a different approach, to illustrate that templates for machines may themselves be part of machine interfaces.

Figure 10.36 shows a non-template subsystem MOUSE-STUFF that provides a template MOUSE-USER-PROGRAM by means of which users may customize a local button, called here GO, to start the mouse action, and to provide the customized click handling while the mouse action continues. GO is customized to visit not only P1 and P2, but also a user-defined button M that provides the user's main agenda for mouse operations. MOUSE-STUFF also provides a button GET-LOC to get the mouse position from an internal position tracker. Not shown is the way in which the different user-defined buttons exchange information (following the paradigm of this book, they would likely do it through some shared data abstraction in the user's domain, supported by a store manager box). The mouse action stops when M's agenda terminates. This is not necessarily an optimum solution to this problem, but simply illustrates a style of solution. It might be better to put both the click handler and the position tracker in the body of MOUSE-STUFF, so that the mouse position could be provided directly as a parameter of the handler's visit to P2, instead of requiring the user to get it separately as shown here.

Figure 10.37 shows the hidden, shared position tracker in MOUSE-STUFF, called MOUSE-LOCATION-MGR, that supplies positions to GET-LOC.

Figure 10.38 shows the MOUSE-USER-PROGRAM template containing the click handler. The diagram is intended to indicate that the click handler waits for the first click, then waits for either a click or a timeout, whichever comes first; only if the second click occurs does it visit P2-CLICK. We are on the edge here of stretching the limits of the structural notation in indicating sequencing; this is an example of processing requirements depending on history that is better handled for design purposes by a plug-in state machine. Doing this with an ACM is left as an exercise for the reader.

> IMPLEMENTATION IMPLICATIONS: Figures 10.39, 10.40, 10.41, and 10.42 map the interesting parts of MOUSE-STUFF to Ada. To use this package, the application programmer only has to write the code for the mainline procedure and the two click procedures, together with a main program that transfers control to the package, and then write some declarations to **with** the package and **instantiate** the customized procedure. Details are left for the reader.

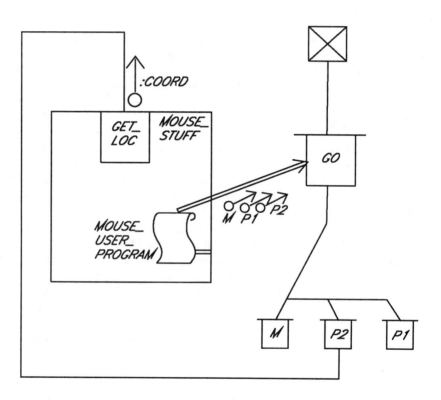

Figure 10.36: A MOUSE HANDLING SUBSYSTEM

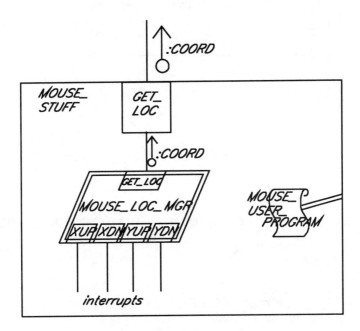

Figure 10.37: MOUSE-STUFF PROVIDES A SHARED POSITION TRACKER

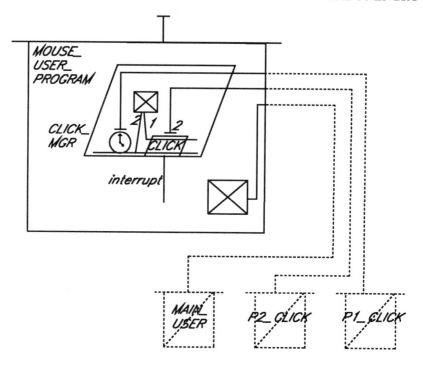

Figure 10.38: THE NATURE OF THE HIDDEN CLICK HANDLER

```
package MOUSE_STUFF is
  type COORD is .....;
  procedure GET_LOCATION (X,Y: out COORD);

  generic
    with procedure P1CLICK;
    with procedure P2CLICK;
    with procedure MAIN_USER;
  procedure MOUSE_USER_PROGRAM;

end MOUSE_STUFF;
```

(specification from Figure 10.36)

Figure 10.39: ADA MOUSE-STUFF SPECIFICATION

```
task MOUSE_LOCATION_MGR is
   entry XUP;
   for XUP USE AT .......;
   entry XDN;
   for XDN USE AT .......;
   entry YUP;
   for YUP USE AT .......;
   entry YDN;
   for YDN USE AT .......;
   entry GET_LOCATION(X,Y: out COORD);
end MOUSE_LOCATION_MGR;
```

(position-tracker task specification from Figure 10.36)

Figure 10.40: SPECIFICATION OF THE ADA POSITION TRACKER TASK

```
task body MOUSE_LOCATION_MGR is

  type LOCATION is record
    X,Y:COORD;
  end record;

  function INIT_COORD return LOCATION;
  LOC:LOCATION:=INIT_COORD;
  function INIT_COORD return LOCATION is seperate;
begin
  loop
    select
      accept XUP;
      LOC.X:=LOC.X + 1;
    or
      accept XDN;
      LOC.X:=LOC.X - 1;
    or
      accept YUP;
      LOC.X:=LOC.X + 1;
    or
      accept YDN;
      LOC.X:=LOC.X - 1;
    or
      accept GET_LOCATION(X,Y: out COORD);
      do X:= LOC.X; Y:= LOC.Y;
      end GET_LOCATION;
    end select;
  end loop;
end MOUSE_LOCATION_MGR;
```

(position-tracker task body from Figure 10.36)

Figure 10.41: BODY OF THE ADA POSITION TRACKER TASK

```
procedure MOUSE_USER_PROGRAM is
--
--THIS TASK MANAGES CLICKS
--AND DISPATCHES APPROPRIATE ROUTINES
--
  task CLICK_MGR is
    entry CLICK;
    for CLICK use at .....;
  end CLICK_MGR;

  task body CLICK_MGR is
    LOC_TIME:DURATION:=2.0;
  begin
    loop
      accept CLICK;
      select
        accept CLICK;
        P2CLICK;
      or
        delay LOC_TIME;
        P1CLICK;
      end select;
    end loop;
  end CLICK_MGR;
begin
  MAIN_USER;
end MOUSE_USER_PROGRAM;
```

(click handler task from Figure 10.38)

Figure 10.42: THE ADA HIDDEN CLICK HANDLER IS A TASK

10.6   TELLERS AND CUSTOMERS IN A BANK

Tellers and customers in a bank relate the template and instance ideas to an everyday example. The figures that follow are assumed to be self-explanatory, except for the points of particular interest highlighted below.

Figure 10.43 sets the stage by illustrating the static customization of tellers with wicket numbers (which as noted earlier is not directly possible in Ada). Then we gradually generalize the problem towards dynamic solutions. The Ada reader may wish to experiment with mapping these designs to Ada.

Figure 10.44 suggests how installation customization may be accomplished by the dispatcher assigning wicket numbers on startup (following which tellers always use the same wicket number) (this would represent a possible Ada mechanism explicitly).

Figure 10.45 shows how wicket numbers may be allocated by the dispatcher when asked by the teller.

Figure 10.46 shows that if tellers are installed dynamically, then they may be distributed to customers, while still being used in the bank context.

Figure 10.47 shows that if customers are installed dynamically, then they may be distributed to tellers for servicing from the bank context.

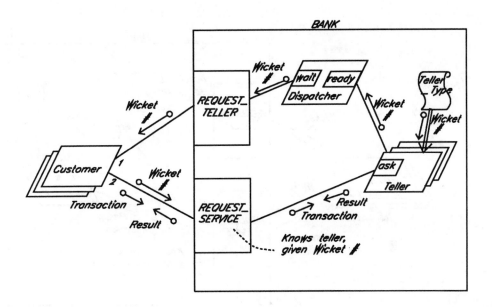

Figure 10.43: STATIC CUSTOMIZATION ON INSTALLATION

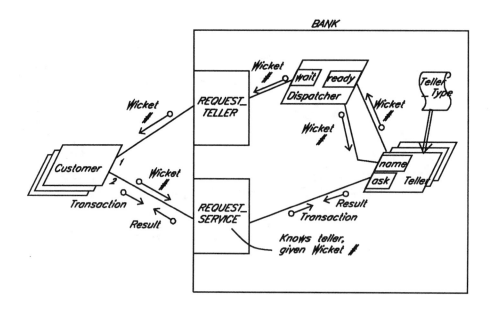

Figure 10.44: EXPLICIT INITIALIZATION ON STARTUP

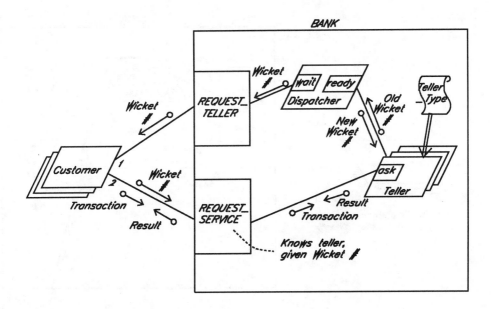

Figure 10.45: DYNAMICALLY ASSIGNED WICKET NUMBERS

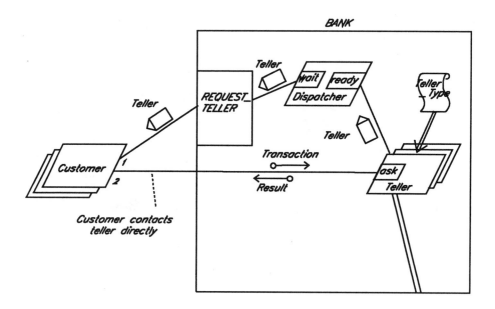

Figure 10.46: DYNAMICALLY INSTALLED TELLERS

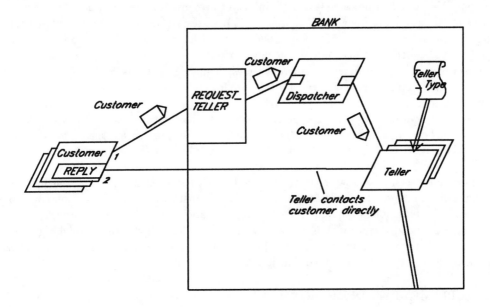

Figure 10.47: DYNAMICALLY INSTALLED CUSTOMERS

10.7   DYNAMICALLY-INSTALLED ACTIVE MACHINES VS. ACTIVE ADTS

What is the relationship between dynamic installation of boxes — as in the game of life case study of Chapter 6 (Figure 6.23), and the printer support subsystem earlier in this chapter (Figure 10.23) — and type managers, like those in Figure 10.1 that represent the programming abstraction of an abstract data type (ADT)? This issue is addressed here in the context of an example from computer communications.

Figure 10.48 illustrates dynamic installation of boxes in a computer communications example. This is a layered communication system along the lines of the one in Chapter 7. The **Li** boxes are subsystems that support communication over dedicated physical links; they may be viewed as link drivers. The link layer box provides an interface for installing and using a variable number of **Li** boxes. The **Ni** boxes are higher level subsystems that support, say, virtual circuits multiplexed over physical links. They might also be gathered together in network layer box, but this is not shown.

Links may go up and down at different times, requiring that link handlers be installed and removed dynamically. Assuming all links are logically identical, links may be installed from a common template. Configuring the installation correctly requires that link boxes know which network boxes to send upgoing messages to, and network boxes know which link boxes to send downgoing messages to. The idea expressed in the figure is that network boxes "send themselves" to link boxes after the links are installed, and vice versa, to accomplish this purpose. A variant of the notation is used here that is only cosmetic: instead of undifferentiated instance flow icons that must be distinguished by naming, the instance flows are given shapes that indicate the nature of the instances (this convention could be extended to include, for example, parallelogram and trapezoid shapes, representing robots).

The recommended approach is to stick with figures like Figure 10.48 for design capture, and map them to implementation using ADTs, without explicitly drawing diagrams representing the latter, as described and justified below.

IMPLEMENTATION IMPLICATIONS:

Dynamic installation of boxes is not directly possible in Ada (where boxes are interpreted as packages), but is in object oriented programming (where boxes are interpreted as "first class objects", in other words objects that may be dynamically installed and passed around from place to place in the program).

For Ada design, dynamically installed boxes should be viewed as useful design-level abstractions that may be mapped to abstract data types (ADTs) for implementation. This may be done by making a type definition for the internal machinery of the design-level box that treats everything in it, including robots (tasks in Ada), as one data structure, putting this definition, along with a pointer to it, as a private type in the specification of the package that will implement the ADT, and then dynamically creating instances as needed. Thus an ADT package operating on different dynamically created instances of the type it supports achieves much of the effect of dynamically installed boxes, each of which operates on different private instances of internal machinery. The only opera-

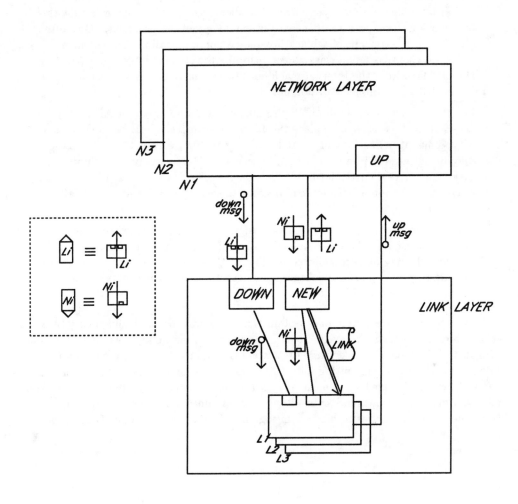

Figure 10.48: SENSIBLE MACHINE DYNAMICS IN A COMMUNICATIONS SYSTEM

tional difference is that the ADT package itself cannot be passed from place to place, or removed.

Given that the Ada implementation will be an ADT, why start from a different design level abstraction (dynamically installed boxes)? The answer is that this is a more natural way to conceptualize many practical problems. One often starts with the concept of a black box (say a communications link manager, as in Figure 10.48) as a first class object. Ripping the concept in two by separating the interface from the internal machinery to get an ADT, as suggested above, is best left as an implementation detail.

For the particular example of Figure 10.48, the mapping to an ADT may be accomplished as follows. Replace the **Li** boxes with a single **L** box that acts as a type manager like that of STACK3 of Figure 10.1, except that its instances may be active (the idea is that each instance is a data structure containing the tasks that drive a particular link). This only works if the original **Li** boxes had only stores and robots inside them, because these map to dynamically installable objects in Ada.

Another Ada solution is to map the design into a different design that eliminates dynamic installation completely. Eliminating it changes the nature of the problem. It may be accomplished for Figure 10.48 by interpreting the **Li** boxes as parameterized generic packages, and resorting to fixed structures to make linkages between the **Li** boxes and the **Ni** ones.

Figure 10.48 is an example of a system that, in a way, dynamically restructures itself while it is running. One can imagine particular physical links going down and new handlers being installed for backup links while the system is running. However, the dynamic restructuring is very limited, amounting only to the existence, or not, of instances of machines that will be used in fixed ways when they are installed, and whose templates are known. *Real* dynamic reconfiguration, like installing new machines according to new templates that require new glue structures to bind them together, is outside the scope of this book.

Part VI

CONCLUSIONS

Chapter 11

CONCLUSIONS

11.1 BROAD THEMES

Some broad themes are visible in this book:

- AN ENGINEERING DESIGN PERSPECTIVE IS NEEDED FOR TIME-INTENSIVE SYSTEMS: The design of *TIME*-intensive systems is an engineering activity by any reasonable measure: complexity, cost, scale of effort, and potential disastrous impact of design errors on life and property; therefore methods used in traditional engineering provide appropriate inspiration. In traditional engineering, the synthesis of form is aided by well understood pictorial notations and methods which not only have clear relation to what is to be built and how it is to work, but also have underlying formality; these contribute to engineering design cultures in the workplace. This perspective pervades the entire book.

- ARCHITECTURE = PLACE + TIME: This "equation" captures in a stylized fashion the essence of the Architectural Design process advocated in this book. The process devotes equal effort to design issues in the *PLACE* (structure) and *TIME* (temporal behaviour) domains.

- DIAGRAMS ARE THE FIRST PROTOTYPES OF THE SYSTEM UNDER DESIGN: The MachineCharts notation provides a means of treating diagrams as the first *PLACE-TIME* prototypes of the system under design, that may be executed by walk throughs, or by a workbench, without generating a target implementation. The concept is called visual prototyping.

- STRUCTURAL REGULARITY IS APPROPRIATE FOR SOFTWARE AS WELL AS HARDWARE: Regular structures with visible interaction idioms are easier to understand, explain, and test. The amorphous, jelly-like nature of so much software may not actually be a necessary property of software, but only a product of the way it is currently created.

- PLUG-IN TEMPORAL BEHAVIOUR SEPARATES CONCERNS: Plug in ACMs (Abstract Controller Machines) provide a means of inserting abstract temporal behaviour specifications, developed during requirements analysis and preliminary design, into concrete machinery developed during detailed design, in a manner that preserves their separate identity, thus providing both modularity and requirements traceability. ACMs are covered in Chapters 3, 6, and 9.

- COMMON SENSE REPRESENTATIONS ARE NEEDED BY PRACTICAL ENGINEERS: The notation and approach of this book aims to provide practical engineers with a common sense way of representing the structural form and temporal behaviour of systems under design that treats software and hardware components of the system in a uniform manner, and that is suitable for detailed design of the software components. That it is able to do so in practice has been demonstrated by the fact that, where it has been tried, it has proved to be useful to communicate the essence of design alternatives to clients and managers, to serve as a basis for the client signing off on a particular alternative.

- COMMON SENSE IS NOT THE SAME AS INFORMAL: The diagrams of this book can be just as formal as any other way of specifying systems, in the sense that they have precise *TIME*-domain semantics, given proper annotation. However, their roots are in the way practical engineers think about systems, rather than in formal methods. An underlying philosophy of the book is that they can provide common sense windows through which practical engineers can access formal methods (although the formal methods themselves are outside the scope of the book).

- WIDE-SPECTRUM NOTATIONS MAKE DESIGN THINKING PORTABLE: The MachineCharts model of black boxes and buttons is easily stretched and extended to include other implementation technologies than Ada. For example, as was demonstrated in Chapter 5, detached buttons provide general models of glue that may be mapped to synchronous technologies like Ada by attaching the buttons to actors (e.g., entries attached to tasks), or to asynchronous technologies like those often supplied by real time executives by transforming them into reactors (e.g., semaphores or mailboxes). As another example, as was demonstrated in Chapter 10, dynamically installed black boxes may be mapped to abstract data types for Ada implementation, or to objects for object-oriented programming. In these and other ways, design thinking becomes portable between widely different implementation technologies.

- CAD TOOLS ARE NEEDED: CAD tools are needed to help with teaching and learning the approach, and to make it practical as the primary design capture mechanism in industry. Tools need to support both the structural and temporal behaviour aspects at a level of abstraction above implementation technology. In other words, one should not have to fill in program details and compile and execute a program in an intended implementation language to experiment with behaviour.

11.2 PRACTICALITY

11.2.1 SCALE UP

Will the visual techniques of this book scale up for large problems? The answer depends on what is meant by "scale up". If it means full workbench support for visual design capture, visual temporal behaviour specification and exploration, industrial strength code generation, and life cycle integration for the largest problem you can think of, then the answer is we don't know yet, because workbenches to provide this level of support do not exist yet. However, if scale up means only that the modes of conceptualization can be applied to large problems, then the answer is surely yes.

Large software systems tend to have their bulk elsewhere than in the *PLACE* and *TIME* domains that have been the main concern of this book; their bulk tends to be in the *WORK* domain, where the detail of computation and data processing resides. (Read any large multitasking program and see how little space, relatively, is devoted to task interactions and their control.) Therefore, separation of *PLACE* and *TIME* concerns from *WORK* ones, as advocated by this book, tends to scale the problem down in size, thereby helping to reveal the "small problems struggling to get out" mentioned in its opening paragraphs. In present software practice, *TIME*-domain and *WORK*-domain concerns tend to be intertwined in the mainline programs that correspond to MachineChart agendas, so keeping them separate requires a definite effort to do things differently. Programming languages do not provide the means for such separation, so one has to rely on notations and methods.

Recursive decomposition provides a way of breaking a large system into units that are individually intellectually manageable. The intellectual problem that remains is combinatorial complexity when the units are combined. Combinatorial complexity can be reduced by some of the techniques of this book (regular form, regular glue structures, standard interaction idioms, etc.). Even so, getting a "total system" view of a large system by "flipping through" pictures of its components, particularly if they are contained in multiple windows on a workstation screen, is hard. A workbench must, therefore, be able to project filtered views of the system under design onto the screen in a flexible manner on demand, or spontaneously while a design is executing. Flattened, collapsed and overlay charts, scenario diagrams, visit threads, and moving pictures of dynamically changing structures, are just a few of many possibilities. Research is required in this area.

Most readers may agree that drawing pictures showing structural relationships among the parts of a system may help to make large problems intellectually manageable, but what about scenarios? Some readers may get the impression from this book that they are impractical for any but very small problems, because too many of them are required to show anything, and they are too hard to draw. The number of scenarios will certainly blow up if one tries to cover all possible patterns. However, this is a familiar problem in testing — scenarios are just test sequences depicted visually — that must be solved whether a system is small or large. All this book does is move the test sequences earlier in the life cycle, and show them in pictorial form. The drawing problem is a real one without automated support, but a good tool could make it almost effortless.

Although the book focuses on small problems as examples, the *issues* revealed by these small problems scale up to much larger ones.

11.2.2 SIMPLICITY

Is the notation simple enough for practical engineers to want to use? Experience indicates that it is. However, it can appear daunting at first to the uninitiated, who see only the apparently large number of icons that have to be learned. In fact, only a small fraction of the total number contain the essence of the notation. Of the rest, some are used only in particular design phases, some provide redundant declaration of intended temporal behaviour (like type declarations in strongly typed programming languages are redundant), some are synonyms for other icon combinations, some are placeholders for detail, and some indicate aspects of implementation intent.

Focusing on the core of the notation, namely its icons for expressing system structure during detailed design, and stripping this core down to its essence by eliminating temporal declarations, reveals that the essential subset is very small and simple. It requires only half a dozen icons for diagrams showing interface relationships — box, robot, work button, gate button, finger, and parameter — and only another three for the internal details — engine, pull finger, and store. These icons (Figure 4.1) all have precise temporal semantics and provide the scaffolding for the rest.

Adding four more basic icons, as follows, brings the total number of icons needed for initial detailed design to thirteen. Splitting robots into two categories, actor and reactor, to distinguish active peers from passive glue adds one icon to the basic nine (Figure 4.1). Waiting place markers to highlight places where waiting is the rule add another. Choice frames to identify first-come-first-served waiting patterns when there are many places to wait add a third. And timers to indicate balking or timeout on waiting add a fourth. These additional three icons are members of the temporal annotation set shown in Figure 4.7. An extra icon, a balk finger, is not included in this count, because it is just a synonym for timeout with zero time, and is therefore not actually a different icon.

Three icons that are useful for the later stages of detailed design to indicate exceptions, reuseable components, and dynamic structures. — jabs, templates, and install arrows — can be ignored when learning the notation for the first time, and can be left out of presentations to audiences interested more in concepts than implementation-oriented details.

Other icons that provide a transition from requirements analysis to design (e.g., events), that serve as placeholders for details (e.g., channels, ports), or that provide icing on the annotation cake (e.g., foreign, transient) are useful for the serious designer, but are not needed to convey the essence of a system under design to an audience that is not interested in details.

Thus the essence of the notation is contained in a dozen or so icons that are easily learned by anyone. Using them effectively to synthesize good designs is not easy, but understanding what they mean when presented with a diagram containing them is. Therefore, the essence of a design can be presented to a colleague not concerned with details, or to a client or manager, by masking out some icons in detailed design diagrams. A workbench could easily mask out categories of icons on request for this purpose.

11.2.3   EDUCATION

The visual approach of this book requires, for many people in the industrial software workplace, a new way of thinking that takes some time and training to learn. Experience has shown that people educated in this approach in school become enthusiasts that push it in the workplace. This kind of bottom-up push is needed for the methods to become widely used. It can be fostered by education, and by seeding an organization with an experienced enthusiast or two. It will not be created by dumping tools into an unprepared workplace.

The latter approach is likely to lead to the perception that pictures are just an additional form of documentation overhead, rather than the core of a new way of doing things.

11.2.4 MANUAL USE

Automation is not necessary for the approach of this book to be useful for practical design exploration in the workplace in "back of the envelope" style. All that is required is a group of engineers who understand the approach and can communicate ideas to each other using it. The author's colleagues and students have used it this way for years, as have many industrial users. Diagrams can be drawn by hand or by widely available diagram-drawing systems. Even when a workbench is available that supports design capture, people will scribble ideas on blackboards, whiteboards, backs of envelopes, and so forth, before going to the workbench to capture them. For this reason, some of the notational conventions have been deliberately chosen to make manual use of the notation easy.

Even if fully automated support for the approach proves to be impractical in the short term, the style of thinking this book encourages, and the "language" it provides for communication of design ideas among people, should be helpful for any size of project.

11.2.5 AUTOMATION

The concept of a designer's workbench supporting the Architectural Design approach, complete with the ability to explore temporal behaviour at the design level, pervades this book. The term "workbench" is used, instead of "tool", because the concept is one of a set of tools that support the entire process. Making a workbench with tools to support the Architectural Design process is a much larger proposition than building a drawing tool that is capable of translating pictures into skeleton code. No such workbench is available commercially at the time this is being written.

Different modes of workbench use are required for design exploration and implementation specification. The design exploration mode needs to be less concerned with capturing everything that will be in the implementation (the visual-syntax-of-code view of pictures), and more concerned with temporal behaviour exploration. In fact, visual syntax for code can get in the way, by encouraging people to become too preoccupied with capturing all the details.

Temporal behaviour specification and exploration requires integrated support for complementary, redundant ways of representation (annotations on structure charts, timeline threads on structure charts, scenarios, state machines, ...). A designer should only have to draw the meaning once, using whatever form is appropriate, and have a tool draw other compatible forms when desired, for explanation, presentation, documentation, design analysis, design execution, or implementation purposes. Furthermore, a tool should be able to integrate the temporal behaviour forms with structural forms stored in a design data base, and provide visual projections of the information from different perspectives to help the designer see relationships. This kind of workbench assistance involves only information retrieval, static analysis and drawing, not actual design execution; therefore, it can be performed on incomplete designs.

For example:

- Given an event scenario, and a cross reference listing of events corresponding to visits or returns from visits, a tool should be able to draw a visit scenario, or its equivalent threaded form on a structure chart.

- A designer should be able to "draw" visit scenarios in linearized form by tracing patterns on a structure chart with a mouse, or follow patterns on a structure chart in threaded form by moving a cursor along the time axis of a linearized scenario.

- A tool should provide assistance in creating Abstract State Machines (ASMs) from scenarios by enabling a person to move a cursor along the time axis of a linearized scenario, identifying segments of the scenario with states; the tool could then draw a preliminary transition diagram itself.

- A tool could show visit threads on a structure chart corresponding to state transitions in a requirements ASM, by making use of the event-visit cross reference list and other information in the design data base.

- Relationships between structure charts, scenarios and state machines could be shown in the context of a complete set of structure charts representing all levels of recursive decomposition of the system under design, or in projected form, perhaps showing only robots at all levels of decomposition, leaving out all boxes and work buttons.

- Assistance could be provided in helping the designer to ensure that interface, interaction and transaction scenarios at different levels of recursive decomposition are compatible with each other, by allowing them to be explored in relation to each other in some revealing way.

- Assistance could be provided to the designer in composing ACMs from sets of test-sequence ASMs that describe different examples of required external behaviour, and in providing the "boilerplate" to plug the resulting ACMs into designs and implementations.

Still more assistance could be provided by a workbench that can execute or analyze fully annotated designs. For example:

- The temporal behaviour of the detailed design could be checked for consistency with requirements scenarios (expressed either in scenario or test-sequence ASM form).

- Additional nuances of temporal behaviour could be explored by generating new scenarios to answer *what-if* questions.

- Formal methods could be applied to investigate issues such as reachability and deadlock.

MachineCharts components have temporal semantics that makes them executable for this purpose when properly annotated, although the mechanism of execution is not discussed in this book. However, observe that executability is only part of the picture; a workbench also needs to provide the kind of pre-execution support indicated earlier.

11.2.6 METHODS

Tools should assist designers with the use of design methods and paradigms supported by the workbench (more than just checking correct diagram syntax). For example, they could point out missing design steps, or fill in "obvious" (to people) design details or modifications within the context of some design paradigm.

11.2.7 ARTWORK

While it may be true that pictures show relationships in a way that text cannot, actually drawing them can be highly labour-intensive, as the author can testify after having drawn all the ones in this book. Scribbling them on the back of an envelope or a blackboard is quite different from entering them into a workstation, where attention has to be paid to details that might be left out on the back of the envelope.

Therefore picture-drawing front ends need to have knowledge of the kind of pictures being drawn, and the intelligence to fill in "obvious" or "standard" artwork semi-automatically, and to perform some aspects of layout and routing automatically, particularly when diagrams are being edited; otherwise, engineers in a hurry to experiment with design ideas will simply become annoyed with having to spend too much time on artwork. To be avoided at all costs is forcing designers to redraw something they have already entered elsewhere in different form.

11.2.8 REUSEABILITY OF DESIGNS

Reuseability is one of the dominant concerns of the 80s, but in current practice is limited to libraries of passive code objects (e.g., generic procedures and packages in Ada, classes in object oriented programming languages, modules in Modula-2, subroutine libraries in many other languages). *TIME*-intensive systems need both more and less than this: more because they need active components for multitasking and multiprocessing; less because code is at too low a level of abstraction (or too specialized for particular languages and/or operating systems). Design-level abstractions are needed that can be mapped into different implementation targets, either because different projects have different implementation constraints, or because a company's implementation technologies change with time. In other words, reuse designs as well as code. Design level component libraries stand a good chance of having longer useful lifetimes than code libraries as implementation technologies change, so they may be worth a considerable amount of effort to build.

Factors contributing to their usefulness will be (1) common sense nature of the design representations, so they can be easily understood, (2) wide spectrum nature of the design representations, so they can be easily mapped to different implementation technologies, (3) wide spectrum nature of the components themselves, so they can be used in a wide variety of projects, (4) availability of documented, systematic design methods for using components in design, so the uninitiated can learn how to do it; (5) suitability for use in CAD workbenches. The essentials of all these factors are present in the material presented in this book. The work of building design-level libraries of components remains to be done.

One can visualize the emergence for particular application domains (e.g., communications, robotics, ...) of parameterized standard components and of parameterized standard architectures that use the components in a regular fashion, all expressed in a notation like in this book. The result would be like specification sheets for hardware components that show connection structures and timing relationships.

11.3   SOME IMPORTANT TOPICS HAVE NOT BEEN COVERED

Bringing to a close a book with such a wide scope as this one inevitably leaves some important topics inadequately covered, or not covered at all. These are left either for the reader to work out, or the author to write more about in the future. Particularly noteworthy ones are as follows:

- Requirements Analysis. That there is a natural continuum between requirements analysis and preliminary design has been pointed out, but a detailed exposition of the relationship between the Preliminary Design part of the Architectural Design process and "traditional" requirements analysis methods is missing. Abstract Controller Machines (ACMs) provide a link between temporal behaviour specifications developed during requirements analysis and concrete machinery developed during detailed design, but the details of the alignment of ACMs with powerful requirements analysis tools like StateMate have not been described.

- Data Structures. Conspicuously missing has been a treatment of the subject of data structures. Data structures have been dismissed as details to be hidden behind interface facades or deferred as the concern of the *WORK* parts of agendas. The MCL language described in Appendix A is a step in the direction of including data structures in the process. However, visual representations of data structures would also be useful as part of an integrated visual approach.

- Formal Temporal Semantics of MachineCharts. The temporal semantics of MachineCharts has been presented in this book in the same style as its treatment of the intended temporal semantics of designs, namely by example, with scenarios. While this may satisfy the reader that the basic chart icons do have precise temporal semantics, it does not show how to build executable or analyzable MachineCharts models. A hint of one approach being taken at Carleton is given in Appendix A. Another possibility is to use Harel's StateCharts to formalize the temporal semantics of the basic icons of MachineCharts, and then to use a StateCharts tool as an execution vehicle. The reader may imagine other possibilities.

- Object Oriented Methods. Relationships to object oriented methods have been mentioned in a few places, but not explored. MachineChart components may be viewed as "objects" and the Architectural Design process may be viewed as a form of "object oriented design", except that a cornerstone of object oriented methods, namely inheritance, has not been included in the scope of the book. This is because the way the term "inheritance" is commonly used in the object oriented programming community has more to do with code reuse than with the design-level, *TIME*-domain and *PLACE*-domain issues that are the major concerns of this book. There is no reason why diagrams representing inheritance hierarchies could not be added to MachineCharts, but they would be in the template world, and would therefore be drawn separately from the kinds of operational diagrams drawn in this book. We may imagine the templates of this book as being the net results of an inheritance hierarchy of templates (corresponding to classes) that might exist "above them". To be developed is a concept of inheritance of temporal behaviour in relation to the way in which the term "temporal behaviour" is used in this book.

- Other Implementation Technologies. Relationships between the techniques of this book and other implementation technologies than Ada, including software ones such as combinations of conventional programming languages and real time executives, and hardware ones such as VHDL, have been suggested, but not explored.

- Verification of Temporal Behaviour. The visual techniques for conceptualizing and exploring behaviour given in this book, while helpful, provide no magic for solving difficult problems such as verifying that some complicated observed temporal behaviour pattern produced by an executing design is consistent with some simpler behaviour pattern (or set of patterns) expressed as a requirement in scenario or state machine form. Such verification would have to be performed by people who understand both the design and the requirements. Verification of temporal behaviour may be assisted by formal analysis methods that can be used to investigate matters such as reachability and deadlock, given an appropriate formalization of the information in a MachineCharts design.

11.4 THE LAST WORD

The material of this book can be taken in the following ways:

- As a primer on visual techniques that can help a designer to organize his or her thoughts, and communicate them to others, while designing systems, whether or not the techniques are supported by tools.

- As a description of a practical design process for *TIME*-intensive systems called Architectural Design that focuses attention on *TIME*-domain and *PLACE*-domain concerns.

- As a requirements definition for a designer's workbench that supports the Architectural Design process.

The essential content of this book is intended to be in its pictures, as befits a visual paradigm, which is why there are so many figures. The words are there for the novice. Practical experience with the notation has shown that in a workplace culture that understands the notation and approach, few words are necessary to convey design ideas to others and to record them for documentation purposes.

Part VII

APPENDICES

Appendix A

ANNOTATING MACHINECHARTS

A.1   INTRODUCTION

An annotation language called MCL (Machine Charts Language) is under development as part of the TimeBench project in the author's department at Carleton University. (TimeBench is a research and development effort into methodologies and tools for designing and verifying the design of reactive, concurrent systems.) MCL is an incomplete language for annotating diagrams to flesh out operational details, such as agendas of engines, actions of state machines, and operations on data. MCL was not used to annotate diagrams in the body of the book because MCL was evolving as the book was being written; however, the existence of something like MCL is implied by much of the book, and it seems appropriate to give some details here. This appendix, which is a condensation of a report by the author and two colleagues, Ron Casselman and Gerald Karam, describes the nature of preliminary MCL, and gives some examples of its use.

A.2   OVERVIEW

A number of observations influenced the design of MCL:

- *Graphics is a useful design abstraction but text may be more appropriate in some cases.* It was decided that a textual language was needed for defining details of function; including data manipulation and the evaluation of conditions, that are difficult to define graphically. Examples of places where text is appropriate are the agendas of engines and the enabling conditions and actions performed by state machines.

- *MachineCharts must be the focal point of the design specification; other description techniques must align with it.* MCL is an incomplete language in the sense that it cannot exist outside of a MachineChart context. As such, MCL has no syntax for the structural information that can be described using MachineCharts; the context for a fragment of MCL code is provided by its association with a MachineChart icon. If Ada were used instead of MCL, there would be a large duplication of information

489

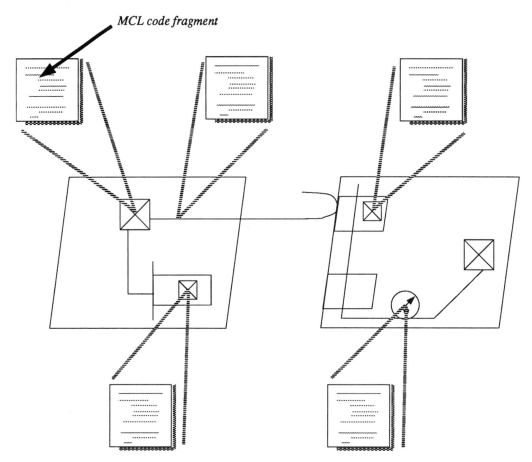

Figure A.1: INTEGRATION OF MCL WITH MACHINECHARTS

and the possibility of inconsistent design specifications. Design checkers could be used to verify the consistency of a design, but this adds an unnecessary element of complexity. A simpler approach, based on different but complimentary descriptions techniques, results in a uniform view of the design process and a simpler CAD tool.

Figure A.1 shows the association of MCL code fragments with various MachineChart icons. The execution semantics implied by Figure A.1 are that an MCL code fragment is executed when its MachineChart context becomes activated. For example, the code for a button engine is executed when the button is pushed, the code for a balking push is executed if the balk occurs, the code for a box is executed when the system is initialized or the box is installed, etc. (In the TimeBench toolset, MCL will be integrated with MachineCharts through text editor windows associated with individual icons.)

There are times when it is desirable or necessary that hooks to the structural information be included in the MCL code. Structural hooks are desirable to give context to the designer without referring to the diagram. For example, consider coding the agenda of a button engine. In this case, information about the names and types of data objects visible to the button may be helpful. This information will be generated on request by TimeBench and may appear as comments or as uneditable text regions in the MCL code. Structural hooks are necessary when the placement of the hook gives sequencing information. For example, button pushes must be placed in sequences of MCL statements. In TimeBench, this will be done by invoking a command in the text editor which is sensitive to the structural information maintained graphically. The code for the button push will be automatically inserted. The line of code for the button push may be deleted, copied or moved in whole, but its contents may not be altered. In addition, the MCL compiler will complain about any button pushes that appear in the MCL code and not on the MachineChart diagram, to ensure that the textual and graphical information remain consistent.

- *The language should be small and easy to learn yet capable of expressing complex data operations easily.* This requirement led to the adoption of SETL's intrinsic data types. The important aspects of MCL's intrinsic types are covered later.

- *The language should be flexible and unrestrictive to ease design specification.* MCL is weakly typed in comparison to Ada. This allows details about data typing to be deferred until implementation.

- *Since Ada is an important target implementation language, mappings to Ada must be reasonable and automatable.* Ada syntax and semantics have been adopted by MCL where appropriate.

- *The language should not focus on implementation details, however, it should be an appropriate starting point for implementation.* This requirement lead to the exclusion from MCL of many language features commonly found in implementation languages. For example, resource requirements are not an issue; dynamic data types expand and shrink as necessary, there are no compiler directives or representation clauses.

The final result is a small, data rich programming language for expressing sequences of executable statements within a MachineChart context. The next section introduces MCL through an example. After this some features of the MCL language are discussed.

A.3 MCL TUTORIAL

This section describes a MachineChart and MCL solution to the Five Dining Philosophers (FDP) problem.

Figure A.2 shows a context diagram of the Five Dining Philosophers problem. A philosopher is either eating spaghetti or thinking. To eat spaghetti a philosopher requires both his left and right forks. Since philosophers share forks, the forks are a critical resource. The challenge is to design a fork allocation scheme that is free of deadlock and starvation.

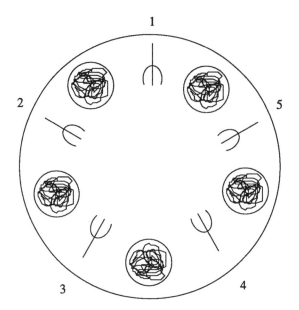

Figure A.2: FIVE DINING PHILOSOPHERS

A MachineCharts structure diagram for the Five Dining Philosophers problem is given in figure A.3. The philosophers are represented as a pool of robots. The **ForkAllocator** is represented as a robot with two push-pull (gate) buttons in its interface; namely, **GrantForks** and **ReturnForks**. **GrantForks** is a push-pull (gate) button family with five family members - one for each philosopher. Each member of the **GrantForks** family is guarded, to individually block hungry philosophers when their forks are unavailable. When a philosopher desires to eat he pushes his member of the **GrantForks** family. When he returns from the push he has been granted permission to eat, i.e., he has picked up his forks. When the philosopher is finished eating he returns his forks by pushing the **ReturnForks** button.

This solution to the Five Dining Philosophers problem uses a token passing scheme to ensure fair fork allocation. A single token is passed around the table as forks are returned. A philosopher may not pick up his forks if the token is at his right. When a pair of forks is returned and the token is on the philosopher's left, it is propagated from left to right. This stops a hungry philosopher from starving his neighbors.

Figure A.4 shows the MCL code in pop-up windows that completes the details of the **ForkAllocator**. Arrows point from the graphical icons to their code fragments. The text in the bold typeface will be automatically generated by the TimeBench tool and may not be altered.

The MCL code for the **Main** engine contains a comment. A comment begins with a pair of hyphens and extends to the end of the line. **Main** loops forever servicing the requests of the philosophers.The looping construct follows the syntax of Ada. The argument to the **pull** statement identifies the choice frame; in this case **sel**. Executing this **pull** statement

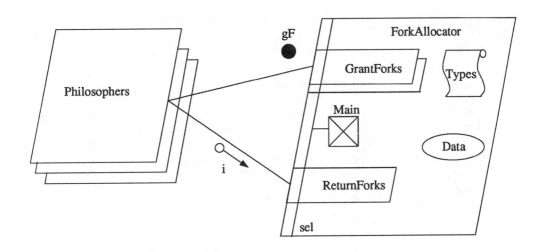

Figure A.3: MACHINECHART DIAGRAM FOR FDP PROBLEM

has the same semantics as executing a selective accept in Ada.

The type definition template **Types** contains the definition of two types; namely, *To-kenRing* and *ForkList*. Both are defined to be lists of boolean values. In Ada, data objects of type *TokenRing* and *ForkList* would be considered to be of different types. In MCL, however, *TokenRing* and *ForkList* are considered to be equivalent types since their underlying representations are the same. Data objects of equivalent types may be freely combined in expressions and statements without type conversions. Note that there is no dimensioning information given for the list types since MCL handles the issues of resource management for composite data structures like lists implicitly - lists will expand and shrink as necessary as elements are added and removed. In an attempt to keep the language simple, MCL does not allow constraints or default values for type definitions.

The data objects *Token* and *Forks* are declared and initialized in the MCL code for the data declaration **Data**. Almost all data elements must first be declared in a MachineChart diagram before they can be used in an MCL specification. Some exceptions include loop counters and indices of push-pull (gate) button families.

Token is defined to be of type *TokenRing*, a list of boolean values, which maintains the placement of the token as it circles the table. The first element of *Token* is set to true to show the initial placement of the token (to the left of philosopher one). *Forks* is defined to be of type *ForkList*, a list of boolean values, which maintains the availability information for the forks. All of the forks are marked as being available. *Token* and *Forks* will be initialized when the robot **ForkAllocator** is created, in this case during system startup. After initialization the length of *Token* and *Forks* will be 5.

The push-pull (gate) buttons, **GrantForks** and **ReturnForks**, that are connected to

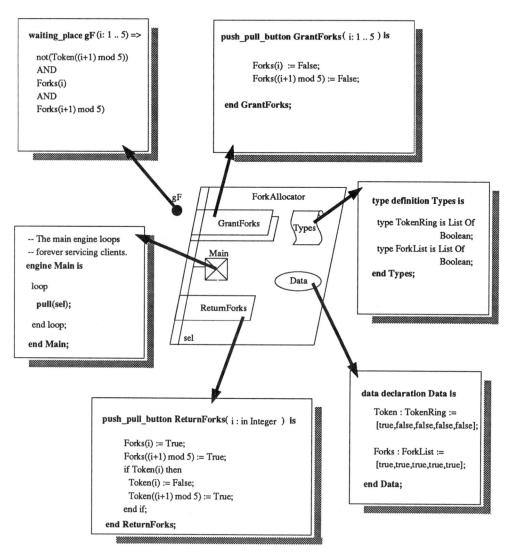

waiting_place gF (i: 1 .. 5) =>

   not(Token((i+1) mod 5))
   AND
   Forks(i)
   AND
   Forks(i+1) mod 5)

push_pull_button GrantForks(i: 1 .. 5) is

    Forks(i) := False;
    Forks((i+1) mod 5) := False;

end GrantForks;

-- The main engine loops
-- forever servicing clients.
engine Main is

 loop

  pull(sel);

 end loop;

end Main;

type definition Types is

   type TokenRing is List Of
               Boolean;
   type ForkList is List Of
               Boolean;
end Types;

push_pull_button ReturnForks(i : in Integer) is

    Forks(i) := True;
    Forks((i+1) mod 5) := True;
    if Token(i) then
     Token(i) := False;
     Token((i+1) mod 5) := True;
    end if;
end ReturnForks;

data declaration Data is

   Token : TokenRing :=
   [true,false,false,false,false];

   Forks : ForkList :=
   [true,true,true,true,true];

end Data;

ForkAllocator

GrantForks

Types

Main

Data

ReturnForks

sel

gF

Figure A.4: MCL CODE FRAGMENTS FOR FDP PROBLEM

the interface of a robot are similar to task entries in Ada. Push-pull (gate) buttons are treated as structural elements separate from the engine agenda of the robot. In Ada, the accept statement, which names the entry, is part of the task mainline.

The first line of **GrantForks'** code segment shows the syntax for specifying a push-pull (gate) button family. A push-pull (gate) button family is used so that philosophers may be individually blocked from acquiring their forks when their forks are unavailable. The variable i, called the family member identifier, is separated by a colon from a discrete integer range. The discrete range specifies the number of members in the family. The code segment of each family is identical except that each member has a unique value for the variable i from the discrete range. Note how the variable i is used to index into the *Forks* list.

Each member of the **GrantForks** family is guarded by a member of the waiting place family **gF**. Like members of a push-pull (gate) button family, each member of a waiting place family has a unique integer valued identifier. The family identifier is helpful here in expressing the logic of the waiting place symbol. The logic is that a philosopher may acquire his forks if the token is not at his right and both of his forks are free.

The final piece of MCL code is for the push-pull (gate) button **ReturnForks**. A push-pull (gate) button family is not required as the philosophers do not need to be individually blocked when returning forks. Each philosopher provides an integer variable i to identify himself. The syntax of the *if* statement is the same as in Ada. The purpose of the *if* statement is to propagate the token from a philosophers left to his right if the token is at his left when he returns his forks.

The above example should give the reader a flavour for the MCL language. The remaining sections of the report will discuss some particulars of the MCL language.

A.4   THE MCL LANGUAGE

A.4.1   SIMPLE DATA TYPES

MCL supports the following simple data types: Integer, Real, Boolean, String, and Enumeration. The operations on these types are:

- addition, subtraction, etc. for integers and reals,

- equality, inequality and assignment for booleans,

- concatenation, substring extraction, etc. for strings and

- successor, predecessor and value operators for enumerations.

These data types may also be used in boolean expressions (in the style of Ada) when combined with logical operators.

Some of the data typing rules of Ada are relaxed. For example, integers and reals may be combined in the same expression without any explicit type conversions. Unlike C, integers and reals may not be treated as booleans, so the following is a semantic error.

```
while (1) loop
...
end loop;
```

Unlike Ada, MCL does not have syntax for constraining the range, precision or accuracy of data types or data objects except for the limitations imposed by the underlying machine. This is in an effort to keep MCL small and focused above implementation details.

Any data item may de declared to be a constant by adding the keyword **constant** to the object declaration. A constant is a read only data object and it is a semantic error to assign a constant a value.

A.4.2 COMPOUND DATA TYPES

MCL supports the following compound data types: Record, List and Set. The syntax for defining a record type and for selecting a component of a record are adopted from Ada. Absent, however, are variant records and record discriminants. The list and set data types are derived from SETL. The power of the SETL types is reduced somewhat for inclusion in MCL. In particular, the elements of a list or set must be of the same type in MCL, and can be of mixed types in SETL. The reason for the restriction is so that mappings to strongly typed languages like Ada are reasonable and automatable.

List and sets are the most complex (and powerful) of the MCL data types and deserve further examination. A list or set may contain elements of any type (including other lists or sets) but all the elements must be of the same type. Lists and sets are dynamic in the sense that they will expand or shrink as needed as elements are added or removed.

LISTS

A list is an integer indexable sequence of elements.

```
type IntList is List Of Integer;
A : List of Integer := [1,2,3,4];
B : List of IntList := [[1,2,3], [4,5,6]];
```

Data object **A** is declared to be a list of integers and is initialized with the list literal [1,2,3,4]. A list literal is formed by enclosing a sequence of elements in the list brackets []. List literals may be used in expressions as constants. The data object **B** is slightly more complex than **A**; it is a list of lists of integers. These data objects are used in the following examples.

- **Extracting an element from a list.**

```
i := A(2);        -- i gets 2
i:= B(2)(2);      -- i gets 5
```

- **Extracting a sequence of elements from a list.**

```
B(1) := A(1 .. 2);       -- B is now [[1,2], [4,5,6]]
```

The construct A(1 .. 2) extracts the sequence of elements from list **A** in the range 1 .. 2.

- **Modifying a range of elements in list.**

    ```
    A(1 .. 2) := [8,8,8];      -- A is now [8,8,8,3,4]
    ```

    The sequence of elements of **A** in the range 1 .. 2 are assigned [8,8,8]. Note how **A** automatically expanded.

- **Inserting a sequence of elements into a list.**

    ```
    A(2 .. 1) := [8,8,8];      -- A is now [1,8,8,8,2,3,4]
    ```

    The elements of list [8,8,8] are inserted before the left index of the slice range (2 .. 1). The list **A** is automatically expanded.

- **Appending a sequence of elements to the end of a list.**

    ```
    A(#A+1 .. #A) := [5,6,7];      -- A is now [1,2,3,4,5,6,7]
    ```

    The #A operator returns the length of the list.

- **Inserting a sequence of elements at the start of a list.**

    ```
    A(1 .. 0) := [8,8,8]      -- A is now [8,8,8,1,2,3,4]
    ```

- **Truncating a list.**

    ```
    B(2)(2) := Nil;      -- B is now [[1,2,3], [4]]
    ```

    MCL defines the special constant **Nil** as the end of a list. Assigning **Nil** to B(2)(2) truncates the elements **5,6** from the list **B**.

- **Concatenating lists.**

    ```
    A := A + B(1);      -- A is now [1,2,3,4,1,2,3]
    ```

- **Looping over all elements of a list.**

    ```
    for i in A loop
      ...
    end loop;
    ```

    The loop parameter **i** is an automatic variable that takes on the successive values of **A**. The type of **i** is derived from the contents of **A**. The looping constructs of MCL are derived from Ada with the above extension to allow for looping over the elements of lists and sets.

The above examples are simple enough; it is when several of the list operations are combined that power of MCL becomes evident. Suppose we wished that the first two elements of **A**, concatenated with the first element of **B**, be inserted into **B** between the first and second element. This can be expressed easily in MCL as follows:

```
B(2 .. 1) := A(1 .. 2) + B(1);
-- B is now [[1,2,3], [1,2,1,2,3], [4,5,6]]
```

SETS

A set is an unordered, nonindexable collection of elements. Sets never contain duplicate elements.

```
type IntSet is Set Of Integer;
A : Set of Integer := {1,2,3,4};
B : Set of IntSet := {{1,2,3}, {4,5,6}}
```

Data object **A** is declared to be a set of integers and is initialized with the set literal {1,2,3,4}. A set literal is formed by enclosing a collection of elements in the set brackets {}. Data object **B** is a set of sets of integers. These data objects are used in the following examples.

- Finding the cardinality of a set.

```
i := #A;       -- i gets 4
```

- Set Union.

```
A := A + {4,5,6};       -- A is now {1,2,3,4,5,6}
```

Note that duplicates are automatically removed from a set.

- Set Difference.

```
A := A - {1,2,3};       -- A is now {4}
```

A gets the set of all elements that belonged to **A** but not to {**1,2,3**}.

- Set Intersection.

```
B := B * {{1,2,3}, {8}};       -- B is now {{1,2,3}}
```

- Adding an element to a set.

```
B := B with {8};       -- B is now {{1,2,3}, {4,5,6}, {8}}
```

- Removing an element from a set.

```
A := A less 2;       -- A is now {1,3,4}
```

- Iterating over the elements of a set.

```
for i in A loop
  ...
end loop;
```

The automatic variable **i** will be assigned each element of the set **A**. The order of iteration over the set is undefined.

As in the last section, a more complicated example is presented to demonstrate the power of MCL. Suppose we wished to compute the cardinality of the set resulting from adding the set **A** to the set **B** intersected with the set **{{1,2,3,4},{4,5,6}}**. This can be expressed in MCL as follows.

```
i := #((B with A) * {{1,2,3,4}, {4,5,6}});
-- i gets 2
```

A.4.3 CONTROL STRUCTURES

The control structures of MCL: *if*, *case* and *loop*, have been derived from Ada.

An example of an *if* statement is given below. The condition of the *if* statement must be a boolean valued expression. In this example, the *if* statement is testing whether an element is a member of a list.

```
if x in [1,3,4,2] then
...
elsif x >= 4 then
...
else
...
end if;
```

The *case* statement is used for choosing an alternative from a list of alternatives. As in Ada, the alternatives must be discrete, exhaustive and of the same type as the case expression. To ensure that the alternatives are exhaustive MCL requires that the *others* alternative always occur as the final alternative. The case expression must be a discrete type, meaning integer or enumeration. The following example shows the syntax of a *case* statement.

```
case i is
when 1 .. 4 => ...
when 5 => ...
when others => ...
end case;
```

MCL has three types of *loop* statements; simple, while and for. The simple and while loops are identical to Ada. An example of each loop is given below.

```
Simple Loop                While Loop
loop                       while x in [1,3,4,2] loop
   ...                         ...
   exit when => ...        end loop;
end loop;
```

The for loop is like that of Ada except that it has been extended to include iteration over the elements of lists and sets. An example of a for loop iterating over the elements of a list is given below. When iterating over a list the elements of the list are chosen in order. When iterating over a set there is no guarantee on the order that the elements will be chosen.

```
for x in [1,3,4,2] loop
   ...
end loop;
```

MCL makes a copy of the list in the iteration so that modifications to the list in the body of loop does not effect the iteration scheme.

A.5 DISCUSSION

The description of MCL given here is not complete, but is sufficient to convey the essence. The aim is that diagrams in the style of the body of the book, annotated with MCL statements, will provide a basis for execution of designs, before target code is generated, and also for later generation of target code.

Appendix B

SUPPLEMENTARY PROBLEMS

B.1 INTRODUCTION

Here are some supplementary problems on which to exercise your knowledge of the design method and notation. Notational exercises aim to explore features of the notation more deeply than was done in the body of the book. Design exercises are small design problems that exercise your knowledge of the notation. Design case studies are more realistic system design problems that are interesting in their own right, not just as exercises for the notation. Implementation exercises are for programming enthusiasts. Finally, for those who have read "System Design With Ada", some suggestions for revisiting it in light of the new material of this book are provided.

B.2 NOTATIONAL EXERCISE: SEMANTICS OF VISIT CHAINING

Illustrate by visit scenarios the sense in which collapsed charts (Figure 4.6) retain the same visit-chaining semantics as the charts from which they were derived, in spite of the disappearance of work buttons from the visit paths.

B.3 NOTATIONAL EXERCISE: REACTORS AS PROTECTED BOXES

Real time executives often provide primitive reactors like semaphores and mailboxes, but may not provide the means to implement more general ones directly. In such cases, a general reactor may be implemented as a box with one internal semaphore to provide mutual exclusion and other internal semaphores or mailboxes to provide waiting places.

Express one of the general reactors in the book in this manner (e.g., the one in Figure 5.14).

B.4   NOTATIONAL EXERCISE: MESSAGE-SCREENING IN REACTOR MAILBOXES

Observe that the reactor glue structures in Figure 5.5 do not support the equivalent of screening waiting-side visitors to waiting places. The individual waiting place reactors shown in the figure do not jointly support such screening, because the non-waiting visitor must pick which one to visit before visiting it. The mailbox reactor shown in the figure does not support such screening, because the waiting visitor waits for the first message to come along, and cannot screen what kind of messages it wants in advance. Such screening is easy to do with the Ada-oriented model of attached gate buttons joined by choice frames. There may be occasions where the same sort of flexibility is required of reactor-based glue structures.

Devise and explain a generalized mailbox solution to this problem that will support screening of messages, and relate it explicitly to an equivalent attached-gate-button solution.

B.5   NOTATIONAL EXERCISE: DESIGN TRANSFORMATION

Following the approach of Chapter 5 (in particular, Figures 5.3, 5.4, and 5.5), transform a different Ada-oriented design with attached gate buttons than the client-server one illustrated in the figure into a design with reactor glue replacing the attached buttons. The idea is to find a design that might be more appropriate for implementation with a separate real time executive that supports, say, semaphores and mailboxes (or some similar set of asynchronous primitives). Show the steps in the transformation process, to make it clear how the transformation was achieved. Choose a design from the body of this book, or from one of the problems of this appendix.

Alternatively, take a non-Ada design from your experience and transform it into an Ada-oriented one using the reverse approach.

B.6   NOTATIONAL EXERCISE: ABSTRACT CONTROLLER MACHINES

B.6.1   SEMAPHORE ACM

Develop an ACM approach to specifying the internal logic of a mutual exclusion semaphore, taking note of the ACM solutions to both the control flag problem of Chapter 3 and the readers-writers problems of Chapter 9. Particularly note that the semaphore WAIT button is purely a waiting place that will be decoupled from the ACM in the same way the writer WAIT button is decoupled from it in the solution of Figure 9.35. Draw necessary state transition diagrams and structure charts, and map the results to Ada.

B.6.2 MOUSE ACM

Redesign the click handler of the mouse example of Chapter 10 to use an ACM to describe the click-action sequencing rules, following the pattern of the ACM examples given in Chapter 9. Map the result into Ada.

B.6.3 READERS-WRITERS ACM

As suggested under the heading "READSTARVE-1 ACM" in Chapter 9, the interface of Figure 9.35 may be changed in two ways to avoid critical races among writers: by making the waiting place into an array; and by using double cold waiting. Verify the statement that only the details of PERFORM need to be changed to accommodate the two new interfaces.

Demonstrate that the "READSTARVE-2" asymmetric interfaces of Figures 9.43 and 9.44 may be driven by an ACM derived from Figure 9.26.

Devise an appropriate state machine and ACM for the "NOSTARVE" example of Figure 9.

B.7 NOTATIONAL EXERCISE: TYPE MANAGERS

Draw a type manager machine called BOARD_SUPPORT inspired by the board manager machine of the game-of-life example of Chapter 6 (Figure 6.13). BOARD_SUPPORT is to provide not only the basic board manipulation operations of BOARD which are applicable to "any" board, but also creation and deletion operations for boards. Unlike BOARD, BOARD_SUPPORT will not store boards internally; therefore, it will not provide the operations which distinguish between "old" and "new" boards; clients must arrange this for themselves using operations offered by BOARD_SUPPORT for "any" board.

Adapt the existing sequential design of Chapter 6 to use BOARD_SUPPORT, without changing the LIFE box. The idea is to statically install an instance BOARD of BOARD_SUPPORT following the pattern of Figure 6.14. However, the instances will not fit exactly into the old design, because the interface of the template is different from the old BOARD interface shown in Figure 6.13. One approach is to fit the new interface into the existing design without modifying the LIFE box, by providing some kind of shell box either between LIFE and BOARD, or surrounding BOARD. Draw a new design following this pattern, showing how the shell box interacts with LIFE and how its internals interact with BOARD.

Draw another design that changes LIFE to accomodate the new BOARD interface. Show how the new internal details of LIFE would be different from the implied internal details before.

B.8 NOTATIONAL EXERCISE: DYNAMICALLY INSTALLED ACTIVE SUBSYSTEMS I

Draw a detailed diagram of a typical cell box in Figure 6.23, including one of the packaged canonical glue structures at the end of the chapter, showing all interface details.

Write an Ada program skeleton showing how to implement the dynamically installable cell box that you have drawn as an active abstract data type in Ada, along the lines suggested at the end of Chapter 10.

B.9   NOTATIONAL EXERCISE: DYNAMICALLY INSTALLED ACTIVE SUBSYSTEMS II

Suppose the frame and physical layers of the FTU system described later are to be dynamically installable for different links, following the general idea of the partial sketch at the end of Chapter 10. Assuming that you have already designed an FTU system, redraw the key FTU diagrams showing this new approach and illustrate how to map the result to an Ada implementation that uses active abstract data types.

B.10   DESIGN EXERCISE: ASYNCHRONOUS MAIL AND MEETINGS

B.10.1   A MAIL TYPE MANAGER: MAILROOM

Draw a design for a MAILROOM box to be used by client robots for sending and receiving "mail", according to the requirements outlined below. Explain the normal operation of MAILROOM using visit scenarios.

MAILROOM is a type manager for mail instances called "envelopes", supporting operations to provide and fill empty envelopes and to send, receive, read and destroy full ones. Envelopes are exchanged via fixed, internal mailboxes that have "well-known" external names, which must be provided as parameters of the appropriate mail operations (a "well-known" name is one which is known by all clients without prior interaction with MAILROOM). Every sent mail item has two address components: a destination mailbox and an optional return mailbox (the latter is the place to send a reply, if one is required). These addresses are the only mail data that is looked at by MAILROOM; everything else is hidden in the "envelope". The receive operation provides a full envelope with its internals unread and untouched and the return address.

MAILROOM has no control over who sends or receives from these mailboxes, but simply arranges that mail operations on them are handled correctly, which includes: queuing receivers in FIFO order for mail from whichever mailbox they designate; routing mail from senders to the correct mailbox; arranging mail to be picked up in the correct order by currently waiting receivers, if there are any; holding mail in FIFO order for later pickup; ensuring that receivers for one mailbox do no wait in line behind receivers for other mailboxes. Note that envelopes themselves are not active, so button queues are not where they will be queued; queue store managers are required.

B.10.2   AN APPLICATION OF MAILROOM: MEETING_ROOM

Apply MAILROOM to providing meeting support for multiple visiting clients to a MEETING_ROOM box (the idea is that MEETING_ROOM uses MAILROOM to provide communication).

Properties of MEETING_ROOM are as follows:

- Meetings may be dynamically created and destroyed by clients of the MEET-ING_ROOM box using services of its interface. (Note that it is the responsibility of clients to ensure that meetings are not destroyed while still in progress). There may be many meetings in progress at once.

- Clients use meetings to exchange information with each other in a race-free fashion. A client may bring information to a meeting and leave immediately, wait to receive information from a meeting, or do both, in one visit to MEETING_ROOM.

- Clients may time out on waiting for information from a meeting. Note that this requires dealing with the situation where the timeout occurs while the result is "on the way"; handling this situation does not necessarily mean getting the information to the timed out client (after all, the client made the decision to leave, so presumably it did not care at this point), but it does mean making sure no consequential confusion can result due to the existence of stale information.

Draw the internal structure of MEETING_ROOM, and show its relationship to MAIL-ROOM, for the case where there is no timeout. Explain the essence of the operation by one or more visit scenarios. (Hint - A dynamically created meeting requires a "chairperson" inside MEETING_ROOM. Why?)

Now draw a design with timeout and explain by a timing diagram how the situation is handled where the timeout occurs while the requested information is "on the way". (Warning - Timeout is *not* provided by MAILROOM.)

B.11 DESIGN CASE STUDY: PLAIN OLD TELEPHONE SYSTEM (POTS)

The problem is to design the essence of POTS in MachineChart terms. To keep things simple, imagine there are only three telephones in the world, and one telephone exchange; furthermore, assume that what happens while a call is in progress is outside the scope of this design problem; only control sequences are of interest. The idea is to capture the essence of the control mechanisms using MachineChart peer robots, interfaces, and glue structures. Don't worry about the physical nature of the telephone transmission; simply imagine that there will be some underlying means of transmitting the control signals that are required by your design. Familiarity with the telephone system enables terms like "call", "caller", "answer", "hangup", "off the hook", "dial tone", "ring", and so forth, to be used in describing both the requirements and the design. Here is a partial list of requirements.

- A called phone may respond, not respond, or be busy.

- A caller may choose to abandon an unsatisfied call attempt after a certain length of time.

- A failure by a user to obey proper telephone protocol (such as failing to hang up after a call) should not prevent the other party to a completed call from making other calls.

- There should be no deadlocks in the system, such as might be caused by two parties simultaneously calling each other, thereby inadvertently activating some mutual waiting machinery.

- It should not be possible to "cross wires" on calls.

Refinements like call queuing and later automatic callback, or call waiting (temporarily suspending a current call while receiving another) may be added at your discretion.

B.12   DESIGN CASE STUDY: DIGITAL WATCH

A digital watch is to be implemented using a general purpose microprocessor programmed in Ada. You are required to provide the design.

Inputs are as follows:

- An ADJUST button which toggles the watch in and out of states in which values may be modified.

- A MODE button which sequentially moves the watch through different modes: normal time, alternate time, alarm, timer, stopwatch, and perhaps others.

- A FUNCTION button which has different functions depending on the mode (e.g., increments or decrements timer and alarm settings).

- A periodic time pulse of the finest time granularity needed by the watch.

Outputs are as follows:

- Normal time display.

- Alternate time display (alternate time zone).

- Alarm display (alarm setting is relative to whichever time of day display type is selected (normal time, or alternate time)).

- Timer.

- Stopwatch.

B.13   DESIGN CASE STUDY: ELEVATOR CONTROL

An n-car elevator system is to be installed in a building with m floors. The system is to be computer controlled and the computer system and control software are to be supplied by your firm. The electromechanical machinery and the sensors are assumed given, except there is some latitude in specifying the signals to be provided to the control computer or computers.

To avoid confusing different kinds of "buttons" in the physical world and the design world, the physical ones will henceforth be called *visit-buttons* and *call-buttons*. The former are on a panel in each car; they are used to select a floor to visit. The latter are on wall panel next to the elevator doors on each floor of the building; they are used to call for a car going in a particular direction to stop on that floor.

General requirements are as follows:

- Each car has a set of visit-buttons, one for each floor. These illuminate when pressed and cause the car to visit (i.e., stop at) the corresponding floor eventually. The illumination is cancelled when the corresponding floor is visited.

- Each floor has two call-buttons (except that ground and top have only one each), one for up and one for down. The call-buttons illuminate when pressed; the illumination is turned off when a car visits the floor and is either travelling in the desired direction, or visiting the floor with no requests outstanding. In the latter case, if both call-buttons are illuminated, only one should be cancelled, depending on which direction is to be serviced first (your design must provide a place for a decision mechanism).

- When a car has no requests to service, it should remain at its final destination (or go to a holding floor), with its doors closed, and await further requests.

- All requests from floors must be serviced eventually, with all floors given equal priority.

- All requests from within cars must be serviced eventually, in the direction of travel.

- Cars may go out of service unexpectedly, when the emergency-button is pressed. There is a mechanism to restore the car to service.

Develop a MachineChart design which you can convincingly demonstrate will form a suitable framework for satisfying the above requirements. You will need to

- identify the abstract events associated with the physical elevator machinery,

- identify the information needed by the scheduling algorithm, the "home" of the algorithm, and how it will get the information it needs in its "home" (but do not try to design an optimal algorithm),

- perform appropriate structural and behavioural modularizations,

- describe inter-component protocols and show how they act together to provide a framework for correct scheduling, without going into details of the scheduling algorithm itself.

To avoid getting bogged down, leave out the following:

- Fine detail, such as the protocol for door opening and closing, which may simply be conceptually bundled as "floor service".

- Details of the scheduling algorithm (the problem is to design the form of the system such that there is a place where the scheduling algorithm can be put).

- The physical nature of the interface devices which give signals to the controlling computer system from visit-buttons and call-buttons and which are given control signals from the computer system.

- Details of the physical distribution of the computer system or the physical way in which the signals are transmitted to and from cars in motion.

- Allocation of the MachineChart components to different physical computers.

Some aspects of this problem to consider are as follows:

- The application has both a high degree of real concurrency and a high degree of connectivity. The concurrency might lead one to contemplate a behaviourally distributed design with a robot (task) for each elevator and floor (and possibly even more than this). The connectivity might lead one to adopt a behaviourally centralized design with only a few, or even no, robots (tasks). There is no "correct" solution, but only a continuum of more or less appropriate ones.

- The problem contains timeout and race possibilities which need to be handled correctly, for example:

  - Timeout: A car should not sit for an indefinite period in a state where it is assumed to be servicing a floor (waiting with its door open for someone to push its visit-buttons).

  - Race: A visit-button may be pushed after the control mechanism has timed out and directed the car in a different direction from that requested by the visit-button.

- Reliability is an issue. A degraded mode of operation should be possible in which each car can operate independently of central scheduling.

B.14 DESIGN CASE STUDY: FILE TRANSFER UTILITY (FTU)

Design a File Transfer Utility (FTU) that will support the bidirectional transfer of ASCII files over a dedicated serial communications link between a pair of computers.

The human interface for the FTU will enable human operators to ask for files to be sent, or for received files to be retrieved, while file i/o is proceeding for other outgoing or incoming files. Outgoing files will be transmitted automatically from a send queue in FIFO order. Incoming files will be automatically stored and notification of their arrival spontaneously provided to the human interface by the FTU, without any action being required by the human operator. Simple commands will enable a human operator to add one or more files to the send queue, to check the status of the queue at any time, and to remove files from the queue. (Assume the existence of an appropriate file subsystem, with an appropriate interface.)

Sending proceeds as follows. Sending of the first file is triggered by the human operator. Thereafter, as long as there are files in the send queue, sending proceeds autonomously. When the FTU is ready to send the next file, it first checks for the existence of the file (it does not do this when the file is put in the queue) and informs the human operator either that sending has started, or that the file does not exist. Then, if the file exists, it sends the file name. When an appropriate response is received from the other end, it starts to send the contents. When the file has been successfully sent, it informs the human operator again.

Receiving proceeds as follows. The FTU is always open for reception. The first evidence of an incoming file is the arrival of its name. On receipt of a file name, the FTU notifies the operator that a file is arriving and then creates and opens a file of that name for writing. If a file with the same name already exists locally, then it will be overwritten. After the file transfer is completed, the file is closed and the operator notified again.

Error recovery occurs as follows. If either system detects errors in received data, or failure of the other end to respond to a transmission before a certain timeout period, then file transmission/reception will be abandoned and the human operator notified. If the error occurs on reception, the local receive file will be deleted. The system will then continue normal operation. This is obviously too unsophisticated for a practical implementation, but will do for design-practise purposes.

The FTU must be able to handle files of arbitrary length. In order to guarantee that the sender doesn't get ahead of the receiver, a form of flow control must be implemented. This is accomplished by breaking the file into "frames" containing a fixed number of characters. The sender sends a frame and then waits for the receiver to send back an acknowledgement that the frame was received correctly before sending another one. The following frame types are required: FILENAME, DATA, ACK, NAK, EOF. These may be assumed to be identified by a character at the beginning of the frame. The ACK, NAK, and EOF frames contain only the identifying character.

There is a protocol associated with sending and receiving frames, as follows. Whenever a sending system sends a FILENAME frame, a DATA frame, or an EOF frame, it will wait for some type of acknowledgement (ACK or NAK) to be returned by the receiving system. If an ACK is returned, the sending system will proceed to send the next frame, if any. If a NAK is received instead, the sending system will abandon sending the current file and proceed with sending the next. If, for any reason, the receiving system does not return any acknowledgement after a timeout period, this is also an error; the sending system must time-out and abandon the transmission of the particular file. A receiving system sends a NAK when it discovers something wrong with a received frame.

To separate frame concerns from details of physical transmission, "enveloping" is performed; i.e., frames are enclosed in physical "envelopes" that contain header and trailer characters that must be added for transmission and stripped off after reception. These extra characters are needed to enable the remote system to determine the beginning and end of frames. The convention is that the part of the software that deals with physical transmission does not understand anything about what is in the frame itself, other than that it is a string of characters; e.g., it cannot tell the difference between the different frame types. To deal with this enveloping in a modular fashion, the design will have different subsystems, arranged in layers, as follows:

- The upper layer (the Frame Layer) is responsible for managing the frame protocol, including sending frames, receiving frames, and timing out on acknowledgements. It also retrieves files for transmission and stores them a frame at a time on reception (this is a distortion of the responsibilities of a typical Frame Layer in a practical layered communication system, in that such a Frame Layer would not normally become directly involved in file operations, but it will suffice for design-practise purposes). It interprets the frames it receives according to their type and sends ACKs when appropriate; if the frame code is unrecognizable, it sends a NAK.

- The lower layer (the Physical Layer) is essentially an I/O driver with some additional logic to add enveloping characters on transmission, and to remove them on reception. It may also add characters in the middle of the frame on transmission and remove them on reception, to provide "transparency" in the case that enveloping characters appear in the contents of the file. Details of enveloping characters and the transparency mechanism are not important here. What is important is that any unexpected enveloping character sequences in the input will cause the Physical Layer to discard the current frame (in practice, some other check, like a parity check, or a cyclic redundancy check, would also be performed). It will not send a NAK, because it does not know anything about frame types. The effect will be as if it had received nothing, as if the receiving wire had been cut.

Note that the inadequate error recovery mechanism gives rise to a possibility that one end may be left with a partially received file when a new file starts to arrive (How?). The system must discard such a file and notify the operator.

B.15   IMPLEMENTATION EXERCISE: CONCURRENT LIFE

Implement a complete Ada program for the game-of-life example with concurrent cells, using the material developed earlier by you in solving another problem posed by this appendix, together with the material in the body of the book.

B.16   REVISIT SYSTEM DESIGN WITH ADA

For those readers who have previously read the earlier "System Design With Ada" book, here are some suggestions for revisiting its material.

Redo the FORMS example following the Architectural Design process of this book, using the new notation, paying particular attention to event patterns and scenarios.

Revisit the final designs for the DIALOG example. Assuming that there are KEYBOARD, SCREEN, MESSAGE and CONTROL subsystems, with obvious correspondence to the components in the old structure charts, draw two new charts showing interconnections among these subsystems in terms of channels: the first has directed channels from CONTROL to the other three; the second has a directed channel from KEYBOARD to

CONTROL, and from CONTROL to SCREEN, and a bidirectional channel between MES-
SAGE and CONTROL. Show by drawing the internal structures for each how the first
forces a transporter glue structure and the latter does not.

Prepare a case study for one of the communication examples (COMM, X25), showing
how to apply the methods of Chapter 7 of this book to improving performance by reducing
rendezvous chaining.

Appendix C

SUPPLEMENTARY READING

This appendix identifies reading related to specific aspects of the body of this book. It is not intended to be a bibliography of references for the broad area covered by the book.

"Buhr Diagrams" for Ada, which this book stretches and extends, are described in an earlier book [1]. The Ada subset of MachineCharts provides a better notation and the Architectural Design method a better design process. However, the earlier book has some useful case studies that could be viewed in terms of the new notation and method with little effort.

An overview of the CAEDE workbench (the acronym stands for **CA**rleton **E**mbedded System **D**esign **E**nvironment) may be found in a 1988 paper by the author and several colleagues [2]. The workbench, which was a demonstration-of-concept prototype developed in parallel with the writing of [1], was first demonstrated shortly after [1] was published, and subsequently made its way into a number of large organizations for experimental purposes. Commercial products based on the earlier book and/or inspired by the CAEDE workbench have since appeared on the market (e.g., AdaGen [3], and Teamwork/Ada [4]).

Harel's StateCharts notation [5] has been mentioned a few times in the book, in part because it is a practical state machine notation that avoids the visual explosion of states and transition arcs that so often occurs when complex state machines are drawn with "flat" notations. In principle, the StateCharts notation may be used for ASMs and ACMs in MachineChart design. However, details of fitting StateCharts into the ACM framework and of mapping the result to implementations remain to be described.

However, this is not the only reason for mentioning StateCharts. A commercial tool that supports them, called StateMate [6], provides the best example known to the author at the time of this writing of a tool that supports visual exploration of temporal behaviour in a common sense manner that is appealing to practical engineers. Thus it conveys the style of workbench visualized for MachineCharts in this book.

The Ada Language Reference Manual [7] is, of course, essential reading for the official definition of the language, although not for a tutorial appreciation of it. Watt, Wichmann, and Findlay [8] provide an excellent treatment of Ada programming. The standard reference on abstract data types in Ada is Booch [9]. Ada tasking issues are well described by Burns, Lister and Wellings [10]. The Ada "polling bias" examples of Chapter 8 follow Gehani and Cargill [11]. Ada real time issues are discussed by Brosgol [12]

References

[1] R.J.A. Buhr, "System Design With Ada", Prentice Hall, 1984

[2] R.J.A. Buhr, G. Karam, C.M. Woodside, C. Hayes, "Software CAD : A Revolutionary Approach", IEEE TSE, Vol. 15, No. 3, March 89, pp. 235-249

[3] Adagen is a product of Mark V Systems, Encino, CA

[4] Teamwork/Ada is a product of Cadre Technologies Inc., Providence, R.I

[5] David Harel, "Statecharts: A Visual Formalism for Complex Systems", Science of Computer Programming 8 (1987) 231-274

[6] D. Harel, H. Lachover, A. Naamad, A. Pnueli, M. Politi, R. Sherman, A. Shtul-Trauring, "StateMate: A Working Environment for the Development of Complex, Reactive Systems", Proc. 10th International Conference on Software Engineering, Singapore, April 11-15, 1988 (StateMate is a product of i-Logix Inc., Burlington MA)

[7] Department of Defense, Ada Joint Program Office, "Reference Manual for the Ada Programming Language", ANSI/MIL-STD-1815A, Government Printing Office, Washington, DC, 1983

[8] David A. Watt, Brian A. Wichmann, William Findlay, "Ada Language and Methodology", Prentice Hall International (UK), London, 1987

[9] Grady Booch, "Software Components With Ada", Benjamin/Cummings, 1987

[10] Alan Burns, Andrew M. Lister, Andrew J. Wellings, "A Review of Ada Tasking", Springer-Verlag Lecture Notes in Computer Science, Number 262, 1987

[11] N.H. Gehani, T.A. Cargill, "Concurrent Programming in the Ada Language: The Polling Bias", J. Software Practice and Experience, 5, 1984

[12] Benjamin M. Brosgol, "International Workshop on Real-Time Ada Issues: Summary Report, Ada Letters, Vol III, No 1, Jan/Feb 88

Appendix D

GLOSSARY

ACM (Abstract Controller Machine): A machine that, given an abstract event, returns an abstract action (or set thereof); used by concrete machinery to determine what to do next (in this book, always contains a hidden, internal abstract state machine (ASM)).

Active: A temporal term: depending on context, indicates the temporal state of having an engine running, or the opposite of passive.

Activity: The process of doing work, while active.

Actor: A machine with the *TIME* domain property of being autonomous and self-directing, and the *PLACE* domain properties of providing containment and hiding. An abstraction of autonomous components in implementation technologies (e.g., software tasks or processes).

Agenda: The sequential program of an engine.

Alarm: An error to be handled out of normal operating sequence.

ASM (Abstract State Machine): The term used in this book for formalisms that express the rules governing the effect of events on the state of something, and of the state on the processing of events; represented in this book by state transition diagrams.

Avoidance: Closing a waiting place by having the actor on the non-waiting side ignore the place while a waiting condition is in effect.

Asynchronous: An interaction between actors that does not require mutual waiting.

Attached Button: A button that is attached to the interface of a box or robot.

Balk: In an attempted synchronous interaction with another machine, abandon the attempt immediately if the other machine is not already waiting; synonym for timeout for a zero time period.

Black Box: Any machine that provides containment, hiding, and an interface.

Box: A black box without operational semantics of its own (apart from self-initialization); all its operational semantics are provided by interface components, or internal ones (other than its engine for self-initialization, if it has one).

Button: A machine that, from the outside, offers a single operator that may be triggered by other machines (see also work button and gate button).

Channel: A structural placeholder for connection details.

Choice Frame: A notation for grouping gate buttons and/or fingers to indicate that a choice must be made among them while the system is running; an unconstrained choice frame indicates uncommitted waiting for the first interaction that can occur; a constrained choice frame indicates that a pre-interaction choice must be made among them (implying that any waiting is of the committed variety).

Clock: An icon indicating timeout, delay, or periodicity.

Close: Impose a waiting condition at a waiting place (see also avoidance and screening).

Cold Waiting: A style of waiting at a waiting place that implies being "left out in the cold" (in other words, completely ignored) while a waiting condition is in effect.

Collapsed: A term applied to a projection of a tree (or subtree) of structure charts onto the single structure chart at the root of the tree (or subtree), in the process eliminating boxes and collapsing work buttons into fingers, producing a chart exposing peer actors and associated glue structures.

Committed Waiting: A form of waiting that commits to where to wait among a set of possible waiting places, without knowing which ones may have events ready and which ones may not, thereby possibly allowing unecessary waiting to occur (in other words, allowing waiting for an event at one waiting place of the set, while events are arriving at other ones); opposite of uncommitted waiting. May be characterized as *visit-before-wait*.

Connection: Anything connecting two machines (e.g., finger, channel).

Cycle: An icon indicating repetitive activity, that may be attached to a finger, an engine, or an entire machine.

Data: Data abstractions are represented by machines whose buttons define the permitted operations on the data. Without internal storage, the result is a type manager machine, representing the programming concept of an abstract data type (ADT); with internal storage, it is a store manager machine.

Delay: Suspension of activity by an actor for a specified time period, the possibility of which is shown visually by a clock icon connected by a finger to the actor's engine.

Detached Button: A button that is not part of the interface of another machine, but stands alone as a machine in its own right.

Dynamic: A structural term, implying that components of structure are installed while the system is running.

Engine: A primitive, sequential machine that provides the motive power for the activity of the machine to which it belongs; can never stand alone; is implicitly at the leaf level of structural decomposition for a tree of structure charts (note that, unless there are also other leaf level components in a machine, drawing the leaf level explicitly is unecessary).

Environment: The source of a system's events and the sink for its responses.

Event: Abstract unit of interaction between machines; in the *PLACE* domain, a directed path of interaction between a source place and a sink place; in the *TIME* domain, an occurrence of an interaction.

Expose: Make an internal component of a machine part of its interface. Done visually in two ways: by directly attaching the component to the interface (as with buttons); or by connecting the component to the interface by means of a special icon.

Face: The push side of a button.

Faceless: A machine with its interface not yet defined.

Finger: A directed connection from one machine to the interface of another (the direction is implied by context), which provides a locus for interactions.

Fixed: A structural term: opposite of dynamic; synonym for static.

Flattened: A term applied to the projection onto a single structure chart of the internal details "underneath" it in the structure chart tree.

Foreign: A machine designed "elsewhere", internal details of which are not accessible in this structure chart tree.

Form: A term indicating the nature of the information diagrams are intended to convey, in both the *PLACE* and *TIME* domains; thus we speak of "structural form" and "temporal form", the former indicating how the system is composed of parts, and the latter the patterns of interaction among the parts.

Functional: Pertaining to the *WORK* domain.

Gate Button: A button that requires both a push and a pull to start its engine, thus imposing synchronization among multiple, concurrent visitors. An abstraction of shared operators in implementation technologies, access to which is controlled (e.g., Ada entries, and operators provided by monitors and real time executives to perform functions such as message sending and receiving, and semaphore signalling and waiting).

Glue Structure: Concrete machinery interposed between peer actors, enabling them to communicate with each other, composed from gate buttons, reactors, subsidiary actors, and fingers (ignoring boxes and work buttons).

Ground: An icon attached to an actor to indicate that it is intended to behave like a reactor (redundant, because the reactor icon suffices, but useful sometimes when designing for multitasking technologies that do not have explicit reactors, like reference-manual Ada).

Handler: The part of an engine that handles alarms.

Immediate Button: Synonym for Work Button.

Install: Making an instance of a template in a particular place; may be static or dynamic; indicated by an install arrow icon, with an associated template, pointing at the installed instance.

Instance: A component installed in a particular place from a template, shown in place by an ordinary machine icon, with the fact that it is an instance indicated by showing an install arrow pointing at it, with an associated template icon.

Instance Flow: A parameter that, when passed from one place to another, provides access to an instance; may be shown visually using a universal instance flow icon, or using icons in the shape of the instance machines themselves with attached arrows indicating the direction of flow. (There is deliberately no notation for the means by which this may be accomplished in software, namely pointers.)

Interaction: A term indicating what happens when a connection is activated.

Interface: The set of buttons, fingers, and exposed internal components, seen from outside a machine, that provide all of the possible ways of connecting it to its environment.

Interlocked: A term applied to an interaction between machines that requires a visiting actor to stop running while the visited machine's engine is running; synonym for synchronous.

Jab: An icon indicating a path for either an asynchronous interaction, or an alarm interaction (the distinction is indicated by context). (Note that a path for an asynchronous interaction can always be represented using an intermediate reactor, so a jab for this purpose is redundant, but nevertheless useful when designing for implementation technologies that support asynchronous interactions directly.)

Linear: A term that identifies a glue structure composed of a set of gate buttons associated with a single choice frame, without any direct interaction being possible among the buttons themselves (thus the buttons are "strung out linearly" along the choice frame).

Machine: Any MachineChart component containing, either implicitly or explicitly, at least one engine in the structure chart subtree "underneath" it.

Meeting: An interlocked, or synchronous, interaction between robots (less restrictive than Rendezvous). Meetings are 2-way, unless warm waiting or nonlinearity is present, when they may be multi-way in a phased sense.

Mixed: A term applied to event scenarios in which activities are represented only by active segments of timelines, without explicit start and stop events (the term implies that the information content in the scenarios is conveyed by mixed patterns of events and activity segments).

More: An icon used to indicate that the complete interface of a machine (foreign or instance) is not shown in the particular place where it is installed, because not all of the interface is used.

Nonlinear: A term applied to a glue structure of gate buttons and choice frames that does not obey the linearity restrictions.

Notifier: A term identifying a style of transporting events between machines in which the source of the events delivers them to the sink, thereby acting as a notifier, instead of the sink requesting them from the source, and possibly having to wait.

Open: Remove a waiting condition at a waiting place (how this is done depends on whether closing was by avoidance or screening).

Order: Temporal order of interactions, indicated by numbering connections.

Overlay: A projection of a structure chart that does not show all of its details.

Parameter: A data item or template instance associated with a connection, that is passed from one machine to another at the start or end of an interaction, depending on the direction of the associated arrow.

Passive: A temporal term indicating a machine that has no autonomous activity of its own (e.g., a box with only internal data is passive, and so is a reactor).

Peer: A term used to indicate machines that are identified as primary ones early in the design process, before glue structures and interfaces have been put in place; usually refers to actors.

Place: When printed as *PLACE*, a term identifying the design domain concerned with system structure; otherwise, denotes a particular location in the structure of a system under design.

Plug-In: Indicates something that can be inserted into a prepared place; such as an ASM into an ACM.

Polling: Synonym for busy-waiting; an undesirable form of waiting in reactive systems.

Port: Place where a channel connects to a machine; placeholder for connection details.

Priority: The only prioritization having a direct effect on MachineChart semantics is prioritization of buttons within choice frames (waiting place buttons are normally assumed to have higher priority). Otherwise priority annotations are useful mainly for indicating implementation intent.

Proactive: A term identifying an actor with only fingers on its interface, and no buttons.

Protect: A term implying no possibility of conflicting use by concurrent actors.

Protocol: Rules governing temporal ordering of interactions between machines.

Pull: Visiting a gate button from the body side; must be paired with a push for an interaction to occur.

Push: Visiting any button from the face side; for a work button, an interaction occurs immediately; for a gate button, must be paired with a pull for an interaction to occur.

Push Button: Synonym for work button.

Push-Pull Button: Synonym for gate button.

Queue: FIFO queues are implicitly associated with both push and pull sides of gate buttons.

Reactive: A term identifying an actor with only buttons on its interface, and no fingers (a reactive actor is the same as a reactor only if the additional constraint is imposed of it being active only during meetings on its buttons, which is symbolized by grounding the actor icon); also used as a general term to indicate a system that must respond to events.

Reactor: A constrained form of robot that is like an actor in providing protection for its internal machinery, but unlike an actor in not having any autonomy of its own; may also be viewed as a protected box (in fact a reactor may be constructed by using a semaphore to control access to the buttons of the box). An abstraction of components in implementation technologies that provide controlled access to shared operators (e.g., semaphores, mailboxes and monitors).

Recursive Decomposition: Designing a system as a composition of subsystems, a subsystem as a composition of subsubsystems, etc., in such a way that each subsystem, subsubsystem, etc., may be viewed as a system in its own right, to which all of the design techniques and representations apply.

Release: A term indicating the removal of a waiting condition on a warm waiting place; the term open conveys the same meaning, when applied to such a place.

Remove: Reverse of install.

Rendezvous: A term reserved for meetings between actors.

Replicate: Install identical instances in the same place.

Robot: A term identifying a machine that is either an actor or a reactor (used only when the difference is unimportant to the point being made).

Routing Chart: A concrete structure chart with the details of its interfaces and connections contained in, and hidden by, channels and ports.

Satisfied: A term applied to a visit, indicating that it has resulted in an interaction.

Screening: Closing a waiting place by masking it out of a choice frame.

Scenario: A timing diagram showing either discrete event/activity patterns, or continuous visit waveforms.

Shadow: A term applied to the visual representation of replicated instances, by overlapping them.

Sink: Destination of events.

Source: Origin of events.

Sporadic: Cyclic, but not periodic; indicated visually by a cycle icon associated with a finger, engine, or actor.

State: The persistent condition of a machine between temporal events at that machine that determines how the machine will respond to future events; may be changed by the occurrence of events; sometimes the word *mode* is used by other authors to indicate this concept.

State Machine: See ASM.

Static: A structural term: opposite of dynamic; synonym for fixed.

Store: An icon serving as a placeholder for stored data (the notation provides no explicit visual notations for the structure of data). See also Data.

Structural: Pertaining to the *PLACE* domain.

Structure Chart: A diagram showing interconnected black boxes. Abstract S.C. - drawn during preliminary design, showing event paths in relation to faceless black boxes. Concrete S.C. - drawn during detailed design, showing all interface and connection machinery in place, in terms of buttons and fingers.

Subsystem: A system whose environment is a set of peer subsystems that are themselves part of the design problem.

Synchronous: Synonym for interlocked; opposite of asynchronous.

System: A machine whose environment is given, and does not have to be designed.

Template: Pattern for constructing and installing instances.

Temporal: Pertaining to the *TIME* domain.

Thread: Trace of visits through structure.

Time: When printed as *TIME*, a term identifying the design domain concerned with *when* things occur, either relatively or absolutely (in other words with the temporal aspect of behaviour); otherwise, indicates wall-clock time.

Timeline: A line associated with a particular machine in a scenario.

Time-Intensive: Denotes systems for which *TIME* domain concerns may be separated from *WORK* ones and treated before them in the design process, in conjunction with *PLACE* domain concerns.

Timeout: Terminating a visit before it is satisfied, after a specified time period has elapsed.

Transaction: Sequence of visits threaded through one or more components to accomplish some application purpose.

Transactor: A peer actor responsible for shepherding a transaction through part or all of a system.

Transporter: A glue actor responsible for transporting an event from a source to a sink, to free the sink from having to wait at the source for the event.

Tree: Relationship among a set of structure charts reflecting recursive decomposition of systems into subsystems, subsystems into subsubsystems, etc.

Uncommitted Waiting: A form of waiting that does not commit to where to wait among a set of possible waiting places, thereby avoiding the possibility of waiting for an event at one waiting place of the set, while events are arriving at other ones; opposite of committed waiting. May be characterized as *visit-after-wait*.

Visit: An attempt to interact with another machine, which may be immediately satisfied, or not, depending on the nature, and possibly the state, of the component being visited.

Waiting: Implies non-busy waiting for events; the term as used in this book does not generally include incidental waiting caused by latency and congestion, which are assumed to be small enough to be negligible (an assumption that must be tested in the implementation).

Waiting Place: A place on one side or the other of a gate button, where waiting occurs for an event coming from "elsewhere" (implying that it arrives by some mechanism outside the button).

Warm Waiting: A style of waiting at a waiting place that implies *not* being "left out in the cold" (in other words, not ignored until the waiting condition is removed, but interacted with first to get information about why waiting is required).

Work: When printed as *WORK*, identifies the design domain concerned with *what* the system must do (in other words with the functional aspect of behaviour); otherwise indicates functionally oriented activity.

Work Button: A button that requires only a push to start its engine, thus imposing no synchronization among multiple, concurrent visitors. An abstraction of unprotected, reentrant operators in implementation technologies (e.g., software procedures and functions).

INDEX